STAGE ONE BO

NORTHWICK PUBLISHERS

14, BEVERE CLOSE, WORCESTER, WR3 7QH, ENGLAND

Telephone Number: 0905-56876

STAGE ONE BOOKS

Other books in the series:

STAGE ONE LAW
AUTHOR P. GERRARD B.Sc., Ph.D., A.I.B.

STAGE ONE COST ACCOUNTING
AUTHOR G. J. WICKINSON-RIDDLE B.A., F.C.A.

STAGE ONE BOOKS

STAGE ONE FINANCIAL ACCOUNTING

W. HARRISON F.I.B., Cert.Ed.

Principal Lecturer in Business Studies
Worcester Technical College.

NORTHWICK PUBLISHERS

NORTHWICK PUBLISHERS

ISBN 0 907135 11 0

Printed in Great Britain by
Richard Clay (The Chaucer Press) Ltd,
Bungay, Suffolk

First Impression 1983

CONTENTS

PREFACE

New text books on Accounts appear on the bookshelves every year, all with their own styles of presentation and sequence of topics – so why the need for *another* book on Accounts?

Over the past 17 years I have made a careful study of students' needs and problems in this subject, particularly at the early stages – the "foundation" levels – and I have noted with concern how many students struggle, and how others appear to do well without fully *understanding* what they are doing. The latter type students invariably come "unstuck" in the next stage of study.

Like any subject, *the basics are the most important.* The students must understand what they are doing and *why* they are doing it. With a firm foundation in the basics, the development of the subject becomes "plain sailing". The first stages – i.e. STAGE ONE – are the most important of all.

Many text books on Accounts *assume* a knowledge which often is not there, and the result is that the subject is "glossed over" from the students' point of view – he/she resorts to "formula" and memory which, in Accounts, has no future!

I have tried in this book to spell out the subject, with the concentration on WHY as well as HOW. In the first chapter I stress the fact that good memory and formula have no major place in this subject, and I have proved this to my own students with their full subsequent endorsement of what I have said.

The subject is presented as I teach it, and I apologise in advance for any "splitting of infinitives" or the use of verbs and pronouns in the wrong sequence – I am teaching you Accounts, not English!

To the female reader I apologise for the use of he, him, his, throughout the book – it would be impossible for me, and boring for the reader, to cover both male and female descriptions in my address of everyone concerned.

One final point – before you start reading, I want you to arm yourself with a thick pad of paper (A4 or foolscap size), because this is a practical subject, and I want you to "doodle" a lot as well as tackle the exercises. Novels are meant to be read in bed or in front of the TV, but not this kind of book!

This book is designed for the student of GCE "O" and "A" levels, BEC National Diplomas and Certificates, and the first stages of any business professional examination. Also, of course, for the person who is just interested in the subject, for various reasons.

Grateful acknowledgement for the use of past examination questions is due to The Association of Accounting Technicians, The Association of Certified Accountants, The Associated Examining Board, The Institute of Bankers, The London Chamber of Commerce and Industry, The Royal Society of Arts, and The London University Entrance and School Examinations Council. The answers to the questions in the text are my own, and no responsibility for the accuracy or method of working attaches to any of these named bodies.

Finally, sufficient thanks cannot be recorded on paper to my family, Joan, David, Philip and Bella, for their tolerance and understanding during the period of writing this text – also to my colleague and good friend, David Cox, for his encouragement and advice, and to his wife, Jean, for her immaculate typing.

Spring 1983 William Harrison

CHAPTER 1

INTRODUCTION TO THE BALANCE SHEET

Unlike many of the other subjects you have studied, or are at present studying, Accounts does not require the reading of large chunks of text and the taking down of copious notes, nor does it require feats of memory or mathematical genius – provided you can add and subtract and work out simple percentages (try to do this without the use of a calculator!) you will have no problems with the "maths side" of Accounts. There is very little to memorise and no need to work to formula.

What does it require then? It requires a knowledge and thorough *understanding* of some basic principles, and practice in applying these principles to varying situations. That is why you must work through as many of the exercises in this book as possible and not be in too much of a hurry to resort to the answer the moment you get stuck! Sorting it out yourself is a very valuable exercise in developing the ability to think clearly and logically. You must not be tempted to develop your own "formula" for each accounting topic as this involves unnecessary memorising, and as your memory can only cope with so much, you will find that there is a limit to the extent you can develop your studies in Accounts. Also, reliance on "formula" means that you are not *understanding* what you are doing and the first time you come across an unusual or unfamiliar situation you won't know how to cope.

Your study of Accounts therefore is going to involve the learning and understanding of certain principles and progressive practice in applying these principles to practical situations. Most of these principles are covered in the first 10 chapters of this book. Thoroughly understand them and the rest of your studies will be "plain-sailing"! You will appreciate the significance of what I have just said later on in your studies – I guarantee that!

DEFINITIONS

A good start would be to look at a few definitions of terms which you will be constantly using throughout your study of Accounts (memorise these – just some of the very few things you will need to memorise).

ASSETS: These are things OWNED by a business which have a value;

examples are premises, equipment, motor vehicles, stock and of course cash or a balance at bank.

LIABILITIES: These are amounts OWED, by a business, to various people, firms and organisations. You could think of liabilities as being the direct opposite of assets.

BALANCE SHEET: this is simply a *list* of all the assets and all of the liabilities of a business at a certain point in time – i.e. what a business *owns* and what it *owes*.

DEBTORS: These are people and organisations who owe money to the business. For example, if a business sells goods to Brown *on credit* (which means that Brown will pay for the goods at a later date), then Brown is a debtor of the business until he pays up. Debtors are treated as assets in the balance sheet of a business because a business in effect owns those debts due to it.

CREDITORS: These are amounts owed *by* a business to others. If a business buys goods on credit from Jones, then Jones becomes a creditor of the business until the debt is paid. As such, Jones will appear on the balance sheet of the business as a *liability* (i.e. something *owed*).

THE BALANCE SHEET

We know that this is a list of all assets and liabilities of a business at a certain point in time, so let us build one up from the point we start an imaginary business. We will list the business assets on the right-hand side and liabilities on the left-hand side of our sheet of paper,

e.g.

Balance Sheet as at (date)

Liabilities	£	*Assets*	£
	–		–
	–		–
	–		–
	Total		Total

It is not important whether the assets and liabilities are presented this way round or the other way round, or in fact in vertical form with the liabilities underneath the assets, or vice-versa!

Think now of the term "*Balance* Sheet". You know what balancing means – the same weight or stresses on both sides. Think of the old "balance" scales – the brass (usually) ones with a shallow dish suspended on each side by chains – put the same weights on each dish and the scales will balance.

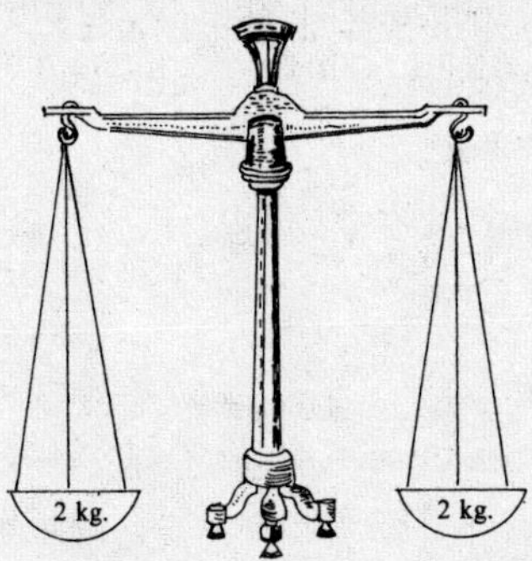

A *Balance* Sheet must balance in the same way, so imagine that the *totals* for each side of the balance sheet above represent the dishes on the scales.

e.g.

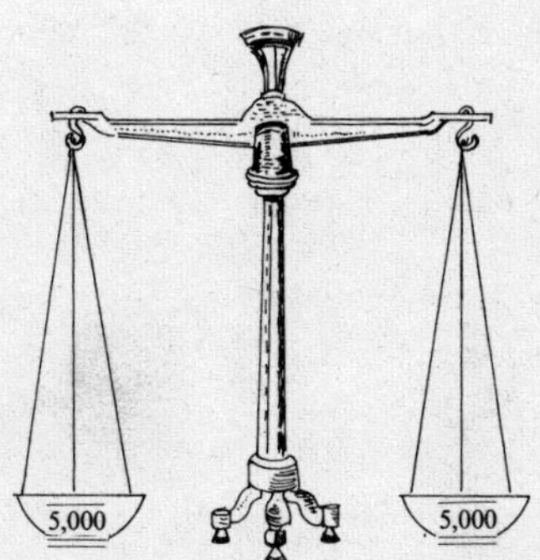

The two sides must *always* balance with each other – if they don't, then something is either missing in the balance sheet or wrongly recorded. There is never any exception to this statement.

Let's now start your business with £30,000 in cash which has been left to you by a rich aunt. You are going to invest this cash in *your* business, now. Therefore the first balance sheet as at *now* will look like this:

Balance Sheet of Business as at Now

Liabilities	£	*Assets*	£
		Cash	30,000
	–		30,000

It doesn't balance! Why? Has your business got any liabilities; in other words does it owe anything at this stage? Of course it does – it owes £30,000 *to you*! The balance sheet is that *of the business* and the business owes *you* the money you have invested in it. The balance sheet must therefore appear:

Balance Sheet of Business as at Now

Liabilities	£	*Assets*	£
OWING TO OWNERS	30,000	Cash	30,000
	30,000		30,000

The amount owing by the business to the owners is known as the **CAPITAL** of the business and this figure also represents the worth, or value, of the business.

Now, during Day 1 spend some of that cash on other assets – say, £10,000 on equipment and £5,000 on stock (for re-sale). That's all you do on Day 1 so your balance sheet at the end of Day 1 looks like this:

Balance Sheet as at end of Day 1

Liabilities	£	*Assets*	£
Capital	30,000	Cash	15,000
		Equipment	10,000
		Stock	5,000
	30,000		30,000

Note that your business is still worth £30,000 – it still owes you £30,000 – all that has happened is that the structure of the assets has now changed. The business has less cash but it has other assets to replace the cash gone out. It has simply swapped an asset (cash) for other assets (equipment and stock) – *total* assets remain the same.

In theory (forgetting wear and tear and second-hand values for the present) the equipment and stock could be sold for cash (£15,000) which, added to the existing cash (£15,000), would produce the £30,000 to pay you back if you decided to finish the business.

On Day 2 you sell £1,000 of your stock for £1,000 cash (you haven't got the idea of making profits yet!) and then you sell £600 of your stock for £600 on credit to Smith. At the end of the day the business balance sheet looks like this:

Balance Sheet at end of Day 2

Liabilities	£	*Assets*	£
Capital	30,000	Cash	16,000
		Equipment	10,000
		Stock	3,400
		Debtor – Smith	600
	30,000		30,000

What has happened? Cash has increased by the sale of £1,000 of stock for £1,000 cash – stock has gone down by the amount of stock sold, £1,600 – and the business has a new asset in the form of a debtor who owes the business £600 for stock bought and not yet paid for. As the debtor is as a result of trading (i.e. buying and selling) he is referred to as a "Trade Debtor". Note that the business is still worth £30,000 – all that has happened is that the structure of the assets has changed. Also, because the items have been correctly recorded, the balance sheet still balances!

On Day 3 you buy £200 of stock and pay cash, and you buy a further £400 of stock from Jones on credit. You also pay £10,000 of the cash into a business bank account. At the end of Day 3 the balance sheet is drawn up:

Balance Sheet as at end of Day 3

Liabilities	£	*Assets*	£
Capital	30,000	Cash	5,800
Creditors	400	Bank balance	10,000
		Equipment	10,000
		Stock	4,000
		Debtors	600
	30,400		30,400

Cash has been depleted by £10,200 (£200 paid for stock and £10,000 paid into the bank). Stock has increased due to the two purchases and as £400 of stock was not paid for, the business is showing a liability to a trade creditor of £400. There is no need to show the names of debtors and creditors in the balance sheet – just the grand total of each.

Note that the balance sheet still "balances" but at a new figure. The business still owes you £30,000 and is therefore still worth £30,000. If the business was sold up the assets would be sold for cash, the bank balance drawn out, and the debtors would be asked to pay up. This would give you £30,400, out of which you would have to pay the creditors £400, leaving £30,000 for the business to pay back to you (i.e. your capital, being what the business is worth).

One way of interpreting the above balance sheet would be to say that the business has £30,400 of assets and that the owner has provided £30,000 to finance these assets, the other £400 being provided by trade creditors.

The worth, or value, of any business is its total assets (in this case £30,400) less its liabilities other than capital (in this case £400). In other words capital = worth. Provided you know all the assets and liabilities of a business you can always work out capital (the worth of the business). Remember this point.

Let's now take the balance sheet a stage further. On Day 4 the debtors pay *by cheque* the sum of £200, and you pay the creditors *in cash* the sum of £300.

Balance Sheet at end of Day 4

Liabilities	£	*Assets*	£
Capital	30,000	Cash	5,500
Creditors	100	Bank balance	10,200
		Equipment	10,000
		Stock	4,000
		Debtors	400
	30,100		30,100

Note that debtors and creditors have reduced by the amounts received and paid and that cash and bank have changed. Cheques paid out or received will affect the *bank* balance – not cash. Your business is still worth £30,000 which is what it owes to you (i.e. capital).

NOTE THE CHANGE

In the above examples various changes have been made to the balance sheet items according to the transactions made. However, each set of alterations made has left the balance sheet "in balance" – i.e. the same weights on each side of the scales. This is because *every* transaction has had one of the following effects on the scales.

WE HAVE EITHER:

(a) Added the same amount to assets and to liabilities, i.e. to both sides of the scales

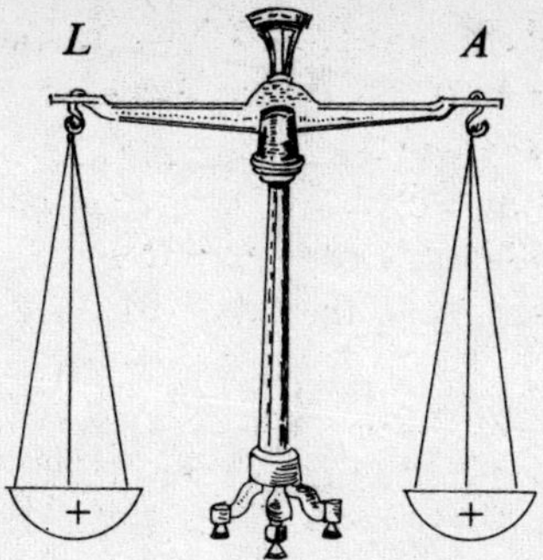

as in the transaction when the business was started with £30,000 cash, and the business therefore acquired an asset cash (£30,000) *and* a liability, capital (£30,000). Also the transactions on day 3, when the business acquired an asset, stock (£400), and at the same time a liability, creditor (£400).

OR

(b) Added a certain amount to the assets and in the same "breath" taken the same amount *off* the assets,

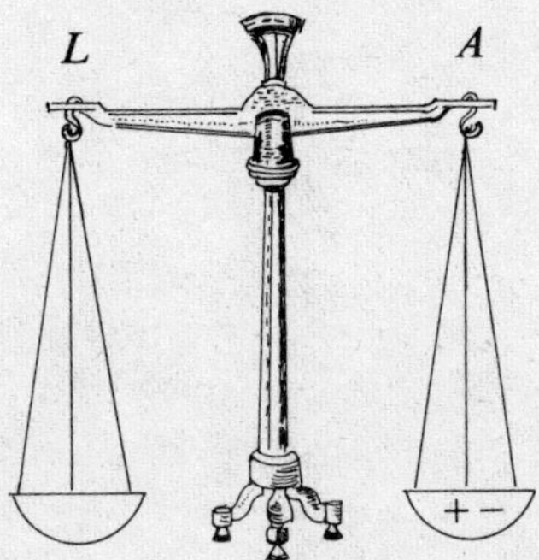

as in the transaction on Day 1 when £15,000 cash left the business but was immediately replaced by £15,000 of other assets (equipment and stock). Also the selling of stock for cash on Day 2, the buying of stock for cash on Day 3 and the transfer of cash to a bank account on the same day, and the payment by debtors on Day 4.

OR

(c) Taken the same amount off both sides of the scales

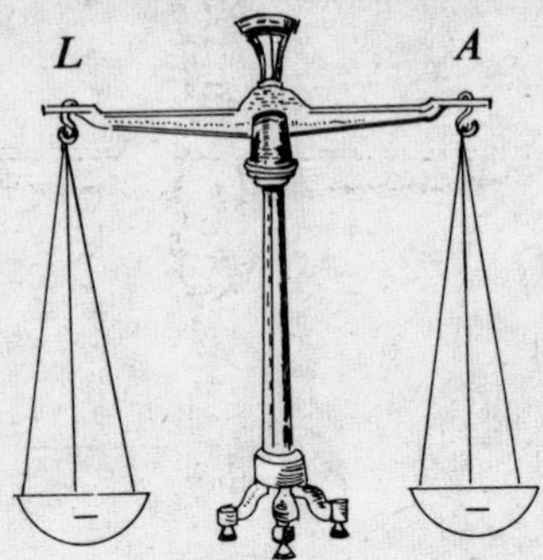

as in Day 4 when creditors were paid in cash – an asset was "lost" and a liability was "lost".

OR

(d) Added to the liabilities and at the same time taken the same amount off the liabilities.

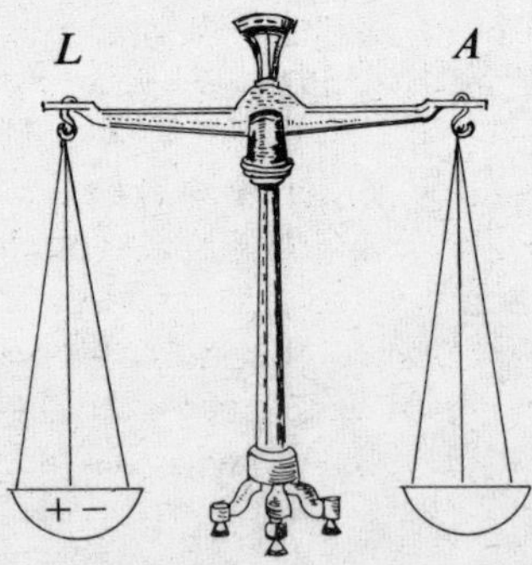

We haven't yet had a transaction which has this effect, but we will later on.

The four effects on the "scales" are the only possible permutations which will keep the scales in balance, e.g.

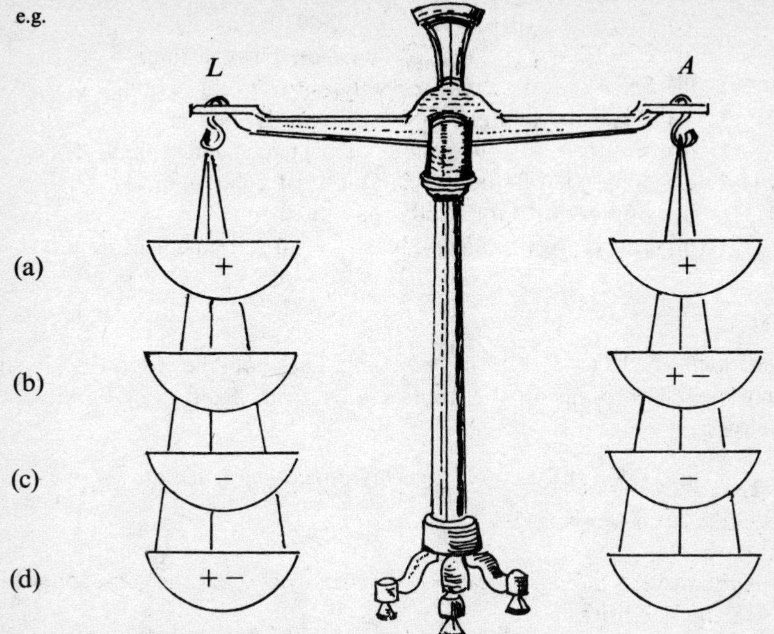

Every single transaction you will ever come across will, when recorded, have one of the above effects on the scales – i.e. on the balance sheet, and the balance sheet will always finish up balanced provided the transactions are recorded correctly!

In thinking in this way we are thinking of the theory behind a "double-entry" system of recording transactions – this double-entry system is the basis of every proper accounting system throughout the world and has operated successfully in businesses for about 500 years. So it's good and tested! Very soon we are going to formalise this system in a practical way but first you must work some exercises on what we have done to date.

EXERCISE 1.1

From the following transactions prepare balance sheets as they would appear *at the end* of Day 1, 2, 3 and 4, after recording each day's transactions.

Day 1 (i) You start your business with £60,000 in cash.
(ii) Buy shop premises for £30,000 – pay cash.
(iii) Buy shop fittings for £4,000 – pay cash.

Day 2 (i) Buy stock (for re-sale) for £2,000 – pay cash.
(ii) Pay £20,000 cash into a business bank account.
(iii) Sell £800 of stock for £800 *on credit* to J. Todd.
Day 3 (i) Buy £500 of stock *on credit* from D. Nixon.
(ii) You receive £300 cheque as part payment from J. Todd.
Day 4 (i) Sell £600 of stock to B. Dunn for £600 *on credit*.
(ii) Buy cash till for £350 – pay by cheque.
(iii) Pay D. Nixon £500 in cash in full settlement of debt.

EXERCISE 1.2

Indicate which category of recording each of the following transactions fall into, using the transactions from Exercise 1.1 above, as follows:

Day 1 (ii); Day 2 (ii); Day 2 (iii); Day 3 (i); Day 3 (ii); Day 4 (iii).

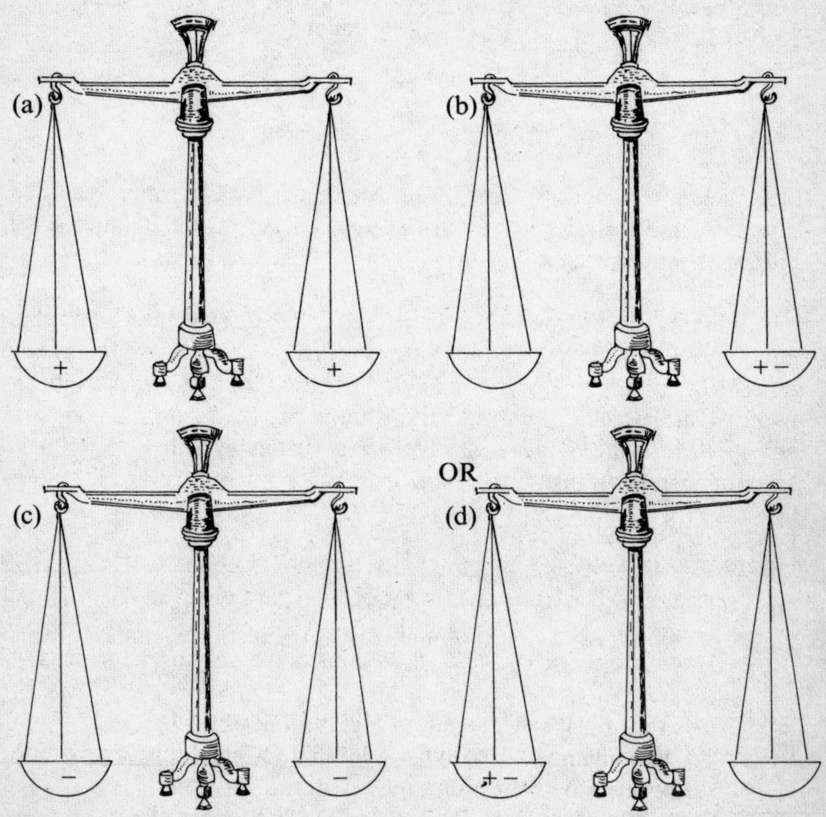

EXERCISE 1.3

The following transactions take place in June:

June 1 P. Gerrard started business by depositing £60,000 into a business bank account.
June 3 Bought shop fittings for £4,000, paying by cheque.
June 6 Bought stock (for re-sale) for £3,000 from E. Doyle, on credit.
June 7 Sold £600 of stock for £600, received cash.
June 10 Bought office desk for £100, paid cash.
June 14 Purchased stock (for re-sale), £400 paid by cheque.
June 20 Sold £1,000 of stock on credit to M. Tanner, for £1,000.
June 23 Paid cheque to E. Doyle £1,800 as part settlement of account.
June 27 Received £700 cash from M. Tanner as part settlement of account.
June 28 Purchased premises for £30,000, paid by cheque.
June 30 Sold £900 of stock for £900 to G. Devlin on credit.

Prepare a balance sheet for P. Gerrard as at 30th June.

EXERCISE 1.4

Prepare a balance sheet for T. Dillingham after taking account of the following transactions:

Oct. 1 T. Dillingham started business by depositing £20,000 into a business bank account.
Oct. 4 Borrowed £30,000 from Heath Finance Ltd to purchase shop premises. Purchased premises the same day.
Oct. 7 Bought shop fittings for £6,000 – paid cheque.
Oct. 9 Purchased stock for resale, £5,000 on credit from P. Collins & Co.
Oct. 12 Sold £3,000 of stock for £3,000 cash.
Oct. 15 Paid £2,500 cash into the business bank account.
Oct. 19 Bought office equipment for £2,000 – paid cheque.
Oct. 23 Bought office furniture for £8,000 – paid cheque.
Oct. 25 Paid cheque for £3,500 to P. Collins & Co. as part settlement of the account.
Oct. 26 Repaid £15,000 by cheque to Heath Finance Ltd.
Oct. 28 T. Dillingham won £5,000 in a lottery and paid this cheque into his business bank account.
Oct. 29 Sold £800 of stock to R. Parker for £800, on credit.

EXERCISE 1.5

N. Thorn started business as manager of the pop group, "Sludge". He invested in his business £10,000 in cash on 1st May. During May the following transactions occurred:

May 2 Purchased motor vehicle for £8,000 – paid cash.
May 4 Paid £1,000 into a business bank account.
May 6 Purchased office furniture for £600 – paid cheque.
May 10 Bought various types of amplifying equipment for £4,500 – paid cheque.
May 22 Purchased music shop with loan monies received from Beeton Enterprises Ltd, £22,000.
May 23 Purchased stock of sheet music for £900 – paid cheque.
May 24 Purchased musical instruments for £2,000 on credit from Bancroft & Co.
May 26 Cash sales of music, £400 (cost to Thorn, £400).
May 28 Sold two violins to Appleby for £600 (cost to Thorn, £600).
May 30 Realising that there is no future in his business Thorn purchases a fast "business car" for £9,000 with a cash loan from Foolhardy Finance Co.

Show the balance sheet of N. Thorn as at 31st May.

CHAPTER 2

BALANCE SHEET DEVELOPMENT

PROFITS

Using the Balance Sheet at the end of Day 4 let us now realise that there is no point in being in business unless we make profits, and this can only be done by *trading* (i.e. buying and selling) – so let's trade profitably!

Balance Sheet at end of Day 4

Liabilities	£	*Assets*	£
Capital	30,000	Cash	5,500
Creditors	100	Bank balance	10,200
		Equipment	10,000
		Stock	4,000
		Debtors	400
	30,100		30,100

On Day 5 we sell £1,000 of stock for £1,500 and receive cash. Try now to visualise what happens to our balance sheet – stock (asset) will reduce by £1,000 and cash (asset) will increase by £1,500 so our total assets have increased by a new £500. Our scales are out of balance unless we do something else. Has every aspect of the transaction been recorded? No! A £500 profit has just been made but has only been recorded so far in the guise of an increase in cash. Who has made this profit? The business, – not you! Who does this profit belong to? *You* of course, as the owner of the business. Your business is making profits for *you*. Surely, therefore, your business now *owes you* a further £500 (you can draw it out later if you want!) How can this fact be recorded? Well, if the business owes something, its balance sheet must show this as a liability. Before this profitable transaction, your business owed you (capital) £30,000 – it now owes you £30,500, so let's increase capital by £500. The balance sheet now looks like the example on page 14. It balances because everything has been recorded – the reduction in stock, the increase in cash and the increase in capital. Note that your business is now worth £500 more than it was at Day 4 and this increase in value is represented, at the moment, by £500 extra cash.

Balance Sheet at end of Day 5

Liabilities	£	*Assets*	£
Capital	30,000	Cash	7,000
Plus profit	500	Bank balance	10,200
	——	Equipment	10,000
	30,500	Stock	3,000
Creditors	100	Debtors	400
	——		——
	30,600		30,600
	═══		═══

The overall effect of this last transaction has been to increase assets by £500 *net* and to increase liabilities by £500, i.e.

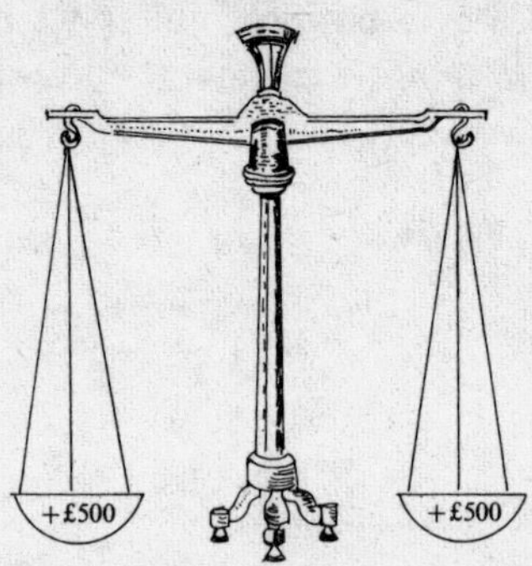

Don't proceed further until you fully understand what we have just done.

Let's move now to Day 6 when we pay the rates, £400, in cash. What happens? Cash is reduced by £400. Has another asset replaced this £400 to bring the balance sheet back into balance? No! – the money has left the business and there is nothing to show for it – the business has in effect lost £400 for good. It hasn't swapped £400 cash for something else like furniture – it has *paid an expense* (quite different than paying for an asset!). The value of the business goes down by £400 and in the same

Balance Sheet at end of Day 6

Liabilities		£	*Assets*	£
Capital		30,000	Cash	6,600
Plus Profit	500		Bank balance	10,200
Less Expenses	400	100	Equipment	10,000
	—	——	Stock	3,000
		30,100	Creditors	400
Creditors		100		
		——		——
		30,200		30,200
		═══		═══

Note – an asset has been reduced (£400) and a liability has been reduced (£400).

way that the business owes *you* any profits made (recorded as an increase in capital) *you* must stand any losses *it* makes (recorded as a decrease in capital). In effect, the £500 profit made yesterday has been cut back to only £100 profit, because we had to pay the rates to make the £500 profit!

i.e.

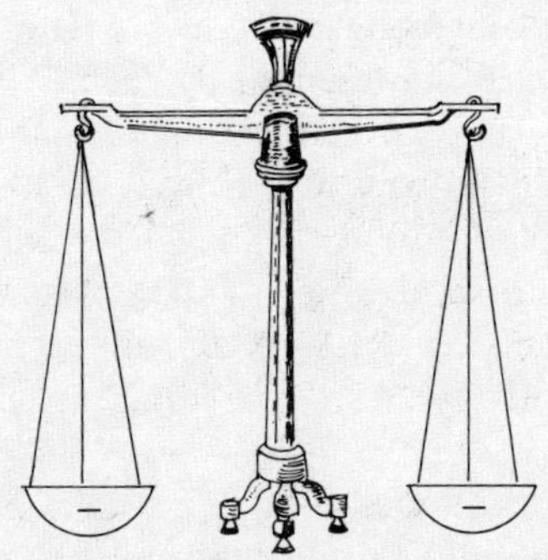

CAPITAL AND REVENUE EXPENDITURE

Study this last example carefully and think of the impact of different kinds of spending. Buying an asset simply involves swapping cash or bank balance for some other asset – *total* assets remain the same. The business is no worse off for the spending because the assets have value, which could, if necessary, be turned back into cash by simply selling the assets concerned. (Forget for the moment wear and tear and second-hand values – we'll deal with that aspect later.)

However, when cash is paid out for things like rent, rates, wages, light and heat etc. the cash leaving the business is *not* replaced – nothing tangible comes into the business (like a table) which could be resold if necessary. Such payments are forms of (necessary) losses, properly called **expenses**. They are really payments for services rendered and include, besides those already mentioned, such things as insurance premiums, repairs, travelling and hotel expenses, petrol for the firm's vehicles, stationery, packing materials, etc. The three latter items, petrol, stationery and packing materials, may bring to mind the purchase of assets because you *do* get something tangible for your money – *but they don't last* – they are quickly consumed in the course of business so within no time at all you have nothing to show for your spending, quite unlike your machinery, furniture, premises, etc. which are definite assets which last. Such items as petrol, stationery, packing materials and similar are therefore always treated as expenses.

If tomorrow morning you leave for work, or college, with £10 in your pocket, then we could say that you are *worth* (forget the clothes you are wearing!) £10 on leaving home. On the way you buy a pen for £4. How much are you worth when you arrive at work/college? The answer is, £10, made up of assets, £6 cash and £4 pen. No worse off!

The day after you leave home again with £10 cash and this time you get a taxi to work/college which costs you £4. How much are you worth when you arrive? Only £6, represented by cash. Although the taxi gave you a valuable service (like rent, rates, light, heat, wages, etc.) that £4 is now gone and there is no way of getting it back.

The first day you paid for an asset. The second day you paid an expense. Paying for an asset is known as **CAPITAL EXPENDITURE** – paying an expense is known as **REVENUE** (or current) **EXPENDITURE**, and in a business both types of spending must be kept separately recorded.

Naturally any business hopes that its revenue expenditure in a year will be less than the amount of profit made in the same period on buying and selling goods, so that some profit is left over (the *net* profit).

Note that in the balance sheets we have drawn up so far, capital expenditure is recorded on the assets side of the balance sheet while revenue expenditure reduces the profit made on buying and selling.

When you thoroughly understand all of the above, try the following exercises.

EXERCISE 2.1

On 27th June the balance sheet of Cox and Co. appeared like this:

Balance Sheet as at 27th June

Liabilities	£	*Assets*	£
Capital	40,000	Machinery	20,000
Creditors	3,000	Office Furniture	8,000
		Stock	6,000
		Debtors	4,000
		Bank	5,000
	43,000		43,000

The following transactions took place in the next few days:

June 28 Paid creditors £800 by cheque.
Sold £2,000 of stock for £3,200 – received cash.
Sold £600 of stock for £900 on credit to Simpson.

June 29 Received £2,500 in cheques from various debtors in settlement of their accounts.
Paid wages, £100, in cash.
June 30 Paid electricity bill, £60, by cheque.
Sold £400 of stock for £600 – received cash.
Paid rent and rates, £700, by cheques.

Show the balance sheet as it would appear at 30th June after all the above transactions have been accounted for.

EXERCISE 2.2

A company has the following assets and liabilities at 31st December:

Premises £40,000; Creditors £3,000; Stock £8,000; Amounts owed for rates at 31st December £350; Cash in hand £2,100; Balance at bank *overdrawn* £4,300; Debtors £5,000; Equipment £6,000.

Required:

(a) How much is the company worth – i.e. what is its capital?
(b) If, six months later, the capital has increased by £7,000 what reasons could account for this?
(c) If, six months later, the capital has decreased by £5,000 what could be the reasons for this decrease?

EXERCISE 2.3

Which category of expenditure do the following payments fall into? Indicate with a tick.

	CAPITAL EXPENDITURE	REVENUE EXPENDITURE
Purchase of office furniture		
Payment of rates		
Purchase of delivery van		
Tax and insurance for van		
Repairs to machinery		
Petrol for van		
Decoration of office		
Extension to factory		

EXERCISE 2.4

Classify the following items as capital or revenue expenditure. In each case give reasons for your classification.

(a) An extension of railway tracks in the factory area.
(b) Wages paid to machine operators.

(c) Installation costs of new production machine.
(d) Materials for extensions to foremen's offices in the factory.
(e) Rent paid for the factory.
(f) Payment for computer time to operate a new stores control system.
(g) Wages paid to X's own employers for building the foremen's offices.

(A.E.B. "O" Level)

EXERCISE 2.5

C. Horne started business as a shoe shop retailer on 1st June with £40,000 deposited in a business bank account.

June 2 Purchased shoes for £4,000 from Meeks & Co. on credit.
June 4 Sold shoes which had cost, £80 for £110 – received cash.
June 6 Paid rent for shop, £120 by cheque.
June 7 Purchased more shoes for cash, £60.
June 9 Sold the shoes purchased on 7th June for £100 – received cash.
June 10 Bought shop fittings for £2,500 – paid cheque.
June 14 Sold shoes (cost £2,400) to Jones on credit, for £3,000.
June 18 Paid cheque, £2,500 to Meeks & Co. as part settlement of account.
June 20 Purchased premises for £27,000 – paid cheque.
June 22 Paid wages, £140, by cheque.
June 23 Purchased clogs from J. Harrison for £210 on credit.
June 26 Sold shoes and clogs which had cost £110 for £190 – received cash.
June 29 Paid insurance premiums on premises, £70, by cheque.
June 30 Bought office typewriter for £150 – paid cheque.

Prepare C. Horne's balance sheet as at 30th June.

CHAPTER 3

KEEPING ACCOUNTS

In the past two chapters we have been building up balance sheets from given information, changing assets and liabilities according to the transactions being dealt with, and showing the final position at the end of the day or month. This is a system of accounting which could be effective, but can we really sit down at the end of each day and draw up an amended balance sheet based on what has gone on during the day? To take account of the *changes* in assets and liabilities which have occurred during the day is going to be an impossible task to do daily. What we need is some system of recording *changes* that occur, *as they occur*, so that any time we want to look at our overall financial position we can look at our records and see *at a glance* what we have got in the way of various assets and liabilities. This information can then be set out in the form of a balance sheet and, if the changes (movements) in assets and liabilities have been recorded correctly, our balance sheet will balance!

Right then, we need a simple system whereby we can record changes as they occur, without the necessity of doing balance sheets all the time. In fact, in practice, we need only draw up a balance sheet once a year and the information which we need to prepare that balance sheet will be provided, *at a glance*, from the system of recording we are going to set up.

To do this we must have an **ACCOUNT** for every single asset and liability we have or incur. This account can be a simple sheet of paper or card, and it will be kept initially (until we go on to the computer!) in a box or metal tray which is called the **LEDGER**. Hence the term, 'ledger accounts' (accounts kept in the ledger). This account will record the changes that occur in that particular asset or liability, *as they occur*, and *each* asset and *each* liability will have its own separate account – i.e. one for cash, one for bank, one for equipment, one for capital, etc. The debtors and the creditors will necessitate having a separate account for each debtor and for each creditor because we will need to know, at a glance, how much we owe to Jones and how much Brown owes to us at any point in time. Whenever we decide to prepare a balance sheet from the information in the accounts we can add up all the debtors and all of the creditors and show one total for each on the respective sides of the balance sheet.

What form should these accounts take? The asset or liability in question can only go up or down in amount – i.e. increase or decrease – so let us have two sides to our account, one to record increases and one to record decreases. A convenient form would be as follows:

Name of Account – (e.g. Cash)

£	£
1,000	400
300	100

If we use the left-hand side of the above account for recording increases in cash, and the right-hand side for decreases in cash we can clearly see from the above that at present we have £800 of cash, and if we were presenting a balance sheet at this point the £800 would show on our balance sheet as an asset "cash". Note at this point that the information for the balance sheet is only obtainable from these accounts, which have been daily recording changes (movements) in the relevant asset or liability as those changes occurred. As a result we know at any point in time what the business has *got*, and what it *owes*.

About 500 years ago someone decided that accounts would take the above form and that the left-hand side would be called the "*debit*" side and the right-hand side the "*credit*" side, abbreviated *DR* and *CR* respectively. We are stuck with that decision so do remember it!

The same person also decided that the **acquisition of an asset should be recorded on the debit side** of an account. Imprint this on your mind and don't forget it. From this follows naturally, a simple set of rules:

(i) To record an increase in an asset (e.g. acquisition of cash, or cheques, or a machine or a debtor, etc.) an entry must be made on the debit (left) side of the relevant asset account.

(ii) To record a decrease in an asset (e.g. payment of cash or cheques, or getting rid of a machine, or reduction of a debtor's account when he pays off part of his debt, etc.) an entry must be made on the other side – the credit (right) side.

By recording this way we only need to look at the *difference* between the two sides and we know how much of that particular asset we have got left at the moment (£800 cash in the above example).

If we regard liabilities as being the *opposite* of assets, as I suggested earlier in this book, then surely when recording changes in our liabilities a reverse procedure should apply – i.e. credit (right) entries for acquisitions (increases) in the liabilities, and debit (left) entries for reductions in liabilities. An increase in creditors for example, (e.g. due to purchase of more stock on delayed payment terms) would be recorded on the credit side of the relevant person's account (e.g. Jones, our creditor) and the same with an increase in Capital account due to profits; whilst a reduction in a creditor's account (e.g. as a result of paying off some of our debt) would be recorded on the debit (left) side of that creditor's account, and so on.

Therefore, knowing the fact that an increase in an asset is recorded as a debit entry, the rules for all entries in the accounts follows naturally *and should not need memorising*:

i.e. To record an increase in an asset – debit the account.
To record a decrease in an asset – credit the account.
To record an increase in a liability – credit the account.
To record a decrease in a liability – debit the account.

Remember that the *difference* in the two sides of the account represents what the business has *got* or what it *owes*. Obviously therefore an asset account (Office furniture, Debtors, Cash, Bank, etc., etc.) should always have a greater amount on the debit side than on the credit side, otherwise it's not an asset! If the bank account has more credit entries than debit entries then it is no longer an asset – it is a liability in the form of a bank overdraft (more has gone out of the bank than has gone in). In other words, an asset account must have a net *debit* difference on the account (more debits than credits) whilst a liability account must have a net *credit* difference on the account (more credits than debits). Such differences are referred to as "*balances on the account*".

Do not proceed further until you have thoroughly "digested" all the points made in this book so far.

APPLYING THE "RULES"

Let us now put these "rules" into practice, with our new business – the following transactions take place in June:

June 1 We start business with a £60,000 legacy in cash.
June 4 Our business purchases premises for £40,000 and pays in cash.
June 10 Purchase machinery for £3,000 – pay cash.
June 17 Purchase office furniture £400 – pay cash.
June 24 Purchase a typewriter for £300 *on credit* from XYZ Ltd.
June 27 We introduce a further £5,000 in cash to the business (got from a second rich aunt!) as additional capital.
June 28 £15,000 of cash is paid into a business bank account.
June 29 Purchase second typewriter for £250 – pay by cheque.
June 30 Pay XYZ Ltd. £200 on account, by cheque.

Let us record these transactions *as the occur* in our ledger accounts following the "rules" previously explained.

LEDGER ACCOUNTS OF OUR BUSINESS

DR — Cash Account — CR

		£			£
June 1	Capital	60,000	June 4	Premises	40,000
June 27	Capital	5,000	June 10	Machinery	3,000
			June 17	Office furniture	400
			June 28	Bank	15,000

DR — Capital Account — CR

		£			£
			June 1	Cash	60,000
			June 27	Cash	5,000

DR — Premises Account — CR

		£			£
June 4	Cash	40,000			

DR — Machinery Account — CR

		£			£
June 10	Cash	3,000			

DR — Office Furniture Account — CR

		£			£
June 17	Cash	400			

DR — Typewriters Account — CR

		£			£
June 24	XYZ Ltd.	300			
June 29	Bank	250			

DR — XYZ Ltd. Account — CR

		£			£
June 30	Bank	200	June 24	Typewriters	300

DR — Bank Account — CR

		£			£
June 28	Cash	15,000	June 29	Typewriters	250
			June 30	XYZ Ltd.	200

Check every entry in the above accounts according to the 500 year old rules. Use the dates as your reference to each transaction and tick each entry as you agree with it. Note that in the accounts, a description, or details, of each item is given – e.g. the £40,000 entry on the credit side of cash (June 4th) relates to "premises" and the corresponding debit entry in Premises Account on June 4th details "Cash" being paid. The details of the corresponding entry must always be stated.

Do *not* proceed until you have checked and agreed each entry in the accounts.

DOUBLE-ENTRY

Look carefully now at the entries in the accounts – what do you notice? – What pattern emerges? Answer – every single *debit* entry in the accounts is matched by a corresponding *credit* entry somewhere else in the accounts – or, if you like every single *credit* entry is matched by a corresponding *debit* entry somewhere in the accounts.

You are using a **DOUBLE-ENTRY** system of recording information in the accounts (i.e. a debit to match a credit and vice-versa). For every £1 debit recorded there must be a corresponding £1 credit recorded somewhere. This is an accounting system which is impeccable for accuracy of recording, and in 500 years no one has come up with a better system – even sophisticated computers use the double-entry system as their base. Many a complicated transaction you may come across in your advanced studies (even degree and post degree standards) can be solved by resorting to "double-entry".

In *all* accounts there is double-entry – there is *never* an exception to the rule – if there is not exact double-entry (e.g. £141.98 of debit entries matched by £141.98 of credit entries) in the accounts, then the accounts are not portraying a true picture of what has gone on. **There is never an exception to this rule.**

Also, if double-entry is not adhered to accurately, a balance sheet will never balance (indicating something is wrong) at the time you are listing the information given by the accounts.

Now refer back to the permutations of the "scales" of the balance sheet. If you don't add to both sides of the scale, or take off both sides of the scale, or add to one side and take the same amount off the same side, your scales won't balance – something has not been recorded correctly. Double-entry in the accounts is the practical equivalent of these effects of pluses and minuses on the scales, so if double entry is carried out properly your scales will always balance on the information taken from the accounts.

From the accounts above we can now, on the 30th June, prepare a balance sheet – i.e. a statement of our business's assets and liabilities. Our balance sheet is *not* an account – it has no debit or credit side – it is simply a *statement* of the information portrayed by our business's accounts – the information is taken *from* our accounts and shown on our balance sheet. If our accounts have been kept correctly (on the double-entry principle) then our assets will equal our liabilities on our balance sheet – i.e. our balance sheet will *balance*. The "up and down" effects on the two "dishes" of our balance sheet "scales" are related to the debit and credit entries in our accounts, and provided double-entry has been carried out properly in our accounts, our balance sheet will balance on the information profided by the accounts, *viz*:

Balance Sheet of our Business as at 30th June

Assets	£	*Liabilities*	£
Capital	65,000	Premises	40,000
		Machinery	3,000
		Office Furniture	400
Creditors	100	Typewriters	
		(i.e. Office Equipment)	550
		Bank	14,550
		Cash	6,600
	65,100		65,100

Check carefully the figures in this balance sheet with the information portrayed by the accounts in our ledger. Without the accounts to refer to we could not have prepared such a balance sheet.

Now the balance sheet is filed away for future reference but our accounts stay where they are in the ledger and will go on recording future changes as they occur from tomorrow.

When you thoroughly understand what we have been doing, have a go at the following exercises.

EXERCISE 3.1

From the following information write up the accounts of Checkley and from these accounts prepare a balance sheet as at 31st May.

May 1 Mr Checkley starts a retail business with £40,000 in cash. On the same day he buys shop fittings for £4,000 and pays cash.
May 2 He buys cash till for £300 on credit from T.S. Ltd.
May 3 Purchase of office equipment for £700 – paid for in cash.
May 8 £30,000 cash is paid into a business bank account.
May 12 £300 cheque is paid to T.S. Ltd. in full settlement of the account.
May 14 More office equipment bought for £600 paid for by cheque.
May 20 Shop fittings installed at a cost of £900 by T.S. Ltd., payment to be made at the end of June.
May 31 New counter for shop erected at a cost of £650 – payment made by cheque.

EXERCISE 3.2

From the following information write up the accounts of Doyle and then prepare a balance sheet as at 31st October.

Oct. 1 Mr Doyle starts business as a demolition contractor with £70,000 in cash and his private motor van valued at £5,000.
Oct. 3 Equipment bought for £8,000 – payment made in cash.
Oct. 5 £60,000 cash is paid into a business bank account.
Oct. 7 Loose tools purchased on credit from XYZ Ltd. for £1,400.
Oct. 9 Land is bought for £20,000 – payment by cheque.
Oct. 14 Mobile office bought for £4,500 – payment by cheque.
Oct. 18 Office fittings bought for £850 on credit from O.S. Ltd.
Oct. 20 Cheque paid to XYZ Ltd., £800 as part payment of debt.
Oct. 28 More equipment bought for £22,000 – payment by cheque.
Oct. 31 £3,000 cash taken from business bank account to hold as a "float" for future cash expenses.

EXERCISE 3.3

Write up the accounts of Riddle from the following and prepare a balance sheet as at 31st December.

Dec. 1 Mr Riddle starts a printing business by bringing into the business £20,000 in cash, his own personal motor vehicle valued at £4,300, and various desks and chairs for the office, acquired from home and valued at £100.
Dec. 2 Pays £15,000 cash into a business bank account.
Dec. 4 Purchases machinery for £2,000; pays cash.
Dec. 5 Purchases storage racks for £400; pays cash.
Dec. 6 Receives cheque for £10,000 from ABC Finance Ltd., being a loan repayable over 5 years.
Dec. 10 Purchases small "warehouse" for £18,000; pays by cheque.
Dec. 16 Mr Riddle brings his personal typewriter into the business; valued at £300.
Dec. 20 Purchase office furniture for £500; pays by cheque.
Dec. 25 Buys more machinery for £7,000; pays by cheque.
Dec. 26 Mr Riddle has a good day at the races, winning £2,500, of which he invests £2,000 cash in his business.
Dec. 27 He pays all cash in hand, with the exception of £200 which is to be held as a "float", into the business bank account.

EXERCISE 3.4

You employ a very inexperienced book-keeper who, since you started in business a few days ago, has recorded the following in your accounts:

DR		Cash Account		CR
	£			£
Sept. 1 Capital	10,000	Sept. 3	Office furniture	600
Sept. 7 Machinery	2,000	Sept. 16	,, ,,	200
Sept. 25 Capital	1,000		LTS Ltd.	450
		Sept. 28	Bank	5,000
		Sept. 30	Machinery	1,500

DR	Capital Account		CR
Sept. 1 Cash	£10,000	Sept. 25 Cash	£1,000

Office Furniture

Sept. 16 Cash	£200	Sept. 3 Cash	£600

Machinery

	£	
Sept. 7 Cash	2,000	
Sept. 30 Cash	1,500	

Loose Tools

Sept. 12 LTS Ltd.	£900	

LTS Ltd.

	£	
Sept. 12 Loose Tools	900	
Sept. 16 Cash	450	

Bank Account

Sept. 28 Cash	£5,000	

Required

Re-write these accounts as they *should* have been entered, and prepare a balance sheet as at 30th September from the information portrayed by the revised accounts.

CHAPTER 4

TYPES OF ACCOUNTS

In the last chapter you learned how to record transactions which affect assets and liabilities, and all the accounts you drew up were either accounts of an asset or a liability. The proper name for such accounts is **REAL ACCOUNTS**. Cash, Bank, Jones (Debtor), Todd (Creditor), Machinery, Premises, Capital, etc. – all these are *real* accounts.

What other accounts are there other than real accounts? There are **NOMINAL** accounts – not real because they don't represent either an asset or a liability. Instead they simply *store up information* needed to work out a profit or loss at the year end. Such accounts would be headed "Purchases" (of goods for resale), "Sales" (of those same purchases), Rent, Rates, Wages, Light and Heat and other such expenses.

In the same way that it is impossible to do balance sheets every day as a means of accounting (hence the use of real accounts to record movements in assets and liabilities), it is also impossible to work out the profit every time a sale is made like we did in previous examples. Imagine, at the end of the day, working out the cost of the goods sold during the day, and comparing this with what we have sold these goods for in order to work out the profit. Impossible! Therefore we need a system which will allow us to quickly calculate the profit or loss over a period of time – we only need to do this say once a year, but at the end of the year the information needed to calculate profit or loss must be readily available, and it will be if we keep a set of *Nominal* accounts.

What information will we need at the year end? We will need to know what stock we have purchased (for resale), i.e. we will need to know the total of the year's "Purchases of Stock", and the total of the year's "Sales of Stock". Obviously the difference between what the stock cost us and what we sold it for will represent our *main* profit, our **GROSS PROFIT**. We will also need to know what expenses we incurred during the year on rates, wages, etc. (i.e. our *revenue* expenditure). These expenses will obviously have to be taken off our gross profit figure to arrive at our final profit for the year – i.e. our **NET PROFIT**.

The nominal accounts will have to readily give us all of this information at the year end, so therefore all purchases, sales and payments for expenses must be recorded in these accounts on a daily basis *as they occur* so that at any point in time it is only a matter of adding up the items in these accounts to give us all the information we need to calculate the profit or loss for that particular period covered by the accounts.

The appearance of these nominal accounts will be just like the real accounts with a debit (left) side, and a credit (right) side, but how will we know which side of purchases account, or sales account, or wages account to enter on? The rules we know for recording changes in assets and liabilities (i.e. to record an increase in an asset, debit the asset account, etc. etc.) will not apply, because we are not dealing with assets and liabilities. Even our purchases of goods for re-sale are not assets, because by the time we reach the end of the year then, hopefully, what we purchased will have "gone" – been sold – only that part of our purchases which still remains unsold will be treated as a temporary asset (we will deal with unsold stock later on, but for the present will assume that *all* of our purchases will be sold during the year leaving no unsold stock at the year end).

When entering *any* item in *any* account the rules of 'double-entry' must always be adhered to – there is never an exception to this if we want to maintain accurate records. So, let's see what happens when we purchase or sell goods, or pay an expense.

Say that we purchase goods (for re-sale) for £500 and pay in cash. An entry must be made in the cash (asset) account to record the decrease in cash and according to our "rules" this will have to be a credit entry, *viz*:

DR	Cash Account		CR
			£
Assuming we already have some cash on this side	June 4	Purchases*	500

* "Purchases" must be written in the account to show what the £500 payment relates to.

Double-entry means that we must now put a *debit* entry of £500 somewhere. Where? The most obvious place – in a *Purchases* account, *e.g.*

DR		Purchases Account	CR
June 4	Cash*	£500	

* Note the cross reference to show clearly that the purchase of goods was for cash.

Let us now purchase £1,000 of goods (for re-sale) *on credit* from Smith & Co. Dealing again with the real account first (i.e. the creditor, Smith), let's enter up this account. We are increasing what we *owe*, a liability, so we credit the account *viz*:

DR	Smith & Co.		CR
	June 5	Purchases*	£1,000

* Again a cross reference to which the £1,000 relates – i.e. "purchases".

The double-entry is again the recording of the purchase which has taken place, and must obviously be a debit entry to complete double-entry *viz*:

DR		Purchases Account			CR
		£			
June 4	Cash	500			
June 5	Smith & Co.	1,000			

It should now be apparent to you that any purchase of goods for resale which takes place will be credited to either cash or a creditor and will always be debited to Purchases account. It is the entry in the *real* account, as per our "rules", which will determine which side of the respective *nominal* account is entered on, so if when dealing with transactions, you enter up the real account first, per the "rules", you can't possibly get the entry in the nominal account on the wrong side!

Let us now have two sales, one for cash £800, and one on credit to Jones for £1,400. Dealing with the real accounts first (Cash and Jones) we must debit them *viz*:

DR		Cash Account			CR
June 10	Sales	£800			

DR		Jones			CR
June 10	Sales	£1,400			

In both cases we have increased an asset – therefore debit entries. The double-entry must be credits in the relevant account, *viz*:

DR		Sales Account			CR
					£
			June 10	Cash	800
			June 10	Jones	1,400

It should now be apparent that *all* sales will involve a debit entry in either cash or a debtor's account, and a credit entry in sales account. You don't need to memorise this fact – it should be natural and obvious if you have carefully studied the text to here.

Finally, let us pay wages in cash £100, and rent in cash £150. The entries are as follows:

DR		Cash Account			CR
					£
			June 30	Wages	100
			June 30	Rent	150

DR		Wages Account	CR
June 10	Cash	£100	

DR		Rent Account	CR
June 10	Cash	£150	

Note that a *separate* nominal account is used for each type of expense. This way we can see clearly what has been spent on each type of expense – far better than lumping everything together in one expense account. Note also the cross references in the accounts showing clearly where the other part of the double-entry lies.

In the above examples we have entered in three real accounts (Cash, Smith and Jones) and in four nominal accounts (Purchases, Sales, Wages and Rent). If we wanted to know our gross and net profits at 30th June we would "collect" the following information from our nominal accounts; remember that in practice these accounts would contain many more entries than shown in this single example, but the entries would all be on the same sides of the accounts – just more to add up!

		£
Total Sales		2,200
Total Purchases		1,500
GROSS PROFIT		700
less expenses	£	
Wages	100	
Rent	150	250
NET PROFIT		450

What has gone on in the real accounts does not affect our profit figures – the information in the real accounts is for our balance sheet when we do one.

Before we look at a comprehensive example, to bring everything we have learned together, let me stress that all the above references to "purchases" and "sales" have meant purchases of goods for re-sale and sales of goods for re-sale. If in the middle of all these I had said "we purchase premises for £30,000" or "we sell machinery for £10,000" then, unless we were in business to buy and sell premises or machinery for profit, these transactions would *not* be entered in our nominal accounts of "Purchases" and "Sales". They would represent purchases and sales of *assets* and would be entered in the real accounts (i.e. Debit Premises Account, and Credit Cash or Bank, or Debit Cash or Bank and Credit Machinery).

In other words, if say a butcher purchases meat, he will debit his "Purchases Account" (nominal account) but if he purchases a new refridgerator he will debit his Refrigerator or Equipment account (real account), because this would be a purchase of an asset which will show on his balance sheet. Similarly, if he sells meat this will be entered in Sales Account, but when he eventually sells his fridge the entry will be in the asset account. "Purchases" means purchases of that which he buys with the intention to re-sell at a profit.

Let's now put all this into practice.

EXAMPLE

May 1 J. Snow starts business as a bookseller with £50,000 in cash.
May 2 Buys premises for £30,000 cash.
May 3 Buys shop fittings for £2,500 cash.
May 4 Pays £15,000 cash into a business bank account.
May 5 Purchases books for £3,000 – pays by cheque.
May 7 Pays rates by cheque £160.
May 9 Purchases office furniture for £1,000 – pays cheque.
May 12 Sales of books for cash £940.
May 14 Purchases books for £4,200 on credit from B.S. Ltd.
May 16 Pays insurance premiums of £90 by cheque.
May 17 Pays wages in cash £430.
May 19 Purchases books for £800 from N.P. Ltd. on credit.
May 20 Cash sales of books £2,100.
May 21 Sells books for £4,100 on credit to I.D. Ltd.
Buys more office furniture for £800 – pays cheque.
May 22 Pays wages in cash £490.
Pays £65 cash for stationery.
Pays £140 electricity bill by cheque.
May 27 Cash sales of books £2,400.
Credit sale of books to JB Ltd., £1,650.
May 28 Pays cheque £2,100 to B.S. Ltd. in part settlement of account.
Receives cheque for £1,300 from I.D. Ltd. in part settlement of account.
May 31 Sales of all remaining books in stock for £830 cash.

We are going to enter the above transactions in J. Snow's accounts. It is important that you tick off every transaction and understand the entries that are made. Ideally, enter up the accounts yourself and then check off with the following – this will be far more effective.

ACCOUNTS IN J. SNOW'S LEDGER

REAL ACCOUNTS

DR — Cash Account — CR

Date	Particulars	£	Date	Particulars	£
May 1	Capital	50,000	May 1	Premises	30,000
May 12	Sales	940	May 3	Fittings	2,500
May 20	Sales	2,100	May 4	Bank	15,000
May 27	Sales	2,400	May 17	Wages	430
May 31	Sales	830	May 22	Wages	490
			May 22	Stationery	65

DR — Capital Account — CR

Date	Particulars		Date	Particulars	
			May 1	Cash	£50,000

DR — Premises Account — CR

Date	Particulars		Date	Particulars	
May 1	Cash	£30,000			

DR — Shop Fittings Account — CR

Date	Particulars		Date	Particulars	
May 3	Cash	£2,500			

DR — Office Furniture Account — CR

Date	Particulars	£	Date	Particulars	
May 9	Bank	1,000			
May 21	Bank	800			

DR — Bank Account — CR

Date	Particulars	£	Date	Particulars	£
May 4	Cash	15,000	May 5	Purchases	3,000
May 28	I.D. Ltd.	1,300	May 7	Rates	160
			May 9	Office Furniture	1,000
			May 16	Insurance	90
			May 21	Office Furniture	800
			May 22	Electricity	140
			May 28	B.S. Ltd.	2,100

DR — I.D. Ltd. Account — CR

Date	Particulars		Date	Particulars	
May 21	Sales	£4,100	May 28	Bank	£1,300

DR — B.S. Ltd. Account — CR

Date	Particulars		Date	Particulars	
May 28	Bank	£2,100	May 14	Purchases	£4,200

DR — J.B. Ltd. Account — CR

Date	Particulars		Date	Particulars	
May 27	Sales	£1,650			

DR — N.P. Ltd. Account — CR

Date	Particulars		Date	Particulars	
			May 19	Purchases	£800

NOMINAL ACCOUNTS

DR		Purchases Account			CR
		£			
May 5	Bank	3,000			
May 14	B.S. Ltd.	4,200			
May 19	N.P. Ltd.	800			

DR		Sales			CR
					£
			May 12	Cash	940
			May 20	Cash	2,100
			May 21	I.D. Ltd.	4,100
			May 27	Cash	2,400
			May 27	J.B. Ltd.	1,650
			May 31	Cash	830

DR		Rates			CR
May 7	Bank	£160			

DR		Insurance			CR
May 16	Bank	£90			

DR		Wages			CR
		£			
May 17	Cash	430			
May 22	Cash	490			

DR		Electricity			CR
May 22	Bank	£140			

DR		Stationery			CR
May 22	Cash	£65			

You will notice from the above that all entries in the Purchases Account and in expense accounts are always debit entries. This is inevitable if you consider that all purchases and payments of expenses must either be by a payment from bank or cash (which must be a *credit* entry in bank or cash in order to reduce that asset) *or* be on credit (which means that some creditor's account must be *credited* to show that money is owing to that person) – in which case the other account (purchases or expenses) must be *debited* to complete the double-entry.

Sales account always consists of credit entries because the corresponding part of a sales transaction must either be receipt of cash or cheque (debit cash or bank) or, if a sale on credit, the creation of a debtor (debit the person concerned).

The accounts in J. Snow's ledger are giving him a progressive record of what is happening in his business and from the information contained in the accounts he will be able to work out his profit and prepare a balance sheet whenever he wants.

Before we do that for him, in the next chapter, you should have some practice in writing up accounts yourself, so when you thoroughly understand this chapter, tackle the following exercise and *file your answer* as you will need it later on.

EXERCISE 4.1

Write up the accounts of J. Brunsdon from the following information. Keep your real accounts separate from your nominal accounts.

March 1 J. Brunsdon starts business as a retailer of video equipment with £45,000 in cash.
March 3 Buys shop premises for £28,000 – pays in cash.
March 4 £15,000 cash is paid into a business bank account.
March 5 Stock of video equipment purchased for £8,000 on credit from V.S. Ltd.
March 6 Shop fittings purchased for £1,200 – payment by cheque.
March 7 Assistants wages paid in cash, £60.
March 8 Office furniture purchased for £600 – payment by cheque.
March 10 Cash sales of video equipment for £1,600.
March 12 Stationery paid for in cash £48.
Insurance premium paid by cheque, £65.
March 14 Credit sales of video equipment to PTS Ltd. for £1,930.
March 18 Rates paid by cheque, £280.
March 20 Cash sales of video equipment for £4,120.
March 21 Wages paid in cash £270.
March 22 Purchases of video equipment for £3,000 – paid for by cheque.
March 23 Advertising costs, £140, paid in cash.
March 24 Cheque for £700 received from PTS Ltd. as part payment of account.
March 25 Payment by cheque of £4,000 to VS Ltd. as part payment of account with them.
March 26 Remaining stock of video equipment sold for £7,940 to PTS Ltd. on credit.
March 27 Wages paid by cheque £310.
March 28 Paid £4,000 cash into the business bank account.
March 31 Electricity bill, £214 paid by cheque.

EXERCISE 4.2

Write up the accounts of B. Rawle from the following. Keep real accounts separate from nominal accounts.

May 1 B. Rawle starts business as the sole proprietor of a music shop, with £40,000 in cash.
May 2 Pays £30,000 cash into a business bank account.
May 4 Purchases sheet music for £3,000, on credit, from J. Mortimer.
May 6 Buys various musical instruments for £4,000, from E. Williams; pays by cheque.
May 7 Pay assistants' wages in cash, £80.
May 10 Pays rent of £60 by cheque.
May 12 Sells sheet music for cash, £180.
May 16 Purchases display units for £1,000, pays by cheque.
May 18 Pays £1,200 cheque to J. Mortimer as part settlement of account.
May 20 Sells a trombone to P. Spiro for £480, on credit.
May 24 Purchases musical instruments at auction, £2,200, for cash.
Nay 25 Buys various shop fittings for £600, pays cheque.
Sells musical instruments to the Dickens School of Music for £4,400 on credit.
May 26 Pays wages in cash £210.
Sells sheet music for cash £450.
May 27 Receives part payment, £100 cash from P. Spiro.
May 28 Pays for advertising £30, by cheque.
Sells various musical instruments for cash, £4,600.
May 30 Sells all the remaining stock of sheet music and instruments to Job Lots Ltd. for £6,800.

EXERCISE 4.3

J. Green starts business as a wholesaler of electrical equipment on 1st June with £80,000 in cash. Post his accounts for the month of June and keep this record safe, and in neat form, as you will need to use these accounts again after reading the next chapter.

June 2 Purchases warehouse for £40,000, pays cash.
June 3 Purchases stock of electrical equipment for £7,000 on credit from ABC Supplies.
June 4 Pays £30,000 cash into a business bank current account, and 5,000 into a business bank deposit account.
June 6 Sales of electrical equipment for £2,400, receive cash.
June 7 Pays rates £620 by cheque.
June 10 Buys motor van for £3,500, pays cheque.

June 12 Purchases petrol for £18, pays cash.
Pays van tax £85 by cheque.
Pays insurance on van £150 by cheque.
June 16 Pays wages £310 in cash.
June 18 Purchases packing machinery for £400, pays cheque.
June 20 Sales of electrical equipment to Ames and Co. for £2,400 on credit.
June 22 Purchases electrical equipment for £3,000 from ABC Supplies on credit.
June 24 Pays telephone bill, £80 by cheque.
June 27 Pays wages in cash £280.
June 28 Sells all remaining stock of electrical equipment for £7,500 to Jaynes on credit.
June 30 Pays general expenses of £800 in cash.

EXERCISE 4.4

Write up the accounts of J. Denver, painter and decorator, from the following. File your neat copy of these accounts as you will need these accounts again after reading Chapter 5.

Nov. 1 Denver started business with a cash legacy of £2,000.
Nov. 2 Purchases ladders for £70, pays cash.
Nov. 4 Purchases various equipment for £40, pays cash.
Nov. 6 Pays insurance premiums of £60 in cash.
Nov. 7 Pays £1,500 cash into a business bank account.
Nov. 10 Purchases paint and wallpaper for Job. No. 1, for £90, on credit from WPS Ltd.
Nov. 16 Completes Job No. 1 and receives £200 cash from customer.
Nov. 18 Pays assistant's wages, £40 in cash.
Nov. 20 Purchases materials for Job No. 2 for £160 – pays by cheque.
Nov. 26 Completes Job No. 2 and issues bill for £540 to his customer, J. Dodd, for payment in one month's time.
Nov. 27 Purchases second-hand van for £800 – pays cheque.
Nov. 29 Pays account of WPS Ltd. in full, by cheque.

EXERCISE 4.5

D. Bragg starts in business on 1 February as a retailer of office equipment and stationery. He intends to work from home and has £500 capital in cash to start with. Post his accounts from the following information and file these neat accounts for use again after completing the next chapter.

Feb. 1 Purchases stationery from AB Suppliers Ltd. for £200, on credit.

Feb. 3 Buys desk for his office at home, £70, pays cash.

Feb 4 Buys delivery van for £900, on six months' credit, from XYZ Garage Ltd.

Feb. 6 Cash sales of stationery £180.

Feb. 8 Purchases stationery from AB Suppliers Ltd. for £600, on credit.

Feb. 10 Cash sales of stationery £260.

Feb. 15 Purchases office equipment (for resale) £800, on credit from AB Supplies Ltd.

Feb 16 Borrows £5,000 from his uncle, W. Williams, who gives a cheque for this amount. The whole of this £5,000 is to be used in D. Braggs business and is deposited in a bank current account.

Feb 18 Rents a small building for storage and pays £60 rent in advance by cheque.

Feb. 20 Sells office equipment to J. Stone for £700 on credit.

Feb. 24 Pays for service of van, petrol, and tax amounting to £160, by cheque.

Feb. 25 Cash sales of stationery, £420.

Feb. 26 Pays assistant's wages in cash, £30.

Feb. 27 Pays £1,000 cheque to AB Suppliers Ltd. in part settlement of account.

Feb. 28 Sells all his remaining stock of stationery and equipment for £700, cash.

CHAPTER 5

TRADING AND PROFIT AND LOSS ACCOUNTS

I want you now to refer back to the accounts we drew up for J. Snow at the end of the last chapter. I said that we could calculate his profit and prepare his balance sheet at any time from this information, so let's do this at the end of May (normally this would be done at the end of the year).

From the information contained in the nominal accounts we can calculate profit or loss for the month of May, *viz*:

		£
Total Sales		12,020
Total Purchases		8,000
GROSS PROFIT		4,020
Less Expenses:	£	
Rates	160	
Insurance	90	
Wages	920	
Electricity	140	
Stationery	65	
		1,375
NET PROFIT		2,645

This statement is, in practice, shown in the form of an *account* with all the rules of double-entry being adhered to. You will soon appreciate why this is necessary, to ensure accuracy and to highlight any errors which may occur. The account used to find the profit is drawn up at the end of each financial year and is called a "Trading and Profit and Loss Account". It will summarise the effects of trading throughout that particular period, which in our case is not a year, but the month of May.

We are now going to formally *transfer* all of the information from the nominal accounts to the "Trading and Profit and Loss Account for the month ended 31st May" so that when we have finished, all of the information which is at present scattered over many different nominal accounts, will all be "under one roof", that of the "Trading and Profit and Loss Account". Note the word "transfer" – this means moving something from one account to *the same side* of another account. Therefore, if we transfer the totals from the nominal accounts to the Trading and Profit and Loss Account, all the debit totals on nominal accounts will finish up on the debit side of the Trading and Profit and Loss Account, and the credit totals on the credit side. Once the transfers have taken place there should be nothing left in the nominal accounts – everything will be in the Trading and Profit and Loss Account.

Let's see how this works. First of all we will transfer Purchases and Sales to the Trading and Profit and Loss Account.

DR Purchases CR

		£			£
May 5	Bank	3,000	May 31	Transfer to	
May 14	BS Ltd.	4,200		T and P & L a/c	8,000
May 19	NP Ltd.	800			
		8,000			8,000

DR Sales CR

		£			£
May 31	Transfer to T and		May 12	Cash	940
	P & L a/c	12,020	May 20	Cash	2,100
			May 21	ID Ltd.	4,100
			May 27	Cash	2,400
			May 27	JB Ltd.	1,650
			May 31	Cash	830
		12,020			12,020

DR Trading and Profit and Loss Account for period ending 31st May CR

	£		£
Purchases	8,000	Sales	12,020

NOTE:

(i) The £8,000 of debits which used to lie in Purchases Account now lies on the debit side of Trading and Profit & Loss Account, the £12,020 of Sales on the credit side.

(ii) Double entry – an £8,000 credit entry matched by an £8,000 debit entry, and £12,020 debit entry matched by a £12,020 credit entry.

(iii) Both sides of Purchases and Sales Accounts add up to the same figure – this is our check to show that the right amounts have been transferred. Note that these additions are on the same horizontal lines to keep the accounts neat.

The Purchases and Sales Accounts are now "closed off" – there is no longer anything in them – they have been "ruled off'. Having given us the necessary information they have done their job of storing up information throughout the period of the month (normally a year), and that information has been passed on to the periodically prepared Trading and Profit and Loss Account. These same account sheets will be used again for the next period's purchases and sales of course, but the double-ruled lines underneath the totals will ensure that nothing relating to May (in our example) will get mixed up with subsequent periods.

Now we will do exactly the same to the other nominal accounts – we will *transfer* the information to the Trading Profit and Loss Account and close off the nominal accounts, *viz*:

DR		Rates			CR
		£			£
May 7	Bank	160	May 31	Transfer to P & L a/c	160
		160			160

DR		Insurance			CR
		£			£
May 16	Bank	90	May 31	Transfer to P & L a/c	90
		90			90

DR		Wages			CR
		£			£
May 17	Cash	430	May 31	Transfer to P & L a/c	920
May 22	Cash	490			
		920			920

DR		Electricity			CR
		£			£
May 22	Bank	140	May 31	Transfer to P & L a/c	140
		140			140

DR		Stationery			CR
		£			£
May 22	Cash	65	May 31	Transfer to P & L a/c	65
		65			65

DR Trading and Profit and Loss Account for period ending 31 May CR

	£		£
Purchases	8,000	Sales	12,020
Rates	160		
Insurance	90		
Wages	920		
Electricity	140		
Stationery	65		
Net Profit	2,645		
	12,020		12,020

NOTE:
(i) Double entry on the transfers of expenses.
(ii) Proper ruling off of the expense accounts in the ledger so that they are ready to start recording the next period's transactions. At the moment they show nothing in them, all the information having been transferred to the T. and P & L account.
(iii) The figure for Net Profit is the *difference* between the cost of purchases and expenses and the selling price of the goods – the difference between the two sides of the account. Once this difference has been inserted in the account both sides add up to the same amount – a check on accuracy. The account is "ruled off".

Double-entry has been observed throughout – except for the double-entry for the net profit of £2,645! Where is the corresponding credit for £2,645? What account do you think should be credited with this amount? Think carefully about this before you carry on reading.

Who does this profit belong to? The owner of the business, J. Snow. At present his Capital Account in the real accounts section of the ledger (refer back) reads "credit balance £50,000", but we now know that his business owes him the profit as well – therefore his Capital account should be credited with the net profit for the month (normally a year) so completing the double-entry to the debit in the T and P & L a/c and so showing the true current position.

Therefore:

DR Capital Account CR

			£
	May 1	Cash	50,000
	May 31	Net Profit from P & L a/c	2,645

Note that this is the only entry we have made in any real account during the end of month (year) recordings.

It may have struck you that the above T and P & L a/c shows a net profit which agrees with the original "primitive" statement we prepared but it does not show the *gross* profit. It *should*, because the gross profit shows the profit on pure buying and selling (ignoring the expenses involved), whilst the net profit shows the final position after paying the necessary expenses. It is possible to have a very large gross profit, if you can buy cheap and sell at a large percentage increase, but if it is necessary to incur large costs in order to *sell* the goods (e.g. advertising, labour costs, large rents etc.) then you may well finish up spending more on "overheads" than you have gained in the original buying and selling of your goods, and so you make a loss. In these circumstances you have got to "prune" your expenses without affecting your sales if you are to stay in business. It is therefore very important to know your *gross* and your *net* profit.

The T and P & L a/c we have drawn up can easily "throw out" the gross profit figure by "balancing the account off" after purchases and sales have been entered, and then continuing the account to allow for the expenses. The account will then be in two parts, the first part being the Trading Account ("trading" means buying and selling) and the second part, the Profit and Loss Account, *viz*:

DR — Trading and Profit and Loss Account for period ending 31 May — CR

		£		£
TRADING ACCOUNT	Purchases	8,000	Sales	12,020
	Gross Profit c/d	4,020		
		12,020		12,020
PROFIT & LOSS ACCOUNT	Rates	160	Gross Profit b/d	4,020
	Insurance	90		
	Wages	920		
	Electricity	140		
	Stationery	65		
	Net Profit to Capital a/c	2,645		
		4,020		4,020

NOTE:

(i) The gross profit is simply the difference between purchases and sales, and by taking the difference, and inserting it on the debit side, we have proved our arithmetical accuracy by showing that the "light" side of the account needed £4,020 adding to it to make it agree with the other side (£12,020). Obviously then, the credits (sales) exceeded the debits by £4,020 and this net result has started off the Profit and Loss Account (credit side), the debits for Rates, Insurance, etc. having the effect of reducing this commencing gross profit, so leaving the final net profit of £2,645. All of your future preparations of T and P & L a/cs should be shown in this way.

The note c/d means "carried down" and b/d means "brought down". We have simply "stopped" the account mid-way and drawn up a net overall picture at this point, the picture showing that, at this stage, there are £4,020 more credits than debits – i.e. we have sold for £4,020 more than the goods sold actually cost us.

You will see now why, in the transfers of expenses of rates, etc., I have stated in these accounts "Transfer to P & L a/c" not "Transfer to T and P & L a/c". Purchases and sales are transferred to Trading Account, all the other expenses to Profit and Loss Account.

Before you proceed further you should now use the accounts you prepared to Exercise 4.1 and 4.2 to prepare Trading and Profit and Loss Accounts for the relevant periods. Transfer the nominal accounts to Trading and Profit and Loss account and transfer your final net profit to the Capital Account. Don't decide to do this later – do it now! You should finish up with the following answers:

Exercise 4.1	*Gross Profit £4,590*	*Net Profit £3,203*	*Capital £48,203*
Exercise 4.2	*Gross Profit £7,710*	*Net Profit £7,330*	*Capital £47,330*

LOSSES

In all our examples and exercises to date we have always finished up with a Net Profit – i.e. our gross profit has been *more* than the total of expenses incurred in making that gross profit. It does happen though, that sometimes the expenses add up to more than the gross profit, in which case a *loss* has been made, e.g.

DR Trading and Profit & Loss Account for the year ended 31st December CR

	£		£
Purchases	18,000	Sales	30,000
Gross Profit c/d	12,000		
	30,000		30,000
Various expenses		Gross Profit b/d	12,000
(detailed)	14,000	Net Loss to Capital a/c	2,000
	14,000		14,000

The double entry (i.e. the debit) to the credit entry in the Profit and Loss Account will be recorded in Capital Account, so reducing capital – i.e. the business now owes less to the owner than before because the business has lost some of the capital put into the business by the owner.

BALANCING OFF ACCOUNTS

Now let us proceed with J. Snow's accounts. We have prepared his Trading and Profit and Loss Account for May and all his nominal accounts are now closed off. The only accounts remaining in his ledger which still have something in them are the real accounts – the assets and liabilities.

The Cash, Bank, Premises, Shop Fittings, Office Furniture and various debtors and creditors have been quite unaffected by what we have just been doing – we finished at the end of May with, for example, Shop Fittings £2,500, and JB Ltd. owing J. Snow £1,650. Obviously the next period (June) will start off with Shop Fittings £2,500, JB Ltd. owing £1,650, etc., etc. In other words the assets and liabilities at 31st May will *continue* into the next period, so we are certainly *not* going to close off these accounts. What we are going to do though is to make them more readable, so that we can see at a glance just how much J. Snow has in cash, how much he owes to BS Ltd., etc. In other words we are going to "balance off" these accounts.

Taking Cash Account as an example – it takes some time to work out the difference between the two sides, showing that J. Snow has £7,785 in cash at the 31st May (i.e. £7,785 more debits than credits in this asset account). Now, rather than continue recording in this account in June, so that we have even more figures to add up at the end of June, let us now consolidate all the figures to date into *one* net figure. If we have £7,785 more debits than credits at 31st May, then let us start off June showing a debit entry (debit balance) of £7,785 so that the figures for May transactions never need to be added up again! This is how we balance off the account at the end of a period:

DR — Cash Account — CR

		£			£
May 1	Capital	50,000	May 1	Premises	30,000
May 12	Sales	940	May 3	Fittings	2,500
May 20	Sales	2,100	May 4	Bank	15,000
May 27	Sales	2,400	May 17	Wages	430
May 31	Sales	830	May 22	Wages	490
			May 22	Stationery	65
			May 31	Balance c/d	7,785
		56,270			56,270
May 31	Balance b/d	7,785			

PROCEDURE FOLLOWED:

(i) The "heaviest" side was added up (the debit side) to arrive at £56,270.

(ii) The other (credit) side was then added up (no total shown in the account itself) to £48,485.

(iii) This showed that there were £7,785 more debits than credits in the account – i.e. a *debit balance* of £7,785.

(iv) The difference of £7,785 was then added to the "lighter" (credit) side of the account (Balance c/d) so bringing the two sides of the account "into balance" (i.e. the debit side *and* the credit side both added up to £56,270 (both sides checked for accuracy).

(v) The balancing figure of £7,785 was then carried down to the debit side of the account (Balance b/d) thereby clearly showing *at a glance* that the next period starts off with £7,785 in cash. The double-ruled lines underneath the totals on each side ensure that May's figures need never be added up again.

Note double-entry, even in the balancing off of an account – *credit* cash £7,785, *debit* cash £7,785 – there is *never* an exception to double entry in the accounts.

At the end of a period all real accounts are "balanced off" so that their balances can be seen *at a glance* (no need for mental arithmetic).

Having balanced off the Cash Account the rest of the real accounts will be balanced off, *viz*:

DR Bank Account CR

		£			£
May 4	Cash	15,000	May 5	Purchases	3,000
May 28	I.D. Ltd.	1,300	May 7	Rates	160
			May 9	Office Furniture	1,000
			May 16	Insurance	90
			May 21	Office Furniture	800
			May 22	Electricity	140
			May 28	B.S. Ltd.	2,100
			May 31	Balance c/d	9,010
		16,300			16,300
May 31	Balance b/d	9,010			

DR I.D. Ltd. CR

		£			£
May 21	Sales	4,100	May 28	Bank	1,300
			May 31	Balance c/d	2,800
		4,100			4,100
May 31	Balance b/d	2,800			

DR J.B. Ltd. CR

May 27	Sales	£1,650			

DR Capital Account CR

		£			£
May 31	Balance c/d	52,645	May 1	Cash	50,000
			May 31	Net profit from P & L a/c	2,645
		52,645			52,645
			May 31	Balance b/d	52,645

DR Premises CR

May 1	Cash	£30,000			

DR Shop Fittings CR

May 3	Cash	£2,500			

DR		B.S. Ltd.			CR
		£			£
May 28	Bank	2,100	May 14	Purchases	4,200
May 31	Balance c/d	2,100			
		4,200			4,200
			May 31	Balance b/d	2,100

DR		Office Furniture			CR
		£			£
May 9	Bank	1,000	May 31	Balance c/d	1,800
May 21	Bank	800			
		1,800			1,800
May 31	Balance b/d	1,800			

DR		N.P. Ltd.			CR
			May 19	Purchases	£800

All the real accounts now show *at a glance* the balance on them. Note that the Capital Account was added up – £52,645 of credits, and no debits, therefore an amount of £52,645 had to be placed on the debit side to bring the account "into balance" (i.e. make both totals of sides agree) – the double entry is a credit to the account of £52,645 showing clearly that Capital *starts the next period* with a credit balance of £52,645 (i.e. there were £52,645 more credits than there were debits in the last period). Note also that nothing has been done to J.B. Ltd., Premises, Shop Fittings or N.P. Ltd. accounts – this is because there is only *one* entry in them and therefore the balance of these accounts *can* be seen at a glance. It would be pointless to do the following to J.B. Ltd.'s Account:

DR		J.B. Ltd.			CR
		£			£
May 27	Sales	1,650	May 31	Balance c/d	1,650
		1,650			1,650
May 31	Balance b/d	1,650			

but if you want to – then do it!

J. SNOW'S BALANCE SHEET

The accountant of the firm can now quickly prepare a balance sheet of J. Snow as at 31st May from the information contained in the real accounts, *viz*:

Balance Sheet of J. Snow as at 31st May

Liabilities	£	*Assets*	£
Capital	50,000	Premises	30,000
Add Net Profit	2,645	Shop Fittings	2,500
		Office Furniture	1,800
	52,645	Debtors	4,450
		Bank	9.010
Creditors	2,900	Cash	7,785
	55,545		55,545

Note – the fact that the balance sheet does balance, shows that double-entry has been faithfully recorded in the accounts and therefore indicates accuracy of recording. Note also how the Capital account balance is shown – not just a bare balance but a "breakdown" of how it has changed in the period.

The above balance sheet faithfully reproduces the information contained in the real accounts but it only *notes* this information. The balance sheet is *not* an account – it has no debit or credit side – it is simply a *statement* of the information shown by the accounts. Nothing has been transferred to the balance sheet from the accounts – the information has simply been *noted.* Quite different from our dealing with the nominal accounts, when we transferred everything to the Trading and Profit and Loss Account so leaving the nominal accounts empty. The real accounts *continue* into the next period but the record of purchases, sales, wages, etc. in May do not! June will have its own purchases, sales, etc., but it will still have the assets and liabilities left over from May.

Study carefully the accounts of J. Snow, step by step, don't just look at them – study them!

SUMMARY

The accounts are written up daily as the transactions take place. The asset and liability accounts (i.e. the real accounts) record changes in the assets and liabilities, whilst purchases, sales and expenses are recorded in the nominal accounts as they occur. Double-entry for every transaction!

At the end of the period (normally a year) the nominal accounts are written off by transferring the amounts in them to a "Trading and Profit and Loss Account". This leaves the nominal accounts "empty" – "ruled off" – all the information now being in the Trading and Profit and Loss Account. The net profit, or loss, is then transferred to Capital Account.

The real accounts are now balanced off to make easy reading, and the balances of these accounts are then *shown* in the balance sheet – debit balances as assets, credit balances as liabilities. You should now take out of your file the accounts you prepared for Exercises 4.1 and 4.2, and balance off the real accounts, before preparing balance sheets as at 31st March. When you have done that, and checked your work, you should work the following exercises.

EXERCISE 5.1

Take from your files the accounts you wrote up for Green (Exercise 4.3), Denver (Exercise 4.4) and Bragg (Exercise 4.5).

From these accounts prepare Trading and Profit and Loss Accounts for each trader, for the months in question, and prepare their individual balance sheets as at the end of the relevant months.

Note that after preparation of the Trading and Profit and Loss accounts, the nominal accounts should be "closed" – i.e. no balances remaining. Where necessary balance off the real accounts before preparing the balance sheets, so that the balance is readable *at a glance*.

EXERCISE 5.2

Post the following transactions to the ledger accounts of J. Rose and then prepare a Trading and Profit and Loss account for the month of May by transferring the balances of the nominal accounts. Finally prepare a balance sheet from the remaining real accounts (properly balanced off) as at 31st May.

May 1 Started business with £10,000 in the bank.
May 2 Bought goods (for resale) on credit from Smith £1,200, and Tomkins, £1,600.
May 4 Sold goods for cash £450.
May 5 Paid rent £70 by cheque.
May 7 Bought office furniture for the business, £2,400, paid cheque.
May 10 Bought delivery van for £3,100, paid cheque.
May 12 Paid the account of Tomkins by cheque.
May 14 Paid insurance and tax on van, in cash £270.
May 16 Purchased goods (for resale) from Palmer for £1,500 – paid him immediately by cheque.
May 18 Sold goods to P. Sheriff for £2,900 on credit.
May 23 Paid wages in cash £120.
May 25 Sold goods to Braintree for £800 on credit. Sold goods to Appleby for £950 on credit.
May 26 Purchased more office furniture for £140, paid by cheque.
May 27 Petrol bill for month, £80, paid by cheque.
May 28 Sold *all* remaining stock of goods for £1,700, received cash.

May 30 Paid to Smith (supplier) a cheque for £2,100 – a mistake having been made by transposing the amount actually owed to Smith. (Note – this error was not discovered by either party until 6th June).

EXERCISE 5.3

John Ellerwood, sole trader, has asked you to help him to prepare a Trading and Profit and Loss Account for the year 19–7, and a balance sheet at the year end, but he is unwilling to let you have access to his actual accounts (you suspect he doesn't keep any). He does, however, give you the following information:

FOR 19–7	£	*At end of 19–7*	£
Actual Purchases	2,600	Total Debtors	830
Interest paid on loans	50	Total Creditors	620
Rent and Rates	400		
Wages	900	Loans	2,000
Insurances	60	Office Furniture	900
Actual Sales	3,600	Motor Van	2,600
Light and Heat	280	Bank Overdraft	1,300
Telephone	110		
Van Expenses	340		
Stationery and postages	40		
Stolen from cash till	10		

NOTE: Capital of J. Ellerwood at the start of the year was £1,600.

EXERCISE 5.4

Post the following transactions to the ledger accounts of B. Jones and then prepare a Trading and Profit and Loss account for the month of June and a Balance Sheet as at 30th June.

June 1 Started business as a butcher with £50,000 in the bank.
June 3 Purchased premises for £40,000 – paid cheque.
June 4 Bought shop fittings for £3,500 – paid cheque.
June 6 Purchased meat for £2,800 on credit from Meat Suppliers Ltd.
June 8 Cash sales of meat, £650.
June 10 Bought delivery van for £4,200 by cheque.
June 12 Cash sales of meat, £800.
June 14 Paid rates £370 by cheque.
June 16 Paid wages of assistant, £90 by cheque.
June 24 Cash purchases of meat £500.
June 26 Paid wages in cash £70.
June 27 Sold meat on credit to Rowland for £1,900.
Paid cheque to Meat Suppliers Ltd, £1,400.
June 28 Sold remaining stock of meat to Rowland for £1,100.

CHAPTER 6

THE TRIAL BALANCE

You should now know how to enter up accounts (called "posting") to record transactions as they occur – i.e. to record movements in assets and liabilities, and to record information in the nominal accounts for the purpose of calculating profit or loss later on.

Obviously errors are going to be made in the accounts at times – no one is perfect – in which case the accounts are not going to record the true picture of what has gone on. A serious error could cause profits to be over, or under-stated, and it is crucial that a business shows a correct profit figure for obvious reasons.

What we *do* know, is that if transactions have not been properly recorded, observing double-entry, then the balance sheet will not balance at the end of the year, but if we wait until the end of the year to find out, then it means checking the entries for all transactions which have taken place throughout the year. This could take days in even a small business, and it is therefore essential that checks for accuracy are made periodically throughout the year, on a monthly or even weekly basis, depending on the volume of transactions in that business. Then, at any check point it will only be necessary to check the recording of transactions as far back as the last check point.

Without a doubt, well over 90% of the errors made in any set of accounts will be errors of double-entry – (i.e. a credit without a corresponding debit, or vice-versa, or a different amount debited than credited, etc.

If we can therefore, periodically, take a check on the accuracy of double-entry then we have gone a long way towards checking the overall accuracy of our accounts. As there should be a debit for every credit and vice-versa, we could simply add up *all* debit entries in *all* accounts, over say the past month, and then add all credit entries. If total debit entries equal, in amount, total credit entries, this will prove that double-entry has been observed in "posting".

This could be a long job, however, so why not, on the "check date", get a lower paid member of staff to "balance off" the accounts at that date so that every account will then display *one* figure representing a surplus of debits over credits, or vice versa, i.e. the balance of that account. If you then simply add up all debit *balances* and all credit *balances* they should, hopefully, agree and you have proved your double-entry. Far simpler for you than listing every single debit and credit entry – simply list the net balances of each account.

In doing this you are putting the *balances* in your accounts "on trial", and if you list these balances on a piece of paper next to the name of the account to which each balance relates, you have produced a "Trial Balance". The set-out of such a statement (it is *not* an account) is as follows:

Trial Balance as at 31 October

	Debit Balances	*Credit Balances*
	£	£
Capital		57,000
Premises	40,000	
Equipment	8,000	
Cash	3,000	
Bank		2,000
Trade Creditors		5,000
Trade Debtors	7,000	
Rates	500	
Wages	4,500	
Sundry Expenses	1,000	
	64,000	64,000

NOTE CAREFULLY:

(i) *Every* account in the ledger is named, and its balance is shown under the respective heading of debit or credit balance.

(ii) The order of the accounts doesn't matter – just as the information comes from the ledger.

(iii) The fact that debit balances agree with credit balances shows that there has been a debit entry for every credit entry (in amount), and vice-versa, in the postings to the accounts.

(iv) The bank balance is an overdraft – a credit balance.

(v) The above statement is *not* an account – it is simply an interim summary of the information portrayed by the accounts. Having seen that it balances (i.e. agrees) you could throw the statement away, but in practice you would file it so that when you do another Trial Balance, as at 30th November, you have the evidence that the balances agreed on 31st October and you need therefore only check "postings" (entries in the accounts) *since* 31st October.

DIFFERENCES BETWEEN TRIAL BALANCES AND BALANCE SHEETS

A popular examination question is "What is the difference between a Trial Balance and a Balance Sheet?" Well, they are both *statements* (*not* accounts) of information contained in the ledger at a particular date. They both show the balances of *all* accounts in the ledger at that date. In the Trial Balance they are shown as simply balances (debit or credit) whereas in the Balance Sheet they are shown not as debit and credit balances, but as assets and liabilities respectively. A Trial Balance would obviously be prepared immediately *before* attempting a Trading and Profit and Loss Account and Balance Sheet at the year end, to prove the accuracy of the accounts, and at this stage the accounts would contain balances for real *and* nominal accounts. By the time the Balance Sheet is prepared, however, the nominal accounts will have had their balances *transferred* to the Trading and Profit and Loss Account, in order to calculate profit or loss, so that when the Balance Sheet is being prepared, the only accounts remaining in the ledger *with a balance still on them* will be the accounts representing either assets or liabilities (i.e. the real accounts). The nominal accounts have just been "closed off" by transfer.

During the year then, a Trial Balance will be prepared periodically to check accuracy to date in the accounts. At the end of the financial year of the business (i.e. the last day, 31st December, or whatever), a Trial Balance will be prepared and when that agrees, the nominal accounts will be transferred to a Trading and Profit and Loss account for that year. After the net profit or loss has been transferred from this annual account to Capital Account, a Balance Sheet will be prepared from the remaining accounts in the ledger with a balance still on them. That is the order of events at year end – Trial Balance as at *that date*, Trading and Profit and Loss Account for that *period*, and finally, Balance Sheet as at *that date*.

Go back now to the accounts we prepared for J. Snow (pages 32/33). Prepare from them a Trial Balance as at 31st May *before* the nominal accounts were transferred to Trading and Profit and Loss Account. Your Trial Balance should look like this, but do it *now*!

Trial Balance of J. Snow as at 31st May 19..

	Debit Balances	*Credit Balances*
	£	£
Cash	7,785	
Capital		50,000
Premises	30,000	
Shop Fittings	2,500	
Office Furniture	1,800	
Bank	9,010	
Debtors	4,450	
Creditors		2,900
Purchases	8,000	
Sales		12,020
Rates	160	
Insurance	90	
Wages	920	
Electricity	140	
Stationery	65	
	64,920	64,920

There is nothing wrong in balancing a nominal account, if you want to, for the purpose of preparing a Trial Balance, so that at the end of the relevant period the balance of that account is transferred to Trading and Profit and Loss Account, e.g.

DR J. Snow's Sales Account CR

		£			£
May 31	Balance c/d	12,020	May 12	Cash	940
			May 20	Cash	2,100
			May 21	I.D. Ltd.	4,100
			May 27	Cash	2,400
			May 27	J.B. Ltd.	1,650
			May 31	Cash	830
		12,020			12,020
May 31	To Trading a/c	12,020	May 31	Balance b/d	12,020
		12,020			12,020

Note that while the balance of Sales Account (and other nominal accounts) is *transferred* to Trading and Profit and Loss Account at the period end, the balances on the real accounts are *carried down* to start off the next period, e.g.

DR		Office Furniture			CR
		£			£
May 9	Bank	1,000	May 31	Balance c/d	1,800
May 21	Bank	800			
		1,800			1,800
May 31	Balance b/d	1,800			

ERRORS NOT REVEALED BY TRIAL BALANCE

Whilst the Trial Balance will reveal errors in double-entry, there are certain types of errors which the Trial Balance will not reveal.

If, for example, a sale of goods on credit is made to Johnson for £400, and your posting clerk credits sales account £400, but debits *Jensen's* account, £400 instead of Johnson, then double-entry *is* correct, but with a posting in the wrong account! Your trial balance will obviously not highlight this error. In the same way, if a butcher purchases a cash till, and his bookkeeper debits "purchases" account instead of debiting "shop equipment" account, this serious error will not be revealed by the Trial Balance.

These two types of errors are called "Errors of Commission" and "Errors of Principle" respectively. The latter error is where a real account is posted instead of the nominal account being posted or vice-versa – i.e. the wrong *section* of the ledger is posted (but posted on the right side!).

Another error which the Trial Balance would not reveal is where *nothing* is posted, no debit, no credit – i.e. the transaction is omitted from the accounts altogether. This is an "Error of Omission".

If, say, a purchase of equipment occurs for £600 cash and the entry in the accounts is posted as credit cash *£60* and debit equipment *£60*, then although double-entry has been observed, *with the wrong amount*, this error will not be revealed by the Trial Balance. The use of wrong amounts is classed as an "Error of Original Entry".

"Compensating Errors" will not be "thrown out" by the Trial Balance either. For example, if the debit side of any account is understated by, say, £10, and, at a later stage in posting accounts, a credit side of an account is understated by the same amount, then the original error will be compensated for by the subsequent error. There are numerous permutations of this kind of error and it is possible that many errors could occur in the accounts and be compensated for by other errors the other way, so that the *net* result of all the wrong postings is that the same *total* amount has been debited as has been credited. These are the worst types of errors!

Finally, if the accounts are posted the "wrong way round" – e.g. a sale to Brown is *debited* to sales (wrong!) and *credited* to Brown (wrong!) then double-entry *has* been observed but the wrong way round. This is an "Error of Reversal" and should not happen!

Try to remember the "official" description of these errors which the Trial Balance will not reveal.

Having read this last section you may well wonder, why do a Trial Balance when it will not reveal all of these errors? The answer is that these kind of errors will quickly "come to light", and will be corrected. When you send an invoice to Jensen, for example, instead of Johnson, you will soon be made aware of your error! Similarly, the other errors described will quickly be identified in most cases.

The Trial Balance will prove accuracy to a very large degree, locating the bulk of the errors, and no system of accounting can do better than this.

IN THE EXAMINATION

Having entered up (i.e. "posted") the accounts of a trader over a period of time, periodic checks on accuracy of double-entry will have taken place at suitable dates by taking out a Trial Balance. Just before the trading and profit and loss accounts are prepared for the end of the financial year, another trial balance will be prepared as a final check on accuracy. *This* trial balance will show the balances on *all* accounts immediately prior to transferring the nominal accounts to Trading and Profit and Loss Account (so "closing them off"), and *showing* the balances of the real accounts on the balance sheet.

If the examiner does not want to test your ability to write up the accounts as transactions occur (as in Chapter 5 exercises), but simply wants to test your ability to prepare "final accounts" (i.e. Trading and Profit and Loss Accounts) and Balance Sheets, he will *in effect* write up the accounts himself, and prepare his own trial balance from the balances on the accounts he has "written up". He will then present you with a Trial Balance showing the balances of all the accounts he has "written up" and ask you to prepare a Trading and Profit and Loss Account and Balance Sheet *from the information given.*

You have simply got to use this information to prepare what the examiner wants. You have to *imagine* the accounts he has written up, and "imagine" the transfer of nominal account balances to Trading and Profit and Loss Accounts (so closing them off) and *imagine* the balances remaining on real accounts (for display on the balance sheet). The examiner has done most of the work for you, and given you all the information you need (i.e. balances on accounts) to prepare your "final accounts" and balance sheet. Very many examination questions, asking for preparation of "fianl accounts" and balance sheet are presented in the form of a trial balance, as per some of the following exercises.

EXERCISE 6.1

The figures of the following Trial Balance were extracted from the books of B. Todd, a sole trader, as on 31st December 19–7.

Trial Balance as at 31st December, 19–7

	£	£
Capital (as at 1st January, 19–7)		21,900
Freehold Land and Buildings	28,000	
Motor Van	2,200	
Purchases	60,000	
Sales		82,000
Salaries	9,100	
Debtors	2,400	
Creditors		1,800
Cash in Hand	600	
Cash at Bank	700	
Rates	650	
Insurances	150	
Telephone	100	
Fixtures and Fittings	1,800	
	105,700	105,700

Required:
You are to prepare Trading and Profit and Loss Accounts for the year ended 31st December 19–7 and a Balance Sheet as at that date.

EXERCISE 6.2

Open the necessary ledger accounts (including a bank account) and enter the following transactions in the books of James:

April 1 James commenced business by transferring £6,000 to a bank account.
April 2 Bought fixtures for the shop, £400, paying by cheque.
April 3 Purchased goods on credit from Teal Ltd. to the value of £840.
April 5 Paid £420 by cheque for the first quarter's rent on the premises.
April 8 Cash sales, £400.
April 8 Paid an insurance premium by cheque, £74.
April 9 Paid wages in cash, £45.

April 10 Bought goods for cash, £200.
April 11 Purchased further goods from Teal Ltd. on credit, £600.
April 12 Paid Teal Ltd. by cheque the balance on their account.
April 15 Cash Sales, £210.
April 15 Sold goods on credit to P. Swan, £440.
April 16 Paid wages in cash, £45.
April 18 P. Swan settled his account by cheque.

Balance the accounts (except for those with only one entry) and extract a Trial Balance to check the basic accuracy of your work.

EXERCISE 6.3

John Gardiner who is a sole trader has extracted the following Trial Balance at the close of business on 31st December 19–5:

	DR	CR
	£	£
Purchases and Sales	9,510	14,790
Cash at Bank	3,330	
Cash in Hand	70	
Wages and Salaries	1,050	
Rent and Rates	480	
General Office Expenses	270	
Debtors and Creditors	3,110	2,670
Office Furniture	1,840	
Delivery Van	2,600	
Capital Account 1 January 19–5		4,800
	22,260	22,260

Required:
Prepare the Trading and Profit and Loss Accounts of John Gardiner for the year ended 31st December 19_5, together with a Balance Sheet as at that date.

EXERCISE 6.4

The following is the trial balance of T. Craven, sole trader, extracted from his accounts at 30th June 19_2:

Trial Balance at 30th June, 19_2

	DR	CR
	£	£
Capital		68,500
Premises	40,000	
Furniture and Fittings	9,000	
Equipment	3,000	
Motor Vehicles	6,000	
Debtors	11,000	
Creditors		6,500
Bank	1,500	
Cash	600	
Purchases	24,300	
Sales		33,400
Rent	1,200	
Rates	1,100	
Wages	8,600	
Insurances	400	
General Expenses	1,700	
	108,400	108,400

Required:
Prepare the Trading and Profit and Loss Accounts of T. Craven for the year ended 30th June 19_2, and a balance sheet at 30th June 19_2.

EXERCISE 6.5

The following list of balances at 30th April 19_8, has been extracted from the books of Boheme and Co.

Trial Balance at 30th April 19_8

	DR	CR
	£	£
Capital		83,000
Sales		289,600
Wages	80,900	
Light and Heat	11,000	
General Expenses	6,200	
Insurances	1,800	
Purchases	170,400	
Debtors	34,300	
Creditors		27,600
Premises	80,000	
Fixtures and Fittings	15,600	
	400,200	400,200

Prepare:
Trading and Profit and Loss Account for year ended 30th April 19_8, and a balance sheet at that date.

EXERCISE 6.6

The following trial balance has been extracted by an inexperienced clerk: the *amounts* are correct per the ledger accounts.

Trial Balance

	DR	CR
	£	£
Capital		51,300
Premises	37,000	
Motor Vehicles		8,000
Office Equipment	4,000	
Sales		16,400
Purchases		9,800
Rates		1,100
Wages and salaries		4,100
Insurances	500	
General Expenses	1,400	
Debtors		6,700
Creditors	5,600	
Advertising	700	
	49,200	97,400

Required:
Re-draft the above Trial Balance showing the various accounts under their correct headings of debit balances or credit balances.

EXERCISE 6.7

Simon Atkins, a sole trader, has extracted the following Trial Balance from his books at the close of business on 30th April 19_6:

	DR	CR
	£	£
Sundry Debtors	6,310	
Sundry Creditors		1,760
Purchases	6,280	
Sales		11,640
Wages and Salaries	2,080	
Cash in Hand	140	
Office Furniture	650	
Bank Overdraft	1,480	
General Office Expenses	490	
Capital Account 1st May 19–5		?
	17,430	13,400

Clearly, Atkins is unable to ascertain the balance of the Capital Account at 1st May 19_5 and there are obviously errors in the Trial Balance. The items listed are all correctly described but some are in the incorrect column.

Required:
Draw up the Trial Balance, using the above figures, but entering all the items in which you consider to be the correct column and insert the correct balance of the Capital Account as at 1st May 19_5.

NOTE: Trading Account, Profit and Loss Account and Balance Sheet are NOT required.

EXERCISE 6.8

(a) What is a Trial Balance? To what extent is it a proof of the accuracy of the books?
(b) Indicate three types of error which will not cause the trial balance to disagree, and give an example of each.

(Royal Society of Arts)

EXERCISE 6.9

19_8
Dec. 1 B. Brown started business with £5,000 in a bank account. He purchased furniture and fittings for £1,000 and paid immediately by cheque.
His purchases of stock on credit during the month were:

		£
Dec. 8	T. Smith	400
Dec. 12	R. Gray	300
Dec. 19	B. Coals	140

His sales of stock on credit during the month were:

		£
Dec. 8	R. Pike	600
Dec. 20	T. Trout	700
Dec. 29	R. Pike	400

Cash sales during the month all paid into the bank totalled £900.
Other purchases and payments by cheque were:

		£
Dec. 8	Rent	40
Dec. 19	Electricity	130
	Motor van	1,000
Dec. 20	Packing paper	140

Dec. 29 R. Pike settled his account in full by cheque and Brown paid Smith, Gray and Coals in full by cheque.
Brown purchased additional furniture and fittings on credit from Office Supplies Ltd. for £500.

(a) Set out all accounts, including a bank account, in B. Brown's ledger, and (b) extract a trial balance.

(University of London "O" level)

CHAPTER 7

DISCOUNTS AND RETURNS

DISCOUNTS

When a business sells goods it will normally provide incentives to induce people and firms to buy from them. For example, a manufacturer sells to wholesalers, who will then sell to retailers, who will then sell to the general public. The manufacturer or the wholesaler may want to tempt the next organisation along the line and he will therefore offer a "Trade Discount" – i.e. "buy from me and I'll deduct 10% from the normal price". So the buyer purchases £100 value of goods for only £90. He records in his Purchases Account, *£90*, and the £10 he has saved is reflected in a higher gross profit figure. Think about this – the £10 "gain" is not recorded anywhere – the goods have been bought for £90 and the reflection of this cheap buying shows in the gross profit – i.e. a "hidden" profit.

On the other hand, a retailer may sell to a customer and state that "if this invoice is paid within one month, a 10% *cash discount* will be allowed". Even if the buyer pays by cheque, not cash, he will pay 10% less if he pays up within a certain time limit. This cash discount *is* shown in the accounts, because at the time of selling the seller does not know whether the buyer will take advantage of this offer or not. If he does, then the cash discount *will* show in the accounts.

Example

Mulberry buys from us £100 of goods subject to a cash discount of 10% if the bill is paid within one month. At the time we sell to Mulberry we don't know whether he will take advantage of this offer. Therefore, when the sale takes place our entries in the accounts are:

DR		Sales		CR
		Date	Mulberry	£100

DR		Mulberry		CR
Date	Sales	£100		

Mulberry owes us £100. If two weeks later, Mulberry sends us a payment of £90 (i.e. £100 less 10%) in *full* settlement then we will record this payment thus:

DR	Mulberry		CR
Date Sales	£100	Date Bank	£90

If we don't do anything else, then this account still shows a debit balance of £10 (balance the account off) showing that Mulberry still owes us £10 – but he doesn't – we have "let him off" this amount for paying us promptly. So what must we do? Obviously we must *credit* his account with £10 to close the account. What do we debit with £10 to complete double-entry? Well, what is it? It is a discount which we have allowed to him – so what is more natural than to *debit* a "Discounts Allowed" account! How will this account figure in the ledger? It's an expense as far as we are concerned – we have in effect "given away" £10 for a service rendered (like rates, etc.) – i.e. prompt payment.

DR	Mulberry		CR
	£		£
Date Sales	100	Date Bank	90
		Date Discount allowed	10
	100		100

N.B. Account closed

DR	Discount Allowed		CR
Date Mulberry	£10		

What do we do with expenses at the year end? We transfer them to the debit side of Profit and Loss Account so reducing our ultimate net profit or increasing our ultimate net loss. The "Discounts Allowed" account is therefore a nominal (expense) account which will, at the year end, be transferred to the debit side of Profit and Loss Account.

Suppose it works the other way round. If we purchase goods for £100 from Togwell and he says he will allow 10% for prompt settlement, then when the initial purchase takes place we will record in our accounts:

DR	Purchases		CR
Date Togwell	£100		

DR	Togwell		CR
		Date Purchases	£100

If we settle, say, within the month, we pay a cheque for £90 in full settlement to Togwell. Togwell's account now appears

DR		Togwell			CR
Date	Bank	£90	Date	Purchases	£100

If we don't now debit the account of Togwell with the £10 discount we have received then the account continues to show a credit balance of £10, indicating that we still owe our creditor £10, which is not so! Therefore we must debit £10 to Togwell's account to "close it off". Double-entry? A credit in "Discounts *Received*" Account (nominal account) – the *opposite* of an expense account because this represents a *gain* which will increase profits.

At the end of the year the £10 *credit* balance on Discounts Received Account will be transferred to Profit and Loss Account *viz*:

DR		Discounts Received			CR
Year End	Profit and Loss a/c	10	Date	Togwell	10
		10			10

N.B. Account closed as with other nominal accounts after transfer to Profit and Loss account

DR	Profit and Loss Account for Year		CR
			£
		Gross Profit	xxx
		Discounts Received	10

N.B. The Net Profit will now show £10 more.

Gains will always obviously increase profit and will therefore appear on the credit side of Profit and Loss Account. Rent Received is another example of a gain where, for example, you rent your upstairs office to someone else. When they pay you the rent, debit cash to record the increase in this asset, and credit the nominal account "Rent Received".

At this point, mentally visualise the ledger as a whole, consisting of real accounts i.e. assets (debit balances) and liabilities (credit balances) which at the end of the year are balanced off and *continue* into the next period, and nominal accounts, i.e. expenses (debit balances) and gains (credit balances) which at the end of the year are *closed off* by transfer to Trading and Profit and Loss Account.

RETURNS OF GOODS

Some goods purchased for re-sale may have to be returned because they are the wrong type or are damaged. Such returns are called "Purchases

Returns", or "Returns Outwards" because we are sending them "out" again.

Let us see how returns would be recorded in the accounts. We will purchase goods for re-sale from Ramsay for £100 on credit.

DR	Purchases		CR
Date Ramsay	£100		

DR	Ramsay		CR
		Date Purchases	£100

Two weeks later we discover that £15 worth of goods have been damaged in transit, so we get Ramsay's permission to return them to him. The position now is that we do not owe Ramsay £100 – we only owe him £85, so what must we do to his account? Obviously we must *debit* his account with £15 so reducing our liability to him. What will be the corresponding credit? Well, what is it all about? A "purchases return" or "returns outwards" so let's open such an account (a nominal account because it's not an asset or a liability).

DR	Ramsay		CR
	£		£
Date Returns	15	Date Purchases	100
Balance c/d	85		
	100		100
		Balance b/d	85

DR	Purchase Returns		CR
		Date Ramsay	£15

Note the credit balance on "Purchases Returns" account. It is not a "gain" like rent receive or discounts received – it is really representing a reduction of our actual purchases. Our *effective* purchases from Ramsay are only £85 represented by the *debit* balance of Purchases Account of £100 and the *credit* balance of Purchases Returns account of £15. The two accounts are very related to each other. It is essential that our end of year Trading Account only shows an actual purchase of £85. How can this be achieved, because the purchases account balance of £100 is going to be transferred to Trading Account, debit side. Well, if we also transfer the £15 "Return" to Trading Account at the year end this will finish up on the *credit* side of Trading Account so off-setting part of the £100 on the other side of the account, *viz*:

DR	Purchases			CR
	£			£
Date Ramsay	100	Year end Trading a/c		100
	100			100

DR	Purchases Returns		CR
	£		£
Year End Trading a/c	15	Date Ramsay	15
	15		15

DR	Trading and Profit & Loss Account for year		CR
	£		£
Purchases	100	Sales (say)	140
Gross Profit c/d to Profit & Loss a/c	55	Purchases Returns	15
	155		155

N.B. *Net* Purchases = £85.

The £15 credit effectively reduces purchases to £85, the true position. We have really sold £85 of goods for £140 so making a £55 gross profit.

In practice, the £15 return would not be shown on the credit side of Trading Account, but would instead be shown as a deduction from Purchases within the Trading Account, *viz*:

DR	Trading and Profit & Loss Account for year		CR
	£		£
Purchases	100	Sales	140
Less returns	15		
	85		
Gross Profit	55		
	140		140

By showing it this way we can see *at a glance* that the *net* purchases were £85 and these were sold for £140.

Normally, if you want to reduce the balance of any account you will enter on the opposite side of the account, but this is one of the very few exceptions where, for ease of reading, you actually reduce the balance by using the word "less'.

The exact same principle applies with Sales Returns but obviously with reverse entries, e.g.

Sell goods to Tarr for £80 on credit. Tarr returns £10 of goods as unsuitable. You agree, and you give him a "credit note" to signify this.

DR		Sales			CR
		£			£
Year End	Trading a/c	80	Date	Tarr	80
		—			—
		80			80
		=			=

DR		Tarr			CR
		£			£
Date	Sales	80	Date	Returns	10
				Balance c/d	70
		—			—
		80			80
		=			=
	Balance b/d	70			

DR		Sales Returns (Returns Inwards)			CR
		£			£
Date	Tarr	10	Year End	Trading a/c	10
		—			—
		10			10
		=			=

DR	Trading and Profit & Loss Account for year		CR
	£		£
Purchases	xxx	Sales	80
Less Returns	xx	*Less* Returns	10
	—		—
	xx		70

Note double-entry throughout. Even the unusual procedure of deducting from one side of the above account is the equivalent of double-entry. The only reason for this procedure is to show *actual* purchases and sales *at a glance*.

ALLOWANCES

Instead of unsatisfactory goods being *returned* either inwards or outwards, the supplier of these goods may agree to making an 'allowance' (i.e. a reduction in the original price recorded) so that the goods do not actually have to be physically returned. The treatment of such allowances on purchases or sales of goods is *exactly* the same in the accounts, as for actual returns. The items would simply be described in the accounts as "allowances", rather than "returns".

Study these examples very carefully. Writing up accounts should by now be logical to you (not an academic exercise), with the basic principles learned in earlier chapters being applied to different situations.

Now attempt the following exercises.

EXERCISE 7.1

Thomas Williams, a sole trader, extracted the following Trial Balance from his books at the close of business on 31st March 19_9:–

	DR	CR
	£	£
Purchases and Sales	7,620	13,990
Capital April 1 19_8		2,400
Bank Overdraft		1,450
Cash	30	
Discounts Allowed & Received	480	310
Returns inwards	270	
Returns Outwards		190
Rent, Rates and Insurance	580	
Fixtures and Fittings	3,800	
Delivery Van	700	
Debtors and Creditors	3,970	2,240
Wages and Salaries	2,980	
General Office Expenses	150	
	£20,580	£20,580

Required:
Prepare the Trading and Profit and Loss Accounts for the year ended 31st March 19_9 together with a Balance Sheet as at that date.

(London Chamber of Commerce)

EXERCISE 7.2

George Hart, a sole trader, has the following transactions during the month of October 19_9.

19_9
Oct. 3 Purchased on credit from Textiles Ltd. woollen goods £30, linen goods £20, all less 10% trade discount.
Oct. 6 Sold on credit to Harold Church woollen goods £24, linen goods £16, all less 5% trade discount.
Oct. 10 Purchased on credit from Newtown Warehouse Ltd. cotton goods £38, linen goods £27, no trade discount.

Oct. 13 Purchased on credit from Textiles Ltd. cotton goods £41, linen goods £39, all less 5% trade discount.

Oct. 19 Sold on credit to Ambrose Richards cotton goods £17, linen goods £13, all less 10% trade discount.

Oct. 25 Sold on credit to Harold Church woollen goods £22, cotton goods £16, no trade discount.

Required:
Post the transactions in the Personal Accounts in George Hart's ledger.

(London Chamber of Commerce)

EXERCISE 7.3

The following Trial Balance was extracted from the books of C. Lord on 30th April 19–1. You are required to prepare his Trading and Profit and Loss Account for the year ended 30th April 19_1.

The Trading Account should show Cost of Goods Sold.

Trial Balance at 30th April 19_1

	DR	£
	£	5,000
Loan from W. Paris		16,850
Capital		
Telephone	250	
Wages	2,650	
Bank & Cash	8,800	
Salaries	6,000	
Purchases & Sales	22,000	44,000
Debtors & Creditors	6,000	8,000
Motor Expenses	2,350	
Office Expenses	2,500	
Light & Heat	1,700	
Rates	600	
Premises	17,000	
Fixtures & Fittings	1,800	
Vehicles	2,000	
Sales and Purchase Returns	300	150
Discounts allowed & received	250	200
	74,200	74,200

(Royal Society of Arts)

EXERCISE 7.4

The following Trial Balance was extracted from the books of a sole trader, as at the close of business on 30th September 19_2:

	DR	CR
	£	£
Motor Vans	1,380	
Debtors and Creditors	2,900	1,580
Capital Account 1st October 19_1		4,570
Equipment	2,000	
Wages and Salaries	1,980	
Purchases and Sales	6,580	10,670
Bank	580	
Cash	40	
Rent, Rates and Insurance	330	
Sales and Purchases Returns	410	280
Fixtures and Fittings	550	
General Expenses	200	
Discounts	520	370
	17,470	17,470

Required:
Prepare the Trading and Profit and Loss Accounts for the year ended 30th September 19_2, together with a Balance Sheet as at that date.

EXERCISE 7.5

The following accounts appear in the ledger of B. Rice.

DR J. Reeves CR

		£			£
May 3	Sales	400	May 10	Returns	30
May 20	Sales	200	May 18	Bank	333
			May 18	Discounts	37
			May 23	Allowance	40

DR B. Hopyard CR

		£			£
May 22	Returns	20	May 19	Purchases	120
May 26	Bank	95	May 30	Purchases	210
May 26	Discounts	5			

DR T. Bennett CR

		£			£
May 1	Balance b/d	300	May 20	Bank	300
May 25	Bank (dishonoured cheque)	300	May 30	Bank	300

Required:

(i) Taking each account separately, explain fully the meaning of every transaction recorded.

EXERCISE 7.6

The list of balances given below appeared in the books of B. Barrett following three weeks of trading to 21st February 19_1:

	£
Capital	5,200
Purchases	420
Sales	900
Returns Inwards	100
Fixed Assets	3,500
Bank (Dr Balance)	2,000
L. Cann debtor	500
B. Barker creditor	420

Open the above accounts in Barrett's ledger with the balances shown as at 21st February 19_1.

Transactions for the week ended 28th February 19_1 are summarized below:

Credit Sales		£	*Credit Purchases*		£
Feb. 23	D. Smythe	176	Feb. 24	B. Barker	330
Feb. 26	D. Smythe	198			
Feb. 28	L. Cann	352			
		726			330

Returns Inwards		£
Feb. 27	D. Smythe	55
		55

The following transactions also took place:

Feb. 23 Received cheque from L. Cann £300

Feb. 25 Allowance on faulty goods previously sold for cash, Barrett refunding sum by cheque, £40.

Feb. 28 Cash sales paid into bank, £300.

Feb. 28 Paid B. Barker the amount outstanding on his account up to the 21 February by cheque.

Make all entries in the appropriate ledger accounts. Balance the accounts and extract a trial balance as on 28 February 19_1.

NOTE: A trading and profit and loss account and balance sheet are NOT required.

(Royal Society of Arts)

EXERCISE 7.7

J. Robinson, tailor, had the following transactions during October. All purchases and sales were on credit.

Oct. 4	Purchased from J. Daniels 30 ties at £2 each less 10% trade discount.
Oct. 6	Purchased from W. Wallis 20 boxes of cuff-links at £3·00 each less 12½% trade discount.
Oct. 14	Sold to D. Cox 4 suits at £120 each less 7½% trade discount.
Oct. 15	Paid the account of J. Daniels (see Oct. 4) by cheque, being allowed 5% cash discount for prompt payment.
Oct. 16	Returned to W. Wallis 2 boxes of cuff-links which were damaged. Received Wallis's credit note.
Oct. 20	D. Cox complained that one of his suits was slightly soiled. Agreed to give him an allowance of £15 for this.

Required:
Enter the above transactions in the accounts of J. Robinson.

CHAPTER 8

UNSOLD STOCK

In all of the examples and exercises to date we have always assumed that the goods purchased by a trader have all been sold by the end of the year. There has never been any unsold stock at the year end. This is highly unlikely in practice so let us now look at how we should treat unsold stock at the year end.

If, during a year, we purchase 1,000 units of "whatever", at a cost to us of £1·00 per unit, and in that year we only sell 850 of them at £1·50 each, how much gross profit have we made? If the profit on *each* is £0·50 then we have surely made 850 × £0·50 = £425 gross profit. There can't be any argument about this. The 150 "whatevers" still left in stock will hopefully sell next year – we have got to think like this. We *finish* Year 1 with 150 "whatevers" and therefore we *start* Year 2 with 150 "whatevers". In other words, our "closing stock" for Year 1 becomes the "opening stock" for Year 2.

If we show the above information in the form of a Trading Account we have the following:

DR	Trading and Profit and Loss Account for Year 1		CR
Purchases (1,000 @ £1·00)	£1,000	Sales (850 @ £1.50)	£1,275

If we balance this account we will only show £275 gross profit, which we know is wrong. This is because the above account tells us that 1,000 units have been sold for £1,275 which is *not* true! We have sold *850* units for £1,275 and 850 units only cost us £850 – therefore the gross profit is £1,275 less £850 = *£425*. We have 150 units (at cost of £1 each) left in stock.

An adjustment must be shown in the Trading Account for the unsold stock. This closing stock is shown, at cost, on the credit side of Trading Account thereby "off-setting" the *total* purchases on the other side of the account – i.e. the credit entry for closing stock (£150) reduces the debit entry for total purchases (£1,000). e.g.

DR	Trading and Profit & Loss Account for Year 1		CR
	£		£
Purchase (1000 @ £1)	1,000	Sales (850 @ £1·50)	1,275
Gross Profit c/d to Profit & Loss a/c	425	Closing Stock (150 @ cost £1·00)	150
	1,425		1,425

Now we are showing the true position, but where is the double-entry (i.e. the debit) for the £150? It is in Stock Account, *viz*:

DR	Stock Account		CR
Dec. 31 Year 1 Trading a/c	£150		

to show that on the last day of the year we have an *asset* in the form of unsold stock – i.e. that part of purchases in Year 1 which remains unsold at the end of the year. At the 31st December, Year 1, this unsold stock is treated as an asset and the balance on the Stock Account will be shown on the Balance Sheet as an asset *on that date*.

As I said earlier, the closing stock of one period becomes the opening stock of the next period, so let us continue the above example into Year 2. In Year 2 we purchase 1,200 "whatevers" at £1·00 each and we sell 1,100 at £1·50 each. We know in advance that the gross profit for Year 2 will be 1,100 × £0·50 = £550.

The opening stock for Year 2 is 150 units at cost, i.e. £150, and the closing stock will be 250 "whatevers" at cost, (opening stock 150 plus purchases of 1,200, less sales, 1,100), i.e. 250 units at cost of £1·00 each.

The closing stock we know, is shown on the credit side of Trading Account with a corresponding debit in Stock Account. The opening stock is shown on the other (debit) side of Trading Account, again with a corresponding entry (credit) in Stock Account, *viz*:

DR	Trading and Profit & Loss Account for year ending 31 December, Year 2		CR
	£		£
Opening Stock (150 @ £1·00)*	150	Sales (1,100 @ £1·50)	1,650
Purchases (1,200 @ £1·00)	1,200	Closing Stock (250 @ £1·00)**	250
Gross Profit c/d to Profit & Loss account	550		
	1,900		1,900

We have already agreed the figure for gross profit but let us now look at the double-entries to the stock figures in our Trading Account. These entries are in Stock Account so let us continue our stock account from last year.

DR			Stock Account				CR
			£				£
Dec. 31	Year 1	Trading a/c	150	Dec. 31	Year 2	Trading a/c	150*
			150				150
Dec. 31	Year 2	Trading a/c**	250				

N.B. Double-entry to the Trading Account entries.

Study what has happened in the Stock Account. The closing stock for end of Year 1 has been "cleared out" of the account at the end of Year 2 by transfer to the debit side of Trading Account for Year 2 (i.e. as Opening Stock for Year 2). This leaves the Stock Account "empty" – "closed off" – we have then re-opened Stock Account with the *current* stock figure (i.e. the stock at the end of Year 2) and completed the double-entry by crediting Trading Account. The balance on Stock Account at 31 December, Year 2 is a debit one of £250 and this will be shown in the "Balance Sheet as at 31st December, Year 2" as an asset at that date.

The procedure then, at the end of each financial year, is to "clear out" of Stock Account last year's figure to Trading Account, and insert the new stock figure in Trading Account and Stock Account. These are the only entries which will ever be made in Stock Account. The purchases which take place between each year end are recorded in Purchases Account. The stock account simply arranges adjustments to the Trading Account to allow for unsold purchases at the beginning and end of a year.

Think now about what has just gone on – carefully! When we do a Trial Balance immediately *prior* to commencing our Trading and Profit and Loss Account, the balance on stock account will be the closing stock figure for the *previous year* and this will therefore appear on the Trial Balance. The *new* stock figure as at the end of *this* current year has not yet made an appearance in the stock account, and will not appear until we start the Trading Account (which will be *after* the preparation of the Trial Balance), when we will credit Training Account and debit Stock Account with the new figure. Therefore "closing stock" at 31st December, Year 2 will *not* appear in the Trial Balance as at 31st December, Year 2 but the closing stock at 31st December, Year 1 *will* appear in the Trial Balance because this will be the only balance showing on Stock Account *at this point.*

One last adjustment to be made to the Trading Account shown above.

The information conveyed by this Account (refer back) is that we started on 1st January Year 2 with £150 of stock to which we added purchases in the year of £1,200 – we therefore have £1,350 (cost price) of stock to "play with". As £250 of that £1,350 is *still* unsold at 31st December, Year 2 we have obviously "got rid of" (sold) £1,100 of stock in the year. In other words the "*Cost* of Goods Sold" or "*Cost* of Sales" for Year 2 is £1,100 – as these goods were sold for £1,650 (Sales) we have made a gross profit of £550. In arriving at the "Cost of Goods Sold" (or "Cost of Sales") figure we took the opening stock (£150) and added Purchases (£1,200), then deducted closing stock (£250) to give "Cost of Goods Sold", £1,100. This is an important figure which should ideally "stand out", to be read at a glance, in the Trading Account. In the above form of Trading Account this figure does not stand out, so let's make it stand out.

If, instead of showing Closing Stock (£250) on the credit side of Trading Account, as in our example, we show it as a *deduction* from the debit side items, we will get the same result, but we will also highlight that most important figure, (you'll realise *how* important it is later on), *viz*:

DR Trading and Profit & Loss Account for year ending 31st December, Year 2 CR

	£		£
Opening Stock	150	Sales	1,650
Purchases	1,200		
	1,350		
Less Closing Stock	250		
Cost of Goods Sold	1,100		
Gross Profit c/d to Profit and Loss a/c	550		
	1,650		1,650

All our future Trading Accounts will be in this form.

VALUING STOCK

The figure for the end of the year closing stock is arrived at by physical inspection of the stock then held – i.e. by "stocktaking". The value placed on this unsold stock is usually the **cost price** – i.e. what it cost when it was purchased. There are variations to this rule, such as when the price the stock could sell at is *less* than what was paid for it! This is possible where the stock has deteriorated, or gone "out of fashion" since it was bought. In such cases the stock would always be valued at the **lower** figure of cost and selling price.

The way stock is valued is most important because the valuations placed in the Trading Account have a direct effect on profits. For example, if the year end (closing) stock is undervalued then the gross profit is understated. Think about this and remember that a change in the value of *closing* stock is reflected in the next period's *opening* stock.

CARRIAGE INWARDS

Payment of carriage charges on our purchases is obviously an expense (credit bank or cash, and debit Carriage Inwards account) but at the end of the year the total of carriage inwards charges would be transferred *not* to Profit and Loss Account, together with all of the other expenses, but to Trading Account. The reason for this is that this type of expense is really an additional cost of purchases. If we purchase goods for £100 and have to pay £5 to get the goods to us, then the true position is that these goods have cost us £105, but the two amounts are kept in separate accounts, both of which are transferred to Trading Account at the year end.

Note that Carriage Inwards is the only expense included in Trading Account. All other expenses (including Carriage *Outwards*) are transferred to the debit side of Profit and Loss Account at the year end.

SPECIMEN TRADING ACCOUNT

A Trading Account including everything you will have to show, appears below as an illustration of set-out.

DR Trading and Profit & Loss Account for year ended ...... CR

	£	£		£
Opening Stock		6,000	Sales	60,000
Purchases	30,000		*Less* returns	700
Less returns	500			
				59,300
	29,500			
Carriage Inwards	400			
		29,900		
		35,900		
Less Closing Stock		4,900		
Cost of Goods Sold		31,000		
Gross Profit c/d		28,300		
		59,300		59,300
			Gross Profit b/d	28,300

In the following exercises, where you are asked to prepare "final accounts" this means the Trading and Profit and Loss Accounts for the period in question.

EXERCISE 8.1

The following trial balance was extracted from the books of D. Lancaster, a builders merchant, on 31st December 19_7. Prepare a Trading, Profit and Loss Account for the year ended December 31st 19_7 and a Balance Sheet on that date.

	£	£
Capital 1st January 19_7		22,000
Freehold land and buildings	17,000	
Furniture and fittings	1,000	
Motor vehicles	2,500	
Purchases and sales	50,000	70,300
Discounts Received		100
Vehicle expenses	400	
Stock January 1st 19_7	5,000	
Returns Outwards		200
General expenses	800	
Property expenses including rates	1,200	
Debtors and Creditors	8,000	5,000
Wages and salaries	9,000	
Cash – at bank and in hand	2,700	
	97,600	97,600

NOTE: Valuation of Stock at 31st December 19_7, £6,000.

(University of London "O" level)

EXERCISE 8.2

At the close of business on 31st October 19_2 the following Trial Balance was extracted

	DR £	CR £
Capital Account		6,490
Discounts	100	120
Stock 1st November 19_1	2,040	
Purchases and Sales	8,760	15,530
Debtors and Creditors	3,910	2,090
Purchases Returns		220
Sales Returns	390	
Office Furniture	600	
Wages and Salaries	3,930	
Rent and Rates	720	
Cash at Bank	3,390	
Cash in Hand	50	
General Office Expenses	80	
Travelling Expenses	480	
	£24,450	£24,450

NOTES: (1) Stock 31st October 19_2 – £2,520.

Required:
Prepare the Trading and Profit and Loss Accounts for the year ended 31st October 19_2 together with a Balance Sheet as on that date.

EXERCISE 8.3

George Church is a sole trader whose business year end is 28th February. He was unable to carry out his stock-taking on 28th February 19_9 owing to extreme pressure of business. He was not able to carry out stock-taking until 5th March 19_9, when he valued his stock at £1,970 – *cost price*.

Between the close of business on 28th February 19_9 and the actual stock-taking, the following transactions took place:

(a) Goods sold £178 *selling price*. Of this total, goods with a selling price of £34 were still in Church's warehouse on 5th March 19_9 and these were *included* in the stock-taking figure of £1,970.
(b) Goods purchases £97. Included in these goods were purchases amounting to £22 which were not delivered to Church until after the stock-taking.

The gross profit on all goods is 25% of *selling price*.

Required:
Calculate the value of stock (at *cost price*) as at the close of business on 28th February 19_9.

NOTE: Calculations must be shown.

(London Chamber of Commerce)

EXERCISE 8.4

George Foster is a sole trader whose warehouse, together with the stock, was destroyed by fire on 20th February 19_2. His Trading Account for his last completed financial year was as follows:

DR Trading Account for the year ended 31st December 19_1 CR

	£		£
To Stock 1st January 19_1	2,170	By Sales	9,000
Purchases	8,210		
	10,380		
Less Stock 31st December 19_1	2,880		
Cost of Goods Sold	7,500		
Gross Profit	1,500		
	£9,000		£9,000

According to Foster's records his Purchases from 1st January 19_2 to the date of the fire amounted to £1,510 and his Sales for the same period amounted to £2,580. None of the goods sold was in the warehouse at the time of the fire, but *included* in the Purchases figure of £1,510 were certain goods which were *still in transit*. The cost price of these goods was £120.

The percentage of Gross Profit to Sales for 19_2 was the same as for the year 19_1.

Required:
Calculate the value (at *cost* price) of the stock destroyed in the fire. Your calculations must be shown, but your answer may take the form of a Trading Account for the period 1st January 19_2 to 20th February 19_2.

(London Chamber of Commerce)

EXERCISE 8.5

Denton Ltd. commenced business on 1st January 19_5 and the company's accounts were made up annually to 31st December. The following figures were extracted from the books of account:

	Sales	*Purchases*	*Increase (+) or decrease (−) in stock during year*	*Selling expenses*	*Rent*	*General expenses*
	£	£	£	£	£	£
19_5	36,000	39,000	+12,000	900	3,000	4,500
19_6	54,000	37,500	− 3,000	1,350	3,000	5,250
19_7	78,000	63,000	+ 4,500	1,950	3,000	6,000
19_8	120,000	108,000	+12,000	3,600	6,000	9,000
19_9	150,000	135,000	+15,000	5,250	6,000	11,250

Required:
(a) A statement showing the book value of the stock on 31st December each year from 19_5 to 19_9 inclusive.
(b) Trading and profit and loss accounts in columnar form for each of the five years to 31st December 19_9.

(Institute of Bankers)

EXERCISE 8.6

The following figures are taken from the annual accounts of Grey Moon Ltd. The accounting year of the company ends on 31st March.

	Stock-in-Trade at 31st March	Net Profit for year
	£	£
19_5	31,000	7,000
19_6	24,300	14,900
19_7	42,800	23,100
19_8	32,700	11,400

An examination of the company's records shows that, while the stock-in-trade at 31st March 19_8 was correctly valued at £32,700 there were errors in the valuation of the stock at the end of each of the three previous years. The stock at 31st March 19_4 had been valued correctly.

The stock at 31st March 19_5 was under-valued by £4,000.

The stock at 31st March 19_6 was under-valued by £2,700.

The stock at 31st March 19_7 was over-valued by £5,200.

YOU ARE REQUIRED:

(a) To redraft the above table, setting out all the items at the amounts at which they *would* have appeared in the company's annual accounts if stock had been correctly valued at all relevant dates.

(b) To point out the significance of the contrast between the original amounts and the revised amounts of net profit.

(Institute of Bankers)

EXERCISE 8.7

The following trial balance was extracted from the books of Todd, a trader, as at 31st December 19_4:

	£	£
Capital account		20,600
Purchases	48,500	
Sales		60,900
Repairs to buildings	848	
Motor Car	950	
Car expenses	318	
Freehold land and buildings	10,000	
Balance at bank	540	
Furniture and fittings	1,460	
Wages and salaries	8,606	
Discounts allowed	1,061	
Discounts received		854
Rates and insurances	248	
Bank Charges and Interest	759	
Trade debtors	5,213	
Trade creditors		4,035
General expenses	1,586	
Stock-in-trade 1st Jan. 19_4	6,300	
	£86,389	£86,389

NOTE: Stock-in-Trade 31st December 19_4, £8,800.

You are required to prepare a trading and profit and loss account for the year 19_4, and a balance sheet as on 31st December 19_4.

(Institute of Bankers)

EXERCISE 8.8

The following is a summary of the records of P. Simms for the past 3 years.

	Year Ended 31.12._3	Year Ended 31.12._4	Year Ended 31.12_5	Year Ended 31.12_6
Purchases	—	14,000	17,000	21,000
Carriage Inwards	—	400	600	800
Sales	—	22,000	26,000	40,000
Stock at Year End	1,000	3,000	5,000	7,000

Required:

(a) Prepare Trading Accounts from this information for the years ending 31st December 19_4, 19_5 and 19_6.

(b) Show the stock account as it would appear from 1.1._4 to 31.12._6, properly balanced off at each year end.

EXERCISE 8.9

Your friend informs you that he can supply popular L.P. records to you at £2 each (normal retail price £5 plus).

Having not been in "business" before you see possibilities of making some extra spending money by buying these records and re-selling them to your own colleagues and other friends. You therefore decide to purchase a supply of records (at £2 each) and sell them at £3.50.

Over the next two weeks the following purchases and sales take place.

Week 1	No. of Records Bought	No. of Records Sold
Monday	10	
Tuesday		4
Wednesday		2
Thursday	6	
Friday		2
Week 2		
Monday		6
Tuesday	12	
Wednesday		10
Thursday	8	
Friday		2

CALCULATE your profit or loss for week 1 and week 2.

CHAPTER 9

ACCRUALS AND PREPAYMENTS

You know by now that any expense has the effect of decreasing the net profit for the period. Every expense transferred from the debit side of the respective nominal account to the debit side of the Profit and Loss Account at the year end, has the effect of reducing the final net profit figure shown in this account.

Let us suppose that our business is operating from rented premises and that the rent is £3,000 per annum. Let us "fall behind" with the rent payments so that at the end of the year we have only paid £2,000 of the £3,000 due – i.e. we still owe £1,000 rent for the year in question. In this case our rent account in the nominal ledger appears thus:

DR		Rent Account	CR
During Year	Cash	£2,000	

Having agreed our trial balance we now start to transfer all the nominal accounts to Trading and Profit & Loss Account. If we transfer the above balance of £2,000, our Profit and Loss Account will show a debit for rent of £2,000, and this will have the effect of reducing our final net profit by £2,000. The rent account will now be "closed off" for the year.

Aren't we kidding ourselves? The rent *due for this period* is £3,000 yet we have only reduced profit by £2,000 (the amount actually paid by us). Our final profit will be overstated by £1,000. We can't increase our profits by holding back our bills!

Our final net profit figure should be reduced by the *amount due* for rent for the period in question. In this example, *£3,000* is the rent for the year covered by the accounts, and if we are to show a true profit figure we must debit the full amount of £3,000 to the Profit and Loss Account, *whether we have paid it or not*. Also, if we have not paid the rent in full then the amount still owing (£1,000) should surely show on our balance sheet as "still owing" – i.e. a liability. Otherwise our balance sheet is not telling the true story.

So, how can we achieve a true profit figure in the Profit and Loss Account and a true picture on the balance sheet? The first rule we must observe is that the Profit and Loss Account should be debited with **the**

amount due for that period, *not* the amount paid. In our example therefore we must debit Profit and Loss Account with the £3,000 due, *not* the £2,000 paid. This means that we must transfer *£3,000* from the rent account to the Profit and Loss Account, so the rent account now appears:

DR			Rent Account		CR
During Year	Cash	£2,000	End of Year	P & L a/c	£3,000

Note – the account is not closed off as in all past examples – it still has a credit balance of £1,000. The double-entry to the Profit and Loss Account means that this account will be debited with £3,000, so reducing net profit by this amount. This means that when we come to do our balance sheet, after completing our Trading and Profit and Loss Account for the year, we have a balance in the nominal accounts, *viz*:

DR			Rent Account		CR
		£			£
During Year	Cash	2,000	End of Year	P & L a/c	3,000
End of Year	Balance c/d	1,000			
		3,000			3,000
			Start of next year	Balance b/d	1,000

The balance sheet shows the balances of *all* accounts remaining in the ledger at this stage, so this balance of £1,000 has got to be shown on the balance sheet. As it is a credit balance it must show on the liabilities side of the balance sheet – i.e. as something owing by the business, which is what it is – called an accrual.

Our net profit in the Profit and Loss account is now a realistic one and our balance sheet acknowledges what is still owing. We are showing the full picture.

This is an occasion when a nominal account becomes, at the date of the balance sheet, a liability for a while. Remember that a balance sheet is a statement of *all* balances in the ledger at the time it is prepared – debit balances representing assets and credit balances representing liabilities. Most of the nominal accounts will at this point be "closed off" for the year, but with rent we have an exception because the full amount *due* has not been paid.

Don't forget – you transfer to Profit and Loss Account, *not* what has been paid for expenses but *what is due* for that period. This is the only way to get a realistic profit figure. You can't make profits by being a bad payer, and if you owe money your balance sheet must show this fact!

Let us now pay *more* for an expense than we need do – i.e. let us pay part of next year's rates in advance. The rates per year are £2,000 and during *this* year we have in fact paid £2,700. Our rates account at the year end looks like this:

DR		Rates Account			CR
During Year	Cash/Bank	£2,700			

If we transfer to Profit and Loss Account the whole £2,700, so closing off the rates account, then we are debiting P & L account with £2,700 and reducing our net profit by this amount. But only £2,000 is *due* for the year – the other £700 is payment for *next* year's rates, which is nothing to do with this year's accounts. Only £2,000 should be debited (charged) to *this year's* profits if we are to show a true profit figure. The same rule applies as before – we transfer to P & L Account, *not* what we have paid but what we *should have paid* – i.e. the amount *due* for *this period.* Our rates account now appears:

DR		Rates Account			CR
		£			£
During Year	Bank	2,700	End of Year	P & L a/c	2,000
			End of Year	Balance c/d	700
		2,700			2,700
Start of next year	Balance b/d	700			

Again, we have a nominal account with a balance still left on it after the final accounts have been prepared, and this balance *must* therefore show on our balance sheet. As it is a debit balance it will have to be shown on the assets side of the balance sheet. Is it an asset? Of course it is! At the date of the balance sheet the local authority *owes us* £700, being money paid by us in advance – i.e. a prepayment. These balances 'left over' will be absorbed by next year's transactions.

Finally, let us look at Rent Received (a *gain* to us). If we have 'let' the upstairs office to someone at a rental of £1,200 per year, and by the end of our financial year the tenant has paid us only £1,000, then he still owes *us* £200. The rent received account appears:

DR			Rent Received		CR
			During Year	Cash	£1,000

As *£1,200* is due, this amount must be transferred to P & L Account (credit side, so increasing our profits) if we are to produce a true profit figure. The account after such transfer now appears:

DR			Rent Received		CR
		£			£
End of Year	P & L a/c	1,200	During Year	Cash	1,000
			End of Year	Balance c/d	200
		1,200			1,200
Start of next year	Balance b/d	200			

The proper amount *due* has been taken to P & L account and the balance of £200 will have to show on the balance sheet. A debit balance of £200 must be regarded as an asset, which is exactly what it is. The tenant *owes us* £200 – he is a debtor – i.e. an asset.

If the tenant had paid us, say, £1,500 – i.e. paid £300 in advance, then having transferred the actual amount *due* (£1,200) to P & L account, the balance of £300 would have finished up on the credit side of rent received account. This balance would then be shown on the liabilities side of our balance sheet because we would *owe* at the balance sheet date, £300, to our tenant who had overpaid us for this period.

As I said before, most nominal accounts will be "closed off" after transfers to P & L account, but where money is still owing, either to us or by us, then a balance will remain on the account at the year end which must then appear on our balance sheet, either as an asset or as a liability. This is where a nominal account becomes either an asset or a liability for a short time on a particular date (our year end).

If, in an exercise, you are presented with a trial balance which shows, for example:

	DR	*CR*
	£	*£*
Light and Heat	*400*	

this tells you that the debit balance on Light and Heat account stands at £400, indicating that this amount has been paid in the period. If a note outside of the trial balance then says that £50 is still owing for light and heat at the end of the period, you know that the amount *due* for that period is £450, and it is this amount which is to be debited to P & L account. The £50 still owing will be shown as a liability on the balance sheet. Even though you may not have to prepare the ledger accounts as part of the exercise you should visualise the following:

DR			Light and Heat		CR
		£			£
During Year	Cash	400	End of Year	P & L a/c	450
End of Year	Balance c/d	50			
		450			450
			Start of next year	Balance b/d	50

Remember that the balance of an expense or gain account, as shown by a trial balance, shows what has been paid, or received, *in that period.* Any additional *notes* to the trial balance regarding amounts still owing or paid in advance must then be taken into account in determining what was *due* for that period – i.e. the debit or credit to be made to P & L account. Then show the relevant liability or asset on the balance sheet, showing what is still owing, or what is owing to you, at the balance sheet date.

EXAMPLE

From the following information, calculate *for each item* what figure you would show in the Profit and Loss account (debit or credit) for the year ending 31st December 19_2, and indicate what figure you would show on the balance sheet at 31st December 19_2, and on which side. Show your answer in the following form:

	Debit to P & L a/c for 19_2	*Credit to P & L a/c for 19_2*	*Asset on Balance Sheet at Dec. 31 19_2*	*Liability on Balance Sheet at Dec. 31 19_2*
	£	£	£	£
Item (i)				
etc.				

QUESTIONS

(i) £460 has been paid for wages in the period and £90 is still owing at the end of the period.

(ii) £900 paid for rates in the period, of which £70 is in respect of 19_3.

(iii) Rent *received* in the period was £600 and £120 is still owing at the end of the period.

(iv) At 31st December 19_1, general expenses owing amounted to £40. During 19_2 £390 was paid for general expenses, and at 31st December 19_2, £25 was still owing for general expenses.

(v) At 31st December 19_1, rents received were in arrears (i.e. owing to us), £165. During 19_2 £843 was received from tenants, of which £98 related to 19_3 (i.e. paid in advance).

ANSWERS

	Debit to P & L a/c	*Credit to P & L a/c*	*Asset on Balance Sheet at Dec. 31 19_2*	*Liability on Balance Sheet at Dec. 31 19_2*
	£	£	£	£
(i)	550			90
(ii)	830		70	
(iii)		720	120	
(iv)	375			25
(v)		580		98

In items (iv) and (v) there were arrears at the beginning *and* end of the year, and in solving item (iv) we could have thought like this – '£390 was paid during the year but £40 of this was the settling of *last* year's outstanding debt, so we therefore only effectively paid £350 *in respect of this year*. Despite paying £350 for this year, we still owe £25, so the amount we *should* have paid is £350 + £25 = £375.

This kind of thinking gives us the right answer, but it would be far safer and easier to use an account to calculate the amount to show in P & L account. This would be done by 'building up', bit-by-bit, a general expenses account. Study the following:

DR General Expenses CR

			£			£	
				19_1			
(3)	During			Dec. 31	Balance b/d	40	(1)
	19_2	Cash/Bank	390	*19_2*			
(2)	*19_2*			Dec. 31	To P & L a/c	375	(4)
	Dec. 31	Balance c/d	25				
			415			415	
				19_2			
				Dec. 31	Balance b/d	25	(2)

This account is built up in stages, as numbered. First of all the position at the beginning of the year is recorded – i.e. £40 owed by us. The account therefore *starts off* with a credit balance (a liability) of £40. Leaving a suitable space in the account the position at the *end* of the year is now recorded – i.e. £25 owing. The account must therefore *finish up* showing a credit balance (liability) of £25. The total amount of cash actually paid during the year is then recorded on the debit side, £390. (Imagine a credit to cash or bank account as each payment took place). The only other item to be entered in the account is the transfer at the year end to P & L account, being the amount *due* for this year. Now, as both sides of the account must add up to the same figure when balanced off (in this example, £415), we only need add up the "heaviest" side (the debit side in this case) and insert the "difference" of £375 on the other side. In other words, the missing figure – i.e. the one we don't know at the outset, becomes the figure needed to bring both sides of the account to the same total.

Note that there can only be a maximum of four "happenings" in any expense (or gain) account:

1. The position at the beginning of the period.
2. The position at the end of the period.
3. The amount paid, or received in the case of a gain account such as rent received, during the period.
4. The amount *due* for that period (to be transferred to P & L account).

If you know *any* three of these four things then obviously you can find the fourth by simple deduction. By recording these in an actual account, as above, i.e. by constructing the account from information given, you are less likely to make errors, and the examiner often asks you to show your workings in account form.

If, in the above example, you had been told how much was owed at the beginning and end of the year and how much was *due* for the year (£375) – i.e. 3 things – you could easily have worked out in the account how much cash had been actually paid in the period, £390, – the fourth thing. Know *any* 3 and you can find the fourth!

Make sure that you understand this thoroughly, because the technique of "building up" an account from given information, in order to find missing information, is going to be extremely useful to you in your future studies. The technique can be applied to so many different situations.

Item (*v*)

At the beginning of the year the tenant was £165 in arrears (i.e. he owed us £165 from *last* year's rent). During the year he paid us a total of £843 in cash. At the end of the year he had already paid £98 of *next* year's rent. Let us build up the Rent Received Account to find the missing information, which is how much is *due* for 19_2.

DR		Rent Received				CR	
			£			£	
(1) Start of Year	Balance		165	During Year	Cash	843	(3)
(4) End of Year	To P & L a/c		580				
(2) End of Year	Balance c/d		98				
			843			843	
				Start of next year	Balance b/d	98	(2)

Follow the numbered order. Remember that the transfer to P & L account will finish up on the credit side of P & L account, so increasing profits. The £98 credit balance at the year end "says" that we owe the tenant this amount. At this date this is correct because he has overpaid us for 19_2.

Be careful when dealing with gains. Amounts "owed" are amounts owed *to* us, not by us!

EXERCISE 9.1

The following is the trial balance at 30th September 19_2 of M. Harper.

Trial Balance at 30th September 19_2

	DR	CR
	£	£
Capital 1st October 19_1		12,920
Office furniture	2,816	
Creditors		2,829
Bank overdraft		323
Land and buildings	7,700	
Equipment	1,400	
Vehicles	1,500	
Stock 1st October 19_1	4,400	
Debtors	2,926	
Purchases	21,435	
Sales		31,219
Rent received from sub-tenant		500
Wages	4,304	
Rates and insurances	274	
Light and heat	185	
Sundry administrative expenses	319	
Selling expenses	532	
	47,791	47,791

The following additional information is to be taken into consideration:

(a) Balance owing for wages for the last few days of the accounting year is £95.
(b) Insurance premium pre-paid £32.
(c) The stock at 30th September 19_2 is valued at £7,200.

Required:
Prepare trading and profit and loss accounts for the financial year to 30th September 19_2, showing clearly in the accounts the cost of goods sold and the net trading profit.

EXERCISE 9.2

The following trial balance was extracted from the books of Rodney, a trader, at 31st December 19_7:

	£	£
Capital		24,447
Office furniture	2,148	
Debtors and creditors	7,689	5,462
Sales		81,742
Purchases	62,101	
Rent and rates	880	
Lighting and heating	246	
Salaries and wages	8,268	
Stock in trade 31st December 19_6	9,274	
Insurances	172	
General expenses	933	
Bank balance	1,582	
Motor vans at cost	8,000	
Motor expenses	1,108	
Freehold premises at cost	10,000	
Rent received		750
	£112,401	£112,401

The following matters are to be taken into account:

1. Stock in trade 31st Dec. 19_7, £9,884.
2. Rates paid in advance 31st Dec. 19_7, £40.
3. Rent receivable due at 31st Dec. 19_7, £250.
4. Lighting and heating due at 31st Dec. 19_7, £85.
5. Included in the amount for insurances £172, is an item of £82 for motor insurances and this amount should be transferred to motor expenses.

Required:
A trading and profit and loss account for 19_7 and a balance sheet at 31st December 19_7.

EXERCISE 9.3

H. E. Jervey borrowed £12,000 on 30th April 19_4 to be repaid within seven years. He agreed to pay interest at 10% per annum, the interest to be calculated and paid on 31st October and 30th April each year.

He prepares his accounts annually on 31st December.

The payments were made on the due dates in 19_4 and 19_5. In 19_6 he paid the interest due on 30th April, but he did not pay the interest due on 31st October until 10th January 19_7. On 30th April 19_7 he paid the interest due and also repaid £3,000 of the loan. On 31st October 19_7 he paid the interest due. In 19_8 the interest was paid on the due dates and a further £3,000 was repaid on 30th June 19_8. No charge was incurred because of late payment of the instalment.

Required:
Prepare the Interest Account from the beginning of the transaction until 1st January 19_9.

(London Chamber of Commerce)

EXERCISE 9.4

The following is a summary of the payments for rent and rates made by Evans, a retailer, of his business premises.

		£
19_0		
Nov. 13	Rates paid for 6 months to 31st March 19_1	160
Dec. 31	Rent paid for 3 months to 31st December 19_0	100
19_1		
March 31	Rent paid for 3 months to 31st March 19_1	100
April 22	Rates paid for 6 months to 30th September 19_1	180
July 2	Rent paid for 3 months to 30th June 19_1	100
Oct. 4	Rent paid for 3 months to 30th September 19_1	100
Nov. 5	Rates paid for 6 months to 31st March 19_2	180
19_2		
Jan. 4	Rent paid for 3 months to 31st December 19–1	100

Required:

1. Write up separate accounts for (i) Rent and (ii) Rates as they should appear in Evans' ledger, showing within the accounts the amounts which should be entered in the profit and loss account for the year ended 31st December 19_1. Show the appropriate entries in the balance sheet as at that date.

EXERCISE 9.5

A property of a business was rented at £250 per month payable monthly.

The rent was three months in arrears on 31st December 19_8 and five months in arrears on 31st December 19_9. The rates were £1,200 per annum payable half yearly in advance on 1st April and 1st October in each year. At 31st December 19_8 the rates for the half year to 31st March 19_9 had not been paid, but these arrears were cleared and rates for 19_9 were paid when due.

Required:

(a) Explain the nature of "accruals" and "prepayments" in preparing final accounts. Why may such adjustments be necessary?

(b) From the information above prepare the *combined* rent and rates account for the year ended 31st December 19_9 showing the figures that would appear for rent and rates in the profit and loss account and the figures in the balance sheet at 31st December 19_9.

(A.E.B. "A" level)

EXERCISE 9.6

The following Trial Balance was extracted from the books of Brown at the close of business on 31st October 19_9. Prepare necessary final accounts and balance sheet.

	DR	CR
	£	£
Capital Account 1st November 19_8		5,970
Equipment	1,200	
Loose Tools	1,100	
Stock 1st November 19_8	960	
Purchases and Sales	5,180	12,060
Bank	1,330	
Cash	40	
Wages and Salaries	1,470	
Office Furniture	800	
Rent, Rates and Insurance	580	
Discounts	470	310
Insurances	140	
Heating and Lighting	490	
Motor Vehicles	3,000	
General Office Expenses	110	
Debtors and Creditors	2,950	1,480
	19,820	19,820

NOTES:

(a) Stock 31st October 19_9 – £1,080.

(b) Wages owing at 31st October 19_9, £240.

(c) Rates prepaid at 31st October 19_9 – £30.

(d) Insurances prepaid at 31st October 19_9, £40.

EXERCISE 9.7

T. Jones has occupied a property since 1st May 19_2. Rent has been paid as follows:

30th May 19_2	£150 for the three months ended 31st July 19_2
25th August 19_2	£300 for the six months ended 31st January 19_3
12th February 19_3	£360 for the six months ended 31st July 19_3

During the whole of this period he has sublet part of his property to D. Smith at an annual rent of £360 and has received rent as follows:

31st July 19_2	£90
30th November 19_2	£90
28th February 19_3	£90

Write up separate Rent Receivable and Rent Payable accounts as they would appear in Jones's Books showing the amounts he transferred to his Profit and Loss Account for the year ended 30th April 19_3.

(Royal Society of Arts)

EXERCISE 9.8

(a) From the following information construct a rent payable account *for the year* 19_7, as it would appear in the ledger:

	£
Rent owing at 1.1._7	40
Rent owing at 31.12._7	60
Cash paid for rent during 19_7	730

(b) From the following information construct a rates account *for the year* 19_9, as it would appear in the ledger:

	£
Rates owing at 1.1._9	120
Rates due for 19_9	850
Rates in advance at 31.12._9	70

(c) From the following information construct a rates account *for the year* 19_5, as it would appear in the ledger:

	£
Rates due for 19_5	1,200
Rates paid during 19_5	900
Rates owing at 31.12._5	180

(d) From the following information construct a rent receivable account *for the year* 19_2 as it would appear in the ledger:

	£
Rent unpaid at 1.1._2	30
Rent unpaid at 31.12._2	50
Rent received during 19_2	1,420

(e) From the following information construct a rent receivable account *for the year* 19_1 as it would appear in the ledger:

	£
Rent in advance at 1.1._1	100
Rent due for 19_1	950
Rent received during 19_1	725

CHAPTER 10

DEPRECIATION

If you go out today and buy a brand new car and then decide to sell it tomorrow, you won't get all of your money back! Why? Because your car is now second-hand, and as a result it is worth less than you paid for it. Even though the car is just as sound as it was yesterday, and hasn't had time to show any wear and tear, it is now worth less. It has *depreciated* in value – value has "dropped off" it.

The same thing applies to any machinery you may buy, or furniture, or equipment. Now, in the first two chapters of this book I said that if you buy a machine, or furniture for cash, you simply swap an asset cash for another asset of the same value, machinery or whatever, and you are no worse off for the spending. The assets you have bought will show on your firm's balance sheet at the amount you paid for them.

In reality, those assets you have purchased will not be valued at what you paid for them, even tomorrow! They will have suffered from the effects of "depreciation". One year later when you prepare your firm's balance sheet, those assets you bought earlier in the year will certainly not be valued at what you paid them, and your business *is* worse off.

How can this be reconciled in the accounts and in the balance sheet? If, for example, you buy for cash on Day 1 a machine for £2,000 then the effect, *immediately*, on a balance sheet would be – less cash, £2,000; more machinery, £2,000. No effect on *total* assets, i.e.

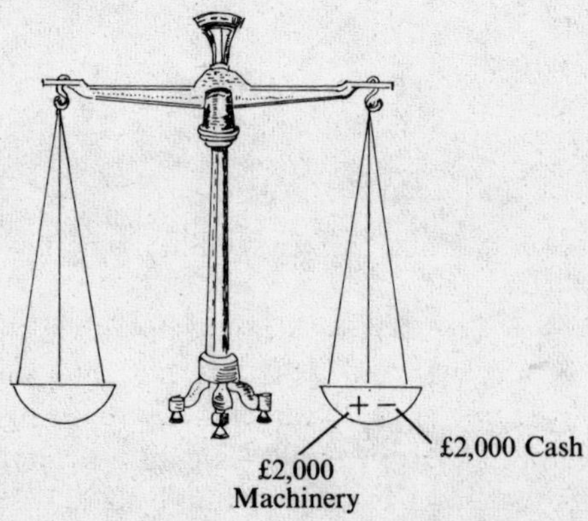

However, in a year's time this is no longer the position. The machinery is now only worth, say, £1,800, and if we still show the machinery on the balance sheet at a value of £2,000 we are "kidding" ourselves. The true picture twelve months hence is:

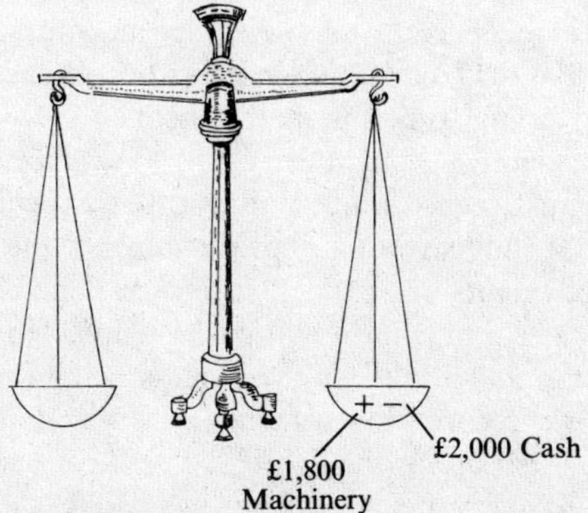

Our scales are out of balance. How can they be brought back into balance? The £200 loss in value of the asset is literally a *loss*. Who has to bear this loss? The owner! Capital must be reduced by £200, because £200 of the money invested in the business has *gone* – it has been taken away by time (*and* wear and tear).

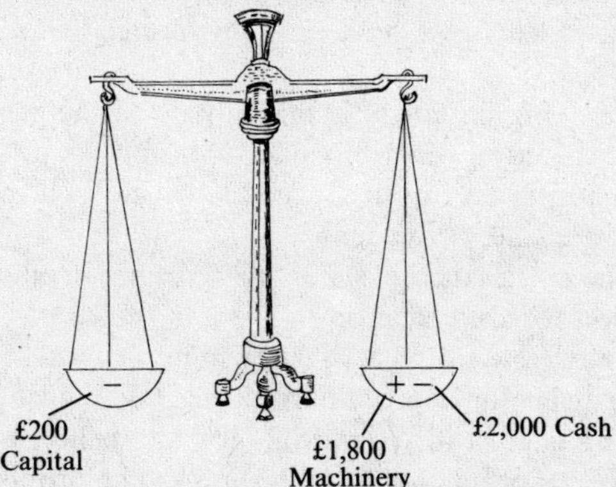

The balance sheet now balances! Everything that has happened has now been recorded.

The £200 loss will not be taken off Capital directly – this depreciation will be treated as an expense (like rent, rates, wages, etc.) and will be debited to P & L account at the year end, so reducing the net profit figure by £200. As the net profit increases capital account, we have in fact *reduced* this increase in capital account by £200, by reducing net profit. Think about this carefully. The final net profit transferred from P & L account to Capital account (so increasing it) is now £200 *less* than it would have been if we had ignored depreciation.

So, the depreciation on assets such as machinery, equipment, vehicles, etc. is caused by passage of time, *and* wear and tear, and the reduction in the value of the asset, because of these factors, must be treated as an expense, which will reduce our ultimate net profit. Wear and tear through usage is obviously going to be the main reason.

We accept that depreciation of an asset is an expense, but we must realise that it is an expense quite unlike other expenses such as rent, rates, wages, etc. It reduces our net profit in the same way, but it does not involve any payments! *No* cash goes out for depreciation. Cash does go out for rent, rates, etc., but not for this item "depreciation", which has happened *naturally* without any payments being involved.

How then do we record this peculiar expense in the accounts? We know that it will finish up on the debit side of P & L account at the end of the period, so reducing net profit, but how does it get there?

First of all let us realise that it does not build up gradually throughout the year, like payments for normal expenses (credit cash/bank, debit relevant expense account). At the *end* of the year we decide how much depreciation has taken place throughout the year and we debit P & L account with this expense. What do we *credit*? The debit item in P & L account is not a *transfer* of accumulated payments throughout the year, as with rent, rates, etc. – we have only just decided to reduce profits by such debit.

What we are doing, in effect, is taking part of the profits away from the business and putting them on one side, and we are going to keep these "stolen" profits in another account called a "Provision for Depreciation of (Machinery) Account".

Therefore, the entries at the *end of the year* are, debit P & L account, credit "Provision for Depreciation of (Asset) Account".

Think carefully now on what is happening. The net profit has been *reduced* by our debit for depreciation in the P & L account. The owner of the business has got to live, and pay for his shelter, food, drink, etc. and his only source of income is the business. The profits are his, and if he wants to draw them out of the business to spend, then he is entitled to. Therefore, at the year end he will look at his net profit figure in the P & L account and this will tell him the maximum amount he can draw out of the business. If we have *reduced* the net profit figure by an item "depreciation of whatever" then we have reduced what he can draw from the business for personal expenses! Yet the debit for depreciation has not necessitated an outflow of cash from the business. We have simply made a "book" entry – debit P & L account, credit "Provision for Depreciation of Asset".

We have, in fact, "forced" the owner to leave cash in the business which he may otherwise have taken away. The cash thus "saved" by the business is *retained* to cover the loss of value in assets through wear and tear, etc. in the period.

Let us look at this more closely. Let's imagine that we set out this morning to the town centre in order to sell fruit to shoppers. On the way to our "pitch" we buy £100 of fruit from the wholesalers and this fruit is put on our barrow (our stall), which cost us £25 to buy.

We arrive at our "pitch" in the town centre and proceed to sell our fruit. At the end of the day we find that we have sold our £100 of fruit for £160, cash. We are therefore £60 better off in cash than when we started. We put this £60 into a tinbox. Then we realise that we haven't paid our assistant, so we give him £20 wages out of our tin box. So far we have made £40 net profit on today's trading and we have this amount in our tin box. Then we realise that we haven't allowed for wear and tear (i.e. depreciation) on our barrow – estimated at £5. So we have only really made *£35* net profit on our day's trading. We cannot ignore depreciation of our barrow through wear and tear, otherwise we do not show a true net profit figure. The wear and tear *has* taken place and we can't ignore it. £35 net profit – how much cash have we got in our tin box? £40! The "depreciation" has had no effect whatsoever on our cash reserves – the payment of wages to our assistant *did*, but not the depreciation.

What is the maximum amount we can take out of our fruit business in cash? The amount shown as net profit, £35! If we take the £35, there will still be £5 left in the tin box which we can't touch! We have been forced to leave £5 in the business which, but for the depreciation consideration, might have been taken away for personal living expenses. Our Trading and Profit and Loss Account would appear:

	£		£
Purchases	100	Sales	160
Gross Profit	60		
	160		160
Assistant's Wages	20	Gross Profit	60
Depreciation of Barrow	5		
Net Profit to Capital Account	35		
	60		60

Note – very important! – our profit for the day is £35. The cash generated for the business is *£40*, – i.e. Net Profit *plus* depreciation. Only £35 cash, maximum, can be taken away by the owner, but there is in fact £40 extra cash in the business as a result of trading. £5 is being retained.

If we do the same thing for the next 5 days, assuming consistent trading each day, and assuming that we, the owners, draw out the net profit shown by the accounts each day to "live on", then in 5 days time we will have £25 cash in our tin box which we can use to replace our worn out barrow with a new one, (read "days" as years to be realistic). So, by debiting P & L account each day with £5 depreciation expense, we have reduced by £5 what we, the owner, can draw from the business each day. The debit of £5 to our P & L account each day for depreciation is a *non-cash debit* – quite unlike other expenses shown in the P & L account (e.g. rent, rates, wages, etc.).

As the double entry to the £5 debit in P & L account is in the form of a credit to "Provision for Depreciation of Barrow" account, the balance on this account at the end of five days (years) will be a credit balance of £25. We know that *any* credit balance at the date of a balance sheet should be shown on the liabilities side of the balance sheet but the practice with accumulated depreciation is to show it as a *deduction* from the asset concerned (in this case "barrow"). Same effect on balance sheet totals! i.e.

DR Balance Sheet as at end of Day 5 CR

Assets	£		£
Barrow (at cost)	25		
Less provision for depreciation	25		
	Nil		

The asset, "barrow" has a *written down value* of nil – i.e. its cost has been consumed by depreciation (wear and tear), but we have in the tin box £25 cash to match the depreciation charges over the 5 days (years), represented by this credit balance on Provision for "Depreciation of Barrow" Account of £25.

At this stage, theoretically, our barrow should be a pile of rubbish (no value) and the entries in the accounts should be (visualise the double entry for each transaction):

DR Barrow A/c CR

		£			£
Day 0	Cash	25	End of Day 5	Provision for Depreciation	25
		25			25

DR	Provision for Depreciation of Barrow				CR
		£			£
End of			End of		
Day 5	Barrow a/c	25	Day 1	P & L account	5
			2	P & L account	5
			3	P & L account	5
			4	P & L account	5
			5	P & L account	5
		25			25

According to the accounts, at end of Day 5 we have no asset "barrow". The amount of depreciation provided each day has been stored in the "Provision for Depreciation Account", and at the end of the life span of the asset has been *transferred* to the asset account, so closing off the account – nothing to show on the balance sheet at end of Day 5. The barrow is a thing of the past!

In the meantime we have got £25 in cash in our tin box. This can be used to buy a new barrow (i.e. to replace the worn out asset) – debit "Barrow A/c" – credit "Cash A/c", so re-opening the asset account "Barrow" with the value of the new asset. Then, we start again with depreciation in each period.

It should be obvious that the Balance Sheet at end of, for example, Day 3 in the above example would show:

Balance Sheet at end of Day 3 (Assets Side)

Assets	£	
Barrow (at cost)	25	(debit balance in Barrow a/c)
Less Provision for depreciation	15	(credit balance – Provision for Depreciation of Barrow a/c)
	10	

The £10 is the "written down value" of this asset at end of Day 3 – i.e. the book value.

You should now fully realise that the effect of debiting P & L account each day, (each year in practice) with the amount of depreciation that has occurred for each asset, is to effectively retain in the business cash (from profits) which might otherwise have been drawn out by the owner. When the asset is worn out, this retained cash can be used to purchase a replacement asset. Is this the object of charging depreciation to P & L account each year? In some cases, yes – in most cases the objective is to simply *recover* the amount originally spent on the asset. In our above example, the barrow cost £25. Over a 5 day (year) period the P & L account showed depreciation £5 each day (year), so forcing the owner to do without that £5 as drawings for personal spending, because the £5 debit to P & L account reduced the net profit which he could draw. The £5 "forcibly" retained in the business each day could be regarded as going towards the eventual *replacement* of the asset, *or* simply as a gradual *recovery* of the £25 originally spent on acquiring the asset. Probably the latter.

SUMMARY

At the end of a financial period, transfer the expenses *due* for the period to the debit side of P & L account (so reducing profit) and transfer the gains to the credit side of P & L account (so increasing profit), then decide on the depreciation that has taken place on various assets held (i.e. the expense of wear and tear). Debit such amounts of depreciation to P & L account (so reducing profit – without an actual cash payment!) and credit "Provision for Depreciation of — (Asset)" Account. At this point you are actually diverting profits (available to the owner) away from the P & L account to a "shelf", where you are going to hold them for future use for the business. When you come to do your balance sheet you will show the asset at cost (as per the account), and you will show the balance on the relevant "Provision for Depreciation" account as a deduction, so showing clearly the written down value of the asset (i.e. – the book-value) in the balance sheet.

As each debit to P & L account for depreciation effectively reduces what the owner can take away from the business, without the business having to make a cash outlay for this entry (unlike wages), this amount of cash (generated from profits in the period) is *retained* in the business to go towards either providing cash to replace the asset when it becomes worn out, or simply to gradually recoup (recover) the original cash outlay when that asset was purchased.

Obviously the amount of wear and tear which takes place each year can not be estimated accurately, and it is usual to calculate depreciation annually on a percentage basis – it can never be 100% accurate. Some cotton mills in Lancashire are still using machinery bought 60 years ago, and the machinery is still "doing the job" yet the accountants, at the time of purchase, probably based their "writing off period" on 15/20 years!

Realising that calculations of wear and tear in a period can never be wholly accurate we must nevertheless have some accepted method to apply to our assets. But before we look at the generally accepted methods used, which assets are we talking about? Does equipment, office furniture and equipment, motor vehicles, plant and machinery depreciate? Yes!

Does stock, debtors, bank balance, etc. depreciate? Ignoring inflation, and assuming that we have got a fairly active business, these latter type of assets don't depreciate because we don't hold them long enough – they are constantly changing.

FIXED AND CURRENT ASSETS

We must therefore distinguish between these different types of assets. Those which we buy for "permanent" use in the business (e.g. Premises, Plant and Machinery, Equipment, Office Furniture, Motor Vehicles, etc.), are termed *Fixed Assets* and are shown under this heading in all balance sheets. Assets which are with us for a short time – i.e. not permanent – such as stock for resale, debtors, bank, prepayments (i.e. payments of expenses in advance) are termed *Current Assets* and these are not subject to depreciation because of their short stay with us. These are shown under the heading of *Current Assets* in any balance sheet. More on this later. Before leaving this subject however, I have quoted Premises (Land and Buildings) as a Fixed Asset. Is this subject to depreciation? It should be, as a fixed asset, through wear, tear and usage, but in reality this asset actually increases in value (i.e. appreciates). In recent years the accountancy profession has decided that the buildings *do* depreciate in value whilst the *land* appreciates in value! Ask any purchaser of his new home whether he bought for a high price the house, or the land. He bought the house!

CALCULATING DEPRECIATION

Anyway, back to the methods of calculating depreciation of fixed assets. Whichever method is used it is going to be a "hit or miss" method, but the accepted methods are as follows:

STRAIGHT LINE METHOD (OR FIXED PERCENTAGE)

This is the most widely-used method, where a fixed percentage of the cost of the asset is "charged" as depreciation each year. If you buy a fixed asset for £10,000 and you consider that the asset has a useful life of, say, 10 years then you will charge £1,000 (10% of cost, £10,000) as depreciation at the end of each year for the next 10 years. If, however, you consider that this particular asset will have a scrap value of, say, £1,000 at the end of 10 years (in which case you must have a very reliable crystal ball!) then you would only "write off" as depreciation *£9,000* over the next 10 years (i.e. £900 per year) and rely on the scrap value of £1,000 to make up the difference on what you have provided.

REDUCING BALANCE METHOD

This is where you take a certain percentage, and apply this, not to the cost of the asset, but to the *reduced value* of the asset year by year. If, for example, you buy a fixed asset for £8,000 and decide on a 10% reducing balance method, then in the first year you will charge depreciation to P & L account (Debit P & L account – Credit "Provision for Depreciation of Asset Account") of £800, but in the second year you will charge 10% of the reduced balance of the asset – in this case 10% of £7,200 – the third year, 10% of £6,480, and so on. Using this method, the asset will never be written off exactly and an adjustment will be necessary in the final useful year of the asset's life to bring the balance of the asset to exactly nil. With this method a different charge for depreciation is made every year, reducing all the time.

There are many academic arguments for using one or other of the above two methods. They *are* academic and not worthy of further comment – depreciation charges in the main are very much a matter of guesswork, but the frightening aspect is the effect of using different methods and time scales to arrive at the amount actually charged in the P & L account, because this reflects on the net profit figure shown in the accounts!

REVALUATION METHOD

This is where, if you have £3,000 of a certain fixed asset at 31st December, Year 1, and *on inspection* at 31st December, Year 2 you find that you have now got only £2,700 of value left in that asset, then the depreciation charge for the year is the reduction of £300.

Obviously this method can only be used for assets which can be valued annually by inspection. The catering trade probably uses this method more than any other trade, where cutlery and crockery are valued at each year end by actual inspection. Any reduction in value held at the year end is treated as depreciation. The depreciation charge will therefore vary from year to year.

Whatever method of calculating depreciation is used, *do* think of a depreciation "charge" to P & L account as being a *diversion* of the available profit to a "shelf" (the Provision for Depreciation Account) to either provide funds for the eventual replacement of that asset or to recoup, (recover), the original outlay of funds for the purchase of that asset.

In the examination, read the question very carefully – it may say that the fixed assets are depreciated by x% *of cost*, or on *reduced balance*. The question may say that depreciation is at x% *per annum*, in which case the asset bought half-way through the current year will only incur a half-year's depreciation (in the current year only, of course).

You may be told specifically to ignore fractions of a year in your calculations. Read the instructions *very* carefully.

EXERCISE 10.1

David Moore, who is a sole trader, decides to purchase a delivery van for the sum of £1,500. He cannot decide whether to write off depreciation of the new van on the "straight line" method or the "diminishing balance" method.

Required:
In order to assist Moore in reaching a decision, draw up the Delivery Van Account for the first three years – taking a rate of 10% for depreciation – as it would appear:

(a) Under the "straight line" method.
and
(b) Under the "diminishing balance" method.

(London Chamber of Commerce)

EXERCISE 10.2

The following is the Profit and Loss Account of Jones for the year 19_4.

Profit and Loss Account

	£		£
Rents and Rates	400	Gross Profit b/d	6,400
Wages	3,000	Rents Received	700
Insurances	100		
Light and Heat	300		
Depreciation	900		
Net Profit	2,400		
	7,100		7,100

(a) How much cash was generated for the business in 19_4 by profits?
(b) If Jones decides to increase the above depreciation charges by 70% in 19_5, what effect will this have on:

(i) the net profit for 19_5, and
(ii) the cash generated from profits in 19_5?

EXERCISE 10.3

G. Brown, a sole trader, extracted the following Trial Balance on 31st March 19_9:

	DR	CR
Capital		2,060
Stock (1.4._8)	1,800	
Purchases	7,400	
Sales		12,940
Discounts	320	110
Rent and Rates	650	
Cash	100	
Bank		830
Returns and Allowances	170	90
Debtors and Creditors	4,200	3,300
Wages and Salaries	3,110	
General Expenses	130	
Motor Vehicles (cost)	3,000	
Provision for Depreciation of Motor Vehicles		2,250
Fixtures and fittings (cost)	1,500	
Provision for Depreciation of Fixtures & Fittings		800
	22,380	22,380

NOTES

1. Stock 31st March 19_9, valued at £2,100.
2. Wages and salaries accrued at 31st March 19_9, £150.
3. Rates prepaid at 31st March 19_9, £60.
4. General expenses owing at 31st March 19_9, £40.
5. Depreciation is to be provided for as follows:
   Motor Vehicles – 25% of cost (straight line method)
   Fixtures and Fittings – 10% of reduced balance.

Prepare Trading and Profit and Loss Account for year ended 31st March 19_9 and a Balance Sheet at that date.

EXERCISE 10.4

Joe Banks, the newly appointed chairman of Blunder Limited, is reviewing the company's accounts for the year ended 30th April, in preparation for his address to the company's forthcoming annual general meeting.

Joe's attention has been drawn to a note prepared by his chief accountant, Ken Popkins:

	£
Net profit for the year ended 30th April	42,000
Plus depreciation for the year ended 30th April	14,000
"Cash flow"	£56,000

Required:

1. Examine and comment on the following points raised by Joe.

(a) How can reference be made to a cash flow of £56,000 when the company's balance sheet at 30th April, shows a bank overdraft of £20,000 compared to a balance in hand of £30,000 last year?

(b) (i) Why does depreciation feature in the cash flow calculation?

(ii) Why is depreciation added to the net profit rather than deducted?

(c) Does a change in the depreciation charge alter the cash flow?

2. Criticise the method used by Ken Popkins to determine cash flow.

(A.E.B. "A" level)

CHAPTER 11

DISPOSALS OF FIXED ASSETS AND REVALUATIONS

DISPOSALS OF FIXED ASSETS

The last chapter showed the necessity of providing depreciation on fixed assets at the end of each year. If this was not done, the net profit for the year would be overstated and the balance sheet would show the asset at a figure higher than its true value – i.e. the asset would continue to show "at cost" year after year.

Imagine that you purchase a delivery vehicle for £4,000 and don't bother to provide depreciation in the accounts. After nearly 4 years, you sell it for £500 cash – the following would be the entries in the accounts.

DR Vehicles CR

		£			£
Year 1			Year 4		
Jan. 1	Bank	4,000	Nov. 30	Cash	500

DR Cash CR

		£			
Year 4					
Nov. 30	Vehicles	500			

Note that since 1st January, Year 1, you have been showing the vehicle on the balance sheet at cost, £4,000 (not a true picture!), and each year your net profit has been quite high (due to no reduction for depreciation), so you have been living well!

Now that you have sold the vehicle for only £500, what are you going to do with the £3,500 debit balance on Vehicles Account? If you leave it there you must show this balance on future balance sheets, and you can't show an asset you haven't got! This £3,500 must be regarded as a loss on the sale of the vehicle, and as such this loss must make its way to the debit side of your end of year P & L account, i.e.

DR Vehicles CR

		£			£
Year 1			Year 4		
Jan. 1	Bank	4,000	Nov. 30	Cash	500
			Dec. 31	To P & L a/c	3,500
		4,000			4,000

DR	Profit & Loss Account for Year 4		CR
	£		£
Other Expenses	6,000	Gross Profit b/d from	
Loss on Sale of Vehicle	3,500	Trading a/c	12,000
Net Profit	2,500		
	12,000		12,000

This loss of £3,500 makes a big "hole" in your profit figure. You won't be able to draw as much for personal spending as you have in the past 4 years! Wouldn't it have been better to have spread this loss of value evenly over the life of the vehicle, so that profits were reduced by a reasonable amount each year? As it is, you have had to bear 4 years accumulated losses all at one go! Your net profits shown over the past 4 years have not reflected the true position of your business. The results of trading are distorted.

Rather than putting a "bit" of profits on the "shelf" (Provision for Depreciation Account) each year, so retaining the equivalent amount of cash in the business – i.e. keeping it away from the owner (you *must* understand this point – if not refer back to the last lesson), you now have to take a massive "chunk" of profits all at once to cover this loss. Certainly £3,500 of cash will be kept in the business this year because of this reduction in net profit, because the debit to P & L account of £3,500 is a *non-cash debit*, like depreciation. It is in fact, depreciation which you *should* have charged over the years, but all in one lump! The entry for the loss is still a *book entry* – Debit P & L Account, Credit Vehicles Account – no cash has gone out in Year 4 for this item of £3,500.

It is very important that you understand this. The gross profit shown, £12,000, is cash in our "tin box", out of which expenses like rates, wages, insurance, etc. have to be paid (i.e. £6,000). This leaves £6,000 in the "box" which, at most, can only be reduced by the owners drawings of £2,500 (maximum), leaving £3,500 in the "box", which must remain in the business to cover the loss of value which has taken place in the asset. This provides the cash (together with the £500 cash received on the sale) to replace the asset, or to recoup the original outlay of £4,000 when you bought the asset 4 years ago, whichever way you want to think of it (better, the latter).

Let us now look at this situation, assuming a prudent policy on your part of providing depreciation each year. When you bought the vehicle you thought it had a life of 5 years so you decided to depreciate it by 20% per annum using the straight-line method. Therefore at 31st December in Year 1, 2 and 3, you debited P & L account with 20% of cost, £800. At 31st December, Year 3 your accounts appear:

DR		Vehicles			CR
Year 1		£			
Jan. 1	Bank	4,000			

DR		Provision for Depreciation of Vehicles			CR
Year 3		£	*Year 1*		£
Dec. 31	Balance c/d	2,400	Dec. 31	P & L a/c	800
			Year 2		
			Dec. 31	P & L a/c	800
			Year 3		
			Dec. 31	P & L a/c	800
		2,400			2,400
			Year 3		
			Dec. 31	Balance b/d	2,400

Over the past 3 years a total of £2,400 of available profits have been put "on one side" for this particular vehicle, representing, you hope, the reduction in value to date. At 31st December, Year 3, the relevant entry on the balance sheet appears:

DR	Balance Sheet at 31st December, Year 3	CR
	Assets	£
	Vehicles (at cost)	4,000
	Less provision for depreciation	2,400
		1,600

This shows a written down value, or "book value" of £1,600. Now, before you provide more depreciation at 31st December, Year 4, you sell the vehicle, in November, for £500. The book value is £1,600 and you only get £500 for the vehicle – therefore you have made a loss of £1,100 on the sale. You have obviously under-estimated the depreciation which has taken place. You should have charged more to profits each year, and your under-estimation must be made up for in Year 4's accounts. The £1,100 loss on sale will have to be debited to P & L account for Year 4. (Considering that you would have been debiting £800 for depreciation anyway next month, had the vehicle not been sold in November, you aren't really far out in your estimation of wear and tear – only £300 over the 4-year period).

THE ENTRIES IN THE ACCOUNTS AT 30TH NOVEMBER ARE AS FOLLOWS:

Vehicles

DR		£	CR		£
Year 1			Year 4		
Jan. 1	Bank	4,000	Nov. 30	Vehicle Disposal a/c	4,000
		4,000			4,000

Provision for Depreciation of Vehicles

DR		£	CR		£
Year 4			*Year 1*		
Nov. 30	Disposals a/c	2,400	Dec. 31	P & L a/c	800
			Year 2		
			Dec. 31	P & L a/c	800
			Year 3		
			Dec. 31	P & L a/c	800
		2,400			2,400

Vehicle Disposals A/c

DR		£	CR		£
Year 4			Year 4		
Nov. 30	Vehicles	4,000	Nov. 30	Cash	500
			Nov. 30	Depreciation	2,400
			Nov. 30	Loss on sale	1,100
		4,000			4,000

Note carefully – the original cost of the vehicle has been *cleared out* of the Vehicles Account to a Disposal Account (a temporary account to record details of the disposal) by transfer of the balance – i.e. from the debit side of Vehicles Account to the debit side of Disposals Account. The balance is now lying in Disposals Account, awaiting disposal. In the above example, the vehicles account is now closed, but obviously there would normally be other vehicles in that account, shown at cost, and there would therefore normally be a debit balance remaining in the account representing the cost price of the vehicles which are still held by the firm.

In the Disposals account, part of the £4,000 is "covered" by the cash received, £500 (imagine the debit to cash). Also £2,400 of the cost is "covered" by the profits put aside over the last 3 years to the Provision Account. These "put aside" profits are now needed, and they are therefore taken *out* of the Provision account (i.e. taken off the shelf), and carried to the Disposal account by double-entry transfer. There would normally still be a credit balance remaining on Provision Account, after the £2,400 transfer, being profits set aside in past years for vehicles *still held*, but in our example we are just looking at this *one* vehicle.

Of the £4,000 originally spent on the vehicle, £2,900 has been covered (by cash, £500, and by past profits put aside, £2,400). The remaining £1,100 *not covered*, must be treated as a "loss on sale" and debited to this year's P & L account. However, as we don't prepare our P & L account until 31st December, this £1,100 must lie temporarily in a "Loss on Sale of Vehicles Account" – debit side.

When the trial balance is drawn up, just prior to preparing the Trading and Profit and Loss Account for the year, this debit item "Loss on Sale of Vehicles – £1,100" will obviously show in the trial balance. It will then be transferred to the debit side of P & L account, so reducing profits for the year. The item could be thought of as "extra depreciation" – i.e. what you *should* have allowed for, but didn't!

Suppose, when you sold the vehicle, that you had got £1,700 for it in cash. Your Disposals Account would then appear:

DR Vehicle Disposals A/c CR

		£			£
Year 4			*Year 4*		
Nov. 30	Vehicles	4,000	Nov. 30	Cash	1,700
Nov. 30	Gain on Sale a/c	100	Nov. 30	Depreciation	2,400
		4,100			4,100

In this case you have provided too much in the way of depreciation charges – the £2,400 together with the £1,700 cash received has exceeded the actual cost of the vehicle by £100. This is a profit, or gain, on sale and can be *added* back to this year's profits in the P & L account – i.e. some of the depreciation which has been taken *out* of profits over the past years, can now be *added back* to profits as this £100 was not required.

Until the P & L account is prepared, next month, the £100 will lie on the *credit* side of a "Gain on Sale of Vehicles" account (note double-entry), and at 31st December it will be transferred to the credit side of P & L account, so increasing profits for Year 4.

Do remember that losses and gains on sales of fixed assets are pure "book" entries in the P & L account – they are not backed by cash in any way. The only cash involved is in the entry "Debit Cash, Credit Disposals Account" for the actual sale proceeds. The other entries are *not* connected to cash.

Look at the following P & L account:

DR	Profit and Loss Account for 19_3		CR
	£		£
Normal Expenses	6,000	Gross Profit b/d	10,000
Depreciation	3,000	(from Trading a/c)	
Loss on sale of fixed asset	1,500	Gain on sale of fixed asset	200
		Net *loss* to Capital a/c	300
	10,500		10,500

Results of the year's trading? Net Loss £300. How much *cash* has been generated from trading in 19_3? Well, the "tin box" had £10,000 cash in it from straight buying and selling (Gross Profit), out of which £6,000 was paid out for normal expenses such as wages, etc., so that leaves £4,000 in the "box", being cash generated from trading. The items "Loss on Sale", "Gain on Sale", and "Depreciation" are all *book* entries with no cash behind them, so the answer *is* £4,000 – i.e. Net Loss £300 with non-cash debits of depreciation and loss on sale added back (so making a positive figure of £4,200), and the non-cash credit of £200 being deducted = £4,000. This aspect of depreciation is *very* important and you should understand it thoroughly.

REVALUATIONS

Land and buildings, as I said earlier, tend to appreciate in value. Suppose you buy a factory in Year 1 for £30,000. It doesn't depreciate, so it is shown in every year's balance sheet at cost £30,000. However, in Year 15 you get a professional valuer in and he values the premises at £60,000. In your balance sheet you should show a "true" picture, so you must now revalue your premises and show them in future in the balance sheet at, not cost, but *valuation* of £60,000.

To bring the premises account up to this figure you must obviously debit the account with another £30,000. But what do you credit? The business has just made a profit *on paper* of £30,000 but it would be wrong to credit the P & L account with this profit of £30,000, as there is not yet any cash "behind" it, and the business certainly does not want this £30,000 mixed up with the net profit figure as the owner may try to draw it out for personal spending! Also, this would distort the true trading results drastically, and the net profit figure would be very misleading. On the other hand, this "book" profit *does* belong to the owner of the business, and the credit entry should therefore be *direct* to his capital account, thereby increasing what the business owes to the owner(s), *viz*:

DR		Premises			CR
		£			£
Year 1	Bank	30,000	Year 15	Balance c/d	60,000
Year 15	Capital	30,000			
		60,000			60,000
Year 15	Balance b/d	60,000			

DR		Capital A/c			CR
		£			£
Year 15	Balance c/d	110,000		Balance b/d	80,000
			Year 15	Premises (Revaluation)	30,000
		110,000			110,000
			Year 15	Balance b/d	110,000

Don't attempt the following exercises until you *thoroughly* understand these last two chapters.

EXERCISE 11.1

On 31st December 19_7 the following accounts appeared in the books of Smallbrook (Engineers) Ltd. The financial year runs from 1st June to 31st May every year.

Machinery and plant:

19_1		£
Jan. 1	Bank	500,000

Provision for depreciation:

19_7		£
May 31	Balance b/d	300,000

On 31st December 19_7 half the machinery and plant was sold for £150,000 cash. New machinery was purchased for cash on 15th February 19_8 for £700,000. At the end of the financial year all machinery is depreciated by 10% of cost. No allowance is made for parts of a year.

Write up the two accounts in Smallbrook (Engineers) Ltd. ledger, and show how the asset would appear in the Balance Sheet on 31st May 19_8. (You may use a separate disposal account if you wish.)

(University of London "O" level)

EXERCISE 11.2

On 1st January 19_8, a company purchased three machines for £1,000 each. Depreciation at the rate of 10% per annum (of cost) has been credited to a "provision for depreciation" account, and the machines have been carried in the books at cost. The company makes up its accounts to 31st December in each year.

On 1st January 19_0, one of the machines was sold for £762. The other two machines were still in use on 31st December 19_0.

You are required to show:

(i) the machinery account and the provision for depreciation account for the three years 19_8, 19_9 and 19_0, and
(ii) to show how the machinery would appear in the balance sheet as on 31st December 19_0.

(Institute of Bankers)

EXERCISE 11.3

(*a*) At 1st March 19_6 the following balances appeared on the ledger accounts of Hill and Co. Ltd:

	£
Van A A/c	1,550
Van B A/c	1,500
Office Equipment A/c	2,100

Each asset account had a corresponding "Provision for Depreciation Account", the respective balances on each being £1,388, £960 and £780.

Van A was originally acquired in December 19_2, and it was considered that it would last six years with a residual value of £50. It is company policy to provide a full year's depreciation in the year of acquisition, and depreciation of 40% per year is calculated on a declining balance.

Van B was acquired in June 19_4 (depreciation at 40% per year on a declining balance) and was sold in December 19_6 for £230. A new van C was obtained for £1,800 (less trade discount 10%), and was expected to have a five year life, and is to be depreciated on a declining balance at 40% per year.

The Office Equipment is depreciated on a straight-line basis at 10% on cost.

Required:
Prepare all the necessary ledger accounts relevant to the above information for the year ended 28th February 19_7.

(*b*) An employee, observing the depreciation balances on the above accounts, notes with relief that "the company has plenty of funds for replacement".

Required:
Comment briefly on the validity of this observation.

(A.C.C.A.)

EXERCISE 11.4

(a) You meet Mr Foolhardy in the bar of his golf club, and when the conversation turns to accounting matters, he says, "It is not my policy to charge for depreciation on fixed assets. The plant in my business is always maintained in first class condition."

Discuss this view.

(b) The balance sheet of Jackson and Co. as at 31st December 19–8, shows motor vehicles as follows:

	£
Motor vehicles at cost	30,300
Less: Depreciation	7,100
Net	£23,200

Vehicles are depreciated on the straight line basis over a five year life. Depreciation is charged pro rata to time in the year of acquisition, but no charge is made in the year of disposal. The disposal account is written up on the last day of each year. During 19_9 the following vehicles transactions took place:

March 31	Purchased	lorry	£6,500
April 30	,,	tanker	£8,400
Aug. 31	,,	truck	£6,500

The lorry was second hand and originally cost £10,000.

Sales of vehicles:

30th April – fork lift truck – £450 – originally cost £3,500 on 31st March 19_7

30th June – saloon car – £75 – originally cost £950 on 30th June 19_5

30th September – dumper – £250 – orginally cost £4,000 on 1st January 19_4.

Your are required to write up the accounts for Vehicles, Vehicle Depreciation and Vehicle Disposal.

(Association of Accounting Technicians)

EXERCISE 11.5

The following trial balance was extracted from the books of Watson, a trader, as at 31st December 19_2:

	£	£
Capital account		9,600
Furniture and fittings	800	
Purchases	48,360	
Sales		62,220
Stock-in-Trade, 1st Jan. 19_2	4,700	
Trade debtors	5,280	
Trade creditors		4,116
Motor vans	1,268	
General expenses	1,469	
Motor expenses	418	
Rent and rates	674	
Equipment	3,750	
Balance at bank	1,415	
Discounts allowed	1,126	
Discounts received		871
Wages and salaries	7,462	
Lighting and heating	85	
	£76,807	£76,807

The following matters are to be taken into account:

1. Stock-in-trade 31st December 91_2, £6,465.
2. Lighting and heating accrued 31st December 19_2, £12.
3. Rates paid in advance 31st December 19_2, £28.
4. The motor vans account appeared in the ledger as follows:

Motor Vans

19_2.			£	19_2.			£
Jan.	1	Balance (old van)	276	Jan.	1	Cash – Sale of old van	208
		Cash – cost of new van	1,200	Dec.	31	Balance	1,268
			£1,476				£1,476
Dec.	31	Balance	1,268				

Provide depreciation on the new van at the rate of 20% per annum.

You are required to prepare a trading and profit and loss account for the year 19_2 and a balance sheet as at 31st December 19_2.

NOTE: Ignore depreciation of furniture and fittings and equipment.

(Institute of Bankers)

EXERCISE 11.6

Charles Rover owns a small factory situated on a trading estate. He uses the reducing balance method of depreciation, for plant, with a 20% write off each year, and maintains a plant account to record all entries concerning the plant.

An extract from the balance sheet as at 30th September 19_7 is as follows:

Fixed Assets	*Cost*	*Depreciation*	*Net*
	£	£	£
Land and Buildings	520,000	—	520,000
Plant	410,100	159,180	250,920
	930,100	159,180	770,920

The Plant account is as follows:

Plant A/c

		£			£
1.10._6	Cost b/d	361,500	1.10._6	Depreciation b/d	122,750
30.6._7	Depreciation on Plant sold	26,300	30.6._7	Cost of Plant sold	53,900
1.8._7	Assets purchased	102,500	30.9._7	Depreciation for the year	62,730
30.9._7	Balance c/f	159,180	30.9._7	Balance c/f	410,100
		£649,480			£649,480

Plant purchased on 12th October 19_3 for £46,800 was sold for £16,212 on 4th December 19_7. New plant costing £81,400, was purchased on 15th May 19_8.

Depreciation is charged in full in the year of purchase, but no depreciation is charged in the year of sale.

Required:

(a) Write up the Plant Account shown above, and a Disposals Account, for the year to 30.9._8

(b) Comment to Charles Rover on his Depreciation Policy.

(Association of Accounting Technicians)

EXERCISE 11.7

The following transactions relate to AJS Limited in respect of plant and machinery:

(i) On 1st March 19_2 machine M.5 purchased for £12,000. The estimated useful life being five years, and having a residual value of £2,000.
(ii) On 1st January 19_3 machine M.6 purchased for £18,000. The estimated useful life being seven years, and having a residual value of £4,000. Assembly and installation costs on the same date were £700.
(iii) On 1st September 19_4 machine M.5 was given in part exchange for machine M.7, the allowance being £4,000. Machine M.7 cost £20,000 with an estimated useful life of ten years and having a residual value of £6,000.

Assume full depreciation expense in the year of purchase, and ignore depreciation expense in the year of sale.

Required:
Plant and machinery account, and the related depreciation and disposal accounts in respect of the three years ending 31st December 19_4.

(I.C.S.A.)

EXERCISE 11.8

Ajax Ltd. owned four machines (A, B, C and D) at 31st December 19_8, viz:

"A" Bought in 19_3 at a cost of £8,000
"B" Bought in 19_5 at a cost of £6,000
"C" Bought in 19_7 at a cost of £10,000
"D" Bought in 19_8 at a cost of £12,000

Depreciation is always provided at 10% of cost, ignoring fractions of years. During the year 19_9 the following transactions take place:

(i) Machine is bought for £9,000
(ii) Machine B is sold for £3,000
(iii) Machine C is sold for £8,500
(iv) Machine A is given in part-exchange towards the purchase of a new machine F. The allowance on Machine A is £2,000 and the balance of the purchase price of machine F, £12,000, is paid in cash.

Required:
Show the following accounts as they would appear in the ledger of Ajax Ltd. after preparation of the final accounts for 19_8. All detailed postings for the year 19_9 should be clearly shown in these accounts.

(a) Machinery Account
(b) Provision for depreciation of machinery account
(c) Machinery Disposals account.

CHAPTER 12

BAD AND DOUBTFUL DEBTS AND MISCELLANEOUS

BAD DEBTS AND PROVISION FOR BAD DEBTS

You sold goods to Mr Thompson many months ago for £150 on credit and he has not yet paid you. You now hear that he has left the country for good. You are not going to get paid. You have a bad debt! Thompson's account appears in your ledger at present:

DR		Thompson			CR
Date	Sales	£150			

If you continue to show this balance as part of total debtors in your business balance sheet you are "kidding" yourself, and everyone else. The account should be written off as bad. You have lost £150. This is an inevitable expense of most businesses – bad debts.

Obviously you must *credit* Thompson's account, so closing it off, and the debit will be in the expense (nominal) account of Bad Debts, *viz*:

DR		Thompson			CR
Date	Sales	£150	Now	Bad Debts	£150
		150			150

DR		Bad Debts			CR
Now	Thompson	150	End of Year	P & L a/c	150
		150			150

From the above you will see that Thompson's balance of £150 was transferred to the debit side of the expense account Bad Debts, together with other nonpayers, and at the end of the year the total bad debts for the year are transferred to the debit side of P & L account, so reducing net profit for that year.

Suppose though, that another of your debtors, Mr Timms, is considered by you as not bad (yet!) but very doubtful. He owes you £80, his account showing a debit balance in your ledger for this amount. Again, if this £80 is included in total debtors in the balance sheet, you are not showing a "true" position. You are hiding your doubts about ever getting this money. You don't want to write off his account to bad debts like Mr Thompson's account, because there is still a reasonable chance of Timms paying you.

We are not talking about a *bad* debt now – only a *doubtful* one, but following the normal conservative conventions of accounting we should make some kind of prosivion, just in case this account does prove to be bad in the future. We should make a provision for *possible* future bad debts.

How can we do this? Well, how did we make a *provision* for depreciation of fixed assets? We are now talking about a form of "depreciation" of our asset, debtors, caused by those who may never pay us. We would not look at Timms in isolation, but would instead look at the *total* of debtors at the balance sheet date and decide that, say, 5% of them are "doubtful".

Just in case these debtors *do* prove to be bad in the future, we are going to take some of this year's profits and put them on one side (i.e. on the "shelf") to cover such possibilities. Therefore, we would debit the year's P & L account with an amount equal to 5% of total debtors and credit this amount to a "Provision for Bad (or Doubtful) Debts" account. Let's say 5% of debtors came to £600.

DR		P & L account for Year 1	CR
Provision for Bad Debts	£600		

DR		Provision for Bad Debts	CR
		End of Year P & L a/c	£600

The effect of these entries is to reduce the net profit figure by £600, but note that the cash of the business is *not* affected in any way by this transaction – no cash goes out, as with most other expenses.

The effect is identical to the effect of providing for depreciation of fixed assets – the owner can now draw less from the business for personal spending. He has been "forced" to leave £600 cash in the business which he otherwise may have taken out. There is £600 cash in another tin box! These profits lying on the "shelf" (in the provision account) will stay there, being unavailable to the owner, as cover for any of these debts which may definitely prove to be bad in the future.

At the end of the next year, 5% of total debtors may come to £700 – i.e. we have doubtful debtors to the extent of £700 yet we have only *provided for*, out of profits in past years, £600. It is necessary therefore to take another £100 of the current year's profits and put these on the shelf *together with the £600 already there*. We must debit this year's P & L account with the *increase* in the provision, and credit the provision for bad debts account, i.e.

DR — P & L account for Year 2 — CR

DR		CR	
Increase in Provision for Bad Debts	£100		

DR — Provision for Bad Debts — CR

DR	£	CR	£
End of Year 2 Balance c/d	700	End of Year 1 P & L a/c	600
		End of Year 2 P & L account	100
	700		700
		End of Year 2 Balance b/d	700

Now, when we get to the end of Year 3 we find that 5% of our debtors comes to only £550. In past years we have *taken out* of P & L account a total of £700, so making these profits unavailable to the owner. But now we don't need so much profit to be lying on the shelf. We can now take some of them off the shelf and put £150 back into this year's P & L account – i.e. make £150 of past years' profits available again to the owner. This would be done by debiting "Provision for Bad Debts" and crediting this year's P & L account with £150, i.e.

DR — P & L account for Year 3 — CR

DR		CR	
		Reduction in Provision for Bad Debts	£150

DR — Provision for Bad Debts — CR

DR	£	CR	£
End of Year 3 P & L a/c	150	End of Year 1 P & L a/c	600
End of Year 3 Balance c/d	550	End of Year 2 P & L a/c	100
	700		700
		End of Year 3 Balance b/d	550

The balance on Provision account is adjusted at the end of each year in line with the considered needs at that time. If the provision needs increasing, it means taking a bit more out of the year's profits (debit P & L account) but, if the provision is too high, then a bit of previous years' profits put aside, can be "put back" into the current year's P & L account (credit it).

In the above example a provision of 5% of total debtors has been maintained. Each business obviously has its own ideas on calculating the provision needed.

How does the credit balance on Provision for Bad Debts account show in the balance sheet? It is shown as a deduction from the current asset "debors". (Like depreciation showing as a deduction from the relevant fixed asset.) Using the example above the relevant section of the balance sheets for the 3 years would appear:

Balance Sheet as at end of year 1

	£	£
Debtors	12,000	
Less provision for bad debts	600	11,400

Balance Sheet as at end of year 2

	£	£
Debtors	14,000	
Less provision for bad debts	700	13,300

Balance Sheet at end of year 3

	£	£
Debtors	11,000	
Less provision for bad debts	550	10,450

Note that the increase or decrease in the provision is debited or credited to P & L account, and the new balance on provision account, after this adjustment, is shown on the balance sheet. The balance sheet as at end of Year 3 clearly shows, at a glance, that although total debtors are £11,000, £550 of these are considered "doubtful".

Don't confuse this with *actual* bad debts, dealt with earlier. As definite bad debts arise, the balance on the debtor's account is written off immediately to the expense account "bad debts", which at the end of the year is transferred to the debit of P & L account, together with other expenses. This obviously reduces total debtors absolutely.

FINALLY

At this point of your studies you have covered the most important aspects of keeping accounts, and preparing various periodical statements. You have, in fact, provided you understand everything to date, and have put your knowledge into practice by doing most of the exercises (ideally all of them), "broken the back" of the subject! The rest of the topics you need to study should prove to be relatively easy. You will simply be applying what you know to different situations.

To complete this section of your studies there are a few more matters to bring to your attention before you wade into the remaining chapters in this book, which simply develop what you already know.

DRAWINGS

Constant reference has been made in the last few chapters to the owner drawing money out of his business to cover his *personal* expenses. The capital the owner invests in the business is credited to Capital account and this amount is expected to *stay* in the business, to be used for purchase of necessary fixed assets. The owner should not normally draw any of this capital for his personal use. However, as profits increase capital, he can of course draw this increase (i.e. the profits), so a typical capital account of a trader could appear thus at the end of a year.

DR Capital account CR

		£			£
End of Year	Drawings	7,000	Start of Year	Balance b/d	20,000
End of Year	Balance c/d	21,000	End of Year	Net Profit (from P & L a/c)	8,000
		28,000			28,000
			Start of Next Year	Balance b/d	21,000

This shows that the owner has *left* £1,000 of profits in the business, and he will probably use the cash behind these profits to purchase another machine, etc., in order to expand. The £1,000 he has left in is really new capital "introduced" for permanent use in the business, so next year he should *ideally* only draw for personal use the profits made in that year.

Obviously, the owner's drawings will take place at regular intervals throughout the year, so a "Drawings Account" (nominal account) will record the drawings as they occur, and then at the end of the year, *total* drawings will be transferred to his capital account in one amount. This relieves the capital account of a lot of unnecessary entries, *viz*:

Drawings Account

DR				CR		
Year 1		£	*Year 1*		£
Jan. 31	Cash	1,000	Dec. 31	Capital a/c	7,000
May 3	Office Furniture	100			
June 30	Cash	2,000			
Sept. 3	Purchases	800			
Oct. 30	Cash	3,100			
		7,000			7,000

Capital Account

DR					CR
Year 1		£	*Year 1*		£
Dec. 31	Drawings	7,000	Jan. 1	Balance b/d	20,000
Dec. 31	Balance c/d	21,000	Dec. 31	Net Profit	8,000
		28,000			28,000
			Year 1		
			Dec. 31	Balance b/d	21,000

Note – the entries in drawings account in January, June and October would have a corresponding credit entry in cash. The entry in May would have a credit entry in Office Furniture, because the owner has obviously taken away from his business, not cash, but some items of furniture for his own use. So the asset cash has not been reduced, but office furniture has. In September he has obviously taken for his personal use, stock (i.e. goods recently purchased), so the business Purchases Account must be reduced by £800 because this amount of purchases is not for re-sale. A credit entry in purchases account will reduce the amount to be transferred to Trading Account at the year end; the amount transferred will be "effective" purchases, *viz*:

Purchases

DR					CR
		£			£
During Year	Various	18,000	Sept. 3	Drawings	800
			End of Year	To Trading a/c	17,200
		18,000			18,000

Whatever the owner takes for his own use will be debited to the drawings account, and the credit will be in the respective account representing what he has taken, which will, of course, be mainly cash or bank balance.

Note – drawings is *not* an expense – it is transferred at the year end to capital account, *not* profit and loss account. Think about this.

SET-OUT OF BALANCE SHEET

In chapter 10 I told you that assets in a balance sheet were shown under two headings – i.e. **FIXED ASSETS** and **CURRENT ASSETS** – fixed assets being those being put to "permanent" use in the business (e.g. premises, equipment, motor vehicles, office furniture, etc.), and current assets being those which were constantly changing as trading took place (e.g. stocks, debtors, bank, cash, etc.).

Current assets could be described as those assets which, in the normal course of trading will be "turned into cash" within a few months at most.

On the other side of the balance sheet, the liabilities are also divided into "groups". Those liabilities which are due to be repaid within the next few weeks, or months at most, are shown under the heading of **CURRENT LIABILITIES** (e.g. trade creditors, bank overdraft, rent owing, etc.).

Any liability which is not due to be repaid, say, within a year, is shown separately to current liabilities under the heading of **LONG TERM LIABILITIES** (e.g. medium- and long-term loans).

Everything else on the liabilities side of the balance sheet will be connected with the owner's capital, which of course heads the list of liabilities.

EXAMPLE

Balance Sheet as at 30th June 19_.

	£	£		£	£
Capital		40,000	*FIXED ASSETS*		
			Premises		40,000
LONG TERM LIABILITIES			Equipment (cost)	8,000	
Long Term Loan		10,000	Less prov. for dep'n	2,000	
					6,000
			Motor Vehicles	5,000	
			Less prov. for dep'n	4,000	
CURRENT LIABILITIES					1,000
Creditors	1,800				
Bank overdraft	1,200				47,000
Accruals	500				
			CURRENT ASSETS		
		3,500	Stock	3,500	
			Debtors	2,500	
			Prepayments	100	
			Cash	400	
					6,500
		53,500			53,500

Study this set-out and note how the *total* of each section stands out clearly.

WORKING CAPITAL

This is the excess of current assets over current liabilities – in the above example the working capital is £3,000. This is a *very* important item which will be studied in detail in chapter 24. For now, just accept that it is important, and know how to calculate what it is. Some examination questions may ask you to show working capital clearly in your balance sheet, in which case simply show the current liabilities as a deduction from current assets on the same side of the balance sheet, *viz*:

Section of Balance Sheet (Assets Side)

		£	£
Current Assets			
Stock		3,500	
Debtors		2,500	
Prepayments		100	
Cash		400	
		6,500	
Less Current Liabilities			
Creditors	1,800		
Bank overdraft	1,200		
Accruals	500	3,500	
Working Capital			3,000

EXERCISE 12.1

During the year ended May 31st 19_2 Thomas Church, a sole trader, incurred the following Bad Debts:

William Smith £25
Arthur Edwards £31
Frank Williams £18
John Frost £43
David Parsons £52

At the close of business on 31st May *19_1* Thomas Church's Provision for Bad and Doubtful Debts had a balance of £130. At the close of business on 31st May 19_2 his Debtors totalled £3,840 and on this date he decided to increase the Provision for Bad and Doubtful Debts to 5% of the Debtors figure of £3,840.

Required

Draw up the Bad Debts Account and the Provision for Bad and Doubtful

Debts Account for the year ended 31st May 19_2 showing the amounts to be transferred to the Profit and Loss Account.

(London Chamber of Commerce)

EXERCISE 12.2

The following balances remain in William Dean's books after completion of the Trading and Profit and Loss Accounts for the year ended 31st May 19_2

	£	£
Capital 1st June 19_1		124,000
Net profit for the year ended 31st May 19_2		13,800
Loan from John Dean (repayable in 10 years)		9,500
Trade creditors		1,950
Expense creditors		270
Premises	110,000	
Stock in trade	25,000	
Trade debtors	2,600	
Balance at bank	1,400	
Cash in hand	20	
Expense items paid in advance	500	
Proprietor's drawings	10,000	
	149,520	149,520

You are required to:

(a) Set out William Dean's Balance Sheet as at 31st May 19_2. Your Balance Sheet should show long term and current liabilities: fixed and current assets.

(b) Write up William Dean's capital account as it would appear in his private ledger for the year ended 31st May 19_2.

(Royal Society of Arts)

EXERCISE 12.3

The following balances were in the ledger of IDA Ltd. on 1st January 19_8:

	£
Provision for depreciation of machinery	50,000
Provision for doubtful debts	4,500
Machinery (at cost)	120,000

On 1st January 19_8 a new machine was purchased costing £50,000. On 31st December 19_8 a machine that cost £4,000 on 1st January 19_6 was sold for £2,000. The company depreciates all machines at 20% on cost each year, including the year of purchase and the year of sale.

On 31st December 19_8, the company's debtors were £105,000 and on this date it decided to write off bad debts of £5,000, and to carry forward a revised provision for doubtful debts on outstanding debtors of 4%.

Required:
For the year ended 31st December 19_8:

(a) the machinery (at cost) account,
(b) the machinery disposals account,
(c) the provision for depreciation of machinery account,
(d) the provision for doubtful debts account,
(e) the appropriate entries in the profit and loss account.

(A.E.B. "O" level)

EXERCISE 12.4

The following trial balance was extracted from the books of Fletcher, a trader, as at 31st December 19_4:

	£	£
Capital account		20,500
Purchases	46,500	
Sales		60,900
Repairs to buildings	848	
Motor Car	950	
Car expenses	318	
Freehold land and buildings	10,000	
Balance at bank	540	
Furniture and fittings	1,460	
Wages and salaries	8,606	
Discounts allowed	1,061	
Discounts received		814
Drawings	2,400	
Rates and insurances	248	
Bad debts	359	
Provision for bad debts 1st Jan. 19_4		140
Trade debtors	5,213	
Trade creditors		4,035
General expenses	1,586	
Stock-in-trade 1st Jan. 19_4	6,300	
	£86,389	£86,389

The following matters are to be taken into account:

1. Stock-in-Trade December 31, 19_4, £8,800
2. Wages and salaries outstanding at December 31, 19_4, £318.
3. Rates and insurances paid in advance at December 31 19_4, £45.

4. The provision for bad debts is to be reduced to £100.
5. During 19_4 Fletcher withdrew goods valued at £200 for his own use. No entry has been made in the books for the withdrawal of these goods.
6. The item "Repairs to buildings £848" includes £650 in respect of alterations and improvements to the buildings.
7. One third of the car expenses represents the cost of Fletcher's motoring for private, as distinct from business, purposes.

You are required to prepare a trading and profit and loss account for the year 19_4, and a balance sheet as on 31st December 19_4.

Ignore depreciation of fixed assets.

(Institute of Bankers)

EXERCISE 12.5

The following trial balance was extracted from the books of Bedford, a trader, at 31st December 19_6.

	£	£
Capital account		17,400
Freehold land and buildings at cost	9,500	
Motor vehicles at cost	2,600	
Provision for depreciation of motor vehicles at 1 January 19_6		1,200
Purchases	71,420	
Sales		93,140
Stock, 1 January 19_6	8,495	
Debtors and creditors	7,281	6,105
Bank balance	798	
Bad debts	440	
Provision for doubtful debts 1 January 19_6		380
Returns inwards	796	
Returns outwards		432
Rent	450	
Salaries	11,084	
Rates and insurance	388	
General expenses	1,424	
Drawings	3,561	
Motor expenses	420	
	£118,657	£118,657

The following are to be taken into account:

(a) Stock in trade 31st December 19_6, £8,869.
(b) The provision for doubtful debts is to be increased by £62.
(c) The depreciation charge on motor vehicles is to be calculated at the rate of 20 per cent of cost.

(d) Rent unpaid at 31st December 19_6 amounted to £150.
(e) Insurance paid in advance 31st December 19_6, £20.
(f) 10 per cent of the total charge for motor expenses and for depreciation of motor vehicles for the year, is to be transferred to drawings.
(g) Charges made by the bank at the end of December 19_6 but not yet entered in the books of the business, amounted to £16.
(h) Goods which cost £14 and were sold to a customer on 30th December 19_6 for £19 were not in good condition when they reached him. It was agreed to reduce the selling price to £4, but no entry was made in Bedford's books before the trial balance was extracted.

Prepare a trading and profit and loss account for the year 19_6 and a balance sheet as at 31st December 19_6.

(Institute of Bankers)

EXERCISE 12.6

(a) What is the difference between "Bad Debts" and "Provision for Doubtful Debts"?
(b) State *two* reasons for creating a "Provision for Doubtful Debts".
(c) R. Browling keeps his books on the financial year January to December. The figures below show his debtors at the end of the years indicated.

	£
January to December 19_4	8,000
19_5	6,000
19_6	9,000
19_7	9,000

He decided to create a provision for doubtful debts of 5% of debtors in December 19_4 and to maintain it at that percentage.

Write up the Provision for Doubtful Debts account for the years ended 31st December 19_4 to 31st December 19_7.

(University of London "O" level)

CHAPTER 13

THE CASH BOOK AND BANK RECONCILIATIONS

THE CASH BOOK

Transactions involving an entry in cash account or bank account are very numerous, and to save time in "posting" the accounts these two accounts are normally kept side-by-side in a "Cash Book" – i.e. 2 accounts in one. The form of this cash book is identical to all other accounts, with a debit side and a credit side, but *each* side has *two* amount columns, one for cash items, and one for bank items, *viz*:

DR *Cash Book* CR

Date	Details	Cash £	Bank £	Date	Details	Cash £	Bank £
Jan. 1	Balances b/d	800	4,900		Purchases		500
	Rent received	100			Jones	60	
	Sales		700		Bank Charges		150
	Brown		600		Drawings	50	
					Wages		200
					Machinery		1,100
				Jan. 31	Balances c/d	790	4,250
		900	6,200			900	6,200
Jan. 31	Balances b/d	790	4,250				

Once you know which side of cash or bank has to be "posted" you just have to be careful that you enter in the correct column on that side! If it's cash going out or coming in, enter under heading "cash", and if it's cheques going out or coming in, enter on the correct side under heading "Bank". What could be easier!

Note the balancing off of the account – deal with the cash columns first and balance off in the normal way, *then* do the same with the bank columns. Note also the "bank charges" item of £150 – this is where *the bank* have taken part of your balance away from you for their charges. The double entry to this is in the expense account "bank charges".

BANK RECONCILIATION STATEMENTS

When you receive your business bank statement the balance showing by the bank should, in theory, agree with the balance shown by you in your cash book (bank column), because the bank have recorded all your payments into and out of bank in the same way that you have. Your cash book (bank column) may show a debit balance of £4,250 (your asset) but the bank statement will show a *credit* balance of £4,250! This is because when you look at the statement the bank have sent, you are looking at a copy of *the bank's* accounts, not yours, and as far as the bank are concerned they *owe you* this £4,250 – you are their creditor, hence a credit balance shown by *them*. Forget their ledger and think of *yours*!

However, the chances are that the balance shown on your bank statement will *not* agree with the balance shown in your bank account. This is because cheques sent out by you in the past week or so will have been entered in your bank account (in the cash book) on the day you sent them out, whereas your bank won't record these payments on your statement until they receive and pay them through the bank clearing system. This will take at least a few days depending how quickly your suppliers, etc. pay them into their bank accounts. At any point in time therefore there will be outstanding cheques sent out by you, but not yet recorded by the bank.

Also, if you pay £2,000 worth of cheques into your bank account today, and you ask the bank for your statement at the same time, then whilst the increase in your bank balance (or reduction of your overdraft) will be recorded in *your* accounts, the bank will not have had time to record it on your statement and this item will therefore not show, yet.

This last example is unfortunately very theoretical, and doesn't happen these days because very few banks are in a position to hand your statement over the counter on request. It's usually sent to you later by post (by which time the item *has* been recorded). An example of where computerisation reduces the quality of a service!

Your bank account (in cash book) will always be "bang up to date" but the bank's record of your account will not be, for the above reasons. Therefore when you get your statement from the bank you must reconcile (i.e. agree) *your* balance with theirs, to prove that all is well.

Study the following example:

DR *Your Cash Book* CR

		Cash	Bank			Cash	Bank
May 1	Balances b/d	—	2,100√	May 3	Wages (cheque 117)		110√
7	Sales		1,700√	10	Purchases (cheque 118)		940
14	Thompson		620√	20	Rates (cheque 119)		420√
31	Simpson		570	21	Harris (cheque 120)		360√
				31	Electricity (cheque 121)		290
				31	Balances c/d	—	2,870
		—	4,990			—	4,990
May 31	Balances b/d	—	2,870				

Your Bank Statement

		Debit*	Credit*	Balance
May 1	Balance			2,100√
May 6	Cheque No. 117	110√		1,990
May 8	Cheques Paid In		1,700√	3,690
May 16	Cheques Pain In		620√	4,310
May 26	Cheque No. 119	420√		3,890
May 27	Cheque No. 120	360√		3,530

N.B. * In the bank's accounts – not yours!

According to you, £2,870 in the bank – according to the bank, £3,530!

Your first job in reconciling these two figures, is to tick off the items in your cash book with the items on your statement, as above. Then you only need concern yourself with the unticked items.

Work now on the assumption that your cash book is "bang up to date". The bank statement is not up to date, so let's bring it up to date, when it should then agree with your up-to-date balance shown in the cash book, *viz*:

Bank Reconciliation Statement at 31 May

			£
Balance shown on bank statement			3,530
Less unpresented cheques:		£	
	118	940	
	121	290	1,230
			2,300
Add amount not yet credited by bank			570
Balance shown in cash book			2,870

You have proved that when the bank statement is up to date, with all unpresented cheques presented and cleared, and all credits entered, it will then agree with your own bank balance – i.e. you have *reconciled* the two differing balances.

Always start your statement with the balance shown by the bank statement, and then bring this balance gradually up to date.

Note, that had the commencing balance on your statement been an overdraft, you would have *added* the two unpresented cheques, because when the bank pay these cheques they will *increase* your overdraft. Similarly, the payment in to bank of £570, when recorded by the bank will *reduce* your overdraft – therefore you would deduct it in your statement.

There are a few occasions when your cash book will *not* be bang up to date. For example, when you receive your bank statement you notice that the bank have charged their commission and interest for the period (amount not known to you until now), or a cheque you paid in last week has been returned unpaid (i.e. "bounced"), or someone has paid *into* your account somewhere else in the country by bank giro credit (credit transfer). Your first knowledge of these various happenings to your account only become known to you when you receive your statement. Another example of your cash book not being up to date would be where you have forgotten to record a regular payment made by the bank on your behalf – i.e. standing orders or direct-debits.

In these cases you should immediately bring your cash book up-to-date – i.e. enter into your cash book these items, so amending the original balance, *then* prepare a reconciliation statement as explained above. Always work on the basis that your cash book is bang up-to-date – if it isn't, then bring it up-to-date *before* commencing your reconciliation statement.

EXERCISE 13.1

From the following information, write up the cash book of J. Day for the month of June, balancing the cash book at the end of June:

June 1 Balances – cash £610, bank £1,470
June 2 Paid J. Brown, cheque for £690 on account
June 4 Paid wages in cash £320
June 6 Paid for new equipment, £750 by cheque
June 10 Received £470 cash from credit customer J. Briggs
June 12 Received rent from tenant £60 in cash
June 16 Bank charges £120 notified
June 18 Received £2,000 cash from sale of old office furniture
June 20 Paid £1,600 cash into the bank account
June 27 Paid cheque for £6,500 for purchase of new fixtures and fittings
June 30 Paid wages in cash £410

EXERCISE 13.2

A. Lefevre received his current account bank statement on 31st May. The statement showed that he had cash in the bank, as at that date, of £1,500. On the same date, the bank column of his cash book showed a credit balance (overdraft) of £4,000.
The reconciliation he carried out showed that the bank had not yet recorded the following items:

(i) cheques drawn payable to suppliers and not yet presented £10,000,
(ii) cash and cheques paid into the bank, not yet credited £3,500,
(iii) the transfer of £3,000 from his deposit account to his current account.

The following items were recorded in the bank current account statement, but not in Lefevre's cash book:

(iv) bank overdraft interest, and commission charges £400,
(v) money sent direct to the bank for the credit of Lefevre's account, by a debtor for goods supplied £900,
(vi) net dividends from U.K. companies, paid direct to Lefevre's bank, £1,500.

Required:
As at 31st May
1. a statement showing the adjusted cash book bank balance,
2. a statement reconciling the bank balance as shown by the bank statement with that shown in the cash book, as adjusted under 1 above.

(A.E.B. "O" level)

EXERCISE 13.3

At the close of business on 31st March 19_9, William Robinson's bank balance according to his Cash Book was £787. This does not agree with the balance at bank as shown by the Bank Statement, and the following items account for the entire difference:

(a) Frank Gibson, one of Robinson's debtors, had paid the sum of £73 direct into Robinson's banking account. This had not been entered in the Cash Book although it was recorded in the Bank Statement on 29th March 19_9.
(b) A bankers standing order for a trade subscription of £25 was paid by the bank during March but the transaction has not yet been shown in the Cash Book.
(c) The following cheques – drawn by Robinson during March 1979 and entered in the Cash Book – has not been presented for payment at

his bank by the close of business on 31st March 19_9: – £34, £41 and £52.

(d) The sum of £112 was paid into his banking account by Robinson on 31st March 19_9 but this item did not appear on his Bank Statement until after that date.

Required:
Prepare the Bank Reconciliation Statement as at 31st March 19_9.

(London Chamber of Commerce)

EXERCISE 13.4

At the close of business on 28th February 19_1 the Cash Book of William Jones showed that he had a balance with his bank of £625. This figure differed from the bank balance as shown on his bank statement. The following matters account for the difference:

(a) On 28th February 19_1 one of his debtors had paid direct to Jones' banking account the sum of £42. This transaction had not been entered in the Cash Book.

(2) During February 19_1 the bank had allowed Jones interest amounting to £54 but this had not yet appeared in the Cash Book.

(3) Certain cheques drawn by Jones during February 19_1 had not been presented for payment by the close of business on 28th February 19_1. These were for £21, £17, £57 and £61.

(4) A standing order for £75 being one quarter's rent had been paid by the bank on Jones' behalf but this had not yet been entered in the Cash Book.

(5) During February 19_1 Jones had paid into his banking account a cheque for £44 which he had received from a debtor. On 28th February 19_1 this cheque had been returned unpaid by the debtor's bank. The appropriate entry appeared on the bank statement but *not* in Jones' Cash Book.

Required:
Draw up the Bank Reconciliation Statement at 28th February 19_1 *commencing* with the Cash Book balance of £625 and ending with the balance as shown on the bank statement.

(London Chamber of Commerce)

EXERCISE 13.5

The cash book of a small business has been written up and closed for the month, showing a credit balance of £490. When the bank statement arrives however, it indicates that on the last day of the month, the firm's account was overdrawn by £873.

An investigation of the situation reveals the following facts:

(i) The bookkeeper had written in an estimated amount for bank interest paid at £620 whereas the true amount was £580.

(ii) Cheques paid to suppliers totalling £376 have not yet been presented at the bank. Payments made into the bank on the last day of the month have not yet been credited by the bank to the company's account. The paying-in book indicates that an amount of £780 is involved but an inspection of cash book shows the amount to have been transposed and entered as £870.

(iii) A cheque paid to Brown for £319 had been entered in the cash book as a receipt.

(iv) A cheque for £143 received from White during the month, had been returned by the bank marked "refer to drawer". It has not yet been written back in the cash book.

(v) Standing Orders to pay rent of £120 appearing in the bank statement have not yet been entered in the cash book.

(vi) The cash book has been undercast by £70 on the receipts side.

(vii) A payment of £398, correctly entered by the bank, was entered in the cash book as £300.

(viii) A dividend warrant for £1,000 on an investment owned by the firm, has been sent direct to the bank, and appears in the bank statement. The firm has received no other communication concerning this amount.

You are required to adjust the cashbook, and complete a Bank reconciliation.

(Institute of Accounting Staff)

EXERCISE 13.6

(a) The cash book of a business shows a favourable bank balance of £3,856 at 30th June. After comparing the entries in the cash book with the entries on the related bank statement you find that:

(i) Cheques amounting to £218 entered in the cash book, have not yet been presented for payment to the bank.

(ii) An amount of £50 entered on the debit side of the cash book has not been banked.

(iii) An amount of £95 has been credited by the bank to the account in error.

(iv) The bank has credited and then debited the bank statement with an amount of £48, being A. Jones' cheque which it forwarded on 1st July 19_7 marked "insufficient funds – return to drawer".

(v) Interest of £10 has been charged by the bank, but not yet entered in the cash book.

(vi) A cheque from a customer entered in the cash book as £88 had been correctly entered by the bank as £188.

Required:

(a) (i) Show the additional entries to be made in the cash book and bring down the corrected balance.

(ii) Prepare a bank reconciliation statement.

(b) Explain the reasons for preparing a bank reconciliation statement.

(A.C.C.A.)

EXERCISE 13.7

On 15th May Mr Lakes received his monthly bank statement for the month ended 30th April. The bank statement contained the following details.

Mr Lakes
Statement of Account with Baroyds Limited
(* Balance indicates account is overdrawn)

Date	*Particulars*	*Payments*	*Receipts*	*Balance*
		£	£	£
April 1	Balance			1,053·29
April 2	236127	210·70		842·59
April 3	Bank Giro Credit		192·35	1,034·94
April 6	236126	15·21		1,019·73
April 6	Charges	12·80		1,006·93
April 9	236129	43·82		963·11
April 10	427519	19·47		943·64
April 12	236128	111·70		831·94
April 17	Standing Order	32·52		799·42
April 20	Sundry Credit		249·50	1,048·92
April 23	236130	77·87		971·05
April 23	236132	59·09		911·96
April 25	Bank Giro Credit		21·47	933·43
April 27	Sundry Credit		304·20	1,237·63
April 30	236133	71·18		1,166·45

For the corresponding period, Mr Lakes' own records contained the following bank account:

Date	*Detail*	£	*Date*	*Detail*	*Cheque No.*	£
April 1	Balance	827·38	April 5	Purchases	128	111·70
April 2	Sales	192·35	April 10	Electricity	129	43·82
April 18	Sales	249·50	April 16	Purchases	130	87·77
April 24	Sales	304·20	April 18	Rent	131	30·00
April 30	Sales	192·80	April 20	Purchases	132	59·09
			April 25	Purchases	133	71·18
			April 30	Wages	134	52·27
			April 30	Balance		1,310·40
		£1,766·23				£1,766·23

Required:
Prepare a statement reconciling the balance at 30th April as given by the bank statement to the balance at 30th April as stated in the bank account.

(A.C.C.A.)

CHAPTER 14

BOOKS OF ORIGINAL ENTRY

DAY BOOKS

I keep stressing that double-entry is essential for every transaction, without exception, if everything is to be recorded properly. However, in certain cases, double-entry can be postponed for a little while, in order to save time.

For example, it is necessary to enter Smith's account the moment a sale to him, or a purchase from him, takes place, so that we know, on a daily basis what he owes us or what we owe him. However, the appropriate double-entry (i.e. the credit to Sales Account or the debit to Purchases Account) could be postponed, because we don't need to know our total sales or purchases on a daily basis (we certainly need to know at the year end).

Therefore, provided someone keeps a note of credit sales and purchases as they occur, these could be posted to sales and purchases accounts in *totals* for, say, a month at a time. In this way there would only be 12 actual postings to each of these accounts in the year instead of hundreds of entries.

A junior member of staff could keep this "note" daily in a book (**A DAY BOOK**), which would *not* be part of the ledger. A suitable ruling would be as follows:

Date	Details	Ref. No.	Amount

Using sales as an example, each credit sale as it takes place could be entered in this book, and at the end of the month a total would be drawn up and this *total* would then be posted to the credit of sales account as "Credit Sales for January", etc. This one entry in sales account for the month's sales would have as its double-entry many, many debits in various debtors accounts, made over the month, all adding up to the same amount that has been credited to sales account, e.g.

Sales Day Book

		Ref. No.	£
May 1	Jones	A21	400·00
May 3	Tomkins	A22	300·00
May 8	Smith	A23	50·00
May 20	Timms	A24	150·00
May 30	Cook	A25	200·00
	Total Credit Sales for May		1,100·00

Jones	
Sales £400	

Tomkins	
Sales £300	

Smith	
Sales £50	

Timms	
Sales £150	

Cook	
Sales £200	

Sales Account	
	Sales for month £1,100

NOTE: The bookkeeper only posts 6 entries (60, or 600 in practice) to the accounts for the month's sales. A junior clerk keeps a note of each credit sale as it occurs in the SALES DAY BOOK, totalling at the month end. Without the use of a day book the bookkeeper would have had to make 10 (or 100 or 1,000) postings to the ledger. Expensive time has been saved! The total debits for the month (£1,100) are matched by one credit (£1,100) at the end of the month to sales account – i.e. double-entry completed.

A Day Book is also usually kept for purchases on credit, and for sales returns and purchases returns. In every case the entry in the relevant person's account is made *immediately* – it is the *other* entry which is stored in the day book, before being posted as part of a total at the month end, to complete double-entry. An example of each of these Day Books should not be necessary at this stage.

The "reference number" in the day book would provide a reference to:

(i) In the case of sales – the filed copy invoice.
(ii) In the case of purchases – the filed invoice received.
(iii) In the case of sales returns – the filed copy of our agreement (called a credit note) to the return.
(iv) In the case of purchases returns – the filed copy of their agreement (credit note) to the return.

So, apart from the advantages regarding posting, a day book gives a quick reference to a piece of paper in your files, which gives full details of the relevant sale, purchase, or return – detail you could never get into the ledger if each sale was posted independently to sales account, each purchase to purchases account, etc.

Remember that day books are *not* part of the ledger – an entry in them is *not* part of the double-entry recording in the accounts.

Cash sales and cash purchases are not entered in the day books, only credit transactions. When a sale or purchase for cash takes place the double entry is carried out at the time – i.e. debit cash/bank, credit sales, etc. You will see the reason for this when we do Control Accounts in Lesson 16.

Another form of "day book" is kept for all discounts allowed and discounts received, so that their totals can be posted monthly, but this is kept by ruling an extra column on each side of the cash book, e.g.

DR *Cash Book* CR

Date	Details	Discounts Allowed	Cash	Bank	Date	Details	Discounts Received	Cash	Bank
		£	£	£			£	£	£
May 1	Balances b/d		100	400					
May 3	Sales		80		May 4	Purchases			700
May 6	Brown	10		90	May 8	Rent		80	
May 23	Jones	5	95		May 12	James	12		108
May 31	Balance c/d		–	372	May 20	Wages		60	
					May 27	Todd	6		54
					May 31	Balance c/d		135	
		15	275	862			18	275	862
May 31	Balance b/d		135		May 31	Balance b/d			372

Note first of all, that a bank balance at the start of May has finished up as an overdraft at the end of May.

Note next, that discounts allowed and received can very conveniently be noted at the time of posting the cash book. For example, when making the entry for James, (a payment to a supplier who has allowed us a 10% cash discount for prompt payment) we credited bank £108 and debited James £108, *viz*:

DR James CR

May 12	Bank	£108	May 1	Purchases	£120

The £12 discount we qualify for must *now* be entered in James' account to close off the debt, *viz*:

DR			Jones		CR
		£			£
May 12	Bank	108	May 1	Purchases	120
May 12	Discount Rec'd	12			
		120			120

However, the double entry (credit to Discounts Received), can be postponed until the end of the month, provided a note is made of the £12 discount in the "Memorandum" column of the cash book. This £12, together with all other discounts received during the month, will be credited to Discounts Received account at the end of the month – same with discounts allowed, but obviously the totals of these will be *debited* to discounts allowed account. In the above example therefore, at 31st May, Discounts allowed account will be debited with £15; Discounts Received credited with £18, to complete double-entry.

The advantage of using part of the cash book as a day book should be obvious – we can see the whole picture at a glance; for example, we can see that Jones paid us £95 and that we allowed him a £5 discount for prompt payment (obviously he owed us £100 originally).

The two "Memorandum" columns are *not* part of the ledger – the entries in these columns are *not* part of double entry recording. Not until those totals of £15 and £18 are *entered* in the accounts of Discounts Allowed and Discounts Received respectively, does double-entry take place!

THE JOURNAL

A day book may be used for sales, purchases, sales returns and purchases returns, and a memorandum column of the cash book for discounts allowed and discounts received. All of these are "records (some in the form of books) of original entry" or "subsidiary records" meaning subsidiary to (not part of) the ledger.

Ideally, *all* transactions in a business should pass through some form of "record of original entry" *before* being actually posted to the ledger.

Therefore, all transactions which have *not* gone through one of the books already mentioned, should pass through another "book of original entry" called the "**Journal**", before being posted to the ledger accounts. For example, if you purchase a machine or a delivery van, or pay off a loan, or transact anything which is not either a sale, purchase, return or discount, then this transaction should pass through the "Journal" before being posted to the ledger.

An example of the Journal:

Journal

Date	Details	Folio	Account to be Debited	Account to be Credited
			£	£
June 3	Office Equipment	G7	1,800	
	M. Supplies Ltd.	C9		1,800
	Being purchase of 2 electric typewriters. Ref. No. XYZ.			

This entry refers to buying some office equipment, and clearly shows that the account of "Office Equipment" is to be debited with £1,800 and the account of the supplier credited with £1,800. It also gives full details of the transaction, this "story" being referred to as the "*narrative*". After the narrative the journal entry is ruled off.

If all transactions (except sales, purchases, etc.) are entered in the Journal in this way, then at the end of the day the Journal book can be handed over to the person in charge of posting the entries in the ledger accounts, who will then follow the instructions in the Journal – i.e. debit Office Equipment £1,800, credit M. Supplies Ltd. £1,800.

The great advantage of the Journal, as with Day Books, is that a great deal of detail can be entered regarding the transaction – detail which you could never get into the ledger accounts without making them look a "real mess". An invaluable source of quick reference in the future in response to queries, etc. In the case of the day book, there was no detail in the book itself but there was a very handy reference to the filed copy invoice, credit note, etc. Even the "memorandum" columns of the cash book for discounts gave an immediate "picture" of what had gone on as I illustrated earlier.

The "folio" column in the Journal could usefully be used to give a quick reference to the number of the account to be posted in the ledger – i.e. Office Equipment account is numbered "G7" in our ledger. A similar folio number could be used in the accounts themselves including the cash book of course, to quickly identify where the double-entry lies, provided each account is numbered.

Very many examination questions will ask you to show the effect of certain transactions "*by Journal entry*". For example, suppose that the transaction is the correction of a debit entry in Brown's account, of £100, for a payment of cash which was in fact a payment made to *Breen*. This transaction was obviously recorded in the ledger as a credit to cash and a debit to *Brown* (instead of Breen). Obviously then, the debit in Brown's account must be cancelled and placed to the debit of Breen's account. You never "cross out" in the ledger accounts – this leaves the accounts wide open to fraud. Instead you must "shift" (transfer) the £100 debit from Brown's account to the debit side of Breen's account, observing double-entry. The accounts will illustrate this, *viz*:

DR Brown (P17) CR

			£				£
June 3	Cash	CB	100	June 4	Breen*	P10	100
			100				100

DR Cash (as part of Cash Book) CR

				June 3	Breen	P19	£100

DR Breen (P10) CR

June 4	Brown*	P17	£100				

* The correcting entry.

As the examiner asked you to show the effect of the correcting transaction *by Journal entry*, your answer would be:

Journal

Date	Details	Folio	Account to be Debited	Account to be Credited
			£	£
June 4	Breen	P10	100	
	Brown	P17		100
	Being correction of error on June 3rd			

You are simply showing by your journal entry what accounts would be debited and what accounts would be credited in the ledger.

Note – in all Journal entries, show the account(s) to be debited first, *then* the account(s) to be credited. Don't forget the narrative – the little story before you rule off the entry – just simply describe the transaction briefly. *What* you say isn't terribly important in the exam, but in practice a full detailed description would be required.

Two final transactions recorded in Journal format. "You pay £900 in cash to contractors for maintenance of your equipment (£600), and for the making of new storage racks (£300). Note that £600 of this cash payment is *revenue* expenditure (an expense), whilst the other £300 is *capital* expenditure (purchase of an asset) because you have got something to replace your spending. You have swapped cash for another asset 'warehouse equipment', valued at £300.

Journal entries to record this:

Journal

		Debit	*Credit*
		£	
July 5	Maintenance	600	
	Warehouse Equipment	300	
	Cash		900
	Being annual maintenance contract and purchase of new equipment		

A journal entry can include half a dozen entries to be debited, and a number to be credited. Provided all the entries are *related* to the same transaction, and the total debits equal total credits, this is fine. For example, if you purchase from ABC Ltd. on credit a typewriter for £800, an office desk for £250, and stationery for £100 the journal entry would read:

Journal

		DR	*CR*
		£	£
July 10	Office Equipment	800	
	Office Furniture	250	
	Stationery	100	
	ABC Ltd.		1,150
	Being purchase of typewriter office desk and stationery		

Or, let us suppose that a trader who has never kept proper accounts, decides that from 1st September he will keep accounts using the double-entry system. At this date he has the following assets and liabilities: Fixtures and fittings £1,400; Office equipment £680; Stock £1,100; Debtors, Jones £40, and Able £75; Cash £60; Bank balance £130; and Creditor, Newman £85.

His brand new accounts will open with these balances and the difference between total assets and total liabilities will of course be the balance of Capital Account.

The Journal entry would appear

Journal

		DR	CR
		£	£
Sept. 1	Fixtures and Fittings	1,400	
	Office equipment	680	
	Stock	1,100	
	Jones	40	
	Able	75	
	Cash	60	
	Bank	130	
	Newman		85
	Capital		3,400
	Being opening of new set of accounts		

EXERCISE 14.1

James Bishop is a sole trader who records all his cash and bank transactions in a three-column Cash Book. The following transactions took place during the month of May

May 1 Cash in hand £27. Cash at Bank £495.
May 3 Paid to A. Johnson by cheque £47 being full settlement of a debt of £50.
May 9 Paid wages, by cheque, £32.
May 12 Received from G. Holt a cheque for £60. This is in full settlement of a debt of £65.
This cheque was placed in Bishop's cash box.
May 17 Received from E. Layton cash amounting to £23 in full settlement of a debt of £25.
May 24 Paid into bank the sum of £70. This *includes* the cheque received from G. Holt on 12 May.
May 26 Paid in cash £32 in full settlement of the amount due to F. Parsons (£35).
May 29 Drew cheque for £25 for office cash.

Required:

(a) Draw up the three column Cash Book for the month of May carrying down the balances for Cash in Hand and Cash at Bank.
(b) Total the two discount columns and state to which ledger accounts these two totals should be posted and also on which *side* of the ledger each entry should be made.

(London Chamber of Commerce)

EXERCISE 14.2

William Andrews, a sole trader, had the following transactions during the month of May

(a) Andrews purchased new office furniture for £240 and gave in part exchange old furniture at an agreed value of £70. Andrews issued a cheque for £170 in settlement. The old furniture appeared in Andrews' ledger at a figure of £85.
(b) Andrews owes £320 to James Gordon in respect of goods supplied. Gordon drew a Bill of Exchange on Andrews for £307 in full settlement of the amount due. The Bill of Exchange is "accepted" by Andrews.
(c) Andrews sold goods amounting to £63 to Herbert Wilson. The entries made in both the Sales Day Book and the ledger gave the figure as £36.
(d) Andrews sold one of his old delivery vans for £150, in cash. This van appeared in Andrews ledger at a figure of £166.

Required:
Draw up Journal entries to record (a), (b) and (d) and to correct the error in (c).

NOTE: Journalise the Cash entries.

(London Chamber of Commerce)

EXERCISE 14.3

William Shipley is a sole trader who records all his cash and bank transactions in a three column Cash Book. For the month of April his transactions were as follows:

April 1 Cash in hand £43. Cash at Bank £449.
April 6 Received a cheque for £55 from A. Jones in full settlement of a debt of £60. The cheque was paid direct into the bank.
April 9 Paid by cheque (£37) the amount due to H. Thompson (£40) being allowed discount of £3.
April 14 Received cash £56 from J. Wilson. This was in full settlement of a debt of £60 due from Wilson.
April 16 The cheque for £55 received on 6 April was returned to Shipley by his bankers as "unpaid".
April 19 Paid into bank the sum of £80 cash.
April 23 Shipley drew a cheque for £68 in favour of A. Gibson. This was in full settlement of a debt of £75.
April 26 Paid salaries by cheque £88.

Required:
(a) Enter the above transactions in Shipley's Cash Book and, at the close of business on 30th April 1980, carry down the balances.

(b) The discount columns should be totalled. You should state to which accounts in the ledger the discount totals should be entered and on which side.

(c) With regard to the transaction on 16th April describe what entry – if any – should be made in addition to the Cash Book entry.

NOTE: Ledger Accounts are NOT required.

(London Chamber of Commerce)

EXERCISE 14.4

The following transactions are carried out by Samuel Hayes, a sole trader, during the month of October:

Oct. 3 Purchased on credit from A. Wise 20 rolls of wallpaper at £2·60 each less 10% trade discount.
(Invoice No. 1.)

Oct. 7 Sold on credit to C. Jackson 15 rolls of wallpaper at £4 each less 5% trade discount.
(Invoice No. 101.)

Oct. 11 Purchased on credit from W. Smith 25 tins of paint at £3 each.
(Invoice No. 2.)

Oct. 15 Sold on credit to J. Shipley 10 rolls of wallpaper at £3·40 each and 5 tins of paint at £4 each – all subject to 10% trade discount.
(Invoice No. 102.)

Oct. 22 Purchased on credit from F. Jones 50 paint brushes at £1·60 each.
(Invoice No. 3.)

Oct. 29 Sold on credit to S. Nichols 5 rolls of wallpaper at £4 each and 10 paint brushes at £2 each.
(Invoice No. 103.)

Required:

(i) Enter the above transactions in the Purchases Day Book of Sales Day Book, as appropriate.

(ii) Post the transactions from the Day Books to the personal accounts in the ledger.

(iii) Post the *totals* of the two Day Books to the appropriate impersonal accounts in the ledger.

(London Chamber of Commerce)

EXERCISE 14.5

The following transactions were carried out by Charles Jones, a sole trader:

(a) Sold one of his delivery vans for cash £320. The delivery van appeared in Jones' ledger at a figure of £360.
(b) Walter Smith owes Jones £290 in respect of goods supplied. In full settlement of this debt Jones drew a Bill of Exchange on Smith for the sum of £287.
(c) Albert Harrison, who owes Jones £160 is declared bankrupt and the sum of £92 is received in final settlement of this debt.
(d) Jones issued a cheque for £90. This was in respect of rent – two thirds being for office accommodation and one third for his private apartment.

Required:
Draw up the Journal entries of Charles Jones in respect of the above transactions.

NOTE: Journalise the cash entries.

(London Chamber of Commerce)

EXERCISE 14.6

During the month of May Robert Potter, a sole trader;

(1) Received Cash £37 from Alfred Jones but credited it in error to the account of Wilfred Jones.
(2) Transferred an unwanted desk to his creditor Martin Ives at an agreed value of £28. This was in full settlement of a debt of £30 due to Ives.
The desk appeared in Potter's ledger at a figure of £33.
(3) Purchased a new delivery van for £1,960 and surrendered his old van in part exchange – at an agreed value of £500. Potter issued a cheque for £1,590 in payment – this to *include* the cost of road tax and insurance for one year.
The old van appeared in Potter's ledger at the figure of £500 which was also the agreed trade-in value.
(4) Sold goods for £83 to Frederick Dawson. This transaction appeared in both the Sales Day Book *and* personal account of Dawson as £38.

Required:
Draw up the Journal entries in respect of (2) and (3) and also to correct the errors in (1) and (4).

NOTE: Journalise the cash entries.

(London Chamber of Commerce)

EXERCISE 14.7

Herbert Bishop is a sole trader who enters all his cash and bank transactions in a three column Cash Book. The following were his transactions for the month of May:

May 1 Cash in hand £31. Cash at Bank £537.
May 5 Received from C. Gordon a cheque for £38 in full settlement of a debt of £40. *This cheque was paid into the bank the same day.*
May 11 Paid to N. Johnson by cheque £56, being in full settlement of a debt of £60.
May 12 Drew cheque for £40 for office cash.
May 13 Paid wages in cash £37.
May 16 Received from G. Layton cash amounting to £39 in full settlement of a debt of £44.
May 25 Paid in cash £18 to J. Gill in full settlement of a debt of £20.
May 29 Paid into bank the sum of £30.
May 29 Paid salaries by cheque £58.

Required:

(i) Draw up the three column Cash Book for the month of May carrying down the balances for Cash in Hand and Cash at Bank.
(ii) Total the two discount columns and state to which ledger accounts these two totals should be posted and also on which *side* of the ledger each entry should be made.

NOTE: Ledger accounts are *not* required.

(London Chamber of Commerce)

EXERCISE 14.8

John Frost, a sole trader, had the following purchases and sales on credit during the month of March.

March 3 Purchased from William Jones 20 tins of paint at £3 each less 5% trade discount.
March 7 Purchased from Arthur Wills 10 bottles of turpentine at £2 each less 5% trade discount.
March 11 Sold to John Adams 12 tins of paint at £5 each less 10% trade discount.
March 17 Sold to Frank Moore 5 bottles of turpentine at £4 each less 10% trade discount.
March 21 Purchased from William Jones 20 paint brushes at £2 each – no trade discount.

March 26 Sold to John Adams 5 tins of paint at £4 each and 10 paint brushes at £3 each, *all* less 10% trade discount.

Required:

(i) Enter the above transactions in the Purchases Day Book and Sales Day Book of John Frost – also posting the items in the personal accounts in his ledger.

(ii) (a) Post the total of the Purchases Day Book to the Purchases Account in Frost's ledger.

(b) Post the total of the Sales Day Book to the Sales Account in Frost's ledger.

(Royal Society of Arts)

CHAPTER 15

CORRECTION OF ERRORS

I said in the last chapter that errors in the accounts should not be crossed out or rubbed out, for security reasons. The errors must be corrected by passing the necessary entries through the accounts. This only applies in practice of course – if you make a mistake in the examination then cross it out or rub it out, neatly!

Suppose we make a sale to Jenson, on credit, for £97, and our book-keeping clerk posts this as £79 in both accounts. This is an error which will not be revealed by the trial balance, but when the error *is* discovered the correcting entries would be, Debit Jenson, £18, and credit sales account £18, *viz*:

Sales

			£
		May 1 Jenson	79
		July 5 Jenson (to correct)	18

Jenson

	£		
May 1 Sales	79		
July 5 Sales (to correct)	18		

ILLUSTRATION

I am now going to show you a set of accounts with quite a few posting errors in them. The asterisks show where the errors are.

Capital

		Balance b/d	£3,350

Equipment

Balance	£2,000		

Stock

Start of Year. Balance	£700		

DR		Bank	CR
	£		£
Balance	650	Mr Y	800
Mr B	351	Rent	75
		Equipment	500
		Rent	75

DR		Sales	CR
			£
		Mr A	420
		Mr B	390
		Mrs C	570

Mr A

Sales	** £240		

Mr B

	£		£
Sales	390	Bank	351
		Discount Allowed	39
	390		390

Mrs C

	£		
Sales	570		
Sales Returns	** 60		

Purchases

	£		
Mrs X	1,100		
Mr Y	800		
Bank	** 500		

Mrs X

		Purchases	£1,100

Mr Y

Bank	* £80	Purchases	£800

DR		Discounts Allowed	
		Mr B	* £39

Sales Returns

Mrs C	£60		

Rent Payable

		£	
Bank	**	57	
	**	—	

Let's assume that we discover the errors marked with a single asterisk, (*), *before* we do a trial balance, prior to preparing the year's final accounts. The errors marked with a double asterisk (**) we don't find until the next year – i.e. *after* this year's final accounts and balance sheet (which is obviously not going to balance!)

The errors (*) would be described in an examination question as:

(i) "A cheque payment to Mr Y, the supplier, of £800 has been recorded in Mr Y's account as £80." From this statement you have got to assume that the *only* error, is in Mr Y's account – i.e. assume that the relevant entry in the bank account was correct.

(ii) "A cash discount of £39 allowed to Mr B was wrongly credited to Discounts Allowed Account." You must assume that the only error is in Discounts Allowed Account – i.e. assume that the corresponding entry in Mr B's account was recorded correctly.

The journal entries to correct these two errors would be:

(i) *Journal*

		DR	CR
Date	Mr Y	720	
	Being correction of error		

Note – this debit *completes* the double entry for this transaction. Nothing need be credited now, because this has already been done as part of the original credit to bank account of £800. Double entry in respect of this transaction is now *complete*.

(ii) *Journal*

		DR	CR
Date	Discounts Allowed	78	
	Being correction of error		

Note – the account is debited with 2 × £39 – one £39 to *cancel* the original wrong credit of £39, and the other £39 to place on the debit side of discounts allowed the £39 which should have been put there in the first place! The balance on discounts allowed account is now a debit one of £39, which is correct. Double-entry has now been completed (i.e. Total credits for this transaction £78, (£39 in Mr B's account and £39 in discounts allowed account) and total debits £78 (in discounts allowed account – i.e. the correcting entry).

Following the posting of the journal entries the respective accounts will appear:

DR		Mr Y	CR
	£		£
Bank	80	Purchases	800
Correction (Bank)	720		
	800		800

DR		Discounts Allowed	CR
	£		£
Correction (Mr B)	78	Mr B	39
		Balance c/d	39
	78		78
Balance b/d	39		

Cross out these two accounts on the previous pages and substitute the above to the ledger.

At this point the other errors remain undiscovered, and as it is the year end we prepare a trial balance for the trader, prior to preparing his final accounts and balance sheet.

Trial Balance at Year End

	DR	CR
Capital		3,350
Equipment	2,000	
Stock (Opening)	700	
Bank		449
Sales		1,380
Debtors	870	
Creditors		1,100
Purchases	2,400	
Discounts Allowed	39	
Sales Returns	60	
Rent	57	
	6,126	6,279

Miles out – as we expected! *We* know where the errors lie which are responsible for this, but in practice we wouldn't, with so many accounts and transactions in them being involved. We would then start checking the accounts by ticking off double-entry, and this would obviously highlight some of the errors, which would then be corrected.

USE OF A SUSPENSE ACCOUNT

Let's assume though, that the errors (**) still remain undiscovered at the point where we have just got to "crack-on" and prepare his final accounts. Look at the trial balance – it is £153 out – too many credits, or too few debits. If we could find a debit balance somewhere, of £153, the trial balance would balance. But we can't – so let's create one! Let's make one up! Such balance would represent the *net* effect of all the errors remaining elusive.

We will in fact, open a new account, and call it "Suspense Account", with a debit balance of £153, *viz*:

DR		Suspense Account	CR
Date Re Trial Balance	£153		

What we are doing is putting £153 (net) of errors in "suspension" and we are going to keep them there until the errors are discovered. It might be just one error of double entry, or it may be a combination of errors of double entry (we know that it's the latter).

There is now another account in the ledger with a balance on it, so it must go on the trial balance statement, and as it is a debit balance, the trial balance agrees!

This balance will stay there whilst the errors remain undiscovered, and in the meantime this balance will have to show on the balance sheet – as it's a debit balance it will have to appear on the assets side, even though it isn't necessarily an asset!

As the errors are gradually found, entries will be made in the suspense account, as part of the correcting entries, and when the last error of double-entry has been corrected the suspense account will be cleared – i.e. closed.

As the days and weeks go by the errors marked (**) will come to light, so let's deal with them. First of all we discover that Mr A's account should have been debited with £420 not £240. Therefore his account must be debited with a further £180, and the double-entry will be in suspense account because we have just found one of the errors which was responsible for the creation of suspense account in the first place. The correction must obviously make some adjustment to the balance on suspense account, *viz*:

Journal

		DR	CR
Date	Mr A	180	
	Suspense a/c		180
	Being correction of error		

Next, we discover that Mrs C should have been credited, not debited, with £60 for sales returns, so we must credit her now with *£120* (think about this – it's like a previous example I showed where an amount was entered on the wrong side of the right account) – double entry is in suspense account, *viz*:

Journal

		DR	CR
Date	Suspense a/c	120	
	Mrs C		120
	Being correction of error		

Note how suspense account balance is "moving around" as we gradually find the errors which together make up a *net* debit balance of £153. When the last error is dealt with, nothing will be left in suspense.

Let us now "discover" all of the other errors of double entry. The £500 debit to purchases account was *not* a purchase (i.e. for re-sale) it was capital expenditure – i.e. purchase of an *asset*, equipment. We must "move" (transfer) the £500 to the right account, equipment account, e.g.

Journal

		DR	CR
Date	Equipment	500	
	Purchases		500
	Being correction of error		

We have taken £500 out of purchases account and put it where it belongs. Why no entry in suspense account? Because this was not an error of double entry – it was simply a matter of the wrong account being debited. Double entry *was* carried out! Therefore this error has nothing to do with the balance on suspense account – it is not in any way responsible! Only the correction of errors of double-entry will involve entries in suspense account.

Next, we discover two errors in rent account. The £57 debit should have been a debit of £75 – an error of double entry (contributing to the balance on suspense) – therefore we must debit rent account with a further £18 and credit suspense.

Journal

		DR	CR
Date	Rent a/c	18	
	Suspense		18
	Being correction of error		

The other error in rent account is the complete omission of £75 paid. Therefore:

Journal

		DR	CR
Date	Rent a/c	75	
	Suspense		75
	Being correction of error		

Look now at the entries to be made in the accounts from the above correcting journal entries. Make the entries "dictated" by the Journal in the relevant accounts – get your pen out – don't just think about it! I'll leave the other accounts to you, but your suspense account should now look like this:

DR		Suspense A/C	CR
	£	Re: Mr A	180
Balance	153	Re: Rent	18
Re: Mrs C	120	Re: Rent	75
	273		273

The account is now closed. The errors in double-entry recording, all contributing to a net debit of £153 in suspense, have *all* been rectified by our correcting journal entries, and there is no longer any need for a suspense account.

If an error of double entry is discovered *before* a trial balance is prepared, then the necessary double entry can be completed without an entry in suspense account, because a suspense account is only opened, or continued, at the time of a trial balance, to bring it into balance!

Note carefully that only correction of *errors of double-entry* affect suspense account. If you never have errors in double-entry recording then you will never have a suspense account! Prepare a trial balance now, using the amended balances in the accounts and it will balance. Try it!

This topic of correction of errors is a very popular area for questions by an examiner for any Stage One examination. Don't be careless in dealing with such questions – think them out very carefully and you will score high marks.

EFFECT OF CORRECTIONS ON NET PROFIT

Besides asking for correcting journal entries, the examiner usually asks you to state the effect of a correction on the previously ascertained net profit. If we use the accounts prepared in the previous pages, it is clear that the net profit figure arrived at in the P & L account is not a true figure. This is because rent account is incorrect at the time of preparing the P & L account – so is discounts allowed account, and purchases account. Therefore the relevant amounts transferred to Trading and Profit and Loss account will be wrong. Remember that it wasn't until much later that these errors (**) were discovered and rectified.

The errors subsequently discovered in Mr A's account and Mrs C's account will not affect our profit figures in any way, because these are errors in real accounts, and whilst these errors will distort our balance sheet figures they will *not* affect profit.

Let's look therefore at the corrections to the accounts which *do* affect previously calculated profit, as mentioned above. You *must* refer back – don't just read on.

Rent account has been "increased" by £93 through the corrections – i.e. we have effectively added £93 to the expense "rent", and therefore our profit for the year (calculated *before* discovery of these errors in rent account) should be *reduced* by £93.

Now, the correction to purchases account. How has this correction affected our previously calculated profit figure? The correcting credit of £500 has effectively *reduced* purchases. If purchases are *reduced*, what happens to the gross profit (and therefore net profit)? Visualise a trading account, or better still get some scrap paper out and construct a trading account, and alter your purchases figures to see what happens to profit. You will then clearly see that a reduction in purchases causes profit to increase, in this case by £500.

The corrections to Mr A's account and Mrs C's account will not affect profit one little bit – the balance sheet figure for "debtors", yes, but not profit. Think very carefully on the effects on profits of corrections to purchases, sales, expenses and gain accounts, and unless instructed otherwise in an examination, use the following format (using the examples dealt with above).

Effect of Corrections on Net Profit

		Increase	*Decrease*
Item (i)	Rent		93
Item (ii)	Purchases	500	
Item (iii)	Mr A	—	—
Item (iv)	Mrs C	—	—
		500	93

Total effect on the previously calculated profit, as a result of corrections = an increase of £407 on the figure shown as net profit in the accounts.

Any question you are faced with on "correction of errors" is a "mark earner" for you in the examination, *provided* you think clearly – use rough paper to *see* what's happening. It is so easy to be careless with this topic and lose valuable marks. As an illustration, when you attempt Exercise 15.8, I guarantee that 95% of you will get the wrong answer (there's a challenge!) – because (i) you won't think about it enough, and (ii) you won't "play around" on rough paper, to see what is actually happening. Place yourself in the 5% of those who get it right first time!

EXERCISE 15.1

Wilfred Oskins, a sole proprietor, had prepared the following trial balance at 31st March 19_0:

	£	£
Capital		53,800
Freehold premises at cost	26,000	
Fixtures and fittings at cost	7,800	
Provision for depreciation on fixtures & fittings (at 1st April 19_9)		3,500
Trade debtors	9,200	
Trade creditors		11,300
Bank	6,500	
Stock 31st March 19_0	13,800	
Drawings	9,500	
Motor vehicle at cost	4,300	
Provision for depreciation on motor vehicle (at 1st April 19–9)		2,400
Gross profit		20,000
Heating and lighting	1,450	
Wages and salaries	7,350	
Advertising	900	
Carriage outwards	700	
Motor vehicle running expenses	1,750	
Rent and rates	2,500	
Cash	1,750	
Suspense account (difference in books)		2,500
	£93,500	£93,500

An immediate investigation revealed the following errors:

(a) the purchases account had been overadded by £500;
(b) I. Jitsum, a debtor, had paid £700 on his account. The amount had been recorded in the cash book, but not in Jitsum's account;
(c) sales returns by O. Swingler of £350 had been recorded in Swingler's account, but not in the sales returns account;
(d) no entry had been made in the bank account for £1,500 paid for rent, although the payment had been recorded in the rent account;
(e) when the total of trade creditors had been calculated, a creditor for £150 had been omitted.

The following additional information for the year was available:

(i) at 31st March 19_0 there were wages and salaries accrued £350 and heating and lighting accrued £190, while £100 of the advertising expenditure had been paid in advance;
(ii) no entry had been made for goods taken by the proprietor for his own use £250 (at cost price);
(iii) depreciation is to be charged on fixtures and fittings at 10% on cost and on the motor vehicle at 20% on cost.

Required:

(a) A suspense account starting with the balance of £2,500 and recording the necessary corrections. (Journal entries are **not** required.)
(b) A profit and loss account for the year ended 31st March 19_0.
(c) A balance sheet as at 31st March 19_0.

(A.E.B. "O" level)

EXERCISE 15.2

R. Blackett's trial balance, extracted at 30th April failed to agree. In early May, the following errors were discovered.

1. The total of the returns outward book £124 had not been posted to the ledger.
2. An invoice received from W. Dawson, £100, had been mislaid. Entries for this transaction had, therefore, not been made.
3. A payment for repairs to the motor van £36 had been entered in the vehicle repairs account as £30.
4. When balancing the account of R. Race in the ledger, the debit balance had been brought down in error as £26, instead of £62.

Required:

(a) (i) Journal entries, complete with suitable narrations, to correct each of the above errors.

(ii) A suspense account indicating the nature and extent of the original difference in the books.
(iii) The incorrect total of the trial balance credit column, given that the incorrect total of the debit column was £10,000.

Required:
(b) **Four** types of errors which do not affect the agreement of the trial balance, giving an example of each.

(A.E.B. "O" level)

EXERCISE 15.3

Oswald Bennett, a sole proprietor, had been advised that his capital account for the year ended 31st December was as follows:

	£
Opening balance	11,500
Net profit for the year	5,750
	17,250
Less drawings	4,900
	12,350

Further investigation showed that the books contained the following errors:

1. A motor vehicle costing £1,100 had been incorrectly debited to material purchases account. Depreciation on the vehicle should have been provided at 20% on cost.
2. Wage payments of £100 to employees had been incorrectly debited to drawings account.
3. Bennett had taken £75 of goods from the business for his own use. No entries had been made in the books.
4. A. Smith, a debtor, had paid £150 on his account but unfortunately the amount had been treated as a payment received in the account of A. Smythe, another debtor.
5. Cash sales of £950 had been omitted from sales account.
6. Rates account had been debited with an amount of £50 instead of the correct amount of £500.

Required:
1. Journal entries recording the necessary corrections, assuming that a suspense account had been opened with a credit entry of £500. (Narrations are not required.)

2. A corrected capital account showing clearly any adjustments to the net profit and/or drawings.

(A.E.B. "O" level)

EXERCISE 15.4

J. Black extracted a trial balance from his books on 31st May 19_7 and found the credit side exceeded the debit side by £250. This difference was immediately entered into a suspense account. The following mistakes were later discovered:

(i) The purchase of a truck had been entered in the vehicles account as £450, instead of £540.
(ii) Cash discount of £5 allowed by W. Jones, a creditor, had not been entered in W. Jones's account.
(iii) £100 property repairs had been entered in error on the debit side of the freehold premises account.
(iv) £200 loan interest charged by the bank had been entered in the bank account, but not posted to an interest on loan account.
(v) £50 received for the sale of an old machine, debited in the cash book, had also been debited to the machinery account.

Draft the journal entries required to correct these errors, and write up the suspense account. Balance the account to show the amount of still undiscovered error.

(University of London "O" level)

EXERCISE 15.5

At the end of the financial year, P. White's trial balance does not agree. The debit side exceeds the credit side by £418·26.

		£
(i)	Sales to R. Williams debited in error to G. Williams	170·64
(ii)	Expenditure on machinery repairs debited to machinery account	145·00
(iii)	The sales total had been undercast by	400·00
(iv)	Money collected from staff for private phone calls had been placed in the petty cash box and added to the balance shown in the book. The amount had then been debited to the telephone account.	9·13

(a) Set out the journal entries required to correct the mistakes.
(b) Write up the suspense account.
(c) Which of the errors is a serious error of principle?
(d) Does error (i) affect the trial balance? If not, why not?

(University of London "O" level)

EXERCISE 15.6

After the preparation of a trial balance, an unexplained difference of DR £210 remains, and a Suspense Account is opened for that amount. Subsequent investigations reveal:

(i) £35 received from A. Jones and credited to his account has not been entered in the Bank Account.
(ii) The owner of the business has taken goods which cost £69 for his own use. No entries have been made for this at all.
(iii) A payment of £47 to M. Smith has been credited to that account.
(iv) Discounts Allowed (£198) and Discounts Received (£213) have been posted to the discount accounts as credits and debts respectively.
(v) Bank Interest received of £111 has not been entered in the bank account.
(vi) £211 owing by A. Able has been debited incorrectly to B. Able.

Required:
(a) Prepare the Suspense Account making the entries necessary to eliminate the debit balance there is. Indicate clearly how you would deal with *all* of the errors discovered.
(b) To what extent is the balancing of a Trial Balance evidence of absence of error?

(A.C.C.A.)

EXERCISE 15.7

George Green is the proprietor of a thriving medium sized engineering business. Whilst he recognises the importance of continued investment in plant to maintain the productive capacity of the business, he does not understand the significance of employing well trained staff to keep proper books of account.

A balance sheet for the firm drawn up by the book-keeper as at 31st December 19_9 is as follows:

		£
Georgie Green – Capital Account		50,000
– Current Account		209
		50,209
Long Term Loan – Jane Kerr (10% interest)		20,000
Profit and Loss a/c		27,613
Trade Creditors		24,891
Bank Overdraft		12,256
		134,969
	£	£
Fixed Assets		87,214
Current Assets		
Stock	13,595	
Debtors	27,495	
Drawings	4,650	
Suspense a/c	1,465	
Cash in Hand	550	
		47,755
		£134,969

Mr Green is unhappy about the above balance sheet and asks you to correct the situation.

Your investigations reveal:

(i) The suspense account balance is the difference on the Trial Balance, drawn up before the accounts were completed.
(ii) The total of page 3 of the purchase day book was carried forward to page 4 as £6,985 instead of £6,895, the ultimate but incorrect total of the day book being posted to the Purchases a/c.
(iii) Interest on the Loan a/c is unpaid.
(iv) The stock sheets were over-cast by £2,000.
(v) An investment of £2,500 has been omitted from the Trial Balance.
(vi) Cash in hand should be £55.
(vii) An invoice for £250 has been included in Stocks and Purchases, but not posted to the personal ledger.
(viii) An item in the Sales Day book of £225, has been posted in the personal account as £425.

You are required to:
(a) write up the Suspense Account; and
(b) produce a corrected balance sheet

(Institute of Accounting Staff)

EXERCISE 15.8

C. Walker's balance sheet at 30th September 19_8 appears below:

	£		£
Capital (1st October 19_7)	6,300	Machinery	5,000
Net Profit for year	3,100	less depreciation	750
	9,400		4,250
		Office Furniture	
less Drawings	2,100	less depreciation	800
	7,300		
Creditors	2,640	Stock	3,000
Bank overdraft	630	Debtors	2,520
	10,570		10,570

Walker then discovers the following errors:

(i) Bank interest of £23 had not been entered in the accounts.
(ii) Stock at 30.9._8 had been undervalued by £170.
(iii) A sale of goods to Brown, £650, had been debited to Brain's account.
(iv) Walker had taken £100 of goods from stock for his own personal use and no entries had been made for this.
(v) A discount allowed of £18 had been wrongly debited to discounts received account.
(vi) Purchase of new office furniture for £175 had been debited to purchases account.

YOU ARE REQUIRED to show your calculation of Walker's *true* net profit for the year – i.e. what it would have been had the above errors not occurred – and to draft a corrected balance sheet as at 30.9._8.

EXERCISE 15.9

(a) An inexperienced bookkeeper has drawn up a trial balance for the year ended 30th June 19_7:

	DR £	CR £
Provision for doubtful debts	200	
Bank overdraft	1,654	
Capital		4,591
Creditors		1,637
Debtors	2,983	
Discount received	252	
Discount allowed		733
Drawings	1,200	
Office furniture	2,155	
General expenses		829
Purchases	10,923	
Returns inwards		330
Rent and rates	314	
Salaries	2,520	
Sales		16,882
Stock	2,418	
Provision for depreciation of furniture	364	
	£24,983	£25,002

Required:
Draw up a "corrected" trial balance, debiting or crediting any residual error to a Suspense Account.

(b) Further investigation of the Suspense Account, ascertained in (a) above, reveals the following errors.

(i) Goods bought from J. Jones amounting to £13 had been posted to his account as £33.
(ii) Furniture which had cost £173 had been debited to the general expense account.
(iii) An invoice from Suppliers Ltd, for £370 had been omitted from the Purchase Account, but credited to Suppliers Ltd account.
(iv) Sales on credit to A. Hope Ltd, for £450 had been posted to the Sales Account, but not to the debtor's ledger.
(v) The balance on the Capital Account had been incorrectly brought forward in the ledger, and should have been £4,291.
(vi) An amount of £86 received from A. Blunt, a debtor, in settlement of his account had been treated as a cash sale.
(vii) Discount allowed has been undertotalled by £35.

Required:
Prepare Journal Entries correcting each of the above errors and write up the Suspense Account.

(c) There are several types of error which will not affect the balancing of a trial balance; these include errors of omission, commission and principle.

Explain what is meant by these terms and give an example of each.

(A.C.C.A.)

EXERCISE 15.10

The trial balance of Henry Curran extracted from his books at 31st December 19_3 failed to agree. The amount of the difference on the books was credited to general expenses account, and the following accounts and balance sheet were prepared:

Trading and Profit and Loss Account

	£		£
Stock 1st January 19_3	1,536	Sales	30,173
Purchases	21,842		
	23,378		
Less Stock 31st December 19_3	1,218		
	22,160		
Gross profit	8,013		
	£30,173		£30,173
	£		£
Wages	4,659	Gross profit	8,013
Repairs	287		
Discounts allowed	471		
General expenses	604		
Net profit	1,992		
	£8,013		£8,013

Balance Sheet, 31st December 19_3

	£		£
Capital account (Balance after crediting net profit, £1,992)	2,331	Furniture and fittings	826
		Stock in trade	1,218
		Debtors	1,548
Creditors	1,406	Balance at bank	145
	£3,737		£3,737

The following errors and omissions were afterwards discovered and the books were properly balanced:

1. A purchase invoice for £64 had been completely omitted from the books. The goods were included in the stock at 31st December 19_3.
2. A payment of £82 for new furniture correctly entered in the cash book had been debited to repairs account.

3. As a result of an error of calculation the stock-in-trade at 31st December 19_3 had been under-valued by £200.
4. A bank overdraft of £145 at 31st December 19_3 had been entered on the wrong side of the trial balance.
5. On 1st November 19_3, £118 was received from Gilbert, a customer, in settlement of a debit balance of £122 on his account. Discount allowed amounted to £4. These transactions were correctly entered in Curran's books. On 1st December 19_3, Gilbert by mistake sent a second cheque for £118 which was entered in Curran's cash book and credited to Gilbert's account which was also credited again with £4 for discount, discount account being debited. The resulting credit balance of £122 on Gilbert's account has been included in the item "Creditors, £1,406".

You are required:

(a) to redraft the trading and profit and loss account, and the balance sheet as they should have been prepared; and
(b) to show your calculation of the amount charged in the accounts for general expenses.

(Institute of Bankers)

EXERCISE 15.11

At the close of business on 31st May 19_5 James Holt, a sole trader, extracted from his books a Trial Balance, but this did not agree. Holt entered the difference in a Suspense Account and then prepared his Trading and Profit and Loss Accounts in the usual way. The Net Profit – as shown by the Profit and Loss Account – was £2,770.

Subsequent to the above it was discovered that the following errors had been made and these accounted for the entire difference in the Trial Balance:

(1) Sales Day Book total £7,160 posted to the Sales Account as £7,610.
(2) Discount received total of £84 had been posted to the *wrong* side of Discount Account.
(3) Wages paid £66 had been debited to Office Furniture Account in error.
(4) Purchases of £125 had been correctly entered in the Purchases Day Book but the personal account concerned had been credited with £152.

Required:

(i) State how, and to what extent, each of the above errors would have affected the Trial Balance e.g.: "Debit overstated £......"
(ii) Calculate the correct Net Profit and show your calculations.

NOTE: Journal entries are *not* required.

(London Chamber of Commerce)

CHAPTER 16

CONTROL ACCOUNTS

Imagine that you started in business on 1st January, and by July of the same year your business has developed considerably. Your ledger is now very large with hundreds of accounts "living" in it. So far, you have been taking out a trial balance each month, to check the accuracy of your double-entry, but as your accounts grow in number this is proving to be very time-consuming, particularly in locating the errors of double-entry which naturally occur.

It would be useful if you could check, periodically, certain *sections* of your ledger, rather than do a full trial balance of the whole ledger. This is difficult, however, because the double-entry aspects of a single transaction extend over the whole range of accounts in your ledger.

But wouldn't it be useful if, in a brief lull in activities, you could say to a junior member of staff, "List (on the adding machine) the total of debtors at present – ignore all of the other accounts." There isn't time to do a trial balance of all accounts, but there *is* time to just add up the debtors' balances. However, the total could not be checked against anything to prove its accuracy, because the relevant double-entry aspects of the entries in the debtors' accounts lie in other accounts (e.g. sales) which haven't been listed!

If someone had been keeping a record on what *should* have been entered in the debtors' accounts to date then you would have something to check against. Suppose, therefore, that a member of your staff kept a "master account" or a "summary account" of all the debtors' accounts, and periodically entered into this "master account" the *totals* to date, on each side of the account, of what *should have been* entered in the individual debtors' accounts. The debit balance of this "master account" should then equal the total of individual debtors' balances in your ledger at any point in time. If the person posting the debtors' accounts has made a mistake in these accounts, then the total balances on debtors' accounts would not agree with the balance of the "master account". Obviously an error such as a debit of £70 to Green's account instead of a debit of £70 to Brown's account would not be revealed, as they are both debtors.

The "master account" (called a CONTROL ACCOUNT) would concern itself with *totals only* of what *should* have been debited to various debtors' accounts for credit sales, and credited to debtors' accounts for cash and cheques received, discounts allowed, sales returns, bad debts written off, etc., in the period in question. This master account would be in effect an *exact "carbon copy"* of all debtors' accounts in the ledger, but showing totals for a period rather than individual entries within that particular period. It would be a "memorandum account" – *not* part of the double-entry system.

The totals, of each type of transaction affecting debtors' accounts, for entry in the master account, would be obtained from the Sales Day Book, Sales Returns Book, Cash Book and various documents.

You could now, by using such a "master account" for debtors, check this particular *section* of your ledger whenever you wanted to, without having to do a full trial balance of all accounts in the ledger. It would be useful therefore to keep *all* debtors' accounts in their own part of the ledger, and this section of the ledger would be called the **"Sales (or Debtors) Ledger"**. The "master account" for this section would be called the **"Sales Ledger Control Account"**, *viz*:

Sales Ledger Control Account

	£		£
Sales	14,000	Bank/Cash	9,000
		Sales Returns	600
		Discounts Allowed	400
		Bad Debts Written off	100

This tells us that, in the period in question, a total of £9,000 *should* have been credited to various debtors' accounts in respect of cash and cheques received; £100 *should* have been credited to various debtors' accounts in respect of bad debts; £14,000 *should* have been debited to various debtors for credit sales made in the period, etc.

If what has been entered in the debtors' accounts matches the totals for the period shown in the above control account, then the total of individual debtors' balances in the sales ledger should come to a total listing of £3,900, to tally with the debit balance shown on the above control account (£3,900).

A similar control could be set up for creditors' accounts, and these accounts should also be kept separate from other accounts in a **"Purchases (or Creditors) Ledger"**. The control account, summarising what *should* have been entered in various creditors' accounts, would be called a **"Purchases Ledger Control Account"**. By using such an account, the Purchases Ledger can be proved any time you wish, without having to do a full trial balance, by simply listing all balances (credit) in the purchases ledger, and checking this total of balances with the credit balance shown on "Purchases Ledger Control Account".

You now have a control account for each of two major sections of your ledger:

(i) The Sales Ledger – *all* debtors' accounts.
(ii) The Purchases Ledger – *all* creditors' accounts.

Each control account is meant to be a "carbon-copy" of what *should* have been entered in that particular ledger, and if the "carbon copy" (showing totals only) does not agree with the original (individual entries in the respective accounts) then some error has been made, and needs to be located.

Study the following example:
At 1st May the total of debtors' balances in the sales ledger of ABC Ltd. was £1,640 and the total of creditors' balances, £1,370. During May the summarised transactions were as follows:

	£
Credit Purchases	9,800
Credit Sales	14,300
Cash Sales	700
Discounts Allowed	300
Discounts Received	200
Returns Inwards	90
Returns Outwards	40
Rent and Rates paid	520
Wages paid	840
Bad debts written off	30
Cash and cheques received from debtors	11,370
Cash and cheques paid to creditors	7,400
Dishonoured cheques	120

Prepare a Sales Ledger Control Account and a Purchases Ledger Control Account from this information, with the two accounts balanced off at 31st May.

Answer

DR Sales Ledger Control Account CR

		£			£
May 1	Balance b/d	1,640		Discounts Allowed	300
	Sales	14,300		Sales Returns	90
	Dishonoured cheques	120		Bad Debts	30
				Cash/Bank	11,370
			May 31	Balance c/d	4,270
		16,060			16,060
May 31	Balance b/d	4,270			

DR — Purchases Ledger Control Account — CR

		£			£
	Discounts Rec'd	200	May 1	Balance b/d	1,370
	Purchases Returns	40		Purchases	9,800
	Cash/Bank	7,400			
May 31	Balance c/d	3,530			
		11,170			11,170
			May 31	Balance b/d	3,530

NOTE: The commencing balance in each account is the total of outstanding debtors and creditors respectively at 1st May – at this point the control accounts are "carbon-copies" of their respective ledgers, the sales ledger and the purchases ledger, but showing *totals*. The credit of £90 in the sales ledger control account means that, according to the day book, £90 altogether *should* have been credited to various debtors' accounts in May in respect of returns – the double-entry of course being in sales returns account.

The credit of £30 for bad debts means that, according to various documents (or the journal), £30 *should* have been credited altogether in May to various debtors' accounts (double-entry in bad debts account of course). In other words, each entry on the debit side of the sales ledger control account is the *total* of those individual items which *should*, if posting has been done properly, have been debited throughout May to various debtors' accounts in the sales ledger. Same reasoning with credit entries, and with the debit and credit entries in the purchases ledger control account.

If what is displayed in the control accounts has been "done" in the respective ledgers, then the total debit balances in the sales ledger at 31st May should, when listed, show a total of £4,270 proving that ledger to be "in order". Purchases ledger individual balances should add up to £3,530 at 31st May.

A note about the entry in the sales ledger control account, of £120, for "dishonoured cheques" (i.e. cheques previously paid into the bank and now returned by the bank unpaid). When these cheques were originally paid into the company's (ABC Ltd.) bank account, the entries were, say,

DR — A. Smith (Debtor) — CR

		£			£
April 25	Balance	120	May 5	Bank	120
		120			120

DR	Bank Account (part of cash book)		CR
May 5 Smith	£120		

Smith has paid his account in full, so closing his account, and increasing the company's asset, bank. Smith's account now says "I owe nothing".

A few days later, Smith's cheque "bounces" – i.e. is returned unpaid, so now Smith *again* owes ABC Ltd. £120, and ABC Ltd's bank account has been reduced by £120. In other words, the original entries made in the accounts, when Smith paid his account, are now cancelled, *viz*:

DR	A. Smith		CR
	£		£
April 25 Balance	120	May 5 Bank	120
	120		120
May 10 Bank	120		

DR	Bank Account		CR
May 5 Smith	£120	May 10 Bank	£120

The posting of the dishonoured cheque has meant a *debit* in the debtor's account, Smith, therefore this should be "copied" in the sales ledger control account.

Why weren't the May transactions for Cash Sales, £700, recorded in a control account? Because the control accounts record what *should* have been done in the accounts of the ledger to which they relate – i.e. the accounts of debtors or creditors – and a cash sale (debit cash, credit sales) does *not* involve an entry in any debtor's or creditor's account; therefore no entry in a control account. The same applies to the items in the question of rent, rates and wages – none of these affect, in any way, either the sales ledger (debtors' accounts) or the purchases ledger (creditors' accounts), therefore they don't affect the control accounts.

To summarise – any transaction which affects (i.e. involves a posting to) a debtor's account is "copied" in the sales ledger control account. Any transaction which involves a posting to a creditor's account is "copied" in the purchases ledger control account. If the transaction doesn't affect either a debtor's or a creditor's account then that transaction is *not* reflected in a control account.

One final example. It sometimes happens that a debtor's account in the sales ledger suddenly acquires a credit balance, or a creditor's account in the purchases ledger acquires a debit balance. This is only a temporary situation caused by a debtor paying more than is needed to settle his account, or by a creditor being overpaid (think of the effect on their accounts). This situation does not affect the control accounts, which are only concerned with checking the *net* debit balances in sales ledger and the *net* credit balances in purchases ledger.

It may, however, happen that Mr Winfield, who is a debtor of your business because you regularly sell goods to him on credit, on one occasion, sells goods *to you* on credit – i.e. he becomes your supplier. This means that you now have an account for him in your sales ledger (as your customer) and an account for him in your purchases ledger (as your supplier). If the purchase from him is a "one-off" transaction then there is no point in having two separate accounts for Winfield, in two separate ledgers. You may decide therefore, to transfer the credit balance of his account in purchases ledger to his account in sales ledger, so retaining the one account in sales ledger. The credit balance transferred will have the effect of "setting off" what Winfield owes on his sales ledger account, *viz*:

SALES LEDGER

DR		Winfield	CR
Balance	£800	Contra	£70

PURCHASES LEDGER

DR		Winfield	CR
	£		£
Contra	70	Balance	70
	70		70

The contradicting ("contra"), entry of £70 effectively closes off the "one-off" account in the purchases ledger, and "sets off" £70 of the £800 owing in the sales ledger – i.e. reduces it to £730.

As these entries affect the sales *and* purchases ledger account, they will obviously need to be recorded in *both* control accounts (to "copy" what *should* have happened – and has!) in the respective ledger accounts. Therefore, a "contra" of £70 will appear on the credit side of sales ledger control account, and on the debit side of purchases ledger control account. This is so that *everything* which should be happening in the two ledgers is being reflected (copied) in the relevant control accounts.

Do remember that control accounts are *not* part of the double-entry system – they are simply summaries of what *should* have gone on in the respective ledgers.

Our ledger is now divided into two distinct parts – a *"sales ledger"* for *all* debtors' accounts, and a *"purchases ledger"* for *all* creditors' accounts. What about all the other accounts – e.g. cash, bank, equipment, sales, purchases, rent, wages, etc., etc.? All of these remain in their own third section of the ledger called the **General Ledger**. You should never find an account in the general ledger with a personal name as its title!

ADVANTAGES OF USING CONTROL ACCOUNTS

We have seen that by using control accounts we can do periodic checks of sections of the overall ledger without having to do a full trial balance. When we *do* prepare our full trial balance, and it does not agree, then instead of checking every transaction in the ledger as a whole, we can set out to "prove" the sales ledger and the purchases ledger on their own by using their control accounts, so pin-pointing where the main errors lie. For example, if the sales ledger and the purchases ledger balances agree with their respective control accounts, then we know that the errors in the trial balance are in the general ledger, and we can concentrate on that ledger. It rarely works out in practice as easy as that (there are usually errors in all three ledgers!), but by having a "self-balancing" system in two of our largest sections of the ledger we can more easily locate, and find, where the errors are.

If there is a sufficiently large sales and purchases ledger then it is worthwhile to sub-divide these ledgers into sub-sections – e.g. "Sales Ledger A–K" (for all debtors' surnames within this range) and "Sales Ledger L–Z". In this case there would be a "Sales Ledger Control Account A–K" and one "L–Z" to control those *parts* of the sales ledger. In a very large business, the ledgers could be sub-divided on an even greater scale. The same applies, of course, to using sectionalised control accounts for the purchases ledger.

Apart from the obvious advantages in being able to "balance" sections of the ledger, the use of control accounts means that *different* people are interpreting the same information. The person who writes up the control account is not likely to be the same person who writes up the ledger accounts, and it is *most* unlikely that two people would make the *same* error – e.g. the transposing of £72 to £27. Having different people doing the "same" job, in different ways, is a good method of "checking".

Control accounts also provide the firm with some kind of defence against an employee's fraudulent tendencies – i.e. the temptation to "fiddle" the books – a check is constantly being made, by another person!

Control accounts are sometimes referred to as "total accounts" or "self-balancing accounts".

EXERCISE 16.1

The balances on the personal ledger control accounts of Galway Ltd. at 31st December 19_7 were as follows:

	DR	CR
	£	£
Bought Ledger	96	56,900
Sales Ledger	97,550	48

The following transactions take place during 19_8:

	£
Purchases	194,720
Sales (including £2,540 cash sales)	251,160
Payments to suppliers	216,100
Allowances made by suppliers	2,880
Interest charged to customers	150
Receipts from credit customers (including £250 cheque dishonoured)	260,090
Bad debts written off (including dishonoured cheque)	1,260
Discounts received	2,520
Discounts allowed	5,860
Refund of customer's overpayment	370

Debit balances on suppliers' accounts at 31st December 19_8 amount to £150, and credit balances on customers' accounts are £230.

Required:
Prepare Galway's sales ledger control account and bought ledger control account for 19_8: carry down the closing balances.

(Royal Society of Arts)

EXERCISE 16.2

From the following details for the month of June 19_4 prepare sales ledger control account and purchases ledger control account.

On 31st May 19_3 the balances in the purchases ledger and sales ledger were £6,200 credit and £2,190 debit respectively.

	£
Credit purchases from suppliers	27,310
Credit sales to customers	19,830
Cash paid to creditors	25,670
Receipts from trade debtors	16,840
Discounts received	835
Discounts allowed	921
Purchases returns	290
Sales returns	320
Bad debts written off	110
Credit balances in purchases ledger transferred to sales ledger	65

EXERCISE 16.3

At the beginning of December the balances on the control accounts which Spadework Ltd. keeps for its sales and purchases ledgers agree with the totals of the balances in the two ledgers, thus:

	Ledger Balances		Control account balance
	DR	CR	
	£	£	£
Customers	19,510	24	19,486
Suppliers	48	11,380	11,332

During the month the following transactions take place:

Purchases	38,944
Sales (including £850 cash sales)	50,232
Payments to suppliers	43,220
Rebates allowed by suppliers	576
Interest charged to customers	30
Receipts from credit customers (including £50 cheque dishonoured)	52,018
Bad debts written off (including dishonoured cheque)	252
Discounts received	904
Discounts allowed	1,172
Refund of customer's overpayment	74

At the end of the month the totals of the balances in the personal ledgers are found to be:

	DR	CR
	£	£
Customers	15,640	40
Suppliers	30	5,606

Write up the two control accounts for the month, and suggest an explanation for any discrepancies between control balances and ledger balances which may be revealed.

(Institute of Bankers)

EXERCISE 16.4

T. Saunders prepared a Purchases Ledger Control Account for April 19_1 from the totals in his subsidiary books. The closing credit balance of the Control Account, which was £4,120, failed to agree with the total of the balances in the Purchases Ledger. The following errors were discovered.

(i) A debit balance of £210 from M. Mahoney's account in the Sales Ledger had been transferred to M. Mahoney's account in the Purchases Ledger, and the transfer had not been entered in the Control Account.

(ii) The total of the Purchases Day Book for April 19_1 had been undercast by £130.
(iii) A credit purchase of £450 from B. Kennedy had been totally omitted from the books of account.
(iv) A cash payment to a supplier T. Flinn of £470 had been correctly entered in the Cash Book but posted to his account at £430.

Required:
(a) Show the Purchases Ledger Control Account after the errors have been corrected.
(b) Calculate the total of the balances in the Purchases Ledger before the errors were discovered.
(c) State briefly **four** advantages of maintaining Control Accounts.

(A.E.B. "A" level)

EXERCISE 16.5

The draft balance sheet at 31st March 19_9 of Tom Brown Limited included the following items:

	£
Purchases ledger control account	24,782 net balance
Sales ledger control account	37,354 net balance

These control account figures, however, did not agree with the position at 31st March 19_9 as shown by the lists of balances extracted from the individual creditors' and debtors' accounts, but the trial balance was agreed and the draft balance sheet balances.

The list of purchases ledger balances at 31st March 19_9 included the following debit balances:

	£
G. Brook	167
K. River	89

The list of sales ledger balances at 31st March 19_9 included the following credit balances:

	£
L. Bridge	642
S. Tunnel	914

Subsequent investigations revealed the following accounting errors:

(i) The sales day book for December 19_8 was overcast by £1,500.
(ii) A credit note for goods costing £160 returned to the supplier, T. Street, in September 19_8, was not recorded in the company's books, but the stock records have been adjusted correctly. According to the

list of balances T. Street is owed £790 at 31st March 19_9.

(iii) A cheque for £900 received from a customer, P. Bridger Limited, in February 19_9, was credited, in error, to L. Bridge.
Note: The account of P. Bridger Limited in the sales ledger shows a debit balance at 31st March 19_9, of £960.

(iv) In February 19_9, a debt due from T. Wood to the company of £600 was written off as a bad debt. Although the debt has been written off in T. Wood's personal account, no adjustment for this has been made in the relevant control account.

(v) A payment of £420 to J. King, supplier, in June 19_8, was debited in the purchases account. The invoices making up this amount were correctly entered in the purchase day book.

Required:
A computation of the corrected balances at 31st March 19_9 of the purchases ledger control account and the sales ledger control account.

(A.C.C.A.)

EXERCISE 16.6

The following information relates to the Debtors' and Creditors' Control accounts for the month of April and is taken from the books of a trading company.

(NOTE: You are advised that not all the following information affects the Control accounts.)

	£
Balances at 1st April:	
Debtors' Ledger (debit)	65,200
Debtors' Ledger (credit)	900
Creditors' Ledger (credit)	37,400
Creditors' Ledger (debit)	100
Credit sales	213,500
Credit purchases	106,700
Cash sales	71,200
Provision for doubtful debts	3,500
Cash received from debtors	179,800
Cash paid to creditors	87,100
Purchases returns	1,500
Sales returns	2,300
Discounts received	2,050
Bad debts written off	700
Bill payable accepted	3,300
Discounts allowed	3,400
"Contras" between Debtors' & Creditors' ledger	1,200
Balances at 30th April:	
Debtors' Ledger (credit)	700
Creditors' Ledger (debit)	150

Required:

(a) Prepare for the month of April **either** the Debtors' Ledger Control account **or** the Creditors' Ledger Control account.

(b) Explain the advantages of Control accounts and say how "contra" items may arise.

(A.E.B. "A" level)

EXERCISE 16.7

(a) What are the purposes of control accounts?

(b) Thornely Ltd. maintains control accounts for its sales and purchases ledgers.

Balances at 31st December 19_8 are:	Debit	Credit
	£	£
Sales ledger	27,124	222
Purchases ledger	375	19,763

Details of transactions during 19_9 are as follows:	£
Credit sales	237,548
Credit purchases	144,137
Receipts from credit customers	228,413
Cash sales	101,485
Payments to suppliers for goods purchased on credit	139,276
Cash purchases	475
Discounts received	1,097
Discounts allowed	1,352
Bad debts written off	2,018
Refund to a credit customer for an overpayment	97

At 31st December 19_9 credit balances on the sales ledger amount to £305 and debit balances on the purchases ledger amount to £164.

You are required to prepare the

(i) sales ledger control account, and

(ii) purchase ledger control account for 19_9.

(Royal Society of Arts)

CHAPTER 17

INCOMPLETE RECORDS

Limited Companies are obliged by law to keep a proper set of accounts, recording everything which goes on in their business. Other businesses, (e.g. sole traders and partnerships), do not have to keep proper accounts. Provided they can satisfy the tax inspector, and the bank manager, as to the amount of profit or loss made by their business for the year, they can keep accounts in a variety of ways – by odd notes, in odd books, in odd fashions! Part of their "accounting system" might well be a series of spikes skewering paid and unpaid invoices and bank statements!

Whilst most firms will keep reasonable records of transactions, from which their accountant can prepare final accounts and balance sheets, the rest won't, and the accountant has got to find a way of calculating profit or loss and preparing a balance sheet from these incomplete records.

How does he go about it? Well, first of all he knows that a trader's capital represents the *difference* between total assets and total liabilities, other than capital (you should have remembered this). He also knows that there are only *two* things which can cause capital to increase – profits and the introduction of new capital. There are also only *two* things which can cause a decrease in capital – losses and drawings.

Therefore, if the accountant (or the trader), constructs a "skeleton" capital account, *viz*:

DR			Capital Account of – (Trader)		CR
		£			£
	Net Loss	–	Start of year	Balance b/d	–
	Drawings	–		Net Profit	–
End of Year	Balance c/d	–		New Capital	–
		–			–
			End of Year	Balance b/d	–

and fills in as many "blanks" as possible, then the remaining "blanks" become *the difference*, to make the two sides of the account add up to the same amount (as they must).

Which blanks can easily be filled in? New capital introduced shouldn't be any problem (the trader will remember this!), nor should drawings. Inspection of bank statements and old cheque stubs and bank paying-in slips should provide this information. Commencing and closing balances to capital account? Capital at the start of the year is simply the difference between total assets and liabilities *at that date*, and whoever prepared the trader's accounts last year should have this information. Capital at the end of the year is a matter of taking stock of what the trader had, and what he owed, at that date – i.e. the difference between the trader's assets and his liabilities at his year-end. Most of his assets can be valued, and paid and unpaid invoices and copy invoices, etc. will soon give the figure for debtors and creditors at the year end date.

All "blanks" are now filled in with the exception of "Net Profit" and "Net Loss" – obviously the business can't have made both, so whichever side of the account demands a balancing figure, dictates a profit or loss!

To summarise – if you know the opening and closing capital figure (and you know what information you need to find "capital", at any date) and you know drawings, and new capital introduced, then you can find net profit or net loss. Easy!

In finding capital at a particular date you could just simply list assets and liabilities on a piece of rough paper, and subtract. However, these "workings" are often asked for in an examination, as part of your answer, and your listings of assets and liabilities would then be presented in the following form:

Statement of Affairs as at 1st January, 19_7

Liabilities		*Assets*	
	£		£
Capital (balancing figure)	13,000	Equipment	7,000
Creditors	2,000	Stock	4,000
		Debtors	3,000
		Bank	1,000
	15,000		15,000

The reason for the heading "Statement of Affairs", to what looks very much like a balance sheet, is that a balance sheet is strictly a list of balances in the ledger, representing assets and liabilities, and as the trader in question does not have "balances of accounts" (because he has no proper ledger) the above description is normally used.

Suppose though, that the trader wants to know his gross profit as well as his net profit. He may even want a full trading and profit and loss account drawing up. In this case we need a bit more information. We need to know purchases and sales, as well as expenses and gains. Opening and closing stocks should not be too difficult to find as valuation of stock is always by inspection or calculation.

What information do we need to find purchases? If we could construct a "purchases ledger control account" covering the year we would have purchases at a glance, e.g.

DR — Purchases Ledger Control a/c — CR

		£			£
	(3) Cash/Bank	9,500	Start of year	Balance b/d	4,000 (1)
	(4) Discounts Rec'd	100		CREDIT PURCHASES	11,000
	(5) Purchases Returns	50			
End of year	(2) Balance c/d	5,350			
		15,000			15,000
			End of year	Balance b/d	5,350 (2)

The information needed to construct this account was:

(1) Creditors at the beginning of the year;
(2) Creditors at the end of the year;
(3) Cash paid to creditors during the year;
(4) and (5) Other items which would affect the creditors accounts overall.

Having inserted this known information, the only figure missing in our constructed account is purchases, and this becomes the balancing figure to the account (to make both sides add up to the same figure). Therefore, if we know the other information we can easily find "purchases" by constructing such an account. If we had been told what purchases were, but not been told what the final figure for creditors was, then the same principle would apply – provided we are given all the figures, expect one, we can always find that missing one by the above process of deduction, using the account as our method.

It is not strictly correct to call the above account a "control account" because we are not using it as a control. A better title to the workings would be "Creditors' Summary" where we are constructing one account to represent *all* creditors.

Similarly, a "Debtors' Summary" could be built up from given information, so providing the missing figure for credit sales, e.g.

DR		Debtors' Summary			CR
		£			£
Start of year	Balances b/d *	6,000		Cash/Bank	19,000 *
	CREDIT SALES	21,000		Discounts Allowed	150 *
				Sales Returns	50 *
				Bad Debts	200 *
			End of year	Balance c/d	7,600 *
		27,000			27,000
End of year	Balance b/d *	7,600			

* – given information. Again, provided we know everything bar any one item, we can find that missing item.

In most examinations, the returns, discounts and bad debts would not be given, indicating that there were none. This makes the calculation even quicker!

This "building up" of an account to find missing information is a technique we used in Chapter 9 for expenses and gains *due* in the period. It is certainly the safest way of calculation – become very familiar with it.

In an incomplete records situation (examination or otherwise), there may be other information given which is not related to debtors, creditors, etc. For example, you may know what sales for the year are, together with opening and closing stocks, but you may not know what the creditors were at the start of the year or what payments were made to creditors during the year. With *two* missing pieces of vital information it is impossible to calculate "purchases" by using a Creditors' Summary Account. However, you may know or be told that the gross profit is always 20% of sales (known as the "gross profit margin"), and this is the "key".

For example, you know that sales for the year are £16,000; opening stock is £2,000 and closing stock £1,000. The "gross profit margin" is 25%. From this information you can start to construct a Trading Account, *viz*:

DR	Trading Account for Year		CR
	£		£
Opening Stock	2,000	Sales	16,000
Purchases	?		
	?		
Less Closing Stock	1,000		
Cost of Goods Sold	?		
Gross Profit c/d (25% of Sales)	4,000		

The question marks are now easily filled in. The total of the credit side of this account adds up to £16,000, therefore the debit side must add up to the same figure (fill it in). Now, working backwards (or upwards!), "cost of goods sold" has *got* to be £12,000 – opening stock plus purchases has *got* to be £13,000, and therefore Purchases has *got* to be £11,000. Only these figures will make the debit side of the account add and subtract to arrive at a final total to the column of £16,000. Fill in these figures for yourself.

There are many variations of the above example. Note, that if gross profit is 20% of sales, then "cost of goods sold" *must* be 80% of sales – this thinking wasn't necessary in the above example, but it could be in another example or question!

The point is, that in an examination, you will be given enough information to calculate missing figures. *Use* that information – construct a trading and profit and loss account *without* figures to start with – just put in the "labels" (i.e. the description of each item). Then, insert the obvious figures given, use the other information given, and the whole thing will start to take shape. Missing figures will display themselves as if by magic by simple processes of adding and substracting. Don't try to do all this in your mind – get it down on paper, then you can see where you are going!

As a final example, a question may tell you the net profit and all expenses, but not gross profit, or its percentage of sales. Once you have inserted your net profit figure and all expenses in your profit and loss account, you have only got to add these up and you have your gross profit figure to take back into your trading account! Think about this one, and remember that you don't necessarily work from top to bottom in an exercise – it's sometimes the other way round! The key to success is always, to "think it out".

EXERCISE 17.1

D. Quox, a retailer, did not keep proper books of accounts, but he was able to supply his accountant with the following information on 1st April 19_8:

	£
Trade debtors	2,400
Bank	7,709
Cash	401
Fixtures and fittings	2,500
Freehold premises	15,500
Trade creditors	2,362
Stock	5,000

Further information was provided on transactions during the year ended 31st March 19_9:

	Cash	*Bank*		*Cash*	*Bank*
	£	£		£	£
Receipts from goods sold	28,450		Payments to suppliers of goods		17,500
Interest from private investment		108	Cash paid into bank	24,400	
Cash receipts paid into bank		24,400	Wage and salaries payments	2,900	
			Rates		590
			Advertising		140
			Insurance		150
			Drawings	150	4,500
			Repairs and decorations	10	375
			Carriage outwards	170	—

NOTES

(a) Fixtures and fittings were to be depreciated by 10% of the book value at the beginning of the year.

(b) Insurance had been paid for the period from 1st April 19_8 till 30th September 19_9.

(c) £150 was still owing for wages.

(d) Discounts allowed for the year were £1,564.

(e) At 31st March 19_9 the following balances were provided:

	£
Stock	4,700
Trade debtors	2,386
Trade creditors	4,562

Required:

1. a calculation of the capital of the business at 1st April 19_8,
2. a calculation of the cash and bank balances at 31st March 19_9,
3. a trading and profit and loss account for the year ended 31st March 19_9 and a balance sheet as at that date.

(A.E.B. "O" level)

EXERCISE 17.2

Summary of the bank account of F. Jarvis, a retailer, for the year ended 30th April 19_7.

	£		£
Balance 1st May 19_6	520	G. Johnson's personal drawings	1,560
Receipts from sales	24,549	Payments for purchase of goods for resale	19,806
		Payments for trade expenses	1,630
		Additional display equipment purchased 1st November, 19_6	140
		Redecoration of G. Johnson's private dwelling	273
		Balance 30th April 19_7	1,660
	25,069		25,069

Additional information at 30th April,	19_6	19_7
	£	£
Trading stock	5,120	4,259
Trade debtors	70	40
Trade creditors	925	827
Fixtures and shop display equipment (at cost less depreciation)	1,260	?
Motor delivery van (at cost less depreciation)	700	?

Jarvis withdrew £200 of the stock for his own consumption. Provide depreciation on fixtures and shop display equipment at 10% per annum and on the motor delivery van at 25% per annum on the book value at the beginning of the year.

Required

From the above information prepare a trading and profit and loss account for the year ended 30th April 19_7 and a balance sheet as at that date.

EXERCISE 17.3

William Jones, a retailer, does not keep a full set of books. He buys on credit but all sales are strictly cash. All takings are paid immediately into his bank account. All payments are made by cheque.

A summary of his bank account for the year ended 31st May 19_7 is as follows:

	£		£
Balance 1st June 19_6	240	Paid to creditors	12,400
Received for cash sales	15,780	Paid for expenses	1,262
		Rent	150
		Drawings	1,800
		Balance 31st May 19_7	408
	16,020		16,020

The following information is also available:

	1st June 19_6	31st May 19_7
	£	£
Creditors for stock	800	900
Creditors for expenses	70	100
Stock in trade	1,000	900
Furniture	200	180

Calculate:

(a) William Jones' Capital on 1st June 19_6.
(b) Purchases for the year ended 31st May 19_7.
(c) Sales for the year ended 31st May 19_7.
(d) The amount chargeable to Profit and Loss Account for expenses for the year ended 31st May 19_7.

Using the figures you have calculated above, prepare a Trading Account and a Profit and Loss Account for the year ended 31st May 19_7 and a Balance Sheet on that date.

(University of London "O" Level)

EXERCISE 17.4

On 1st January 19_9 W. Smith's Balance Sheet was as follows:

	£		£
Capital	50,500	Premises	45,000
Mortgage loan	5,000	Delivery vans	2,400
Creditors for stock	1,750	Stock	4,725
		Bank	4,625
		Rates in advance	500
	57,250		57,250

Mr Smith does not keep any books at all. The only information available regarding his business is to be derived from paid and unpaid invoices, cheque counterfoils and paying-in slips. Any other information required must be estimated. It is, however, definite that no sales are on credit.

From the following information prepare a Trading, Profit and Loss account for the year ended 31st December 19_9, and a Balance Sheet on that date.

	£
Cash paid into bank, proceeds of cash sales	41,526
Cheques drawn for payments to suppliers	28,476
Cash discount deducted	400
Cheques drawn for expense items	1,750
Cheques drawn for private expenditure	8,000

During the year rates amounting to £2,500 had been paid (by cheque) up to 31st March 19_0. This is in addition to the expense items entered above.

Repayments of the mortgage loan have been made by standing order at the bank at the rate of £50 per calendar month, but the account has been debited with £400 interest by the mortgage holder.

On 31st December 19_9 the following figures are available:
Stocks £5,600 Creditors £2,300 Delivery vans £1,500.

(University of London "O" level)

EXERCISE 17.5

The following is a summary of the bank account of Douglas, a trader, for the year 19_9.

Bank Summary

	£		£
Balance Jan. 1, 19_9	412	Payments to trade creditors	13,915
Amounts paid into bank	18,738	Rent and rates	422
Balance, December 31, 19_9	77	General expenses	2,060
		Drawings	2,830
	£19,227		£19,227

The total of cash sales and receipts from trade debtors during 19_9 was £20,625; of this, £18,738 was paid into the bank, £1,250 was paid for wages and £84 was paid for general expenses. Cash not otherwise accounted for is to be treated as taken by Douglas for private purposes.

No discounts were allowed or received and there were no bad debts.

The following information is obtained from the books:

	Dec. 31 19_8 £	Dec. 31 19_9 £
Stock in trade	2,729	3,018
Trade debtors	1,864	1,641
Trade creditors	1,470	1,595
Rates in advance	30	32
Rent outstanding		90
Creditors for general expenses	70	135
Cash in hand	27	51
Furniture and fittings	650	650

You are required to prepare a trading and profit and loss account for the year 19_9, and a balance sheet as on December 31, 19_9.

NOTE: Ignore depreciation of furniture and fittings.

(Institute of Bankers)

EXERCISE 17.6

The Balance Sheet at 30th September 19_9 of John East, a long established trader, is as follows:

	£	£		£	£
Capital account:			Fixed assets, at cost		140,000
At 30th Sept. 19_8		62,000	*Less:* Depreciation to date		96,000
					44,000
Add: Net profit for the year ended 30th Sept. 19_9		16,000	Current assets:		
			Stock in trade	17,000	
		78,000	Trade debtors	6,000	
Less: Drawings		9,000	Amounts prepaid	400	
			Balance at bank	8,500	31,900
		69,000			
Current liabilities:					
Trade creditors	6,200				
Accrued charges	700	6,900			
		£75,900			£75,900

Owing to a long illness, John East has been obliged to leave the day to day operation of his business since early 19_0 in the hands of Peter Pink, a trusted employee.

Although his illness has prevented him keeping his accounting records up to date, John was able to make plans for the year ended 30th September 19_0, which showed that during the year the business bank account would never be in an overdraft situation.

A letter from the bank drawing John East's attention to the fact that his business bank account was £5,000 overdrawn on 30th September 19_0 coincided with the sudden disappearance of Peter Pink. Subsequent investigations implicate Peter Pink whom it would appear has not paid into the business bank account all the monies received from trade debtors; however all necessary payments have been paid correctly through the business bank account.

It has always been the practice of John East to bank all business receipts intact and to make all payments from the business bank account.

It can be assumed that there were no unpresented cheques at 30th September 19_0 and all amounts paid into the bank account on or before 30th September 19_0 were credited by that date.

John East is now endeavouring to determine the amount of cash misappropriated and also prepare the annual accounts for the year ended 30th September 19_0. John East is not insured against loss owing to the misappropriation of cash.

Accordingly, the following information has now been obtained concerning the year ended 30th September 19_0:

(i) stock in trade, at cost, at 30th September 19_0 was valued at £11,000;
(ii) throughout the year, a uniform rate of gross profit was earned of one-third of the cost of goods sold;
(iii) payments for purchases totalled £110,700 whilst trade creditors at 30th September 19_0 were £3,300 more than a year previously;
(iv) administrative expenses payments made during the year totalled £11,200 whilst the amount to be charged to the profit and loss account is £11,000;
(v) establishment expenses payments were £9,400 and establishment expenses prepaid at 30th September 19_0 amounted to £800;
(vi) fixed assets bought and paid for amounted to £20,000;
(vii) depreciation is provided annually at the rate of 5% of the cost of fixed assets held at the end of each financial year;
(viii) John East's cash drawings totalled £10,000;
(ix) trade debtors at 30th September 19_0 amounted to £6,500 and cash sales during the year under review amounted to £82,000;
(x) amounts prepaid at 30th September 19_9 of £400 related to establishment expenses;
(xi) accrued charges at 30th September 19_9 of £700 related to administrative expenses.

Required:
(a) A computation of the amount of cash misappropriated during the year ended 30 September 19_0.
(b) John East's Trading and Profit and Loss Account for the year ended 30th September 19_0 and a Balance Sheet at that date.
NOTE: The Profit and Loss Account should include an item "cash misappropriated".
(c) Explain the importance of determining gross profit as well as net profit wherever possible.

(A.C.C.A.)

EXERCISE 17.7

A. Clark has not kept a full set of accounting records but is able to present the following summary of his bank account for the year ended 31st March 19_2:

Bank Account

19_1		£	19_2		£
April 1	Balance b/d	13,000	March 31	Payments to trade creditors	78,350
	Takings	115,846		Miscellaneous expenses	7,320
				Rent	3,400
				Rates	910
				Equipment	13,000
				Balance c/d	25,866
		128,846			128,846
19_2					
April 1	Balance b/d	25,866			

Before banking his takings Clark withdrew £5,000 cash as drawings and paid miscellaneous expenses of £2,654. During March 1982 Clark's shop was broken into and several days' takings were stolen from the till. Clark is uncertain as to how much cash was stolen and the theft is not covered by insurance. The range of products sold by Clark earn a uniform gross profit of 30% of sales.

The following information is also available:

	1st April 19_1	31st March 19_2
	£	£
Stock	18,000	7,000
Trade creditors	9,000	10,650
Trade debtors	12,000	13,500
Rent prepaid	850	1,200
Rates owing	230	—
Equipment (at valuation)	2,000	14,100

Required:

(a) A trading and profit and loss account for the year ended 31st March 19_2 showing clearly the amount of cash stolen.

(b) A balance sheet as at 31st March 19_2.

(A.E.B. "A" level)

EXERCISE 17.8

Carter owns and operates a small retail shop. From the few records he keeps, the following information is available for the beginning and end of his accounting year:

	30th June 19_9	30th June 19_0
	£	£
Cash in shop till	70	105
Bank overdraft	695	1,350
Stock	2,000	4,600
Owed by customers	920	2,540
Owed to suppliers	2,180	3,730
Loan from wife	2,000	1,500

Additional information:

1. Carter tells you that during the year and before making the weekly bankings of takings he took from the till –
   (a) £50 a week for his personal needs, and
   (b) £40 a week for his assistant's wages.
2. Paid cheques show that all payments from the bank account were to suppliers except –
   (a) a payment of £110 to an insurance company being £80 for the insurance of the shop and £30 for the insurance on Carter's private house, and
   (b) a payment of £750 for furniture for Carter's own house.
3. During the year Carter had paid business expenses of £600 through his separate private bank account.
4. Although no record of it is kept, Carter owns the retail shop, having purchased it on 1st July, 5 years ago for £12,000 and shop fixtures bought on the same date for £3,000. It is agreed that fair rates of depreciation are 5% per annum on cost for the shop and 10% per annum on cost for the fixtures.

Required:

(a) A detailed calculation of Carter's profit for the year ended 30th June 19_0.

(b) A statement of the financial position of his business at 30th June 19_0.

(A.E.B. "A" level)

EXERCISE 17.9

The following information has been taken from the incomplete records of B. Bates, at 31st May 19_4.

(a) Summarised bank account for the year ended 31st May 19_4.

	£		£
Cash banked	14,500	Commencing balance	200
		Rent and rates	500
		Light and heat	300
		Purchase of delivery vehicle	1,200
		Paid to suppliers	8,000
		Drawings	3,000
		Closing balance c/d	1,300
	14,500		14,500

(b) Sales during the year amounted to £14,200; trade debtors at 31st May 19_3 were £2,100 and a year later £1,400.

(c) Trade creditors at 31st May 19_3 were £1,000 and at 31st May 19_4 £2,200.

(d) The gross profit for the year under review was 25 per cent of the cost of sales.

(e) The stock in trade at 31st May 19_4, has been valued, at cost, at £1,060.

(f) All takings during the year ended 31st May 19_4, were banked with the exception of amounts used for the payment of sundry administrative and distribution expenses.

(g) Fixtures and fittings were valued at £3,000 at 31st May 19_3, and a year later at £2,800.

(h) A provision of £100 for depreciation for the year is to be made on the delivery vehicle.

Required:
A trading and profit and loss account for the year ended 31st May 19_4, and a balance sheet at that date.

CHAPTER 18

INCOME AND EXPENDITURE ACCOUNTS

You should, by now, be very familiar with the process of drawing up trading and profit and loss accounts and balance sheets at the end of a trader's financial year. This chapter is not going to ask you to learn something new because it is concerned simply with the profit and loss accounts and balance sheets of clubs and societies.

An "income and expenditure account" is nothing more than the *profit and loss account of a club* and, because you can already draw up profit and loss accounts of traders, you can therefore draw up income and expenditure accounts of clubs! Why the different title? Well, I think that the original idea was to make it comprehensible to club members, who may not know anything about accounts, but the real argument for not calling a club's "profit and loss account" a "profit and loss account" is that clubs and societies are not there to make profits and losses, although they may finish up with an "excess of income over expenditure" i.e. a profit! The whole argument, whatever it is, is ludicrous, as is the title of "income and expenditure account" for what is really a "profit and loss account". The purchase of a new sports pavilion for cash is *expenditure* (according to the dictionary), but would this item appear in the "income and expenditure account"? Certainly not, because it is capital expenditure! No wonder many club members never understand the Treasurer's Report!

Anyway, we are lumbered with this title, especially for examinations, whether we like it or not, but I want you to always *think* of it as "the profit and loss account of a club", and having completed your account, *then* insert the title to satisfy conventions. Also, having worked out your "net profit", try to remember to describe it as "excess of income over expenditure". This will keep everybody happy!

If it's a profit and loss account, then it is subject to the "rules" we know already. You debit it, not with what you have paid for rent, etc., but with what you *should* have paid for that period. Similarly you credit it, not with what you have received, but with what you *should* have received in that period. Any differences of course show on the balance sheet as either assets or liabilities.

A club or society will not normally need a trading account because they don't buy and sell – therefore there will be no gross profit figure to start off your "P and L account", which will consist simply of expenses on the debit side and gains on the credit side of the account. Most of the expenses you are familiar with for traders (e.g. rent, rates, wages, depreciation, etc. etc.) will apply equally to clubs, but the club is likely to have more types of gains than a trader would have – e.g. subscriptions, locker rents, fees paid by visiting teams, donations, etc.

A club will organise dances, raffles, bingo, socials, etc., and each of these will have its own expenses and income from sale of tickets, etc. The rule is that you only show in the P & L account the profit (on the credit side) or the loss (debit side) *on that particular function*. You do *not* show expenses for dance on the debit side and sale of tickets on the credit side – you show the final outcome only. This is so that members can see *at a glance* "profit on dance", "loss on social", etc.

If the club has a bar, then obviously this should make a profit! Only the profit is shown, as one item, on the credit (gains) side of the P & L account. However, in calculating that profit you could prepare a *Bar Trading Account* e.g.

Bar Trading Account

	£		£
Opening Stocks	2,000	Sales	18,000
Purchases	11,000		
	13,000		
Less Closing Stock	1,000		
Cost of Goods Sold	12,000		
Bar Wages	1,000		
Profit on Bar	5,000		
	18,000		18,000

Only the £5,000 profit would appear in your P & L account, but the examiner may well ask you to show a Bar Trading Account as a separate part of your answer. Note bar wages – this is an expense of the bar, not the club. The same would apply to bar cleaner's wages. Do remember, when calculating purchases, to take account of amounts owing to suppliers at the beginning and end of the year (prepare on rough paper a "creditors' summary account" if necessary).

Be *very* careful in calculating subscriptions due for the year. Prepare a "subscriptions account" on rough paper to find the missing figure, using the techniques described earlier in Chapter 9. For example: information given:

Subscriptions due at 1st January 19_4	£40
Subscriptions paid in advance at 1st January 19_4	£15
Subscriptions received during 19_4	£280
Subscriptions owing at 31st December 19_4	£55
Subscriptions paid in advance at 31st December 19_4	£10

Assume that unpaid subscriptions will eventually be paid.

How much is *due* for 19_4 – i.e. how much do we *credit* to P & L account for the year?

Answer

Subscriptions Account

		£			£
(1) Jan. 1	Balance b/d	40	Jan. 1	Balance b/d	15 (1)
(4) Dec. 31	*P & L a/c*	300	19_4	Cash	280 (3)
(2) Dec. 31	Balance c/d	10	Dec. 31	Balance c/d	55 (2)
		350			350
(2) Dec. 31	Balance b/d	55	Dec. 31	Balance b/d	10 (2)

Remember? Four items of information, but only three given to us – the fourth item becomes the "balancing" figure to the account. Refer back to Chapter 9. We are using *exactly* the same technique described there, and the only difference is that we have amounts owing to us *and* by us at the beginning and end of the year. If members have paid more than they need do – i.e. subscriptions in advance – then the club owes the members that amount at that date. Think carefully when dealing with subscriptions.

If the club allows a "one-off" payment by members for "life membership" then, because this receipt by the club does not relate solely to that particular period covered by the accounts, it is normally credited direct to capital account rather than to P & L account.

The balance sheet of a club is exactly the same as a trader's except that "capital" is sometimes described as "General Fund" or "Accumulated Fund".

In examination questions on this topic, much of the information is normally given by an extract of the cash book which is termed a "Receipts and Payments Account" (a sensible description, unlike the other!). Remember that the amounts shown in this account are amounts paid or received in the period in question, not necessarily the amounts *due* for the period.

Before we leave this very straightforward topic, remember to head your Profit and Loss account with the title "Income and Expenditure Account" (*but don't think in these terms*), and describe your "net profit" as "excess of income over expenditure", or, if a "loss", "excess of expenditure over income" (*but don't think in these terms – think* of "net profit" or "net loss" and be realistic!).

EXERCISE 18.1

The following information was prepared by the music society known as The Modern Melody Makers:

Balance Sheet as at 31st December 19_8

Liabilities	£	Assets	£
Accumulated Fund	5,000	Instruments at cost	4,500
New Instrument Fund	3,500	Music Stands	250
Members' subscriptions in advance	80	Investments	3,700
Secretary's expenses owing	155	Members' subscriptions due	170
Expenses owing to members	265	Balance at Bank	480
Insurance premium due	100		
	9,100		9,100

Receipts and Payments for year ended 31st December 19_9

	£		£
Members' subscriptions	540	Transport	840
Fees from concerts etc.	3,230	Upkeep of uniform	110
Sale of instruments	620	Rent of hall	440
Income from investments	270	Repairs to instruments	320
		Expenses of members	790
		Sheet music	95
		Insurance	200
		Secretary's expenses	385
		New instruments	1,150

Required:

(i) Prepare the Income and Expenditure account for the year ended 31st December 19_9, taking into account:
  (a) Rent owing – £40.
  (b) Cost of sheet music is treated as revenue expenditure.
  (c) Instruments are to be depreciated at 6% of their value at 1st January 19_9.
  (d) Subscriptions paid in advance were £90.
  (e) Subscriptions due amount to £210.
  (f) All subscriptions due at 31st December 19_9 were received during 19_0.
  (g) Expenses owing to members amount to £60.
  (h) The surplus is to be divided – £500 to the Instrument Fund and the remainder to the Accumulated Fund.

(ii) Set out the Balance Sheet as at 31st December 19_9.

(London Chamber of Commerce)

EXERCISE 18.2

The following items represented the assets and liabilities of Humberstone Fishing Club as at 1st April 19_9:

balance at bank, £4,320, subscriptions owing from year 19_8/9 £170, boats £42,000, boat equipment £5,500, boatyard premises £25,000, club-house premises £20,000, diesel oil stocks £2,500, heating and lighting owing £170.

The club met for social activities, but their main purpose was off-shore fishing in the North Sea. For the financial year ended 31st March 19_0 the following information was available on their activities:

Receipts	£	*Payments*	£
Balance	4,320	Purchase of new diesel engine for a boat and a complete re-fit (to be capitalised)	3,750
Subscriptions	8,200	Expenses of annual dinner-dance	1,530
From bingo evenings	7,570	Expenses of bingo evenings	3,950
Annual dinner-dance	1,250	Heating and lighting	1,150
Fish sales to members	5,700	Maintenance costs for boats	3,500
From insurance company	4,800	Insurance premiums	1,100
		Miscellaneous expenses	170
		Diesel oil purchases	7,300
		Balance	9,390

Additional information:

(a) The insurance receipt was in respect of a boat lost at sea during the year. (Book value at 1st April 19_9 £5,600.)
(b) Stock of diesel oil at 31st March 19_0 was £1,700.
(c) Amounts owing at 31st March 19_0 were:

heating and lighting	£350
diesel oil	£375

(d) There were no subscriptions in advance or in arrears at 31st March 19_0.
(c) All receipts and payments were passed through the club's bank account.

Required:
(a) A calculation of the capital fund as at 1st April 19_9.
(b) An income and expenditure account for the year ended 31st March 19_0 clearly showing the profit/loss on the bingo evenings and the annual dinner-dance.
(c) A balance sheet as at 31st March 19_0.

(A.E.B. "O" level)

EXERCISE 18.3

The following Trial Balance was extracted from the books of the Evergreen Social Club at the close of business on 31st May 19_1.

	DR	CR
	£	£
Bar Stocks 1st June 19_0	640	
Bar Purchases and Sales	2,950	4,760
Salary of Secretary	700	
Wages of Staff	2,190	
Rates and Insurance	580	
Accumulated Fund 1st June 19_0		5,680
Club Premises	5,200	
Club Furniture and Fixtures	860	
Postages and Telephone	230	
Cash at Bank	420	
Cash in Hand	30	
Subscriptions received		3,770
Sundry expenses	270	
Lighting and Heating	450	
Income from Social events		310
	14,520	14,520

NOTES:

1. Bar Stocks 31st May 19_1 – £810.
2. At 31st May 19_1, subscriptions in arrears amounted to £20. No subscriptions had been paid in advance.
3. Provide for depreciation of Furniture and Fixtures – £60.
4. One third of lighting and heating and one third of wages are to be debited to the Bar Trading Account.

Required:
Prepare the Bar Trading Account and General Income and Expenditure Account for the year ended 31st May 19_1, together with a Balance Sheet as on that date.

(London Chamber of Commerce)

EXERCISE 18.4

The following is a list of the receipts and payments made by the treasurer of the Mayfield Social Club during the year ended 31st May 19_1:

	£
Balance at bank 1st June 19_0	850
Subscriptions received during year	1,200
Profit on sale of refreshments	410
Proceeds of whist drives and dances	175
Rent of hall paid during year	220
Purchase of new games equipment (regarded as revenue expenditure)	210
Cleaners' wages	520
Heating and lighting payments	175
Secretarial expenses	500
Purchase of new furniture	400

The following items are due for the year ended 31st May 19_1 but have not yet been paid:

Rent of hall for one month	20
An electricity account for lighting	25

You are to prepare:

(a) the Mayfield Social Club's Receipts and Payments Account for the year ended 31st May 19_1;
(b) the Mayfield Social Club's Income and Expenditure Account for the year ended 31st May 19_1.

(Royal Society of Arts)

EXERCISE 18.5

The following receipts and payments account for the year ended 31st October 19_0 has been prepared from the current account bank statements of the Country Cousins Sports Club:

		£			£
19_9 Nov 1	Balance b/fwd.	1,700	19_0 Oct 31	Clubhouse:	
19_0 Oct 31	Subscriptions	8,600		Rates and insurance	380
	Bar takings	13,800		Decorations and repairs	910
	Donations	1,168		Annual dinner –	
	Annual dinner – Sale of tickets	470		Catering	650
				Bar purchases	9,200
				Stationery and printing	248
				New sports equipment	2,463
				Hire of films	89
				Warden's salary	4,700
				Petty cash	94
				Balance c/fwd.	7,004
		25,738			25,738

The following additional information has been given:

At 31st October	19_9	19_0
	£	£
Clubhouse, at cost	15,000	15,000
Bar stocks, at cost	1,840	2,360
Petty cash float	30	10
Bank deposit account	600	730
Subscriptions received in advance	210	360
Creditors for bar supplies	2,400	1,900

It has been decided to provide for depreciation annually on the clubhouse at the rate of 10% of cost and on the new sports equipment at the rate of $33\frac{1}{3}$% of cost.

The petty cash float is used exclusively for postages.

The only entry in the bank deposit account during the year ended 31st October 19_0 concerns interest.

One-quarter of the warden's salary and one-half of the clubhouse costs, including depreciation, are to be apportioned to the bar.

The donations received during the year ended 31st October 19_0 are for the new coaching bursary fund which will be utilised for the provision of training facilities for promising young sportsmen and sportswomen. It is expected to make the first award during 19_1.

Required:

(a) An account showing the profit or loss for the year ended 31st October 19_0 on the operation of the bar.

(b) An Income and Expenditure Account for the year ended 31st October 19_0 and a Balance Sheet at that date for the Country Cousins Sports Club.

(A.C.C.A.)

EXERCISE 18.6

The following Receipts and Payments account and other information have been supplied by the treasurer of the Tuff Road Rugby Club for the year ended 31st August 19_8.

	Receipts	£	£		*Payments*	£	£
19_7				19_8			
Sept. 1	Balances at bank			Aug. 31	Groundsman's salary		2,700
	Current account	450			Rent, rates, insurances		1,840
	Deposit account	700			Repairs to pavilion		425
		—	1,150		Petty cash		75
19_8					New rugby equipment		500
Aug. 31	Subscriptions		9,230		Travelling expenses		2,870
	Bar takings		15,510		Printing & stationery		560
	Collections at matches		1,280		Cash register		400
	Donations		5,000		Bar purchases		11,730
	Interest on deposit account		480		Balances at bank		
					Current account	4,250	
					Deposit account	7,300	
						—	11,550
			32,650				32,650

Other information is as follows:

	Aug. 31 19_7 £	Aug. 31 19_8 £
Club Pavilion, cost £16,000 depreciated by 5% annually	4,800	4,000
Bar stocks at cost	1,250	960
Amount due for bar purchases	850	1,910
Amount due for subscriptions	460	720
Subscriptions received in advance	40	55
Petty cash float	30	15

(i) The donations are the result of an appeal for funds to build an extension to the club premises, and the proceeds have been placed on Deposit account.

(ii) Petty cash expenditure is mainly on postal expenses.

(iii) It is the club's policy to write off the cost of rugby equipment as soon as it is purchased. The cash register is to be depreciated by 25%.

(iv) Collections made at matches go towards meeting the revenue expenses of the club.

Required:

(a) An account to show the profit or loss on the bar for the year to 31st August 19_8.

(b) The Club's Income and Expenditure account for the year to 31st August 19_8.

(c) A Balance Sheet at 31st August 19_8.

(A.E.B. "A" level)

EXERCISE 18.7

The Greenfinger Gardeners' Club is a member of the Countryside Gardeners' Federation. The annual subscription payable by member clubs to the federation is 5% of the total subscription income plus 5% of any profit (or less any loss) arising from the sale of seeds and fertilisers for the preceding year.

The receipts and payments account for the year ended 31st December 19_8 of the Greenfingers Gardeners' Club is as follows:

	£		£
Balance at 1st January 19_8	196	Purchase of seeds and fertilisers	1,640
Subscriptions received	1,647	Cost of visit to research centre	247
Sale of tickets for visit to research		Purchase of garden equipment	738
centre	232	Repairs to garden equipment	302
Sale of seeds and fertilisers	1,928	Annual garden show:	
Annual garden show:		Hire of marquee	364
Sale of tickets	829	Prizes	650
Competition fees	410	Balance at 31st December 19_8	1,301
	5,242		5,242

The following additional information is given:

At 31st December	19_7	19_8
	£	£
Subscriptions due and unpaid	164	83
Subscriptions prepaid	324	248
Sale of seeds and fertilisers – debtors	220	424
Purchase of seeds and fertilisers – creditors	804	547
Stocks of seeds and fertilisers – at cost	261	390

Required:
A computation of the membership subscription for 19_9 payable by the Greenfinger Gardeners' Club to the Countryside Gardeners' Federation.

(A.C.C.A.)

EXERCISE 18.8

The treasurer of the Warrington Social Club has prepared the following receipts and payments account for the year ended 30th September 19_1.

19_0		£	19_1		£
Oct. 1	Balance b/d	6,000	Sept. 30	Bar purchases	2,960
	Subscriptions	4,400		Dance expenses	2,000
	Bar receipts	4,500		General expenses	4,750
	Miscellaneous receipts	1,450		Groundsman's salary	5,700
	Dance receipts	4,100		Resurfacing of snooker tables	1,800
				Repairs	370
				Balance c/d	2,870
		20,450			20,450
19_1					
Oct. 1	Balance b/d	2,870			

The following information is also available:

	Sept. 30 19_0 £	Sept. 30 19_1 £
Premises at cost	15,000	15,000
Bar stocks at cost	480	550
Bar purchases owing	310	420
Subscriptions owing	20	100
Subscriptions prepaid	60	80
General expenses owing	170	210
Equipment, cost £5,000, depreciated by 10% on cost per annum	2,000	?

The snooker tables are resurfaced regularly every 5 years and were resurfaced on 1st October 19_0. The cost of resurfacing is treated as capital expenditure.

Required:

(a) The club's income and expenditure account for the year ended 30th September 19_1 showing clearly the profit on bar sales.

(b) A balance sheet as at 30th September 19_1.

EXERCISE 18.9

Bamford Cricket Club treasurer reported the following financial details on the club as on 30th September 19_9.

Clubhouse premises £15,000, fixtures and equipment £6,500, bank £4,650, subscriptions owing for 19_8/_9 £130, travelling expenses owing £55, bar stocks £1,800, capital fund £28,025.

During the first week of October 19_9, the clubhouse premises were burnt down and were declared of no value. An estimated £5,000 of the club's fixtures and equipment were also destroyed. Both the clubhouse, and fixtures and equipment were underinsured. The following amounts were received from the insurance company:

Premises	£5,000
Fixtures and equipment	£2,000

The club decided to raise new funds as soon as possible, by holding weekly bingo sessions. The proceeds would help to finance the building of new premises and the buying of new equipment.

The following financial information was available on the club's activities for the year ended 30th September 19_0.

	Bank		Bank
	£		£
Balance	4,650	Travelling expenses	860
Bar sales	16,750	New equipment	7,000
Subscriptions _8/_9	130	Ground rent	1,250
,, _9/_0	5,540	Heating and lighting	350
,, _0/_1	250	Postages and stationery	59
Receipts from bingo evenings	20,000	Rent of premises for bingo	450
Insurance receipts	7,000	Bingo callers' wages	2,500
Bingo prize money given back to the club	800	Bar purchases	7,840
		Bingo printing expenses	750
Balance	2,939	Payments to contractors	
		New premises	23,000
		New fixtures	6,500
		Bingo prize payments	7,500
	58,059		58,059

(a) At 30th September 19_0 £4,000 was still owing to the contractors for the club's new premises.
(b) Bar stocks were £1,300 as at 30th September 19_0.
(c) The club's bank had agreed overdraft facilities.

Required:

For the year ended 30th September 19_0:
1. a profit/loss statement on the bingo activities,
2. an income and expenditure account clearly showing the profit/loss on each separate activity,
3. a balance sheet as at 30th September 19_0.

(A.E.B. "O" level)

CHAPTER 19

MANUFACTURING ACCOUNTS

So far we have been dealing with the accounts of traders (except for clubs in the last chapter) and we have assumed that goods have been bought by a trader to be sold in exactly the same state, at a profit. The trading accounts of our traders have been concerned solely with the buying and selling of *finished goods.*

Now we are going to look at the manufacturer's accounts—the person who actually *makes* the finished goods from various raw materials. Obviously when he has made the goods, he is going to sell them, perhaps to a wholesaler or direct to the retailer, so he will still need a trading account and a profit and loss account like all the traders we have looked at so far. The *only* difference will be that he is not *purchasing* goods to sell—he is *manufacturing* goods to sell. Therefore, in place of "purchases" in his trading account he will show instead the *cost to him* of manufacturing those finished goods, and the difference between this figure and his sales figure (allowing of course for unsold stocks) will be his gross profit, e.g.

DR Trading and Profit and Loss Account of a Manufacturer CR

	£		£
Opening Stock of Finished Goods	6,000	Sales	30,000
Cost of Manufacturer of goods	20,000		
	26,000		
Less Closing Stock of Finished Goods	4,000		
Cost of Goods Sold	22,000		
Gross Profit c/d	8,000		
	30,000		30,000
(Profit and Loss account dealt with as usual)	—	Gross Profit b/d	8,000

Presumably his cost of manufacture is less than he would have to pay if he bought the goods in a finished state from another manufacturer – if not he is wasting his time!

How does he calculate the cost of manufacture of the finished units? He prepares at the year end a *"Manufacturing Account"* to immediately precede his "Trading Account", and this manufacturing account simply shows his manufacturing costs ("stored up" in nominal accounts throughout the year), the final total being brought down to his Trading Account as "Cost of Manufacture". Before we look closer at this account, what manufacturing expenses will he incur? The main expenses of any manufacturing are materials and labour (together known as "prime cost"). Other manufacturing expenses are power, factory light heat and rates, depreciation of machinery, etc., etc. – any expense connected directly to the *factory* (not the warehouse or office).

The total of these expenses will eventually be transferred to the debit side of trading account (see above), but as the trading account is only concerned with the cost of manufacture of *finished* goods (which can be sold), an adjustment will have to be made in the manufacturing account for goods which are in between the raw material stage and the finished goods stage – i.e. partly finished goods or *work-in-progress*.

Let us study an actual manufacturing account and see how each item "fits in":

DR Manufacturing Account for year ended ...... CR

	£		£
Opening stock of Raw Materials	4,000	Cost of Manufacture of Finished Goods c/d to Trading Account	55,000
Purchases of Raw Materials	28,000		
Carriage Inwards on Raw Materials	500		
	32,500		
Less Closing Stock of Raw Materials	2,500		
Raw Materials Used	30,000		
Manufacturing Wages	14,000		
PRIME COST	44,000		
Indirect Costs			
Power	1,500		
Light and Heat	1,000		
Rent and Rates	1,250		
Depreciation of Machinery	750		
Indirect labour	6,000		
Cost of Manufacture of Finished and Unfinished Goods	54,500		
Opening Stocks of Work-in-Progress	2,000		
	56,500		
Less Closing Stocks of Work-in-Progress	1,500		
Cost of Manufacture of Finished Goods	55,000		55,000

NOTE: All the costs of manufacture are on the debit side of the account – the double-entry (i.e. the credits) to these will be in the nominal accounts described, as their totals are transferred at the year end to manufacturing account. The same principle exactly as with the expenses in the P & L account. The total costs of manufacture of *finished goods* is transferred from the manufacturing account (credit entry to "clear it") to the debit side of trading account in the place where "purchases" would normally appear.

The figure for "raw materials used" (£30,000) represents the raw materials in hand at the start of the year, *plus* the purchases of raw materials during the year, *less* those which haven't been used at the end of the year – i.e. those *used.* Carriage inwards on purchases of raw materials is, of course, an additional cost of purchases.

The manufacturing wages are those wages *directly* connected with the production process, and these, together with the materials used make up the *main* cost of production – i.e. the *prime* cost.

The "indirect costs" need no explanation, except perhaps the indirect labour cost of £6,000. This represents the labour costs of those people not *directly* connected with the actual production process – e.g. foremen, messengers, cleaners, maintenance engineers, "general" help, etc.

The sub-total of £54,500 is the cost of *all* production in the period – the making of finished units (ready for sale) *and* the making of partly finished units (not yet ready for sale). The trading account is only concerned with *finished* goods, and this account compares the cost of such goods with the selling price, to produce a gross profit figure. There is therefore no point in transferring £54,500 to trading account, because part of this figure represents goods which are not yet ready for selling and which must therefore remain in the factory. Hence the final adjustment for these partly-finished goods in the manufacturing account. Having added the opening stock of work-in-progress and deducted the closing stocks, (the normal procedure for any stocks, which you are already familiar with) we are left with a figure of £55,000 representing the cost of manufacture of *finished goods only*. This can now be transferred to Trading Account.

Try to think of the final accounts of a manufacturer as follows: (see opposite).

NOTE: The finished goods, produced in the factory, are then transferred to the warehouse for selling. The goods have left the factory, and if not sold will remain in the warehouse (i.e. Trading Account) until they *are* sold.

If you are ever unsure as to *where* to place an expense then think – "is

Manufacturing, Trading and Profit & Loss Account for year ending . . . .

		£		£
Manufacturing a/c i.e. "The Factory"	Opening Stock of Raw Materials	x	Cost of Manufacture of Finished Goods c/d to Trading Account	x
	Purchases of Raw Mat.	x		
		X		
	Less Closing Stock of Raw Materials	x		
	Raw Materials Consumed	X		
	Manufacturing Wages	x		
	PRIME COST	X		
	Indirect Costs	x		
		X		
	Opening Stock of Work-in-Progress	x		
		X		
	Less Closing Stock of Work-in-Progress	x		
		X		X
Trading a/c i.e. "The Warehouse"	Opening Stock of Finished Goods	x	Sales	x
	Cost of Manufacture b/d	x		
		X		
	Less Closing Stock of Finished Goods	x		
	Cost of Goods Sold	X		
	Gross Profit c/d	x		
		X		X
Profit & Loss a/c i.e. "The Office"	Various Expenses including depreciation of office furniture, etc.	x	Gross Profit b/d	x
			Various Gains	x
	Net Profit	x		
		X		X

it an expense of manufacture, or is it an expense which would be incurred whether the owner was a manufacturer or not?" If the former, debit Manufacturing Account; if the latter, debit profit and loss account. For example, bank charges, advertising, office salaries, etc., are incurred by traders *and* manufacturers – they are not expenses *peculiar* to manufacturers only – therefore they are a P & L account expense. Depreciation of a factory asset is charged to manufacturing account whilst depreciation of an office asset is charged to P & L account.

Obviously, the balance sheet of a manufacturer will be the same as a normal trader. The only difference will be that the manufacturer will show under the heading of "current assets", *three* types of stock rather than one – i.e. stock of raw materials, stock of work-in-progress, and stock of finished goods. Everything else will be the same.

EXERCISE 19.1

The following information was extracted from the accounts of Jimbo Ltd., manufacturers, as at 30th June 19_1. Prepare Manufacturing, Trading and Profit and Loss accounts for the year ended 30th June 19_1. Show clearly the cost of materials used, prime cost, factory cost of goods completed and the cost of goods sold.

	£
Stocks at 1st July 19_0	
Raw Materials at cost	5,900
Finished Goods (at factory cost)	5,400
Purchases for year to 30th June 19_1	
Raw Materials	129,500
Other Factory Materials (indirect)	4,100
Direct Wages	40,300
Factory Fuel and Power	2,800
Heating and lighting of which amount ¾ is chargeable to Factory, ¼ to office	1,600
Fire Insurance, of which amount ½ is chargeable to Factory, ½ to office	1,800
Rent and Rates of Factory	4,500
Rent and Rates of Office	1,500
Factory Salaries	7,000
Sundry expenses and Advertising	5,200
Office salaries	4,000
Provision for bad debts	220
Depreciation: Factory machinery	8,000
Office furniture	700
Sales	265,000

On 30th June, 19_1, the following valuations were made of stocks:

	£
Raw Materials at cost	8,300
Finished goods (at factory cost)	5,600

In addition you are given the following information:
The provision for bad debts to be increased to £320.
£350 was owing at 30th June 19_1, for office rent.

EXERCISE 19.2

Mr R. Reed owns a small workshop in which he manufactures cricket bats in two qualities, 5 star and 3 star. The following information is provided from his records for the year to 31st March 19_2.

	£
Stocks at 1st April 19_1:	
Raw materials	3,860
Finished goods 5 star	1,225
3 star	3,200
Purchases of raw materials	124,514
Carriage on raw materials	320
Workshop wages 5 star	16,000
3 star	48,000
Workshop light and heat	1,300
Workshop general expenses	800
Workshop rent and rates	1,800
Raw materials returned to suppliers	480
Sales 5 star	100,000
3 star	200,000
Stocks at 31st March 19_2:	
Raw materials	1,320
Finished goods 5 star	594
3 star	2,125

Workshop records show that, of the raw materials consumed in production in the year ended 31st March 19_2, £50,894 was used in the production of 5 star and the remainder in the production of 3 star. All workshop costs not allocated are to be apportioned one quarter to the production of 5 star and three-quarters to the production of 3 star.

Required:
For the year ended 31st March 19_2:

(a) a manufacturing account showing clearly the prime cost and the factory cost of goods manufactured for each grade of the product;
(b) a trading account for each grade of the product;
(c) a brief explanation of the significance of the factory cost of goods manufactured.

(A.E.B. "O" level)

EXERCISE 19.3

Arthur Piece, an engineer, ran a manufacturing business, but he did not keep proper books of account. He was able to provide the following information on his activities for the year ended 30th June 19_9.

	£
Balances as at 1st July 19_8	
Creditors for raw materials	15,000
Debtors for finished units	22,500
Stock of finished units	27,000
Maintenance wages owing	1,000
Payments:	
To creditors for raw materials	60,000
Direct manufacturing wages	31,500
Factory heating and lighting	2,500
Factory maintenance wages	12,000
Factory rent and rates	2,000
Direct manufacturing expenses	4,000
Repairs to manufacturing machinery	5,000
Receipts:	
From debtors for finished units sold	196,000
Balances as at 30th June 19_9	
Creditors for raw materials	20,000
Debtors for finished units	20,500
Stock of finished units	31,000

The finished units produced during the year were transferred to the warehouse at factory cost. There was no work-in-progress.

Of the raw materials purchased during the year, nine-tenths were consumed by the factory. There was no opening stock of raw materials.

Depreciation on machinery for the year was estimated to be £9,500.

Required:

For the year ended 30th June 19_9, prepare

(a) a manufacturing account showing clearly **prime cost** and **factory cost** of goods produced;

(b) a trading account.

(A.E.B. "O" level)

EXERCISE 19.4

Carpenters Ltd. manufacture two wooden products *viz* wheelbarrows and step ladders.

The following figures relate to the year ended 31st December 19_7:

	Wheel-barrows £		*Step ladders* £
Sales during year	44,000		33,000
Timber used	7,000		3,500
Nuts, bolts and metal fittings	150		200
Direct wages	14,000		7,000
		£	
Factory power		6,000	
Factory indirect wages		1,500	
Factory rates		3,000	
Administration expenses		14,000	
Selling expenses		7,000	

Prepare an account in COLUMNAR form to show the PRIME COST, THE COST OF PRODUCTION and the NET PROFIT for each item.

Factory expenses are to be apportioned to each item in the ratio of timber used and the other expenses in the ratio of sales.

(University of London "O" level)

EXERCISE 19.5

J. Smallpiece is the owner of a factory. The following trial balance was extracted from his books on 31st March 19_8:

	£ (000's)	£ (000's)
Capital J. Smallpiece 1st April 19_7		50
Loan from T. Smallpiece 1st April 19_7		20
Premises	50	
Machinery and plant at cost	20	
Furniture and fittings at cost	4	
Stocks: Finished goods	6	
Work in progress	nil	
Raw materials	5	
Debtors and creditors	8	6
Balance at bank and cash in hand	3	
Purchases of raw materials	44	
Sales of finished goods		100
Factory wages (direct)	20	
(indirect)	4	
Office salaries	3	
Office expenses	2	
Rates	4	
Machinery and plant maintenance	2	
Cleaning, etc.	4	
Provision for depreciation:		
Machinery and plant		10
Furniture and fittings		3
Drawings	10	
	189	189

The following are to be taken into consideration:

(a) Stocks 31st March 19_8:

	£
Raw materials	4,000
Work in progress	1,000
Finished goods	7,000

(b) Cleaning and rates are to be charged in the proportion of $\frac{3}{4}$ to the factory, $\frac{1}{4}$ to the office.

(c) Interest on loan to be 10% per annum.

(d) Depreciation of machinery and plant by 10% on cost and furniture and fittings by 25% on cost.

Prepare a Manufacturing Account, Trading Account and Profit and Loss Account for the year ended 31st March 19_8 and a Balance Sheet on that date.

(University of London "O" level)

CHAPTER 20

PARTNERSHIP ACCOUNTS

A partnership is defined by the Partnership Act of 1890 as "two or more persons carrying on business with a view to profit". A partnership can be set up with the absolute minimum of formalities and at no cost, but it is obviously desirable for a legal agreement to be drawn up at the outset to make it quite clear what the powers of each partner are, and what proportion of profits each partner is entitled to, or, if losses occur, is liable for.

The accounts of a partnership business (the firm) are kept exactly the same as a sole trader's, and the year end manufacturing (where relevant), trading and profit and loss accounts and balance sheet are prepared in exactly the same way. However, because we now have two, or more, owners of the business we will have two or more capital accounts, one for each partner, showing what capital each has contributed. These capital accounts will be headed with the name of the particular partner and at the year end they will be credited with that partner's share of the profits, or debited with his share of the losses, and will be debited with that partner's drawings. Obviously there will be a separate drawings account kept for each partner, which will be transferred at the year end to that partner's capital account.

The *only* additional requirement in keeping partnership accounts is an *extension* to the profit and loss account, to show clearly how the net profit or loss is divided between the respective partners. With a sole trader we simply take the net profit figure direct to the credit of the sole trader's capital account, but with a partnership this profit needs to be "split up" to show who gets what. This sharing of profits, or losses, is called **"appropriation"** – appropriating the profit amongst the partners.

How is profit appropriated? Two partners, X and Y, may agree that they will share profits and losses equally, but partner X may feel that because he does more work in the business, or has more expertise, than Y, then he should get more of the profits than Y. The obvious answer is for both to agree on a sharing of profits in the proportions of, say $\frac{2}{3}$ to X, $\frac{1}{3}$ to Y, but another answer is for them to share profits equally *after* allowing a "salary" to X of, say, £1,000 per annum. Therefore, out of the net profit available (shown in the Profit and Loss account), £1,000 will *firstly* be appropriated to X, and whatever profit is then left over will be shared equally between them both.

If Y has contributed £20,000 capital to the business and X only £15,000, then Y may feel that he wants compensating for his extra personal outlay, on the basis that this extra money contributed could have been earning interest for him on a personal investment. Again, the obvious way to allow for this would be to let Y have a greater share of the profits by agreeing on an appropriate profit sharing ratio. The only snag with this is, that in a year when losses are incurred, Y would have to bear a larger portion of that loss! The answer is for the partners to agree to allow interest of so much per cent on their capital contributed. This interest would come out of the net profit figure (together with any agreed salaries) *before* a final appropriation (sharing) of the profit left, according to the agreed profit sharing ratios.

In the example of X and Y therefore, it could be agreed that they will share profits and losses equally *after* allowing a salary of £1,000 to X and after allowing interest on capital of say, 10% to each partner. In this way, all is fair to all. X will get his salary for "expertise" and Y will get more interest on his capital than X will.

These appropriations of profits are not paid to the respective partners in cash. Instead, they are made "available" to the partners by credits to their capital accounts at each year end, (just like the sole trader's capital account being credited with the whole of the net profit). Whatever part of these profits are taken away from the business is shown as drawings, on the debit side of their capital accounts. How do these various appropriations of profit find their way to the credit side of the capital accounts? By direct transfer from Profit and Loss account, by the use of an "extension" to the Profit and Loss account we know so well. This extension is called the *profit and loss appropriation account*, *viz*:

Trading and Profit and Loss Account for year ended 31st December 19_7
(Trading account as usual)

DR		CR	
	£		£
Various expenses	8,000	Gross Profit b/d	20,000
Net Profit c/d to Appropriation a/c	12,000		
	20,000		20,000
Salary – X	1,000	Net Profit b/d	12,000
Interest of Capital			
X	1,500		
Y	2,000		
Share of Profits			
X	3,750		
Y	3,750		
	12,000		12,000

NOTE: the net profit is calculated in the Profit and Loss account as usual, and is then carried down to the other side of the Profit and Loss Appropriation account. The debits then show *how* this £12,000 of available profit is appropriated, (shared), amongst the partners. Once the salary and interest on capital has been appropriated (total £4,500) there is £7,500 *left*, to be shared according to agreed ratios, in this case equal.

The double-entry for every debit is a credit in the respective partner's capital account – i.e. those amounts are made available to the partners for them to draw out, if they wish, for personal use.

Note that these are *appropriations* of the £12,000 profit available. If there were *no profits* there would be *no appropriations!* The crediting of salaries, of partners' interest on capital, etc. is dependent on there being enough profits – no profits, no salary, interest or anything for the partners. The total salaries and wages of *employees* in the firm appear in the Profit and Loss account itself (so reducing net profit or increasing net loss), because these are *not* appropriations of profit – they are *charges* against profits which *must* be paid whether profits are made or not. Anything due to partners must come out of the final net profit, if any, and is therefore dependent on there being a net profit to appropriate to them.

The capital accounts may now look like this:

DR Capital Account – X CR

19_7		£	*19_7*		£
Dec. 31	Drawings	6,000	Jan. 1	Balance b/d	15,000
			Dec. 31	P & L a/c (Salary)	1,000
			Dec. 31	P & L a/c (Interest)	1,500
			Dec. 31	P & L a/c	
Dec. 31	Balance c/d	15,250		(Share of Profits)	3,750
		21,250			21,250
			Dec. 31	Balance b/d	15,250

DR Capital Account – Y CR

19_7		£	*19_7*		£
Dec. 31	Drawings	5,000	Jan. 1	Balance b/d	20,000
			Dec. 31	P & L a/c (Interest)	2,000
			Dec. 31	P & L a/c	
Dec. 31	Balance c/d	20,750		(Share of Profits)	3,750
		25,750			25,750
			Dec. 31	Balance b/d	20,750

NOTE: the total year's drawings for each partner have been transferred from the respective partner's drawings accounts, which have recorded the drawings as they took place to give totals at the year end. Both partners have judged the earnings of profits pretty well as they have both drawn almost exactly what the business has made available to them at the year end.

On the balance sheet there will be two capital account balances to show and, as with the sole trader, it is usual to show a "breakdown", *viz*:

Balance Sheet of X and Y as at 31st December, 19_7

Liabilities	£	£	*Assets*	£
CAPITAL ACCOUNTS				
X Balance at 1.1._7	15,000			
Add Salary	1,000			
Interest on Capital	1,500			
Share of Profits	3,750			
	21,250			
Less Drawings	6,000	15,250		
Y Balance at 1.1._7	20,000			
Add Interest on Capital	2,000			
Share of Profits	3,750			
	25,750			
Less Drawings	5,000	20,750		

Note how the final balance of each partner stands out clearly.

USE OF CURRENT ACCOUNTS

In the above example, X had £6,250 of profits made available to him in total, of which he has "taken away" £6,000. He could now have the odd £250, if he wanted, but he should *not* take any more than this, otherwise he will be taking away part of the original £15,000 of capital he contributed to the business as *permanent* capital, which the business presumably needs in order to operate. He is only allowed to take this capital, or part of it, away, with the agreement of the other partners, or on retirement, or of course on the dissolution (ending) of the business. In other words, he is only supposed to draw what is made available to him through profits – in this example a maximum drawing of £6,250.

It is usual to keep the partners' permanent capital *separate* from their share of profits available for drawing (i.e. from salaries, interest on capital, etc.), and this is achieved by each partner having two accounts – a **Capital Account** and a **Current Account**.

The Capital account "holds" the original capital contributed to the business by that partner when he "joined" the partnership, and the only other entries that will ever be made in that account will be if he introduces more new capital (either to help the business over a difficult period or to allow expansion of the business), or if he withdraws some of his permanent capital with the agreement of the other partners, or if he retires and takes his capital away from the business.

The partners entitlement to shares of the profits each year by way of salary, interest on capital and share of remaining profits is appropriated to the credit of the partners' *current* accounts (debit profit and loss appropriation account – credit current account), and the drawings for the year are debited to the respective current accounts. In this way, any credit balance on current account at any time will represent what is available for personal drawings. As the capital is being kept quite separate there is no danger of permanent capital being taken away from the firm by drawings.

Should a partner draw more from his current account than he has in it, the account will obviously show a debit balance – an asset to the firm in that the partner now owes *to the firm* the amount by which his drawings exceed what has been made available to him by the business. This should ideally be made good by a cash payment by the partner to the firm, to clear the debit balance.

The use of capital and current accounts can be likened to someone receiving, say, a £50,000 inheritance, who goes along to the bank and says that he only wants to be able to draw the *interest* from this investment, so leaving the original £50,000 intact. The bank would open a capital account to which the £50,000 would be credited (and left there!), and the yearly interest would be credited by the bank to that person's *current* account (day-to-day account) which could be drawn according to the investor's requirements. Any credit balance on current account would represent "drawable earnings" whilst any debit balance would represent "overdrawings" of earnings which must be repaid.

A partnership's capital and current accounts operate in the same way, the earnings credited to current account being appropriations of profits.

In the above example of X and Y, the Profit and Loss Appropriation Account would be identical to the one shown, but the corresponding credits would be in the partners' *current* accounts rather than their capital accounts, *viz*:

Capital A/c – X

	19_7		
	Jan. 1	Balance b/d	£15,000

Capital A/c – Y

			19_7		
			Jan. 1	Balance b/d	£20,000

Current A/c – X

19_7		£	*19_7*		£
Dec. 31	Drawings	6,000	Dec. 31	P & L a/c (Salary)	1,000
Dec. 31	Balance c/d	250	Dec. 31	P & L a/c (Interest)	1,500
			Dec. 31	P & L a/c (Share of Profits)	3,750
		6,250			6,250
			Dec. 31	Balance b/d	250

Current A/c – Y

19_7		£	*19_7*		£
Dec. 31	Drawings	5,000	Dec. 31	P & L a/c (Interest)	2,000
Dec. 31	Balance c/d	750	Dec. 31	P & L a/c (Share of Profits)	3,750
		5,750			5,750
			Dec. 31	Balance b/d	750

Now X and Y can see, *at a glance*, that they still have £250 and £750 available to them respectively from past profits. If either decide that they will *leave* that amount in the firm to "help it out", then the amount should be transferred to Capital account to become part of permanent capital (debit Current Account – credit Capital account). Otherwise the balances remain on current account for future drawings if required.

Any interest on capital agreed upon, is of course calculated on the *capital* account balances.

The appropriate balance sheet would now appear: (see opposite)

The *whole* picture at a glance!

In an examination you will be given instructions, or it will be obvious, as to whether current accounts are to be used. Usually they are, but some questions indicate that everything is to go through the capital accounts.

INTEREST ON DRAWINGS

The partners usually draw money from the firm at regular intervals throughout the year to cover their *personal* expenses, and these are

Balance Sheet of X and Y as at 31st December 19_7

Liabilities	£	*Assets*	£
CAPITAL ACCOUNTS			
X			15,000
Y			20,000
			35,000
CURRENT ACCOUNTS			
X Balance at 1.1._7	—		
Add Salary	1,000		
Interest on Capital	1,500		
Share of Profits	3,750		
	6,250		
Less Drawings	6,000		
			250
Y Balance at 1.1._7	—		
Add Interest on Capital	2,000		
Share of Profits	3,750		
	5,750		
Less Drawings	5,000		750
			36,000

recorded in their drawings accounts as they happen. In doing this the partner is assuming that the firm is making profits as the year "ticks along" – if it isn't, then he will finish up with a large debit balance on his current account at the year end!

Some firms try to "discourage" the partners drawing money (profits) too early in the year, because whilst the firm has possession of this money it can be using it to its own advantage. This discouragement is achieved by *charging* the partners *interest* on their drawings, calculated as so much per cent *per annum*. This means that, assuming a year end of 31st December, if a partner draws £1,000 on 31st March he will then be charged x% of £1,000 for 9 months (i.e. up to the year end). If he can hold off his personal spending of this £1,000 until 31st October, then he will only be charged x% of £1,000 for 2 months.

This interest on drawings is obviously a gain to the firm (interest *received*) for the benefit of the partners overall, and as such, it should be *added* to the amount of profit available for appropriation to the partners, at the same time being charged to the partners who incurred the interest charge. This means that whilst a partner will be charged (i.e. a debit to his current account) with the interest he has incurred, he will get some of this charge back again through the increase in the firm's available profit, of which he will get a share! A simple example:

Profit and Loss Appropriation Account

	£		£
Share of Profits		Net Profit b/d	8,000
Smith	4,300	*Interest on Drawings*	
Jones	4,300	Smith	400
		Jones	200
	8,600		8,600

NOTE: Assuming no salaries or interest on capital agreed on, and the partners sharing profits and losses equally, Smith has had his current account debited by £400 – i.e. the amount made available to him for drawings has been reduced. However, as Smith's *and* Jones' "payment" of interest to the firm has increased the profits they can share by £600, Smith has in fact been credited with £300 *more* than he would have got, had interest on drawings not been charged to them both – same with Jones. £600 of extra profits has been made available to *both* partners, and each are entitled to one-half of this. So Smith has, in effect, only suffered (in favour of Jones) to the extent of £100; Jones has gained £100, at the expense of Smith. Think carefully about this.

Remember that the double-entry to all items shown in the Profit and Loss appropriation account lies in the respective partner's current account, or capital account if current accounts are not being used.

PROVISIONS OF THE PARTNERSHIP ACT 1890

As I said earlier, whether salaries are to be allowed to certain partners, or interest on capital allowed to all partners, or interest to be charged on drawings, are matters for the partners to agree themselves, preferably in writing. Similarly the ratios in which they are to share the remaining profits or losses should be agreed upon.

In the event of any of these matters *not* being agreed upon, then the provisions of the Partnership Act of 1890 come into play and these decide on what will be, *viz*:

In the absence of any agreement to the contrary:

(i) Profits and losses will be shared equally.
(ii) Partners will not receive salaries or interest on capital, or be charged interest on drawings.
(iii) Any loan given to the firm by a partner will receive interest at 5% per annum.

With regard to loans to the firm by partners, this would be where a partner did not want to introduce more permanent capital to the business, but was willing to lend money for a certain period. Normally the rate of interest would be agreed on, but if not, the Partnership Act states that 5% could be insisted upon.

Interest on such a loan would be debited to appropriation account (i.e. "payment" of it would depend on sufficient profits being made) and credited to that particular partner's current account. In the balance sheet the amount of the partner's loan would appear as a liability of the firm *after* capital and current accounts had been shown.

LOSSES OF FIRM

Where a net loss for the year occurs, this will obviously be brought down from profit and loss account to the *debit* side of the appropriation account, *viz*:

Profit and Loss Appropriation Account

	£		£
Net Loss b/d	4,000	*Share of Loss*	
		Smith	3,000
		Jones	1,000
	4,000		4,000

Assuming that the agreement is to share profits and losses in the ratios of $\frac{3}{4}$ and $\frac{1}{4}$, Smith will have his current account *debited* with £3,000 as his share of the loss. The question of salaries and interest on capital doesn't arise even if agreed upon, because there is no profit to share!

EXERCISE 20.1

M and P, partners in a retail business, had the following partnership agreement:

		£
(a) Salaries per annum:	M	6,000
	P	5,000

(b) Interest on fixed capitals at 10% per annum.
(c) Profits and losses to be shared equally.

Their capital and current account balances as at 1st June 19_9 were respectively:

		£			£
Capital account	M	24,000	Current account	M	3,500 *cr*
Capital account	P	10,000	Current account	P	2,520 *cr*

The following financial information was available for the year ended 31st May 19_0, after the preparation of the profit and loss account.

		£
Drawings per month	M	520
Drawings per month	P	400
Net profit for year (before appropriation)		25,000
Shop premises at cost		23,000
Motor vehicles at cost		7,400
Bank		8,100
Cash		3,490
Trade debtors		6,310
Trade creditors		4,020
Stock		11,700
Provision for depreciation of motor vehicles		2,000

Required:

(a) A profit and loss appropriation account for the year ended 31st May 19_0.

(b) A balance sheet as at that date.

Pay particular attention to layout and presentation. The partners' current accounts may be submitted or, alternatively, the details can be shown on the balance sheet.

(A.E.B. "O" level)

EXERCISE 20.2

A and B, two businessmen, decided to form a partnership. They agreed that they would retain their own regional selling areas and be responsible for their own sales. The partnership agreement provided that:

(a) Each partner is to be credited with a commission of 10% on his own annual sales. The commission is to be treated as an appropriation of profits.

(b) All other expenses would be treated as expenses of the whole business.

(c) Profits and losses to be shared equally.

A and B commenced joint operations on 1st January 19_8 by providing the following capitals:

A Cash £10,000
Stock of goods for sale £3,000
Premises £15,000
Motor vehicle £4,000

B Cash £6,000
Stock of goods for sale £5,000
Fixtures and fittings £2,000
Motor vehicle £3,500

For the year ended 31st December 19_8, the following financial information was available.

		£
(i)	Purchases	71,550
	Sales by A	67,500
	Sales by B	47,600
	Advertising	750
	Rent and rates	1,550
	Heating and lighting	350
	Wages and salaries	7,500
	Financial charges	395
	Carriage inwards	2,700
	Sales returns to A	1,500
	Sales returns to B	1,600
	Drawings A	15,000
	Drawings B	11,000

		£
(ii)	Heating and lighting owing at 31st December 19_8	75
	Rent and rates paid in advance at 31st December 19_8	350.

(iii) Motor vehicles are to be depreciated by 20% per annum on their book valuations.
Fixtures and fittings are to be similarly depreciated by 10% per annum.

(iv) Closing balances at 31st December 19_8

	£
Cash	3,145
Bank	8,300
Trade debtors	17,510
Trade creditors	11,750
Stock	14,540

Required:

(1) A trading, profit and loss and appropriation account for the year ended 31st December 19_8.

(2) A balance sheet as at 31st December 19_8.

(A.E.B. "O" level)

EXERCISE 20.3

Smith, Jones and White are in partnership sharing profits and losses in the ratio of 2:2:1 respectively.

During the year ended 31st December 19_4 the net trading profit of the firm was £8,400 and the partners' drawings were:

	£
Smith	2,000
Jones	1,900
White	1,500

Interest is charged on partners' drawings as follows:

	£
Smith	63
Jones	57
White	45

Interest is allowed on partners' capitals at the rate of 6% per annum. Jones is entitled to a salary of £900 per annum. The partners agreed that Smith should withdraw £1,000 from his capital at 1st July 19_4 and that White should contribute a similar amount as at that date.

The balances on the partners' accounts at 1st January 19_4 were:

	Capital Accounts all credit balances	Current Accounts
	£	£
Smith	11,000	600 credit balance
Jones	7,000	400 debit balance
White	6,000	300 debit balance

Required:
Prepare the partnership profit and loss appropriation account and the partners' capital and current accounts for the year ended 31st December 19_4.

EXERCISE 20.4

A and B were in partnership as manufacturers of engineering components. They shared profits and losses in the ratio of 3:1, but B received in addition an annual salary of £4,600 because he was engineering works manager as well as having his normal partnership duties.

The following were the balances in the financial books as at 1st May 19_7:

	£
Freehold and buildings	20,000
Trade debtors	8,000
Bank overdraft	5,900
Office rent and rates owing	350
Stocks: Raw materials	3,500
Finished goods	7,500
Trade creditors	6,000
Plant and machinery at cost	15,000
Motor vehicles at cost	8,000
Provisions for depreciation:	
Plant and machinery	7,000
Motor vehicles	2,500
Cash account	1,500
Advertising paid in advance	250

The balances on the capital accounts for A and B at 1st May 19_7 were in the ratio 2:1.

For the financial year ended 30th April 19_8 the following information was available:

(a) Finished goods were sold at 25% above the trading cost of sales. All goods were manufactured in the business.

(b) Monthly drawings had been made as follows:

A £800
B £500

(c) Depreciation for the year had been calculated as follows:

Plant and machinery	£3,000
Motor vehicles	£3,000

(d) Expenses adjustments necessary at 30th April 19_8 were:

In arrears	Direct manufacturing wages	£800
	Office salaries	£100
	Printing and stationery	£60
In advance	Office rent and rates	£150

(e) Stock of finished goods at 30th April 19_8 was: £12,000

(f) Payments made during the year:

	£
Vehicle expenses	1,250
Advertising	100
Bank overdraft interest	520
Printing and stationery	120
Offices rent and rates	2,000
Office salaries	2,500
Distribution salaries	6,000

(g) Other balances of accounts at 30th April 19_8 were:

	£
Cost of goods manufactured during the year (i.e. balance on the manufacturing account *which has already been prepared*)	124,500
Stocks: raw materials	8,400
Trade debtors	5,000
Trade creditors	4,700
Bank overdraft	7,600
Cash	1,210

Required:
1. Calculate the opening capital account balances for the partners as at 1st May 19_7.
2. A trading and profit and loss account for the year ended 30th April 19_8.
3. A balance sheet (either in vertical or conventional form) as at 30th April 19_8.

(A.E.B. "O" level)

EXERCISE 20.5

For several years until 31st March 19_3 Paul and Mark had been operating as bakers and fishmongers, trading in partnership but without any partnership agreement. The business occupies premises in the centre of a town.

However, from 1st April 19_3 an agreement made by the partners provided for:

(i) interest on partners' capital account balances at 10% per annum;
(ii) Mark to receive a salary of £6,000 per annum;
(iii) bonuses of 5% of gross profit to be credited to individual partners in respect of the departments for which they are responsible; and
(iv) the balance of profit or loss to be divided three fifths to Paul and two fifths to Mark.

Paul is responsible for the baker department whilst Mark's responsibility is for fishmongery.

The partnership's accounting year end is 30th September. All amounts becoming due by the partnership to the partners are credited to the relevant current account.

The following trial balance at 30th September 19_3 has been extracted from the books of the partnership:

	£	£
Gross profit: Bakery department		16,400
Fishmongery department		12,600
Establishment expenses (including fixed assets depreciation)	4,300	
Administrative expenses	5,000	
Partners' capital accounts – at 30th September 19_2		
Paul		20,000
Mark		24,000
Partners' current accounts – at 30th September 19_2		
Paul		2,100
Mark		2,700
Partner's Loan account – Paul – at 30th September 19_2		3,200
Partners' drawings:		
Paul	6,000	
Mark	7,000	
Fixed assets: at cost	43,000	
provision for depreciation at 30th September 19_3		8,000
Stock in trade, at cost:		
Bakery department	3,700	
Fishmongery department	5,300	
Trade debtors	12,000	
Trade creditors		6,500
Balance at bank	9,200	
	£95,500	£95,500

Since preparing the above trial balance, the following discoveries have been made:

(i) a quantity of flour costing £400, which was ordered to be destroyed by the health authorities on 29th September 19_3 was included inadvertently in the bakery department stock valuation at 30th September 19_3;

(ii) the fishmongery department's purchases for the year ended 30th September 19_3 and the stock valuation at that date included goods costing £1,000 which were not received from the suppliers, Cod Supplies Limited, until 3rd October 19_3;

(iii) establishment expenses include £600 cash drawings paid to Mark in August 19_3;

(iv) by agreement with Paul, Mark paid into the partnership on 1st April 19_3 a legacy of £3,800 received from his late father's estate. Unfortunately, this receipt has been credited to the bakery department's sales.

It can be assumed that gross and net profits have accrued uniformly throughout the year under review

Required:

(a) The partnership's Profit and Loss Appropriation Account for the year ended 30th September 19_3.

(b) The partners' current accounts for the year ended 30th September 19_3.
(c) The partnership Balance Sheet at 30th September 19_3.
(d) Explain why it is necessary to treat partners' salaries differently from employees' salaries in the accounts of partnerships.

(A.C.C.A.)

EXERCISE 20.6

Frank Bidmead and Oscar Chester are in partnership sharing profits and losses in the ratio 3:2. At the close of business on 30th April 19_2 the following Trial Balance was extracted from their books:

		DR	CR
		£	£
Capital Accounts	Bidmead		2,000
	Chester		1,400
Drawings	Bidmead	820	
	Chester	760	
Current Accounts 1st May 19_1			
Bidmead			210
Chester			170
Debtors and Creditors		1,860	920
Purchases and Sales		4,170	8,330
Discounts		240	190
Rent and Rates		520	
Wages and Salaries		1,040	
Office Furniture		600	
Stock 1st May 19_1		1,180	
Bad Debts written off		110	
General Office Expenses		250	
Cash at Bank		1,590	
Cash in Hand		80	
		£13,220	£13,220

NOTES:
1. The Capital Accounts are to remain FIXED at the figures shown in the Trial Balance.
2. No interest is allowed on the Capital Accounts.
3. Chester is entitled to a partnership salary of £500 but no entries have yet been made concerning this.
4. Rent prepaid at 30th April 19_2 is £30.
5. Provide for depreciation of Office Furniture £60.
6. Stock 30th April 19_2 £1,020.

Required:
Draw up the Trading and Profit and Loss Accounts for the year ended 30th April 19_2, together with a Balance Sheet as on that date.

(London Chamber of Commerce)

EXERCISE 20.7

William Gilmore and Horace Hall are in partnership sharing profits and losses equally. At the close of business on 31st October 19_2 the following Trial Balance was extracted from their books:

		DR £	CR £
Capital Accounts 1st November 19_1			
	Gilmore		4,000
	Hall		3,000
Current Accounts 1st November 19_1			
	Gilmore		640
	Hall		630
Drawings	Gilmore	900	
	Hall	880	
Stock 1st November 19_1		2,140	
Purchases and Sales		8,760	15,530
Debtors and Creditors		3,910	2,190
Purchases Returns			240
Sales Returns		390	
Office Furniture		600	
Wages and Salaries		3,930	
Rent and Rates		720	
Cash at Bank		3,390	
Cash in Hand		50	
General Office Expenses		80	
Travelling Expenses		480	
		£26,230	£26,230

NOTES:

1. Stock 31st October 19_2 – £2,520.
2. Wages and Salaries accrued at 31st October 19_2 – £40.
3. The Capital Accounts are to remain FIXED at the figures shown in the Trial Balance.
4. Interest is to be allowed on the Capital Accounts at the rate of 5% per annum.
5. There are no partnership salaries and no provision is to be made for depreciation of office furniture.

Required:
Prepare the Trading and Profit and Loss Accounts for the year ended 31 October 19_2, together with a Balance Sheet as on that date.

(London Chamber of Commerce)

EXERCISE 20.8

Smith, Robinson and Brown are partners and they share profits and losses in the proportions of $\frac{1}{2}$, $\frac{1}{3}$ and $\frac{1}{6}$ respectively.

During the year ended 31st May 19_9 their Capital Accounts had remained fixed at the following sums:

Smith	£5,000
Robinson	£4,000
Brown	£2,000

The partners are entitled to interest on their Capital Accounts at the rate of 6% per annum. On 30th November 19_8 Robinson made a loan to the partnership of £6,000. This is in addition to the balance shown on his Capital Account, and it is agreed that this should also bear interest at the rate of 6% per annum.

In addition to the above it is agreed that partners are entitled to partnership salaries as follows:

Robinson	£1,200
Brown	£1,500

No interest is charged on partners' drawings. The Net Profit of the partnership before taking into account any of the above matters was £10,740.

Required:
Draw up the appropriation account of the partnership for the year ended 31st May 19_9.

(London Chamber of Commerce)

EXERCISE 20.9

A. Amos and B. Brown are in partnership, sharing profits and losses in the proportion of two thirds and one third respectively. The following Trial Balance was extracted from their books at the close of business on 28th February 19_9:

		DR	CR
		£	£
Capital Accounts 1st March 19_8:			
	Amos		3,500
	Brown		2,000
Stock 1st March 19_8		2,760	
Purchases and Sales		9,180	18,280
Bank		1,610	
Cash		70	
Rent, Rates and Insurance		460	
Office Furniture		720	
Discounts		830	510
Bad Debts		320	
Partners' Current Accounts:			
1st March 19_8	Amos		430
	Brown		320
Drawings	Amos	2,200	
	Brown	2,400	
Wages and Salaries		3,070	
Debtors and Creditors		3,040	2,210
General Office Expenses		590	
		£27,250	£27,250

NOTES:

(a) Wages and Salaries accrued at 28th February 19_9 – £80.

(b) Rates prepaid at 28th February 19_9 – £40.

(c) Stock 28th February 19_9 – £2,660.

(d) No allowance is to be made for depreciation.

(e) Brown is entitled to a partnership salary of £1,200 but no entries have been made regarding this.

(f) The partners' Capital accounts are to remain fixed at the figures shown in the Trial Balance. All other transactions concerning partners are to be made in the partners' current accounts.

(g) No interest is to be allowed on Capital Accounts.

Required:

Prepare the Trading and Profit and Loss Accounts for the year ended 28th February 19_9, together with a Balance Sheet as at that date.

(London Chamber of Commerce)

EXERCISE 20.10

William Wallace and George Turner were in partnership as general merchants, sharing profits and losses equally and having fixed capitals of

£10,000 and £8,000 respectively. The following Trial Balance was prepared as at 31st December 19_9:

	DR	CR
	£	£
Capital – W. Wallace		10,000
Capital – G. Turner		8,000
Bank Deposit A/c	5,600	
Bank Current A/c		143
Debtors and Creditors	1,478	2,765
Bank Interest		136
Cash in hand	28	
Discounts	224	196
Carriage inwards	128	
Purchases and Sales	14,090	23,538
Carriage outwards	322	
Returns	458	234
General expenses	987	
Premises at cost	8,000	
Wages and salaries	5,610	
Furniture and fittings	1,260	
Insurance	123	
Stock in trade 1.1._9	3,544	
Drawings – G. Turner	1,200	
Drawings – W. Wallace	1,960	
	£45,012	£45,012

The following matters relate to the partnership accounts:

1. Stock in trade at 31st December 19_9 was valued at cost £5,240.
2. Two thirds of wages and salaries are to be allocated to Trading Account and one third to Profit and Loss Account.
3. Prepayments and accruals at 31st December 19_9 were: Prepayment of Insurance £28. Accruals: Carriage inwards £12.
4. Bad debts £38 are to be written off.
5. Furniture and fittings were revalued at £1,134.
6. W. Wallace is entitled to a salary of £1,000 a year.
7. The partners are to be allowed Interest on their capital at the rate of 6% per annum, but no interest is chargeable on Drawings.

Required:
Prepare:
(i) Profit and Loss Account and an Appropriation Account for the year 19_9 assuming a Gross Profit of £7,040.
(ii) The Current Account of William Wallace (assume no opening balance).

(London Chamber of Commerce)

CHAPTER 21

GOODWILL AND PURCHASE OF A BUSINESS

GOODWILL

This is the value of any business over and above that value shown on the balance sheet, even when the assets are shown on that balance sheet at "accurate" values. It is the value placed upon the business's reputation – the value of the customer returning again because he is happy with the service and attention given to him. Goodwill is created by treating customers well in every respect, thereby establishing a reputation.

Look at the following balance sheet.

XYZ
Balance Sheet as at ....

Liabilities	£	*Assets*	£
Capital	85,000	*Fixed Assets*	
Long Term Loan	10,000	Premises	50,000
Current Liabilities		Plant and Equipment	30,000
Creditors	5,000	*Current Assets*	
		Stock	10,000
		Debtors	7,000
		Cash	3,000
	100,000		100,000

Firstly, note how the long term loan is shown quite separate from capital and current liabilities – it has its own place in the balance sheet.

According to the balance sheet this business is worth £85,000. Suppose the owner decides to sell the business as it stands, except for the cash of course. Will he sell for £82,000 (the value of the assets and liabilities except cash)? Not likely – a lot of effort has gone into building up the reputation of this business – whoever takes it over will inherit an established "book" of customers who regularly deal with this particular business.

The vendor (the seller) therefore is going to ask for more than £82,000 for the assets (less cash) and liabilities of the business – he may make the purchase price £100,000 which means that he is selling an additional *asset*, not shown on his balance sheet, i.e. Goodwill, at a price of £18,000.

The buyer who is going to take over the assets and liabilities therefore pays £100,000 for this business and enters into *his own* accounts the values shown on the above balance sheet. The "excess" of £18,000 he has paid for the goodwill of the business represents the purchase of an additional asset, "Goodwill", which he will also enter into his accounts. His journal entry, for ultimate posting in his accounts, on the purchase of the business of XYZ will therefore be:

Journal

	DR	CR
	£	£
Premises	50,000	
Plant and equipment	30,000	
Stock	10,000	
Debtors (individual personal accounts debited)	7,000	
Goodwill	18,000	
Long Term Loan		10,000
Creditors (individual personal accounts credited)		5,000
Vendor's Account (XYZ)		100,000
	115,000	115,000
Being purchase of business XYZ		

Note that the goodwill is the excess of the purchase price of the business over what the assets and liabilities being bought are worth on a balance sheet basis. Goodwill will now appear on the balance sheet of the buyer as a *fixed asset.*

Why credit the vendor's account with the purchase price of £100,000? Because at this point the buyer, whose accounts we are dealing with, *owes* the £100,000 to the vendor (XYZ) for the purchase of his business – i.e. the vendor is a *creditor* of the buyer.

The next journal entry will show how this liability is repaid. If payment is to be made in cash then the following entries will be made in the buyer's accounts.

Journal

	DR	CR
	£	£
Vendor's Account (XYZ)	100,000	
Cash		100,000
Being settlement of purchase price of XYZ business		

Let's now go back to the above example and assume this time that all the assets, except cash, and liabilities of XYZ are being bought, as before, but that the buyer does not agree with the values of various assets as shown by the balance sheet of the vendor (XYZ). Let's assume that the buyer considers premises to be worth £60,000 (not £50,000), plant and equipment to be worth only £18,000 (not £30,000) and stock only £7,000 (not £10,000). The effect of all this is that the buyer gains £10,000 on the premises item but loses £15,000 on the plant and stock – an overall "loss" of £5,000. If the vendor (XYZ) still insists on a purchase price of £100,000, then the buyer is really paying £23,000 over and above the value of what he is getting in the form of assets and liabilities. As far as the buyer is concerned he is paying £23,000 (not £18,000 as before) for goodwill, and the entries in his account will be as follows:

Journal

	DR £	CR £
Premises	60,000	
Plant and Equipment	18,000	
Stock	7,000	
Debtors	7,000	
Goodwill	23,000	
Long Term Loan		10,000
Creditors		5,000
Vendor (XYZ)		100,000
	115,000	115,000

The difference in estimates of value is reflected in the goodwill figure. The vendor is now paid off in full as before.

THE VENDOR'S ACCOUNTS

The accounts of XYZ will obviously need to be closed off because his business now ceases to exist. He is not concerned with the values his buyer places on various assets – he is simply selling everything, assets (except cash) and liabilities at the values shown in his balance sheet, for £100,000 cash.

Go back now to his balance sheet shown on page 239, as it stood before the sale. Every asset shown is represented by debit balances in his ledger accounts and every liability by credit balances. All of these accounts except cash *and capital* are now going to be "closed off" by transferring these balances to *one* account opened for the purpose of this sale, and called a *Realisation Account*. In other words, everything in his ledger which is being bought is going to be put under one "roof", *viz*:

Premises

Balance	£50,000	Realisation a/c	£50,000

Plant and Equipment

Balance	£30,000	Realisation a/c	£30,000

Stock

Balance	£10,000	Realisation a/c	£10,000

Various Debtors' Accounts

Balances	£7,000	Realisation a/c	£7,000

Long Term Loan

Realisation a/c	£10,000	Balance	£10,000

Various Creditors' Accounts

Realisation a/c	£5,000	Balances	£5,000

Realisation A/c

	£		£
Premises	50,000	Loan	10,000
Plant and Equipment	30,000	Creditors	5,000
Stock	10,000		
Debtors	7,000		

Note that all the assets and liabilities being sold are now in the Realisation Account – their individual accounts are closed off – finished with. The balance of the Realisation Account (£82,000 debit) represents the value being sold, and as this is to be sold for £100,000 there is a *profit* of £18,000 for the vendor, XYZ.

The next step is to record the purchase price in the Realisation Account (credit entry) and to debit the buyer's account with £100,000 pending his payment, – i.e. until he pays, he is a debtor. The difference on the Realisation Account of £18,000 will then be transferred to the vendor's capital account as profit, so closing off the Realisation Account which has finished its function. Study carefully the following entries.

Realisation Account

	£		£
Premises	50,000	Loan	10,000
Plant and Equipment	30,000	Creditors	5,000
Stock	10,000	The Buyer	100,000
Debtors	7,000		
Profit on Realisation to Capital a/c	18,000		
	115,000		115,000

The Buyer

Realisation a/c	£100,000		

Capital A/c

			£
		Balance	85,000
		Profit on Realisation	18,000

Cash A/c

Balance	£3,000		

The only accounts now remaining open in the vendor's ledger are capital, the buyer (debtor) and cash. When the £100,000 cash is received the buyer's account will be closed off and the increased cash in cash account will be used to pay off the vendor's capital owing to him by his business. This will close off the remaining accounts, *viz*:

The Buyer

Realisation a/c	£100,000	Cash	£100,000

Cash

	£		£
Balance	3,000	Capital a/c	103,000
The Buyer	100,000		
	103,000		103,000

Capital A/c

	£		£
Cash	103,000	Balance	85,000
		Profit on Realisation	18,000
	103,000		103,000

All accounts are now closed.

If you have been wondering why capital account was not "transferred" to the buyer, together with the other liabilities of the business of XYZ, this means that you did not fully understand the very earliest chapters in this book explaining what capital was! The capital account balance of £82,000 (i.e. the original balance less cash not leaving the business) *was* transferred to the buyer – *in the form of the various assets and liabilities* which were "transferred" to the buyer! Capital, remember = assets less liabilities!

SUMMARY OF PROCEDURES

IN THE BUYER'S ACCOUNTS

He brings into his accounts the various assets and liabilities taken over at the values *he* places on them. The difference between the net value of assets so acquired and the amount paid for those net assets represents the purchase of another asset, "goodwill". If he pays *less* than the considered value then he has *made a profit.*

IN THE VENDOR'S ACCOUNTS

He transfers *all assets and liabilities being sold* to one account, a Realisation Account, and enters in this account the purchase price to be paid. The resulting difference on Realisation Account then represents his profit (or loss), which is transferred to his Capital Account. The capital account is finally "cleared" on receipt of the purchase price monies and the buyer's account is also cleared off.

GOODWILL

Goodwill *is* a fixed asset because it is going to remain permanently in the business. However, the difference between this fixed asset and others, which are in a tangible form, is that if the business goes bankrupt then this "asset" will disappear overnight! The other fixed assets will sell, but with goodwill there will be nothing to sell!

It is considered to be good accounting practice to remove this asset, goodwill, from the accounts and therefore from the balance sheet, as quickly as possible, and the reason for this is "accounting conservatism", where the policy is always to show the worst position rather than the best position. For example, in accounting, *anticipated* profits are never taken into account (they must actually *happen*) but anticipated losses are always taken into account (even though they may not actually happen!).

Goodwill, having appeared in the accounts as a result of buying it, is normally gradually written off by annual debits to Profit and Loss account and credits of goodwill account itself. Profits are therefore being used each year for the purpose of writing down that intangible asset, goodwill. Within a few years the asset, goodwill, will have disappeared from the accounts and therefore from the balance sheet. The goodwill of the business is still there of course, but the business is not "bragging" about it by showing it in the accounts. Anyone inspecting the balance sheet will be looking at tangible assets only.

The worst position is being observed rather than the best, and the inspector of the balance sheet will of course be aware of the goodwill associated with that business, even though it is not shown. Look at the balance sheets of a really first class company and you will rarely see goodwill (unless it has recently been purchased from a business "taken over", and is in the process of being written off), but you know it is there, making the "picture" of that company even better than that already impressively shown on the balance sheet.

Think now of the *effect* of writing down goodwill by a bit each year. The debit to Profit and Loss account is, like depreciation, a "non-cash" debit – it reduces profits but does not involve any cash leaving the business. Like depreciation, this entry in the Profit and Loss account "forces" cash (from profits) which might otherwise have left the business through drawings, to be left in the business. The purpose of this is to *recoup* the amount originally spent in acquiring that asset. The cash is simply being "saved" year by year and when goodwill has been completely written off, the equivalent amount of cash will be "lying" in the business in place of the goodwill item which used to be displayed in the balance sheet.

Obviously the cash "saved" won't remain in this form of asset as someone is bound to spend it in one way or another. *How* it is spent does not matter, because the business will obviously benefit in some way, and the equivalent value of what used to appear as goodwill in the balance sheet will be there in some other form. In effect, as the goodwill is gradually written off to profits this intangible asset is gradually being replaced by something tangible – initially cash (from profits), then into some other form of value. Think very carefully about this before proceeding.

EXERCISE 21.1

I. Dodgem's balance sheet on 31st December 19_8 was as follows:

	£		£
Capital	87,000	Premises	55,000
Trade creditors	8,000	Plant and machinery at cost	
Bank overdraft	15,800	*less* depreciation	21,000
Expenses owing	200	Fixtures and fittings at cost	
		less depreciation	4,000
		Stock	17,000
		Trade debtors	9,500
		Cash	4,500
	£111,000		£111,000

An opportunity had arisen for Dodgem to acquire the business of A. Swing who was retiring.

A. SWING
Balance Sheet as at 31st December 19_8

	£		£
Capital	54,000	Premises	25,000
Trade creditors	9,000	Plant	9,000
		Motor vehicle	3,500
		Stock	11,000
		Trade debtors	6,000
		Bank	8,000
		Cash	500
	£63,000		£63,000

Dodgem agreed to take over Swing's premises, plant, stock, trade debtors and trade creditors.

For the purpose of his own records Dodgem valued the premises at £35,000, plant at £6,000 and stock at £8,000.

The agreed purchase price was £50,000 and in order to finance the purchase Dodgem had obtained a fixed loan for 5 years from his bank, for one half of the purchase price on the condition that he contributed the same amount from his own private resources in cash. The purchase price was paid on 1st January 19_9.

Dodgem also decided to scrap some of his oldest plant and machinery which cost £9,000 with depreciation to date £8,000. This was sold for scrap for £300 cash on 1st January 19_9. On the same date he bought some new plant for £4,000, paying in cash.

Required:

1. The purchase of business account in I. Dodgem's books.
2. I. Dodgem's balance sheet as at 1st January 19_9 after all the above transactions have been completed.

(A.E.B. "O" level)

EXERCISE 21.2

Martin Price and Alfred Wilson are two sole traders who decide to enter into a partnership as from the commencement of business on 1st March 19_0. At the close of business on 29th February 19_0, their respective balance sheets were as follows:

MARTIN PRICE

	£		£
Capital Account	3,460	Office Furniture	720
Creditors	1,240	Stock	1,490
		Debtors	1,730
		Cash at Bank	760
	£4,700		£4,700

ALFRED WILSON

	£		£
Capital Account	3,150	Delivery Van	800
Creditors	910	Stock	2,060
Bank Overdraft	230	Debtors	1,430
	£4,290		£4,290

All the assets and liabilities of both traders were taken into the partnership with the exception of Wilson's bank overdraft.

For the purpose of the partnership, the following are the agreed valuations:

Office Furniture (Price)	£650
Delivery Van (Wilson)	£750

All the other assets are taken into the partnership at the figures appearing in the above balance sheets except that, in the case of Price, Bad Debts to the extent of £110 are written off before the transfer takes place.

Required:

(i) Calculate the opening Capital of each of the partners. (Calculations MUST be shown.)

(ii) Draw up the opening Balance Sheet of the partnership taking into consideration all the information given above.

(London Chamber of Commerce)

EXERCISE 21.3

On 31st March 19_6, Y purchased for £20,750 all the assets of Henderson a trader. At that date the assets shown in Henderson's balance sheet appeared as follows:

	£
Freehold property	7,000
Motor vehicles	3,250
Stock-in-trade	4,500

The freehold property was valued at £9,500 and the motor vehicles and the stock at the amount shown in Henderson's balance sheet.

The price was satisified by paying off Henderson's bank overdraft of £750 and by the issue to Henderson of £20,000 in cash.

Show the entries in the journal of Y.

(Institute of Bankers)

EXERCISE 21.4

J. Halstead started business on 1st January 19_7 with £10,000 in cash. During 19_7 he made a profit of £4,448, and at 31st December, 19_7 his fixed assets were £8,000, stock was valued at £4,261 and debtors were £3,847. At this date the balance at bank was £2,624 and his creditors were £4,284.

On 1st January 19_8 Halstead took over all the assets and liabilities, except bank, of F. Bardfield at an agreed price of £7,800 to be paid in cash.

The assets were taken over at the figures at which they appeared in the balance sheet of Bardfield dated 31st December 19_7, as follows:

Balance Sheet of Bardfield at 31.12._7

	£		£
Capital	4,000	Fixed Assets	4,000
P & L account	2,160	Stock	2,816
Creditors	1,481	Debtors	891
Bank overdraft	66		
	7,707		7,707

Required:

(a) Prepare *journal entries* for Halstead showing the effects in his ledger of purchasing the business.

(b) Prepare journal entries for Bardfield showing the disposal of his business.

(c) Show the balance sheet of Halstead immediately after the purchase.

EXERCISE 21.5

Todd decides to purchase the business of Robinson on 1st January 19_5. He has £15,000 at bank and borrows an additional amount of £2,000 from XYZ Ltd.

Robinson's balance sheet at 1st January 19_5 was:

	£		£
Creditors	1,500	Balance at bank	856
Capital	10,776	Stock	2,400
		Debtors	1,020
		Fixtures	2,000
		Premises	6,000
	12,276		12,276

It was agreed that Todd should take over all the assets, except the balance at bank, and all the liabilities, and that the following assets should be revalued for the purpose of the purchase:

	£
Premises	7,000
Fixtures	1,600

It was also agreed that an amount equal to 5% of the debtors should be allowed for doubtful debts.

Todd agreed to pay Robinson an additional amount for the goodwill of his business on the basis of two years purchase of the average profits for the last five years. These profits were £1,100, £1,255, £1,480, £1,580, £1,645.

The transaction was completed on 1st January 19_5, and R. Todd paid Robinson by cheque.

Required:

1. Show the Journal entries of Todd and his balance sheet on 1st January 19_5, immediately after the transaction.
2. Show the Journal entries for Robinson to close down his business.

CHAPTER 22

PARTNERSHIP ACCOUNTS CONTINUED

NEW PARTNERS

An existing partnership may invite another person to join them, in order to get access to more capital, and the new partner will obviously be expected to inject new capital into the business. Whatever cash the new partner brings in will be debited to cash/bank and credited to his capital account.

The new partner has entered into an established business which has already generated a certain amount of goodwill, which does not show in the accounts, and he is therefore getting the advantage of previous efforts by the original partners. If the business subsequently sells out to somebody else then a price will be put on goodwill, and this will represent a profit to the partners involved in the business. If, for example, a business worth £60,000, according to the balance sheet, is sold for £80,000, this will be the value of the assets less liabilities (i.e. the net assets), *plus £20,000* for goodwill. This £20,000 is, to the partners in the business which is being sold, a profit which they will share in their agreed proportions. But why should the recent new partner take a share of this profit, which he has done nothing towards? This profit belongs to the partners who generated the goodwill in the first place.

If, therefore, the business is sold sometime in the future, the "new" partner is automatically going to get his share of the profit from the sale of the goodwill – which we know he is not entitled to.

To combat this, it is necessary to make adjusting entries in the various capital accounts of the partners *at the time the new partner is admitted to the business*. If, for example, we calculate that the new partner will get, in the event of the business being sold, £2,000 for goodwill which he has had no part in generating, (i.e. it had already been created *before* he joined the firm), then we must reduce his claim on the business assets (represented by the credit balance on his capital account) by £2,000 on the day he joins the firm. In other words, if he contributes £10,000 of capital on joining, then this must be immediately reduced to £8,000 in view of the benefit he immediately receives from the existing goodwill present in the business at the time he joins. The "loss" of £2,000 to the new partner through the debiting of his capital account is "made up" to him by the fact that he immediately has a *claim* of £2,000 on the existing goodwill of the business. Whenever, if ever, the business is sold, the £2,000 will "come back" to him as his share of this particular profit.

If therefore, a new partner joins a firm, this will mean a change in the profit sharing ratios agreed upon, and an immediate adjustment made to all partners' capital accounts in respect of the goodwill in the business.

For example – John and Tim are in partnership, and their valuation of the goodwill of their business is £9,000. At present they share profits and losses in the proportions $\frac{2}{3}$ and $\frac{1}{3}$ respectively. If goodwill is ever sold (i.e. on sale of the business) they will be entitled to £6,000 (John) and £3,000 (Tim) as their share of this profit.

If they now decide to admit David as a new partner, who will contribute £10,000 of new capital in cash, and the agreement is that the new profit sharing ratios will be John $\frac{1}{2}$, Tim $\frac{3}{10}$ and David $\frac{2}{10}$, this means that in the event of the goodwill being sold in the future, John will get one-half of it (i.e. £4,500), Tim will get three-tenths of it (i.e. £2,700), and David will get two-tenths of it (i.e. £1,800).

To get a clear picture:

Goodwill valued at £9,000

In the event of sale of goodwill (together with other net assets),

John gets £4,500 from goodwill
Tim gets £2,700 from goodwill
David gets £1,800 from goodwill.

But we know that John is entitled to $\frac{2}{3}$ of the goodwill (i.e. £6,000) and Tim is entitled to $\frac{1}{3}$ of the goodwill (i.e. £3,000) because these were the profit sharing ratios *before* David entered the firm. David is not entitled to anything, because he has played no part whatsoever in the creation of this goodwill.

Because of the new profit sharing ratios, John is going to "lose out" £1,500 if ever the goodwill is sold, Tim is going to "lose out" £300, and David is going to *gain* £1,800.

It is therefore essential that adjustments are made to the capital accounts of the respective partners *at the time the profit sharing ratios are changed.* Because John will ultimately lose £1,500 we can put this right by crediting his capital account *now* with £1,500 – i.e. increase his claim on the business assets by £1,500. Because Tim will ultimately lose £300 we can credit his capital account now with £300, and because David will ultimately *gain* £1,800 we must *debit* his capital account now in order to reduce his claim on the business assets. Note double-entry – CR John £1,500, CR Tim £300, DR David £1,800.

If David complains that he has invested £10,000 in the firm yet his capital account shows only a liability of £8,200 to him, we can explain to him that the difference is what he has "paid" for the existing goodwill of the business, and that he will get this £1,800 back if ever the business is sold to someone else, or if he retires. In other words, he has "paid" for – $\frac{2}{10}$ of the business's goodwill.

An easier way around this would have been to have opened a Goodwill account (asset) with a debit of £9,000, and to have credited John and Tim's capital accounts with $\frac{2}{3}$ (£6,000) and $\frac{1}{3}$ (£3,000) of £9,000 respectively.

However, as you already know, it is considered bad accounting practice to deliberately open a goodwill account. The only time goodwill appears in the accounts is when it has been purchased from another business and the policy is then to write if off against profits as quickly as possible.

If, therefore, a change takes place in the profit sharing ratios of partners, through the introduction of a new partner, an adjustment should be made in the capital accounts there and then, to adjust for what may happen in the future, or (a better way of thinking) to acknowledge, via the capital accounts, the true rights to goodwill of each partner.

FINAL EXAMPLE

Goodwill of a firm is valued at £12,000. Partners A, B and C have created this goodwill and they share profits and losses equally. D is then admitted to the partnership and the new profit sharing ratios are to be equal (i.e. $\frac{1}{4}$ each):

A is *entitled* to $\frac{1}{3}$ of the goodwill	£4,000
B is *entitled* to $\frac{1}{3}$ of the goodwill	£4,000
C is *entitled* to $\frac{1}{3}$ of the goodwill	£4,000
	£12,000

D is entitled to *nothing*.

New situation on introduction of D:

A will eventually get $\frac{1}{4}$ of the goodwill (he therefore "loses out" £1,000)	£3,000
B will eventually get $\frac{1}{4}$ of the goodwill (he therefore "loses out" £1,000)	£3,000
C will eventually get $\frac{1}{4}$ of the goodwill (he "loses out" £1,000)	£3,000
D will eventually get $\frac{1}{4}$ of the goodwill (he *gains* £3,000)	£3,000
	£12,000

To compensate A, B and C *now*, their capital accounts should be *credited* with £1,000 each, and D's capital account should be debited with £3,000 (i.e. take "off him" *now* what he is not entitled to).

These entries give the benefit of existing goodwill to the partners who have created it. The difference will be made up by their respective shares, of the goodwill under the new agreement. The entries make the new partner "pay" for his share of the goodwill already created before he joined the firm.

DISSOLUTION

A firm may decide to stop trading and "dissolve" the firm for many reasons. The partners may *want* to dissolve their firm, they may *have* to dissolve their firm if they get into financial difficulties, or they may *sell* their firm to a suitable buyer.

SELLING THE FIRM

The accounting procedures necessary to deal with this situation have been dealt with in full in Chapter 21 which dealt with the vendor's accounts. The only difference to what you did in that chapter is the fact that you now have more than one capital account, and possibly current accounts, to close off. This simply means that when the final distribution of cash takes place, it is spread over the various capital accounts according to the balances on them, the balances on current accounts having previously been amalgamated with the capital account balances to show the final claims of partners.

A very simple example will illustrate and revise. David and Philip (partners) share profits and losses equally.

Summarised Balance Sheet of David and Philip

	£		£
Capital Accounts		Fixed Assets	20,000
David	15,000		
Philip	10,000		
Current Accounts			
David	800	Stock	11,000
Philip	2,000	Debtors	5,000
Creditors	9,200	Bank	1,000
	37,000		37,000

David and Philip decide to sell their assets and liabilities except bank balance, to Bella H at an agreed price of £30,000. Expenses of sale will amount to £200.

PROCEDURE

All assets and liabilities being bought are closed off by transfer to Realisation Account, and the purchase price is entered into this account. Costs of realisation are also entered, *viz*:

Realisation Account

	£		£
Fixed Assets	20,000	Creditors	9,200
Stock	11,000	Bella H	30,000
Debtors	5,000		
Expenses (bank)	200		
Profit on Realisation			
David	1,500		
Philip	1,500		
	39,200		39,200

NOTE: The bank account is reduced by the £200 expenses of sale, which as you see from the above has reduced the overall profit on realisation, by £200. Bella H's account will be debited for the present with £30,000 – i.e. a debtor of the firm.

There is no longer any need for current accounts, so the balances of these will now be transferred to their respective capital accounts and the profit on realisation will be credited to each capital account.

When Bella H pays the £30,000 this will go into the bank account, which will then be used to pay off the partners' claims according to their final capital account balances, *viz*:

David – Capital a/c

	£		£
Bank	17,300	Balance	15,000
		Current a/c balance	800
		Profit on Realisation	1,500
	17,300		17,300

Philip – Capital a/c

	£		£
Bank	13,500	Balance	10,000
		Current a/c balance	2,000
		Profit on Realisation	1,500
	13,500		13,500

Bank a/c

	£		£
Balance	1,000	Expenses	200
Bella H.	30,000	David – Capital	17,300
		Philip – Capital	13,500
	31,000		31,000

There is just enough cash to pay the partners off in full, and all accounts are now closed off.

VOLUNTARY OR COMPULSORY DISSOLUTION

If the partners *want* to or *have* to dissolve their firm, and nobody wants to buy the business assets and liabilities as a whole, as in the previous example, then the partners must sell off the assets "piece-meal" and pay off their liabilities from the proceeds.

The procedure is identical in principle, and almost identical in procedure, to that already dealt with.

STEPS

(i) All assets *to be sold* are transferred at book value to a Realisation Account, so closing off those asset accounts.

(ii) The proceeds received from the sale of *each* asset are entered into cash account (debit) and credited to Realisation Account as each sale takes place.

(iii) Expenses of realisation are entered into cash account (credit) and debited to Realisation Account.

(iv) The balance on Realisation Account at this point represents the difference between the transferred book values of the assets being sold, and the proceeds actually received, less of course any expenses involved – i.e. profit or loss. This profit or loss on realisation of assets is transferred from Realisation Account to the respective capital accounts (current account balances already amalgamated with capital accounts).

(v) Cash, increased due to sale of assets, is then used to pay off all liabilities such as creditors, loans, etc. Note that the owners of *any* business are always the *last* to be repaid by the business.

(vi) Finally, whatever cash remains is used to pay off the partners' claims according to their capital account balances.

The above steps should be regarded as a *logical* progression towards closing down the partnership, *not* as formula to be memorised!

EXAMPLE

Look back to the balance sheet of David and Philip. This time the partners are simply going to dissolve the firm themselves.

Assume that fixed assets are sold for only £15,000, stock for £12,000 and that debtors only pay a total of £4,000. Expenses of realisation are £100. The numbers shown relate to the numbers of the "steps" above.

Realisation a/c

		£		£	
(i)	Fixed Assets	20,000	Bank (Fixed Assets)	15,000	(ii)
(i)	Stock	11,000	Stock	12,000	(ii)
(i)	Debtors	5,000	Debtors	4,000	(ii)
(iii)	Expenses	100	*Loss on Realisation*		
			David – Capital	2,550	(iv)
			Philip – Capital	2,550	(iv)
		36,100		36,100	

Bank a/c

		£		£	
	Balance	1,000	Realisation a/c	100	(iii)
(ii)	Realisation a/c	15,000	Creditors	9,200	(v)
(ii)	Realisation a/c	12,000	*Capital Accounts*		
(ii)	Realisation a/c	4,000	David	13,250	(vi)
			Philip	9,450	(vi)
		32,000		32,000	

David – Capital a/c

		£		£	
(iv)	Loss on Realisation	2,550	Balance	15,000	
(vi)	Bank	13,250	Current a/c	800	(iv)
		15,800		15,800	

Philip – Capital a/c

		£		£	
(iv)	Loss on Realisation	2,550	Balance	10,000	
(vi)	Bank	9,450	Current a/c	2,000	(iv)
		12,000		12,000	

Various Creditors' Accounts

(v)	Bank	£9,200	Balances	£9,200

Note that the only difference between a dissolution of a partnership and the sale of *any* business is, that with a dissolution the realisation account records the *individual* proceeds from the sale of each asset, so that the account finishes up showing book values on the debit side and realisation values of those same assets on the credit side. The various liabilities are then paid off quite separately. With a sale of a business the purchase price, in one amount, takes the place of the individual proceeds of sale, and the net value of the assets and liabilities being sold takes up the rest of the account.

Whether it's a dissolution or a sale, *only those assets and liabilities which are to be sold* find their way into the Realisation Account, and are then compared with what they are sold for, individually (dissolution) or collectively (sale of business), to give a difference representing either profit or loss on the ending of the partnership.

GARNER v. MURRAY RULING

If, after amalgamation of current account balances with capital account balances, and after transfer of profit or loss on realisation to capital accounts, a capital account finishes up with a *debit* balance, then this means that the partner concerned owes money to his firm. No cash will be paid to him – instead he must cover his debit balance by bringing in personal cash.

Until he covers his debit balance with cash there will not be enough cash in the business to satisfy the claims of the other partners who have credit balances on their capital accounts. What is due to them cannot be paid in full until the defaulting partner brings in the necessary cash to close his capital account.

What if he can't find any personal cash to bring into the firm? How will the cash *available* be divided between the other partners?

Look at this final extract from the accounts of a dissolved partnership, after all transactions have been dealt with except the final "payout" to partners.

John – Capital

Final Balance	£600		

Fred – Capital

		Final Balance	£6,000

Tom – Capital

		Final Balance	£4,000

Cash

Final Balance	£9,400		

NOTE: If John pays £600 cash into the firm there will then be sufficient cash to pay Fred and Tom their respective claims, and all capital accounts will then be closed off.

If John cannot find £600, then Fred and Tom must bear this debit balance of £600 *themselves*, but in what proportions?

Unless their written partnership agreement dictates what will happen in such a situation, the ruling from an old, but famous, legal case (Garner *v*. Murray) will apply. This ruling says in effect that the debit balance of the partner concerned will be borne by the other partners "*in proportion to their last agreed capitals*".

If, at the last year end, Fred had a capital account balance of £9,000 and Tom £6,000 then these proportions of 3:2 would be the proportions in which Fred and Tom would share John's deficit – $\frac{3}{5}$ of £600 to be borne by Fred and $\frac{2}{5}$ by Tom. The accounts would then be closed off as follows:

John – Capital

	£		£
Balance	600	Fred	360
		Tom	240
	600		600

Fred – Capital

	£		£
John	360	Balance	6,000
Bank	5,640		
	6,000		6,000

Tom – Capital

	£		£
John	240	Balance	4,000
Bank	3,760		
	4,000		4,000

Cash

	£		£
Balance	9,400	Fred	5,640
		Tom	3,760
	9,400		9,400

NOTE: Fred has taken over £360 of John's debit balance, and Tom has taken over the other £240. There is now enough cash to pay their revised claims.

EXERCISE 22.1

A and B were partners, sharing profits and losses in the proportions A three-fifths and B two-fifths. On 1st March 19_5, C was admitted as a partner. He was required to pay £5,000 into the firm's bank account. Of this sum, £3,000 was to be treated as C's capital, and £2,000 as a premium for goodwill. As from 1st March 19_5, profits and losses were to be shared in the proportions A two-fifths, B two-fifths and C one-fifth.

Show the entries in the firm's journal to record the treatment of the £5,000 paid in by C.

No goodwill account is to be opened in the firm's books.

EXERCISE 22.2

Jack and Tom are partners in an old established business. Their partnership agreement provides that:

(a) interest at the rate of 10% per annum is paid on partners' fixed capital.
(b) Tom is credited with a salary of £3,000 per annum.
(c) the balance of the partnership's profits or losses is divided between Jack and Tom in the proportions $\frac{3}{5}$ and $\frac{2}{5}$ respectively.

The balances on the partners' capital and current accounts at 1st January 19_7, were as follows:

	Capital accounts	*Current accounts*
	£	£
Jack	12,000	1,000
Tom	8,000	700

NOTE: All balances are in credit.

During the year ended 31 December 19_7, the partnership net profit, carried to the appropriation account, was £16,000 arising uniformly throughout the year. The partners' cash drawings during 19_7 were as follows:

Jack	£5,000	Tom	£6,000

After reviewing the draft accounts for 1977, Jack and Tom decided to admit their senior clerk, Harry, as a partner with effect from 1st October 19_7.

Harry has been with the business for many years and from the beginning of 19_7 has received a salary of £4,000 per annum payable monthly.

For some years the partnership has used a house owned by Harry for offices and paid him a rent of £1,000 per annum. It has now been agreed that with effect from 1st October 19_7, the property is transferred at its market valuation of £6,000 to the partnership as Harry's fixed capital; this change will mean that Harry is no longer entitled to receive rent.

After stating that there will be no partners' salaries, the new partnership agreement provides that:

(i) interest at the rate of 10% per annum is to be paid on partners' fixed capital.

(ii) the balance of the partnership's profits or losses is to be shared between partners in the proportions Jack $\frac{1}{2}$, Tom $\frac{3}{10}$ and Harry $\frac{1}{5}$.

Required:

1. A statement showing the distribution of the partnership's net profit for 19_7 between Jack, Tom and Harry.
2. The capital and current accounts for the year ended 31st December 19_7, of Jack, Tom and Harry.

(AEB "A" level)

EXERCISE 22.3

Peter, James and John were partners with capitals of £8,000, £10,000 and £2,000 respectively. They shared profits and losses in proportion to their capitals. James retired from the partnership on 31st December 19_0. The partnership deed provided that, in the event of dissolution, goodwill be valued at three years' purchase of the average profits of the last four years. These profits were £2,400, £2,800, £1,600 and £3,200. The Balance Sheet of the partnership on 31st December 19_0, prior to dissolution, was:

Liabilities		£	Assets	£
Sundry creditors		4,000	Sundry assets	9,000
Capital Peter	8,000		Cash	15,000
Capital James	10,000			
Capital John	2,000			
		20,000		
		24,000		24,000

By agreement, James took out of the business *immediately* the car he had been using (book value £1,000) and, on 6th February 19_1, he was paid cash to clear his capital account including his share of goodwill.

Required:

Prepare:

(i) A statement showing the calculations for the value of goodwill.
(ii) A Goodwill Account for the old partnership.
(iii) A Balance Sheet for the new partnership, Peter and John, as at 1st January 19_1.

(London Chamber of Commerce)

EXERCISE 22.4

A, B and C are partners of a trading firm and share profits and losses in the ratio 3:2:1. The firm's balance sheet on 31st December 19_0 was:

		£	£
Fixed Assets			
Freehold Premises			36,000
Motor Vehicles at cost less depreciation			8,000
			44,000
Current Assets			
Stock		18,000	
Debtors		12,000	
Balance at Bank		8,000	
		38,000	
Less Current Liabilities			
Creditors		8,000	
Working capital			30,000
Total			74,000
Partners' Capital Accounts	£		
A	36,000		
B	24,000		
C	12,000	72,000	
Partners' Current Accounts	£		
A	2,400		
B	Dr (1,600)		
C	1,200	2,000	74,000
			74,000

B retired from the Partnership on 1st January 19_1 and agreed to leave half the final balance on his capital account as a short term loan to the firm. The remainder was paid to him in cash immediately.

A and C had agreed to continue in partnership sharing profits and losses in the same proportions as before. Unrecorded goodwill on 1st January was valued at £18,000.

Required:
(i) Capital Accounts of A, B and C
(ii) B's Loan Account

(London Chamber of Commerce)

EXERCISE 22.5 (attempt after Chapter 23)

Thomas Ward and Edward Grant are in partnership, and at 1st January 19_0 they agreed to sell their business to Laws Ltd. The partnership Balance Sheet was as follows:

Balance Sheet as at 31st December 19_9

	£	£		£	£
Capital Accounts	£	£	Fixed Assets	£	£
Thomas Ward	12,000		Freehold Premises		6,000
Edward Grant	8,000		Plant & Machinery		4,500
		20,000	Fixtures and Fittings		1,200
					11,700
Current Accounts			Current Assets		
Thomas Ward	200		Stock	5,000	
Edward Grant	350		Sundry Debtors	6,000	
		550	Balance at Bank	1,250	
					12,250
Current Liabilities					
Sundry Creditors		3,400			
		£23,950			£23,950

Laws Ltd. was a new Company formed to purchase the above partnership business. Its Authorised Share Capital was £150,000, made up of 50,000 8% Preference Shares of £1 each, and 100,000 Ordinary Shares of £1 each.

The Company agreed to take over *all* the assets except the Bank Account, and also agreed to take over the responsibility for payment of the creditors. The Company valued the acquired assets as follows:

	£
Freehold Premises	10,000
Plant and Machinery	3,500
Fixtures and Fittings	600
Stock	4,600

The Company also agreed to pay £5,850, included in the purchase price, for the total debtors taken over. The purchase price was to be £25,000, and the Company proposed to settle this amount by the issue at par of 18,000 £1 Ordinary Shares, issued as fully paid, to the partners, the balance of the purchase price to be settled in cash on 15th January 19_0.

Required:
In the books of the partnership, show the entries necessary, in the following accounts, to close the business:
(i) Realisation Account
(ii) Bank Account
(iii) Partners' Capital Accounts

NOTE: Assume that the share distribution was made in the capital ratio of the partners at 31st December 19_9.

(London Chamber of Commerce)

EXERCISE 22.6

Almond, Beet and Cherry who are partners sharing profits or losses in the ratio of 2:1:1 respectively agree to dissolve the partnership. Their Balance Sheet at 31st December (the date of dissolution), was:

Balance Sheet as at 31st December
(date of dissolution)

	£		£
Capital: Almond	13,000	Premises	20,000
Beet	5,000	Machinery	9,200
Cherry	3,450	Vehicles	2,200
Loan	2,000	Debtors	3,540
Creditors	2,600	Stock	3,260
Mortgage	12,000		
Bank Overdraft	150		
	38,200		38,200

Terms of the dissolution agreement:

1. The loan was repaid.
2. Almond is to take over the premises at a revalued figure of £24,000 and to discharge the mortgage. He also takes one half of the Machinery for £4,000 and the Debtors to the extent of £2,600 for £2,150.
3. Almond is to assume responsibility for the Creditors.
4. Beet is to take over the Vehicles at book value less 20% and the remaining Machinery at book value less 10%.

5. Stock was taken over by Cherry at its market price of £3,900 less 10%.
6. The remaining debtors were sold to a debt collection agency for £600.
7. Expenses amounting to £72 were paid.
8. Final balances of the partners' capital accounts are settled by payments of cash.

Required:
Prepare the Realisation, Bank and Capital accounts.

(London Chamber of Commerce)

EXERCISE 22.7

A, B and C, having traded over many years, have now decided to dissolve their partnership. Their balance sheet as at 30th April 19_2 is as follows:

	£	£		£	£
Capital A	10,000		Fixed Assets		
B	12,000		Premises	25,000	
C	12,000	34,000	Equipment	6,000	
			Fixtures and Fittings	2,000	
			Motor Vehicles	4,000	37,000
Current A	2,800				
B	4,100				
C	(2,600)	4,300			
Current Liabilities			Current Assets		
Creditors	2,000		Stock	3,000	
Bank	3,700	5,700	Debtors	4,000	7,000
		44,000			44,000

Expanders Co. Ltd. agree to take over all of the fixed assets of the partnership except the motor vehicles at a valuation of £45,000. In full consideration Expanders Co. Ltd, pay £25,000 cash into the partnership bank account and, in addition, issue to the partners 30,000 Ordinary Shares of 50p each. A, B and C agree that the shares be distributed between themselves in the ratio of the balances remaining on their capital accounts after realisation.

A and B take over the two motor vehicles at an agreed valuation of £1,200 each. Stock is sold for £2,500 and debtors have paid £3,000. Creditors are discharged for £1,800 and the costs of dissolution are £1,000.

Required:
The following accounts recording the dissolution of the partnership:
(a) the bank account;
(b) the realisation account;
(c) the capital accounts of the partners.

(A.E.B. "A" level)

EXERCISE 22.8

A, B and C have been in partnership for some years sharing profits and losses, one half, one third and one sixth respectively. Their capitals at 1st April 19_8 (no separate current accounts are maintained) were A £95,000; B £69,000; C £38,000.

Their previous accountant retired on 31st March 19_8 and a new one, Dennis Smart, was appointed from 1st April 19_8. During the year to 31st March 19_9 Dennis discovered certain errors previously made in the accounts, namely:

(i) Some years earlier A and B had made fixed loans to the partnership of £12,000 and £15,000 respectively, and the partnership deed provided that these loans carried interest at an annual rate of 10%. Dennis discovered that in the year to 31st March 19_7, the previous accountant had forgotten to provide for loan interest before dividing up the year's profit, and in the year to 31st March 19_8, he had credited interest on A's loan account to B's capital account and vice versa.
(ii) No entry has been made in respect of a partnership motor car taken over by C in January 19_8. C had agreed to take over this car at £1,200, although its net book value at that date was £1,050.

Dennis prepared draft accounts for the year to 31st March 19_9 which showed a profit of £70,000, before charging interest on partners' loans but after deducting Dennis's salary of £5,000. Dennis had so impressed the partners that they decided to admit him as a partner *retrospectively* from 1st April 19_8. He was to bring in capital when he had sold some investments and was to be entitled to a one-tenth share of profits or losses, but was not to receive a salary. No other changes were made in the partnership agreement. Dennis agreed to pay into the business at 31st March 19_9, £6,000 for his share of the unrecorded goodwill. The appropriate amounts were credited to the original partners' capital accounts.

Drawings during the year to 31st March 19_9 were A £21,500; B £17,800 and C £7,400.

Required:
The partners' capital accounts (preferably in columnar form) showing the balance due to each partner at 1st April 19–9, after correcting the errors made in earlier years and after finalising the accounts for the year to 31st March 19_9.

(A.E.B. "A" level)

EXERCISE 22.9

Ash and Beech were partners sharing profits and losses in the proportions Ash two-thirds and Beech one-third. On 1st January 19_0, Oak was admitted as a partner and he paid in £2,550 as capital and £2,100 as a premium for a quarter share of the goodwill. Profits and losses were to be shared in the proportions Ash one-half and Beech and Oak one-quarter each.

The following trial balance was extracted from the books:

Trial Balance, 31st December 19_0

	£	£
Capital accounts at 31st Dec. 19_9:		
Ash		4,500
Beech		2,800
Amount paid in by Oak		4,650
Stock-in-trade 31st Dec. 19_9	1,875	
Debtors and creditors	1,660	1,420
Drawings – Ash	2,610	
Beech	1,530	
Oak	1,390	
Fixed assets	9,700	
Purchases	21,200	
Sales		30,600
Wages and salaries	3,025	
General expenses	840	
Balance at bank	140	
	£43,970	£43,970

The following matters are to be taken into account:

1. It was decided that the stock-in-trade at 31st December 19_9 should have been valued at £2,565, but no entry to reflect this decision has been made in the books.
2. The balance on General Expenses Account (£840) includes a payment of £22 for repairs to Ash's private residence.
3. A sales invoice for £184 dated 30th December 19_0 has, by mistake, been entered in the books twice.

4. No entries have been made in the books for:
   (i) goods, valued at £68 taken by Beech for his private use.
   (ii) business travelling expenses £44 incurred by Oak and paid by him out of his own pocket.
5. The stock-in-trade at 31st December 19_0 was valued at £2,168.

You are required:

(a) To set out the entries in the partners' capital accounts, and
(b) to prepare a trading and profit and loss account for the year 19_0 and a balance sheet as at 31st December 19_0.

NOTE: No partners' current accounts are to be opened, and no goodwill account is to be raised in the books. Ignore depreciation of fixed assets.

CHAPTER 23

LIMITED COMPANY ACCOUNTS

BACKGROUND

We have been concerned so far with the accounts of sole traders and partnerships, and there are many legal differences between these two types of business unit and limited companies. Most of these differences will be covered in your studies of other subjects such as law and economics, but there are certain comparisons that should be made now which will help you to understand what is going on.

Sole trader and partnership type businesses are very easy to form – no formalities or legal documentation are required, even though these may be desirable, nor is any formal system of keeping and presenting accounts required by law.

With a limited company, however, there are many formalities to be observed, not only on the formation of the company but regularly thereafter. Limited companies are subject to the requirements of the Companies Acts of 1948–81 and much of what the company and the directors may do is controlled by these Acts. A limited company's accounts must be properly kept and audited and the annual final accounts and balance sheet must be published in set format. The Acts dictate what information must be shown in these final accounts, which must be "filed" at Companies House for anyone who is interested to see. Many important resolutions passed by the company must also be "filed" for "all the world" to see.

Why such stringent requirements for limited companies and not for sole traders or partnerships? Well, the sole trader or the partners are running their businesses for themselves, and the law does not recognise any difference between them as persons, and the business itself – they are responsible *personally* for any debts their businesses may incur, and if their business assets are insufficient to pay off these debts they will be held *personally* liable for the unpaid debts. This means that they may have to sell their personal possessions in order to pay off unpaid business debts. In other words these owners have *unlimited liability* for the business debts. A supplier who is providing these businesses with stock on credit will not worry too much therefore if he sees fairly meagre business assets lying around, if he knows that the owners have big cars and big houses outside of the business, because if he ever has to sue them for unpaid bills these personal assets could be "called on" by the courts to pay off the business debts.

A limited company (the business, not the persons) is, however, recognised in law as being a legal "person" or a "separate legal entity", and if this business incurs debts its creditors can only sue the *company* as a separate legal "person" – the owners of the business are *not* personally liable for these debts and cannot therefore be sued. It may be necessary for the company's assets to be sold in order to pay off these debts, but if these assets do not realise enough to satisfy the debts in full then the suing creditors must be satisfied with what they get. There is no question of the owners themselves being sued, even if they *do* have big cars and big houses of their own, because they have *limited liability* for their company's debts – i.e. their liability is limited to the amount they have put into the company; they can lose this, but they can not be asked to contribute any more money to cover the company's debts.

These **owners** of the limited company are the people who have bought shares in the company – they are **the shareholders**. Because the company, despite being called a "person", can't act or think for itself, it is necessary for a board of directors to be appointed to act for and on behalf of the company, and for the company's shareholders – i.e. the owners. The directors are responsible for the day to day administration and operation of the business and in many small limited companies the directors and shareholders are one and the same people.

A company therefore gets its capital by issuing shares in itself to various people, and in a large company these shareholders will have no regular contact with the company. Having invested their money in the shares they will let the directors "get on with it", and hope that the accounts will show large profits each year which they will be able to share in. What they receive as their share of profits is called a *dividend*, and is the equivalent of owners' drawings in a sole trader or partnership business.

The stringent requirements of the Companies Acts 1948–81 are designed to protect the shareholders who have invested their money in the company, and to protect creditors of the company who cannot rely on the personal assets of the owners to cover the company's liabilities.

Having bought shares in a company, that person may reach the point where he wants his money back; he needs therefore to sell his shares. The company will *not* buy these shares back (and in fact, in most cases, it is not allowed by law to buy shares back) so the shareholder must find someone who is willing to buy the shares from him. If the shares are "quoted" on the Stock Exchange this is no problem, because the transfer of ownership of the shares is easy via a stockbroker. If, however, the shares are not "quoted", then he has to find his own buyer and will meet other problems, not least of which will be the difficulty of placing a value on the shares. With quoted shares the value is shown daily in newspapers such as the Financial Times, the current values being mainly based on the supply and demand for those shares.

Companies issue shares to get permanent capital for purchase of fixed assets, research, etc., and whoever buys the shares becomes a part owner of that company.

TYPES OF SHARES

Two main types of share are issued by companies.

PREFERENCE SHARES

These carry a fixed rate of dividend, e.g. "x"% Preference Shares, which means that the shareholders will receive at the year end a dividend (share of the company's profit) amounting to "x"% of their holding, even if the company has made such large profits that it could afford to pay a larger dividend. The shareholders are restricted to "x"%. In a good year they will obviously "lose out" by this, but in a poor year for profits they are still entitled to their "x"%, even though the directors may be reluctant to pay any dividend at all that year. The profits must however be large enough to cover the "x"% dividends due – if not, then the preference shareholders do not get their "x"%. If there are no profits this year then no preference dividends are paid.

Assuming that there *are* profits available, the preference shareholders will be paid their fixed dividends *before* any other type of shareholder.

Preference shares are either "Cumulative" or "Non-Cumulative". Cumulative shares allow unpaid fixed rate dividends to accumulate, until there are sufficient profits to pay these arrears of dividends. Non-cumulative shares don't allow unpaid dividends to build up; if there are insufficient profits this year to pay the fixed rate dividend, then the shareholders can not claim *this* dividend in later years.

In the event of the company going into liquidation (the equivalent of a sole trader or partnership going bankrupt) the owners of the company – i.e. the shareholders – are the very last persons to be repaid their capital. Other liabilities of the company will be paid off first. There may be insufficient money left therefore to pay back the shareholders' capital in full, but in a liquidation the preference shareholders will be paid back their capital, as far as possible, *before* any other type of shareholder is repaid.

Preference shareholders therefore get preferential treatment regarding payment of their dividends each year, and repayment of their capital on the winding up of the company.

ORDINARY SHARES

These do not carry a fixed rate of dividend but depend on the volume of profits made. In a good year the directors may declare a large dividend for the ordinary shareholders, whilst in a poor year they may get hardly anything, perhaps nothing. The ordinary dividends are paid *after* the preference dividends if sufficient profits remain.

In the event of liquidation the ordinary shareholders are the very last persons to be repaid their invested capital. In a compulsory liquidation therefore they will be lucky to get much, if any, of their capital returned to them. This is because, in a forced sale, assets rarely realise their book value which means insufficient money to repay all liabilities. Because of this, ordinary share capital is often referred to as "risk capital". Nevertheless most shares issued by companies are ordinary shares, and in a successful company these shareholders fare well.

Both types of share are issued at a certain face-value which can be 10p, 25p, 50p, £1, £5, etc. This is known as the **nominal** value. If a company issues £1 Ordinary Shares at nominal value, or "**at par**", this means that the buyers of the shares are being asked to pay £1 each for the £1 shares. If the £1 shares are issued for more than £1 then they are being issued *at a premium*, and people are quite happy to pay "over the odds" for a successful company's shares. They may therefore pay £1·30 each for a £1 share, but their share certificate will only acknowledge the nominal value – i.e. "John Smith is the registered holder of 100 Ordinary Shares of £1 each".

Whatever rate (%) of dividends are declared at the year end – a fixed rate for preference shares and a variable rate (according to profits) for ordinary shares – this percentage is always calculated on the *nominal* value of the shares, irrespective of what the owners paid for them. If, for example, you buy £1 shares at a 50% premium and an ordinary dividend of say, 15% is declared at the year end, you will receive 15p for every £1 share held. However, as you paid £1·50 for each share you are only receiving 15p for each £1·50 of your outlay, which is a *real* return to you of only 10%.

ACCOUNTS

The keeping of accounts for companies is just the same as for the other kinds of business unit we have dealt with – manufacturing accounts, trading and profit and loss accounts, balance sheets, etc. are prepared in the same way you are used to. The special requirements of the Companies Acts regarding the *published* accounts – i.e. those which will be filed at Companies House and sent to shareholders – will be dealt with at a later stage in your studies. We are concerned now with accounts for "internal" use.

The owners of the company are the shareholders, who contribute capital by buying shares. Obviously we can't have a separate capital account for each owner, as with partnerships. Instead there will be one capital account to represent *all* ordinary shareholders and another capital account for *all* preference shareholders – "Ordinary Share Capital Account" and "Preference Share Capital Account" respectively. The balances of these accounts will show on the balance sheet in the place that capital normally appears.

The profit and loss account, like the partnership, will always have an extension (the appropriation account) to show how the net profit for the year is appropriated, but, unlike the partnership, the whole of the net profit will not be appropriated – some will be left in the appropriation account.

Obviously the main appropriation of profits will be for dividends, *viz*:

Profit and Loss Appropriation Account for Year 1

Dividends Proposed	£		£
Preference	4,000	Net Profit b/d	20,000
Ordinary	10,000	(from P & L a/c)	
Balance c/d	6,000		
	20,000		20,000
		Balance b/d	6,000

NOTE: Of the £20,000 available profit, £14,000 has been appropriated as dividends and the other £6,000 is being left in the business. This £6,000 represents profits from trading and must therefore have been cash at some point in time (i.e. stock turned into debtors, who eventually paid cash). The chances are that it is no longer in cash form, but it is still in the business in *some* form – either increased assets or reduced liabilities – the £6,000 value is somewhere! If the £6,000 *is* still in cash form then, unless the company is planning to spend this on more assets in order to expand the business, or to pay off pressing debts, it may as well pay the £6,000 away as dividends. If, as is most likely, the £6,000 is no longer in cash form then it would be difficult to pay it away as dividends! Whatever form it is in, this value is being left (retained) in the business to help the company in some way or other. The £6,000 still belongs to the owners because the company makes profits for *them*, so the credit balance on appropriation account must show on the balance sheet as a liability of the company to its owners, described as either "P & L appropriation account" or more usually, "retained earnings".

In next year's appropriation account there will already be a balance of £6,000 on the credit side when next year's net profit is carried down, *viz*:

P & L Appropriation Account for Year 2

	£		£
Dividends Proposed		Balance b/d	6,000
Preference	4,000	Net Profit (for year 2)	24,000
Ordinary	12,000		
Balance c/d	14,000		
	30,000		30,000
		Balance b/d	14,000

Note that there is now £30,000 of profits available for appropriation, but it is usual practice to base the ordinary dividend rate on *this* year's profit (£24,000) and not to use previous year's profits for this year's dividends. (The £6,000 was left in the company last year *for a purpose*). The unappropriated profits over the years have now built up to £14,000, so £14,000 of value remains *somewhere* in the business and is acknowledged on the balance sheet as owing to the shareholders.

Leaving profits in the business is like injecting new capital, and the motive for doing this is usually in order to expand – i.e. use the cash behind the profits to increase working capital (see next chapter) or to purchase more fixed assets, etc.

The dividends shown in the above account are described as "proposed", not paid. This is because when the dividends are declared by the directors at the year end, the time when the appropriation account is written up, they are at this point only proposed – they will be paid later on. In the meantime they must "lie" in "proposed dividend" accounts, the balance of these accounts being shown on the balance sheet at the year end as current liabilities – i.e. due to be paid soon. The double entry to the debits in the appropriation account are therefore credits in the respective Proposed Preference and Ordinary Dividend accounts. When the dividends are eventually paid, these accounts will of course be closed off, (credit bank, debit proposed dividend account).

Let us now look at the balance sheet of the company as it might appear in 5 years' time:

Balance Sheet of Tucker Ltd. as at 31st March, 19_4

		£		£	£
Issued Share Capital			*Fixed Assets*		
100,000 Ordinary Shares of			Premises at cost		90,000
£1 each fully paid		100,000	Equipment at cost	120,000	
20,000 10% Preference Shares			Less prov. for		
of £1 each, fully paid		20,000	dep'n	40,000	80,000
Retained Earnings		80,000			
					170,000
Shareholders' Stake		200,000			
Current Liabilities			*Current Assets*		
Creditors	18,000		Stock	37,000	
Proposed Pref.			Debtors	20,000	
Dividend	2,000		Bank	8,000	
Ord. Dividend	15,000				65,000
		35,000			
		235,000			235,000

NOTE: The issued shares are fully described, and the words "fully paid" mean that the whole of the nominal value of the shares has been paid for by the shareholders. Sometimes the company will not ask for immediate full payment, in which case shares of £1 each may be described as, say, "75p called", indicating that the full £1 has not yet been paid; the 25p uncalled portion can be called for any time the company wants this extra money. Such shares are called "partly-paid" shares. The large balance on appropriation account means that profits have been retained, rather than paid out as dividends, on a large scale over the past 5 years. These retained profits are represented *somewhere* on the assets side, probably in the form of equipment – they are certainly not still in the form of cash.

Rather than keeping this accumulation of profits in appropriation account it is usual to keep a large proportion in a separate account called a *General Reserve* account, thereby indicating that these profits have been retained for general purposes. If we therefore transfer £60,000 of retained profits to General Reserve the entries in the accounts will be,

P & L Appropriation a/c

	£		£
General Reserve	60,000	Balance	80,000
Balance c/d	20,000		
	80,000		80,000
		Balance b/d	20,000

General Reserve a/c

		P & L Appropriation a/c	£60,000

and the liabilities side of the balance sheet will now show *two* different accounts making up the total retained earnings of £80,000, as per the above account balances. You might say "why bother to do this?" and I say, "Quite!" It is usual to build up the general reserve on an annual basis. A proportion of the profits in appropriation account would be transferred to general reserve each year, rather than making one big transfer occasionally as in the above example. A typical appropriation account at the year end might appear:

Appropriation a/c

	£		£
Transfer to General Reserve	6,000	Balance b/d	20,000
Proposed Dividend	20,000	Net Profit b/d	30,000
Balance c/d	24,000		
	50,000		50,000
		Balance b/d	24,000

SHARE PREMIUM

I mentioned earlier that successful companies could issue shares at a price above their nominal value – i.e. at a premium – and people would buy these even though their dividend rates would be calculated on nominal values only. When a company issues, say, a 50p share for 75p, the company is in fact making a profit of 25p on each share issued. This profit, as with any profit, belongs to the shareholders (the owners) and should be shown as such on the balance sheet, (a liability of the company). When such shares are issued at a premium, the *nominal value only* is credited to the respective share capital account – the premium is credited to a separate account – a "Share Premium Account." For example, a company issues 100,000 Ordinary Shares of 50p each at a premium of 20% –i.e. 60p per share. The entries in the accounts would be:

Bank a/c

	£		
Ord. Share Capital	50,000		
Share Premium	10,000		

Ordinary Share Capital a/c

		Bank	£50,000

Share Premium a/c

		Bank	£10,000

On the balance sheet, the balance of share premium account would appear as a liability in the "shareholders' stake" section, together with retained earnings and general reserve balances. Remember that only the *nominal* value of the shares goes into the share capital account. The premium is kept separate.

RESERVES

The definition of a "Reserve" is *retained profits*. The profits we have just been dealing with were profits from normal trading (appropriation account balance and general reserve balance) and profits on issue of shares (share premium account balance). These three accounts are Reserves because they hold retained profits.

There are two kinds of reserve.

REVENUE RESERVES – these are made up of retained profits which have originated from normal trading activities – i.e. Profit and Loss appropriation account balance and general reserve balance. Such reserves *are* available for distribution to the shareholders as dividends if the directors so decide.

CAPITAL RESERVES – These are made up of retained profits which have *not* been created by normal trading activities. The best example is share premium account, which is a reserve of profits obtained through selling shares at a price above their face (nominal) value. Capital reserves are not normally available for distribution as dividends, the idea being that shareholders should only receive, by way of dividend, profits made through normal trading.

A profit on the sale of a fixed asset should strictly be credited to a capital reserve account, not P & L account, as this is not a normal trading profit.

Another type of capital reserve is created by revaluing, say, premises. The increase in the value of premises if you remember, (which you should!) was credited direct to a sole trader's or partners' capital account, but with a company the increase in value is credited to a "Revaluation Reserve" (a capital reserve). For example, a company decides to revalue its premises, shown in the accounts at cost, £60,000, to a new value of £90,000.

Premises

	£		
Balance	60,000		
Revaluation Reserve	30,000		

Revaluation Reserve

		Premises	£30,000

Imagine the distortion of profits for the year if the £30,000 had been credited to P & L account! Also, this £30,000 would then have become part of the net profit, and therefore become available for distribution as dividends.

All reserves, whether they are revenue or capital reserves, still belong to the shareholders – the company owes these profits to them, and they therefore appear on the balance sheet as liabilities, being part of the shareholders' stake.

CONCEPT OF RESERVES

It is very important to appreciate that *all* reserves have some representation on the assets side of the balance sheet. For example, the revaluation reserve just dealt with is represented by an increase in the asset, property. The share premium account is represented initially by more cash/bank, and then as this cash is spent on something else the reserve is represented by that something else. The appropriation account balance and general reserve balance are represented, again initially, by more cash, then eventually by something else as this cash is spent. Study the following example:

(i) A company starts business by issuing 50,000 Ordinary shares of £1 each at par –

Balance Sheet

Issued Share Capital			
50,000 Ord. shares of £1	£50,000	Cash	£50,000

(ii) This cash is then used to buy premises:

Balance Sheet

	£		£
Share Capital	50,000	Premises	50,000
		Cash	–
	50,000		50,000

NOTE: The permanent capital invested in the company has been put to permanent use.

(iii) £10,000 of stock is purchased on credit and then is sold for £16,000, on credit.

Balance Sheet

	£		£
Share Capital	50,000	Premises	50,000
P & L account	6,000	Debtors	16,000
Creditors	10,000		
	66,000		66,000

The profit is at the moment represented by the asset, debtors, and when the debtors pay up the profit will become represented by cash.

(iv) Premises are revalued at £60,000. It is also decided to transfer £1,000 to a general reserve and to propose a dividend of £2,000. The debtors settle their accounts in cash.

Balance Sheet

	£		£
Share Capital	50,000	Premises	60,000
Revaluation Reserve	10,000		
P & L account	3,000		
General Reserve	1,000		
	64,000	Cash	16,000
Creditors	10,000		
Proposed Dividend	2,000		
	76,000		76,000

(v) Finally, the creditors are paid in full and the dividend is paid. Equipment is purchased for cash, £4,000.

Balance Sheet

	£		£
Share Capital	50,000	} Premises	60,000
Revaluation Reserve	10,000		
General Reserve	1,000	} Equipment	4,000
P & L account	3,000		
	64,000		64,000

The profits retained in general reserve and P & L account used to be backed by cash – they are now "tied up" in the fixed asset, equipment. In other words, by retaining these profits the company was able to expand, by buying more fixed assets. The share capital and revaluation reserve are of course backed by the premises. Reserves will always be backed, or represented by *some* kind of asset – "it may be a liquid asset" (i.e. "near cash", such as stock or debtors or actual cash), or it may be a fixed asset, in which case the profits concerned are referred to as being "tied up".

DEBENTURES

The owners of a company are its shareholders – the people who have put *permanent* capital into the company by buying its shares. As owners, they have a say in how the company is to be run by voting on varied issues at meetings of shareholders. They can never expect to get their money back from the company (unless they hold redeemable shares, or unless the company goes into liquidation) but they can always sell their shares to someone else. If a company requires more *permanent* capital it will issue some new shares – i.e. invite the public to buy shares, or to increase their existing shares. Quite often though, a company is in need of temporary capital only – capital which is only required for a limited period of time. The obvious answer is for the company to borrow money, and this can be done in a variety of ways. A bank or finance company may lend the required amount or the company may ask the general public to lend money – the company does this by the process of offering for sale DEBENTURES which are acknowledgements, (in the form of a certificate), of money received on loan. Persons buying these debentures are simply lending money to the company. As with all loans they will be repaid at some future date (compare with shares), and in the meantime the lender, (debenture holder), will receive interest at a fixed rate on the loan he has made to the company. This interest is payable *whether profits are made by the company or not*, and this is why the expense "debenture interest" is always charged to the Profit and Loss account proper, and not to the appropriation account. Like rent, rates, wages, etc., this interest *must* be paid, and is therefore a *charge* against profits, not an appropriation of profits. With shares you will remember, payment of dividends is entirely dependent on profits being made, and such payments are therefore *appropriations* of profit.

As debenture holders are simply a special kind of creditor, they do not have any say in the running of the company – i.e. they have no voting powers. Like shares, debentures can be sold to someone else – i.e. the loan transferred – should the holder want his money back before the repayment date.

When anyone lends money they usually wish the loan to be secured in some way, and loans to a company in the form of debentures are usually secured on certain assets of the company (e.g. the premises), which means that should the company be unable to repay the debenture holders on the due date, then the premises would have to be sold to pay off the debenture holders. Debentures so secured are called Mortgage Debentures and most debentures are of this kind.

Unsecured Debentures are referred to as "simple" or "naked" debentures.

Note where debentures and other long-term loans are shown on the balance sheet below. The interest, and earliest and latest dates of repayment of the debentures, are clearly shown.

SPECIMEN COMPANY BALANCE SHEETS

Balance Sheet of XYZ Ltd. as at 31st December 19. .

		£				£
*Authorised Share Capital**			*Fixed Assets*			
10,000 8½% Preference Shares			Goodwill			5,000
of £1 each		10,000	Freehold Premises			
60,000 Ordinary Shares of			at valuation			70,000
£1 each		60,000	Machinery at cost		28,000	
			Less Prov. for			
		70,000	depreciation		12,000	16,000
		£	Fixtures, etc. at cost		8,000	
Issued Share Capital			Less Prov. for			
6,000 8½% Preference Shares			depreciation		2,500	5,500
of £1 each, fully paid		6,000				
40,000 Ordinary Shares of			Trade investments			
£1 each, fully paid		40,000	at cost			5,000
		46,000				101,500
Share Premium		4,000				
Revaluation Reserve		10,000				
Capital Reserve		2,000				
General Reserve		8,000				
Retained Profits		11,000				
Shareholders' Stake		81,000				
Long Term Liabilities						
12% Mortgage Debentures						
1992/95		30,000				
Current Liabilities			*Current Assets*			
Trade Creditors	7,500		Stock		11,000	
Proposed Pref. Div.	510		Debtors	10,000		
Proposed Ordinary			Less Prov.			
Dividend	4,000		for bad			
Accruals	90		debts	1,900		
		12,100			8,100	
			Prepayments		100	
			Bank		1,800	
			Cash in hand		600	
						21,600
		123,100				123,100

* Authorised Share Capital is the maximum shares the company is legally allowed to issue. It is usually shown on the balance sheet like this, purely as a *note*, the total being ruled off.

Balance Sheet of XYZ Ltd. as at 31st December 19. .

		£	£
Authorised Share Capital			
10,000 $8\frac{1}{2}\%$ Preference Shares of £1 each			10,000
60,000 Ordinary Shares of £1 each			60,000
			70,000
CAPITAL EMPLOYED			£
Issued Share Capital			
6,000 $8\frac{1}{2}\%$ Preference Shares of £1 each, fully paid			6,000
40,000 Ordinary Shares of £1 each, fully paid			40,000
			46,000
Reserves			
Share Premium		4,000	
Revaluation Reserve		10,000	
Capital Reserve		2,000	
General Reserve		8,000	
Retained Profits		11,000	
			35,000
Shareholders' Stake			81,000
Long Term Liabilities			
12% Mortgage Debentures 1992/95			30,000
			111,000
UTILISATION OF CAPITAL			
Fixed Assets			
Goodwill			5,000
Freehold Premises at valuation			70,000
Machinery at cost		28,000	
Less provision for depreciation		12,000	
			16,000
Fixtures, etc. at cost		8,000	
Less provision for depreciation		2,500	
			5,500
Trade Investments at cost			5,000
			101,500
Current Assets			
Stock		11,000	
Debtors	10,000		
Less Prov. for bad debts	1,900	8,100	
Prepayments		100	
Bank		1,800	
Cash in hand		600	
		21,600	
Less Current Liabilities			
Trade Creditors	7,500		
Proposed Pref. Dividend	510		
Proposed Ord. Dividend	4,000		
Accruals	90	12,100	9,500
			111,000

The first balance sheet is shown in conventional form. There are many variations of presentation, and one of the most popular formats for limited companies is the preceding version of a *vertical* lay-out, using the same figures. You will note that it shows first of all the amount of permanent and semi-permanent capital at the company's disposal, and then goes on to show how this capital is being used in the business – i.e. in fixed and current assets, less of course the commitments of current liabilities.

EXERCISE 23.1

The following information relates to Beba Ltd for the year ended 30th April 19_0:

	£			£
General reserve	35,000	Trade creditors		38,000
Net trading profit for the year	75,000	Interim ordinary dividend paid		6,000
Profit & Loss Account (credit balance) 19_9	50,000	Preference shares dividends paid		
Share premium account	100,000	Interim	4,000	
		Final	4,000	
			——	8,000
Issued capital		*Authorised capital*		
100,000 8% £1 preference shares	100,000	200,000 8% £1 preference shares		200,000
300,000 £1 ordinary shares	300,000	400,000 £1 ordinary shares		400,000

The directors had proposed that:

(a) £30,000 should be transferred to general reserve;
(b) a final dividend of 10% should be paid to ordinary shareholders.

Required:
A profit and loss appropriation account for the year ended 30th April 19_0 and a balance sheet extract at that date, showing in detail, the total shareholders' funds (i.e. the total shareholders' interest).

Pay particular attention to layout and presentation.

(A.E.B. "O" level)

EXERCISE 23.2

(a) The following balances have been extracted from the books of the Nemesis Company Limited as at 30th September 19_7:

	£
Creditors	6,300
Sales	80,000
Land at cost	18,000
Buildings at cost	38,000
Furniture and fittings at cost	22,000
Bank (credit balance)	6,000
Depreciation – buildings	6,000
– furniture and fittings	10,000
Discounts received	1,764
Unappropriated profit at 1st October 19_6	2,000
Provision for doubtful debts	816
Goodwill	16,400
Cash in hand	232
Stock at 1st October 19_6	14,248
Interim dividend on preference shares	600
Rates	2,124
Wages and Salaries	8,000
Insurance	1,896
Returns inward	372
General expenses	436
Debtors	12,640
Purchases	43,856
Debenture Interest	400
Bad Debts	676
5% Debentures	16,000
6% £1 Preference Shares	20,000
£1 Ordinary Shares	20,000
General Reserve	10,000
Share Premium	1,000

Additional information:

(i) Stock on hand at 30th September 19_7 was £15,546.
(ii) Insurance paid in advance – £100.
(iii) Wages owing – £280.
(iv) Depreciation is to be provided at 10% on cost of buildings, and at 20% on the written down value of furniture and fittings.
(v) Provision for doubtful debts is to be reduced to 5% of debtors.
(vi) Debenture interest outstanding of £400.
(vii) The directors propose to pay a 5% Ordinary Dividend and the final Preference Dividend, and to transfer £8,000 to General Reserve.

Required:
Prepare the Trading, Profit and Loss and Appropriation Account for the period ended 30th September 19_7 and a Balance Sheet as at that date.

(b) Examine the accounts you have prepared in (a) above and then answer the questions below:
(i) How did the Share Premium Account arise?

(ii) How could the goodwill account have arisen?
(iii) What is the rate of return on net capital employed, and what is the significance of this figure?
(iv) Which of the reserves are capital reserves and which are revenue reserves, and what, in principle, is the difference between the two?

(A.C.C.A.)

EXERCISE 23.3

(a) The following terms usually appear in the final accounts of a limited company:

(i) interim dividend,
(ii) authorised capital,
(iii) general reserve,
(iv) share premium account.

Required:
An explanation of the meaning of each of the above terms.

(b) The following information has been obtained from the books of Drayfuss Ltd:

Authorised capital		100,000 8% £1 preference shares 400,000 50p ordinary shares
Profit and loss account balance 1st April 19_8	*cr*	£355,000
General Reserve		£105,000
Issued capital		80,000 8% £1 preference shares (fully paid) 250,000 50p ordinary shares (fully paid)
Net trading profit for the year to 31st March 19_9		£95,000.

The preference share interim dividend of 4% had been paid and the final dividend of 4% had been proposed by the directors.

No ordinary share interim dividend had been declared, but the directors proposed a final dividend of 15p per share.

The directors agreed to transfer to general reserve £150,000.

Required:
The profit and loss appropriation account for the year ended 31st March 19_9

(Ignore taxation).

(A.E.B. "O" level)

EXERCISE 23.4

The following balances were extracted from the books of Homer Traders Limited at 31st March 19_9:

	£
Ordinary shares of £1 each, fully paid	30,000
8% Preference shares of £1 each, fully paid	5,000
Share premium account	4,000
6% Loan stock	5,000
Trade creditors	7,400
Trade debtors	16,500
Sales	240,000
Purchases	211,000
Discounts allowed	250
Discounts received	650
Freehold buildings:	
At cost	25,000
Provision for depreciation	2,500
Fixtures and fittings:	
At cost	32,000
Provision for depreciation	12,800
Stock at 1st April 19_8	21,000
Returns outwards	4,000
Establishment expenses	6,500
Administration expenses	2,800
Selling and distribution expenses	8,350
Bad debts written off	200
Provision for doubtful debts	900
Profit and loss account at 1st April 19_8	18,100
Goodwill	8,000
Bank overdraft	1,250

Additional information:

(i) Depreciation is provided annually on the cost of fixed assets held at the end of the financial year at the following rates:

Freehold buildings	2%
Fixtures and fittings	10%

(ii) The trade debtors balance includes £500 due from K. Smythe who has now been declared bankrupt. In the circumstances, it has been decided to write the debt off as a bad debt.

(iii) The provision for doubtful debts at 31st March 19_9, is to be 5% of trade debtors at that date, after writing off bad debts.

(iv) Establishment expenses prepaid at 31st March 19_9 amounted to £200.

(v) Administration expenses accrued due at 31st March 19_9 amounted to £350.

(vi) The company paid the interest on the loan stock for the year ended 31st March 19_9, on 30th April 19_9.
(vii) Gross profit is at the rate of $16\frac{2}{3}\%$ of sales.
(viii) The company's directors propose that the preference share dividend be paid, and a dividend of 10% on the ordinary shares be paid.

Required:
(a) The trading and profit and loss account for the year ended 31st March 19_9 of Homer Traders Limited and a balance sheet at that date.

(A.C.C.A.)

EXERCISE 23.5

The following trial balance was extracted from the books of Beccles Ltd. at 31st December 19_7:

	£	£
Share capital		200,000
Share premium		40,000
Freehold land and buildings at cost	142,000	
Motor vans at cost	55,000	
Provision for depreciation of motor vans at 1st January 19_7		21,800
Purchases	189,273	
Sales		297,462
Rent and rates	4,000	
General expenses	9,741	
Wages	34,689	
Bad debts	948	
Provision for doubtful debts at 1st January 19_7		1,076
Directors' salaries	25,000	
Debtors and creditors	26,482	16,974
Retained profit at 1st January, 19_7		18,397
Stock in trade at 1st January, 19_7	42,618	
Bank balance	65,958	
	£595,709	£595,709

You are given the following additional information:
(i) the authorised and issued share capital is 200,000 shares of £1 each, which are all issued and fully paid;
(ii) wages outstanding at 31st December 19_7, amounted to £354;
(iii) the provision for doubtful debts is to be increased by £124;
(iv) stock in trade at 31st December 19_7, was £47,288;
(v) rent and rates amounting to £400 were paid in advance at 31st December 19_7:
(vi) it is proposed to pay a dividend of £8,000 for the year 19_7;

(vii) depreciation on motor vans is to be charged at the rate of 20 per cent per annum on cost.

Required:
A trading and profit and loss account for the year 19_7 and a balance sheet at 31st December 19_7.

NOTE: Ignore taxation.

(Institute of Bankers)

EXERCISE 23.6

The following balances were extracted from the ledger of South & North Ltd. as at 31st December 19_9:

	£
Freehold Land and Buildings at cost	65,000
Trade Creditors	27,400
Purchases	185,850
Motor Vans at cost £10,950 less sale on 1st January 19_9	10,500
Trade Debtors	22,810
Delivery expenses	2,526
Sales	269,550
Wages and Salaries	29,600
Share Capital:	
70,000 Ordinary Shares of £1 each fully paid	70,000
Stock in trade 1.1._9	21,000
Directors' fees	9,200
General expenses	9,432
Cash at Bank and in hand	24,930
Rates and Insurance	1,502
Provision for depreciation of Motor Vans to 31.12._8	5,400
Profit and Loss Account CR balance 1.1._9	10,000

The following additional information is given:

1. The Authorised Capital was £70,000.
2. Depreciation on motor vans to be provided at the rate of 20% per annum on cost.
3. Rates in arrear at 31st December 19_9 amounted to £120.
4. A motor van which had cost £1,500 was sold on 1st January 19_9 for £450. The provision for depreciation to 31.12._8 on this van totalled £1,000.
5. Stock in trade at 31st December 19_9 was valued at £17,000 at cost.
6. The net profit for the year 19_9, after all the above adjustments had been made, was £25,380.
7. Goods despatched on "Sale or return", invoiced at £240, had been included in Sales and Debtors in the Trial Balance but were subsequently returned on 5th January 19_0. The invoice price was cost plus 50%.

Required:
Prepare the Balance Sheet of South and North Ltd. as at 31st December 19_9, preferably in "vertical" presentation.

(London Chamber of Commerce)

EXERCISE 23.7

The balance sheets of Helston Ltd. at 31st December 19_9, and 19_0 are as follows:

	19_9		*19_0*	
	£	£	£	£
Fixed assets at cost		202,000		245,000
less depreciation		83,000		105,000
		119,000		140,000
Current assets:				
Stock	25,000		50,000	
Debtors	23,000		29,000	
Bank	12,000	60,000	1,000	80,000
		179,000		220,000
Share capital		100,000		100,000
Retained profit		49,000		83,000
		149,000		183,000
Current liabilities		30,000		37,000
		179,000		220,000

The figure of current liabilities at 31st December 19_9, includes a proposed dividend of £5,000 for the year to that date. No decision has been taken yet about the dividend to be paid for 19_0, and nothing is included in the 19_0 balance sheet for such dividend.

The directors are considering the dividend that should be paid for 19_0 in the light of the excellent results for that year.

Required:
(a) A calculation of the maximum dividend that should be declared for 19_0 if the working capital ratio in the December 19_0 balance sheet, after providing for the dividend, is to be the same as in the December 19_9 balance sheet.
(b) A brief discussion of the financial policy pursued by the directors of Helston Ltd. in 19_0.

(Institute of Bankers)

EXERCISE 23.8

The following trial balance was extracted from the books of Lingford Ltd. as at 31st December 19_9:

	£	£
Share capital		120,000
Share premium		25,000
Freehold land and buildings at cost	87,000	
Motor vans at cost	40,000	
Provision for depreciation on motor vans at 1st January, 19_9		14,800
Purchases	129,938	
Sales		179,422
Rent and rates	2,500	
General expenses	5,842	
Wages	19,876	
Bad debts	542	
Provision for doubtful debts at 1st January, 19_9		684
Directors' salaries	16,000	
Debtors and creditors	16,941	11,171
Stock in trade at 1st January, 19_9	28,572	
Bank balance	24,921	
Profit and loss account as at 1st January 19_9		21,055
	372,132	372,132

You are given the following additional information:

(i) the authorised and issued share capital is 120,000 shares of £1 each all of which are issued and fully paid;
(ii) wages due but unpaid at 31st December 19_9 amounted to £264;
(iii) the provision for doubtful debts is to be increased by £102;
(iv) stock-in-trade at 31st December 19_9, was £38,292;
(v) rent and rates amounting to £300 were paid in advance at 31st December 19_9;
(vi) depreciation on motor vans is to be charged at the rate of 20 per cent. per annum on cost;
(vii) it is proposed to pay a dividend of £5,000 for the year 19_9.

Required:
A trading and profit and loss account for the year 19_9, and a balance sheet as at 31st December, 19_9.

(Institute of Bankers)

EXERCISE 23.9

Fishlines Ltd. is a small private company. From the following information, set out the company's Balance Sheet on 31st December 19_7.

This should be set out in such a way to show within the Balance Sheet (a) the working capital and (b) the net worth of the business.

	£	£
Premises at cost 1st January 19_1	50,000	
Furniture and fittings at cost 1st January 19_1	4,000	
Stock	7,000	
Debtors	3,500	
Cash in hand and bank	8,000	
		72,500
Capital – 45,000 shares of £1 each all issued and fully paid	45,000	
Retained profits	14,000	
Profit and Loss Account Balance	400	
Dividend unpaid	5,000	
Provision for depreciation on premises	5,000	
Provision for depreciation on furniture and fittings	2,000	
Provision for doubtful debts	400	
Trade creditors	700	
		72,500

(University of London "O" level)

CHAPTER 24

CASH AND WORKING CAPITAL

CASH

A Balance Sheet shows the financial state of a business as at a particular date. It has been described as a "photograph" of a business, and these "photographs" are usually taken once a year. In this respect always remember that things can change overnight!

Whilst we can get a certain amount of information as to how a business is progressing, by comparing one year's balance sheet with another, it is often desirable to know what has gone on in the period between the balance sheet dates.

Quite often a trader is puzzled as to why, after a year of good profits, he has a bigger bank overdraft at the year end than he had at the beginning. In explaining to him, we would point out that whilst profits have the effect of increasing cash, via debtors, it is rare that the cash (or bank) balance at the year end has increased by the same amount as profits for the period for the following reasons:

(i) Some of the cash from profits may still be in the form of debtors, or *extra* cash may have been received from debtors.
(ii) Some of the cash may have been applied to the purchase of more stock.
(iii) Some of the cash may have been utilised in paying creditors (who supply stock) or creditors may have been allowed to build up, so *saving* cash.
(iv) Payments may have been made in purchasing fixed assets (such transactions do not of course affect profits) or there may be cash receipts from the sale of fixed assets.
(v) Extra cash may have come in from new issues of shares, or debentures, or cash may have gone out in repayment of debentures and other long term loans.
(vi) Dividends may have been paid out of profits, and so on . . .

All of the above reasons could be summarised in the form of a Cash Flow Statement whereby we show *Sources* of cash and *Uses* of cash in the period. The cash book would of course give us all the information we need, but there would be far too many items to analyse. We need something concise, so that what has happened to cash can be seen almost at a glance. Most of the items in the cash book would refer to receipts from debtors, payments to creditors, payment of rent, wages, etc., etc. If we take *one* figure, the net profit figure for the period, then we have in fact taken the *net* effect of all those numerous items just mentioned, which make up the trading and profit and loss account. This figure will start off our cash flow Statement as a *Source of cash.* All the other figures which go into our statement will simply account for the reasons why the profit figure is not wholly represented by cash at this point in time. The difference between the final totals, "Sources" and "Uses", will account for the difference in the cash (bank) balances at the beginning and end of the period in question.

Let us look at some examples:

Balance Sheet as at start

	£		£
Capital	5,000	Cash	5,000

DURING MONTH 1

A trader buys £2,000 of stock for cash – therefore:

Balance Sheet as at end of Month 1

	£		£
Capital	5,000	Stock	2,000
		Cash	3,000
	5,000		5,000

Cash Flow Statement for Month 1

	£
Sources	
Profits	—
	—
Uses	
Increase in stock	2,000
	2,000

Applications exceed Sources by £2,000 – i.e. cash has decreased by £2,000.

DURING MONTH 2

A trader sells £1,000 of stock for £1,500 cash – therefore:

Balance Sheet at end of Month 2

	£		£
Capital	5,000	Stock	1,000
P & L A/c	500	Cash	4,500
	5,500		5,500

Why has cash increased by £1,500 in month 2, when only £500 profit has been made? Because £1,000 of stock has been converted into cash and an additional £500 of cash has come in from profits.

Cash Flow Statement for Month 2

	£
Sources	
Profits	500
Decrease in Stock	1,000
	1,500
Uses	
NIL	NIL

DURING MONTH 3

£500 of stock is sold on credit for £750

Balance Sheet as at end of Month 3

	£		£
Capital	5,000	Stock	500
P & L A/c		Debtors	750
(£500 + £250)	750	Cash	4,500
	5,750		5,750

Despite a profit of £250, cash remains the same. This is because the reduction in stock of £500, which should have been converted into cash, has been applied to debtors, and similarly with the £250 profit.

Cash Flow Statement for Month 3

	£
Sources	
Profits	250
Decreases in Stock	500
	750
Uses	
Increases in Debtors	750
	750

So once again we have accounted for the "movements" in cash.

DURING MONTH 4

Stock is bought for £800 cash. £400 of stock is sold for £550, on credit.

Balance Sheet at end of Month 4

	£		£
Capital	5,000	Stock	900
P & L A/c	900	Debtors	1,300
		Cash	3,700
	5,900		5,900

Profits of £150 have been made, yet cash has reduced by £800. This is because the whole of the cash which should have been received (£550) has been applied to debtors, and another *£400* of cash has been utilised in increasing stock (if you are wondering what has happened to the OTHER £400 spent on stock – well, this found its way into "debtors" as part of the £550 mentioned above!).

Cash Flow Statement for Month 4

	£
Sources	
Profits	150
	150
Uses	
Increase in Debtors	550
Increase in Stock	400
	950

i.e. a decrease in cash of £800.

DURING MONTH 5

Stock is purchased on credit for £1,000, and is immediately sold for £1,600 on credit. Also, fixed assets are bought for £1,000 cash.

Balance Sheet as at end of Month 5

	£		£
Capital	5,000	Fixed Assets	1,000
P & L A/c	1,500	Stock	900
Creditors	1,000	Debtors	2,900
		Cash	2,700
	7,500		7,500

The cash balance has reduced by £1,000 in month 5. This is because the whole of the cash which *SHOULD* have been received from the sale of £1,600, has been applied to debtors – also, £1,000 of cash has been *SAVED* by purchasing stock on credit (i.e. stock is acquired without having to pay for it there and then, and this is equivalent to a receipt of cash).

Also, of course, £1,000 cash is spent on fixed assets.

Cash Flow Statement for Month 5

	£
Sources	
Profits	600
Increase in Creditors	1,000
	1,600
Uses	
Increase in Debtors	1,600
Purchase of fixed assets	1,000
	2,600

i.e. a decrease in cash of £1,000.

WHAT IT ALL AMOUNTS TO IS THIS:

Sources of cash are:

1. Profits.
2. Increase in creditors (cash is saved – payments "held off").
3. Decreases in debtors (cash benefits – less cash "held" in debtors).
4. Decreases in stock ("saving" of cash as stock is not replaced).

Uses of cash are:

1. Losses.
2. Decreases in creditors (extra payments being made – less credit being taken).
3. Increases in debtors (less cash coming in).
4. Increases in stock (more cash going out for this).

Other Sources are:

(i) Cash from a share/debenture issue/loans.
(ii) Sale of fixed assets.

Other Uses are:

(i) Redemption of Debentures and other long term loans.
(ii) Purchase of fixed assets.
(iii) Drawings of proprietor, payment of dividends to shareholders and payment of tax.

SUMMARY

Any increase in an asset (other than cash) must be at the expense of cash – i.e. a use of cash.

Any decrease in an asset (other than cash) must be a gain to cash – i.e. a source of cash.

Conversely, any increase in a liability must be a gain to cash. Any decrease in a liability must be at the expense of cash.

EXAMPLE

From the following balance sheets we will prepare a Cash Flow statement for the period 19_9.

Balance Sheets

	19_8	*19_9*		*19_8*	*19_9*
	£	£		£	£
Issued Share Capital	30,000	40,000	Fixed Assets (cost)	47,200	64,000
Share Premium	1,500	2,500	Less depreciation	6,200	8,900
General Reserve	4,000	6,000			
Profit & Loss a/c	7,000	10,000		41,000	55,100
	42,500	58,500	Stock	7,000	11,000
Debentures	5,000	3,000	Debtors		
			Bank	5,000	3,700
Creditors	3,500	4,800		1,000	500
Dividends Proposed	3,000	4,000			
	54,000	70,300			
				54,000	70,300

As good a start as any is to calculate the cash flow from profits. The Profit and Loss account has increased by £3,000 *after* transferring to General Reserve £2,000 and after appropriating a dividend of £4,000. Therefore the company must have made a net profit of £3,000 + £2,000 + £4,000 = *£9,000*. This is the figure taken down from the Profit and Loss account proper to the appropriation account, and is therefore *after* charging depreciation in the Profit and Loss account. You know that the entry for depreciation in the Profit and Loss account does not affect the cash in any way (unlike other items in Profit and Loss account such as rent, wages, etc.) – it is a book keeping entry only (DR Profit and Loss, CR Provision for Depreciation account) – a non-cash debit. As we want to know how much cash has come in from profits we must *add* the current year's charge for depreciation, £2,700, on to our calculated net profit figure of £9,000, so making *£11,700*. Then we can look at all the *other* items in our balance sheets.

Cash Flow Statement for 19_9

	£		£
Sources		*Uses*	
Profits	11,700	Repayment of Debentures	2,000
Issue of Shares	10,000	Dividend Paid	3,000
Share premium	1,000	Purchase of Fixed Assets	16,800
Increases in Creditors	1,300	Increase in Stock	4,000
Decrease in Debtors	1,300		
	25,300		25,800

i.e. The Bank balance is £500 worse off than before – check this with the balance sheets.

Note that the dividend *proposed last year* (£3,000) would have been *paid this year*.

A cash flow statement, in this simple form, is a most useful analysis, and an understanding of its construction will be of great benefit to you when answering questions concerned with cash flow. It will also help you to understand the construction of "Sources and Applications of Funds Statements" which will be dealt with in the next chapter.

WORKING CAPITAL

When a business commences to operate, the first transaction is, of course, the injection of capital into the concern. A sole trader provides a sum of money with which to start off his business; the partners in a firm each provide their various sums of money to get the firm started in business;

and the limited company sells its shares in order to get the necessary capital together with which to start trading.

Let us suppose that a particular business concern starts off with a contribution of £10,000 capital, and that £5,000 of this capital is used to purchase premises from which the business will operate, and a further £2,000 is used to buy furniture, fittings and equipment. In other words a total of £7,000 is put into FIXED ASSETS – which are here to stay! The business has not yet started to operate (i.e. by trading or manufacturing) but has simply set itself up. The work has not yet started. Out of the original £10,000 capital provided, £7,000 has been spent on this "setting up" of the business – which leaves £3,000 for the business to *work with.* This is the amount which the business has to utilise to make its profits.

To start with, some of this £3,000 will be used to buy stock – this will subsequently be sold, and the business will then have debtors – the debtors will eventually "pay up" so producing cash, this cash will then be used to pay off the creditors who have provided the business with stock on credit, more stock will then be purchased, then sold, and the debtors will pay up, so creating cash, and so on. All of this activity with the £3,000 left over from the initial capital of £10,000! This £3,000 of capital is WORKING in order to make profits and is the firm's WORKING CAPITAL.

If the business makes some profits then these will increase the capital which the business has to work with, i.e. its working capital. The larger the profits are, the larger the business's working capital will become.

Let us look at an example to see how this works out:

EXAMPLE:

The balance sheet of A Trader at 31st December, Year 1 is as follows:

	£		£
Capital	6,000	Fixed Assets	2,500
Creditors	500	Stock	2,000
		Debtors	1,500
		Bank	500
	6,500		6,500

The balance sheet tells us that out of the initial £6,000 capital provided, £2,500 has been tied up in fixed assets, so leaving £3,500 of capital for the firm to work with, i.e. its working capital.

DURING JANUARY, YEAR 2 the following transactions occur:

	£
Receipts from debtors	1,200
Payments to creditors	400
Purchase of stock on credit	700

The balance sheet at 31st January, Year 2 will now look like this:

	£		£
Capital	6,000	Fixed Assets	2,500
Creditors	800	Stock	2,700
		Debtors	300
		Cash	1,300
	6,800		6,800

Working capital is still the same – £3,500. Why? Because no extra working capital came in from profits (there were none in January) or elsewhere, and no further working capital has been tied up in fixed assets.

DURING FEBRUARY, YEAR 2 the following transactions occur:

£800 stock sold on credit for £1,100
£200 paid to creditors
£750 spent on fixed assets

The balance sheet at 28th February now looks like this:

	£		£
Capital	6,000	Fixed Assets	3,250
Profit and Loss account	300	Stock	1,900
Creditors	600	Debtors	1,400
		Cash	350
	6,900		6,900

Working capital is now £3,050 i.e. £6,000 of capital plus £300 extra capital in the form of retained profits, of which £3,250 has been tied up in fixed assets, thereby leaving £3,050. At the end of January working capital was only £3,500 but it has been increased by the amount of the profits (£300) and then decreased by the purchase of fixed assets (£750).

What do we know about Working Capital then? We know that it is that part of the capital put into a business which is not tied up in fixed assets and is therefore available to work with in order to make profits. And when we talk of capital "put into a business" we don't mean just the initial investment (e.g. the proceeds from shares), but also any new capital which may come into the business (e.g. new issue of shares/loans) *and* any new capital which finds its way into the business (e.g. from profits) and is LEFT IN (e.g. retained profits in the form of Reserves). To sum up this section let us have a look at another balance sheet:

Balance Sheet as at 19_0

	£		£
Issued share capital	10,000	Premises	11,000
Share premium	3,000	Machinery, etc.	4,000
General Reserve	2,000	Stock	7,000
Profit and Loss a/c	4,200	Debtors	2,000
		Bank	2,000
	19,200		
Debentures 1990/95	3,500		
	22,700		
Creditors	3,300		
	26,000		26,000

From this we can say that the capital obtained from issuing shares is £10,000 plus the premium on the issue, £3,000, and that of the new capital generated over the years in profits, a total of £6,200 has been retained in the company. All this makes a total investment of £19,200 by the shareholders. In addition, £3,500 loan capital has been obtained by issuing debentures, which gives us a grand total of £22,700 long term capital.

How much of this is "tied up"? – £15,000 in fixed assets is "tied up". This leaves £7,700 (£22,700 less £15,000) to work with – i.e. the **WORKING CAPITAL.**

How important is WORKING CAPITAL?

It can be described as the circulating blood of a business – once it stops circulating the business is dead – and if there is not sufficient of it, then the business has to struggle for its life. Let me illustrate this:

MOVEMENTS IN WORKING CAPITAL

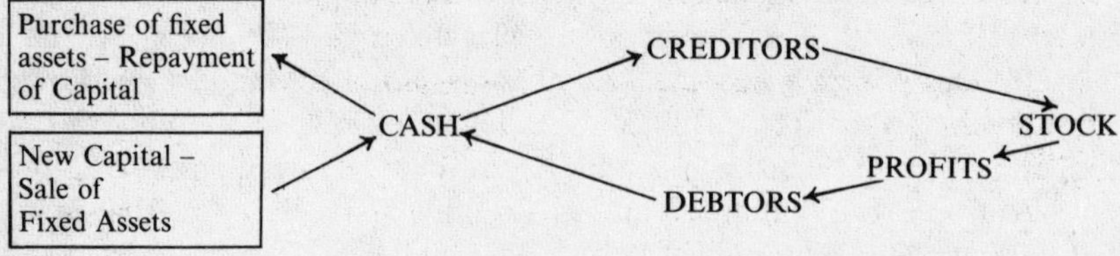

The above shows how working capital revolves, and as it revolves, profits are made (as stock is sold to debtors) – the faster it revolves the faster the profits are made. You will note from the diagram how new capital can be injected into the flow of working capital, and how working capital can leave the flow as capital is repaid (i.e. long term loans being paid off) or fixed assets purchased. All short term loans (e.g. bank overdraft) would be classed as "creditors" as they would soon be due to be repaid.

A business gets into difficulties when working capital is depleted too much. The cause of this could be due to heavy losses being made or it could be due to diverting too much working capital into fixed assets. This latter cause is the most common and is referred to as "overtrading". For example, a business which is getting in a lot of new orders from customers is obviously going to be very pleased with itself, but to satisfy this increased demand for its products, the business may have to erect new factories or machinery or to buy other new fixed assets. This, we know involves depleting the store of working capital, and unless the business has adequate resources of working capital, it may well find that after buying all the additional fixed assets, it has no capital left to work with! This is where the business resorts to heavy borrowing and great reliance on extended trade credit in order to purchase stocks of raw materials and goods. And if the creditors start "pushing" for repayment, the business may find that the only way to repay its debts is to sell some of its fixed assets! The next step is then usually bankruptcy or liquidation as no business can continue to function without its full complement of fixed assets.

If, of course, the depletion of working capital referred to (through buying more fixed assets) is quickly replaced by the extra profits coming in from increased trade, then all is well, and such is usually the case when a business is expanding gradually and steadily. The danger is when the business expands too rapidly (unless its store of working capital is very large, which is unlikely).

A prudent businessman will therefore expand his business at a rate which is consistent with the working capital available, and will know at what point he should "draw the line" by refusing new orders and contracts. Let us look at an example of overtrading:

Balance Sheet of a Company as at 31st December, Year 1

	£		£
Share Capital	50,000	Fixed Assets	35,000
Profit and Loss a/c	10,000	Stock	10,000
		Bank	30,000
	60,000		
Creditors	15,000		
	75,000		75,000

Normal Profits = £7,500 p.a.
Working Capital = £25,000 (i.e. capital of £50,000 plus retained profits of £10,000, of which £35,000 has been "tied up")

The company is offered a contract which would double its normal profits, but which would involve purchasing another factory and equipment at a cost of £80,000. To purchase these fixed assets the company obtains a bank overdraft of £50,000 which, together with its existing bank balance pays for the assets.

Balance Sheet of a Company NOW

	£		£
Share Capital	50,000	Fixed Assets	115,000
Profit and Loss a/c	10,000	Stock	10,000
	60,000		
Creditors	15,000		
Bank	50,000		
	125,000		125,000

Working Capital = MINUS £55,000 (i.e. negative).

The problems are:

(i) Stock must be bought and the company must rely very heavily on credit for this.
(ii) The working capital which has "gone" will only be replaced slowly as profits are made.
(iii) If stock is not turned over quickly there will be no money to pay the creditors bills as they become due, there being no working capital to fall back on.

In effect, the company is now being run mainly with other peoples' *short term* money, these people having a bigger stake in the business than the shareholders themselves have. If these short term creditors do not get paid as the debts become due, they could push the company into liquidation.

The above illustrates how very important it is for a business to maintain an adequate supply of working capital at all times.

You should now have a very good idea of what working capital is, and I want you now to look at it from another angle, which is this:

"Working capital is the excess of total current assets over total current liabilities" – i.e. Current Assets minus Current Liabilities = Working Capital."

If total current assets are £7,000 and current liabilities are £4,000, then the working capital is £3,000. *In other words, if all the current liabilities were paid off in full, there would still be £3,000 of current assets left to work with – the Business is not wholly dependent on its short term creditors.*

Read these words again and consider their significance in the examples we have looked at during the course of this topic.

CHANGES IN AMOUNT OF WORKING CAPITAL

We have already seen some of the things which can increase or decrease the amount of working capital available, such as purchase of fixed assets (decrease); issue of more shares (increase); making of profits (increase) etc.

In deciding whether a certain kind of transaction will affect the amount of working capital available, it might be easier to think of working capital in the terms of "current assets less current liabilities". From this it should be obvious that the amount of working capital will not be affected in the slightest by a transaction that increases or decreases current assets *AND* current liabilities by the same amount; nor by a transaction which increases current assets *AND* decreases current assets by the same amount. Such transactions respectively could be:

(i) Purchase of stock on credit (stock increases – Creditors increase)
(ii) Payment made to a creditor (cash decreases – Creditors decrease)
(iii) Receipts of cash from a debtor (cash increases – Debtors decrease)

In other words, if a transaction does not affect any item OUTSIDE of the working capital "circle" in the following balance sheet, then it does NOT affect the amount of working capital available. All changes caused by transactions (i) to (iii) above occur *WITHIN* the "circle":

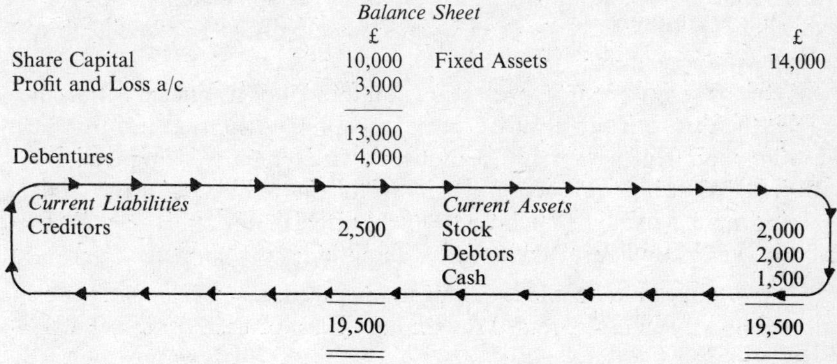

Balance Sheet

	£		£
Share Capital	10,000	Fixed Assets	14,000
Profit and Loss a/c	3,000		
	13,000		
Debentures	4,000		
Current Liabilities		*Current Assets*	
Creditors	2,500	Stock	2,000
		Debtors	2,000
		Cash	1,500
	19,500		19,500

Some examples of transactions which *will* have an effect inside *and* outside of the "circle", and will therefore affect the working capital, are:

(i) New debentures or other long term loans taken out – current assets (cash/bank) increase – current liabilities remain the same, and the result is an increase in working capital.
(ii) Debentures (long term loans) repaid – cash/bank decreases whilst current liabilities remain the same – result is a decrease in working capital.
(iii) Shares issued for cash – current assets increase whilst current liabilities remain the same, and so working capital increases.
(iv) Purchase of fixed assets for cash – cash decreases, whilst current liabilities remain the same – result, a decrease in working capital.
(v) Sale of fixed assets – cash increases, so does working capital.
(vi) £1,000 of stock sold for £1,600 on credit – current assets (stock) decrease by £1,000, whilst current assets (debtors) increase by £1,600. This gives a *net* increase in current assets of £600 and Profit and Loss account also increases by £600. Current liabilities remain the same, and the result is therefore an increase in working capital, of £600. In other words, profit increases working capital and losses decrease working capital.
(vii) The £600 profit in (vi) above is paid out as a dividend – current assets (cash) decrease and Profit and Loss account decreases by £600 – current liabilities remain the same. Result is a decrease in working capital.
(viii) Payment of taxation will cause a decrease in working capital because Profit and Loss account will decrease and so will cash.

NOTE: that all of the above transactions affect some items within the working capital "circle" *and* some items outside of the "circle". They all affect working capital.

We know now that if a transaction confines all of its effects within the circle, then there is no effect on working capital. Also, that if a transaction has an effect within and without the circle then working capital *is* affected. What if a transaction has *all* of its effects outside of the circle? For example, a change in depreciation charges will not affect the "circle" in any way – obviously then such transactions will *not* affect working capital.

Don't interpret what I have been saying about the circle as a set of formulas and just memorise some rules. You must *understand* what is happening so *study* (rather than memorise) what I have said above.

Now think up some transactions yourself and decide how these would affect working capital, if at all. Play around with little balance sheets as above – use plenty of paper and transmit your thoughts, imaginary decisions, etc. to this paper. This is one of the best ways of becoming permanently familiar with *ANY* topic.

CURRENT RATIO (WORKING CAPITAL RATIO)

In deciding whether a business has *enough* working capital it is not sufficient to calculate the amount. For example £30,000 of working capital may be more than enough for a small manufacturing firm, but to a large public company it would be hopelessly inadequate.

A useful indication is to calculate the current ratio, that is, what proportion do the current assets bear to the current liabilities? If the current assets total £12,000 and the current liabilities total £6,000 then the current ratio is two to one, indicating that the current assets cover the current liabilities twice over. The ratio is expressed:

$$\frac{\text{Current assets}}{\text{Current liabilities}} \qquad \text{(Current Assets} \div \text{Current Liabilities)}$$

If the current liabilities are covered twice by the current assets then the business is in a fairly strong position as regards its ability to meet its immediate commitments.

There is no "rule of thumb" here because different types of business require different levels of cover. For example, a retail business dealing in cash sales would require a lower current ratio than a business dealing with long term contracts where the turnover is slow, and in the meantime there is the need to carry large stocks and possibly debtors. If the working capital of the business cannot support much of these stocks and debtors until sales take place and payment is received, then there is a need to rely heavily on "outside support" in the form of short term credit, and too much reliance on short term support can be dangerous. The business must be in a position to satisfy the claims of these short term creditors easily, and hence the need for adequate cover.

Generally speaking, a 1·5 – 2·0 to 1 current ratio would be "reasonable to adequate", whilst a 3 to 1 ratio may indicate that the business is carrying too much stock or too many debtors – in other words the ratio is too high, but always consider the *type* of business.

A business with a very inadequate amount of working capital can only rectify this by gaining access to more *long term* or permanent capital, (e.g. long term loans, share issues, etc.).

EXERCISE 24.1

Harley has been in business for many years, and the following series of balance sheets were prepared from his books:

	19_7	19_8	19_9
	£	£	£
Assets:			
Motor vans	5,300	4,200	5,600
Stocks	6,098	5,436	6,788
Debtors	4,724	3,842	6,036
Bank	1,342	4,292	78
	17,464	17,770	18,502
Sources of Finance			
Capital	12,694	8,052	11,694
Creditors	4,770	9,718	6,808
	17,464	17,770	18,502

Harley's capital account for 19_8 and 19_9 was as follows:

		£			£
31.12._8	Drawings	10,152	1. 1._8	Balance	12,694
31.12._8	Balance	8,052	31.12._8	Profit	5,510
		18,204			18,204
31.12._9	Drawings	9,432	1. 1._9	Balance	8,052
31.12._9	Balance	11,694	31.12._9	Profit	13,074
		21,126			21,126

Harley complains that, despite the high profit in 19_9, his cash position is worse than it was a year earlier.

Required:
A brief report in which you explain to Harley the reasons for his reduced liquidity. The report should be supported by an appropriate financial statement.

(Institute of Bankers)

EXERCISE 24.2

The summarised accounts of Colorado Ltd. for 19_7 are as follows:

Trading and Profit and Loss Account for year ended 31st December 19_7

	£		£
Materials consumed	18,921	Sales	44,120
Wages	12,545		
Depreciation	3,830		
	35,296		
Gross profit	8,824		
	44,120		44,120
Expenses	4,521	Gross profit	8,824
Net profit	4,303		
	8,824		8,824

Balance Sheet at 31st December 19_7

		£			£
Share capital		36,000	*Fixed assets*		
Retained profit		8,420	Buildings at cost		20,000
			Plant (purchased 1.1._5)		
		44,420	Cost	30,640	
Current liabilities			*less* depreciation	11,490	
Raw materials	5,140				19,150
Expenses	270				
		5,410			39,150
			Current assets		
			Stock of materials	4,812	
			Debtors	3,328	
			Cash	2,540	
					10,680
		49,830			49,830

The directors of Colorado Ltd. have decided to embark on a policy of expansion. They consider that the 19_7 turnover can be doubled in 19_8 on the basis of the following estimates and additional information:

(i) a new building costing £20,000 will be required;

(ii) additional plant, with an eight year life, and costing £24,000, will be required;

(iii) the cost of materials consumed and wages will double, and expenses will increase by £2,000;

(iv) at the end of 19_8 stock in trade will have increased to £8,900, debtors to £6,200 and creditors for raw materials to £10,250; expense creditors will amount to £450;

(v) the directors have negotiated a loan of £15,000, with interest at 10 per cent per annum, repayable on 31st December 19_0, and which was received on 1st January 19_8;

(vi) the company's bankers have agreed to provide, on overdraft, any additional funds needed to meet the proposed expansion, but have stipulated that the overdraft must be cleared by 31st December 19_9.

Required:

(a) A summary bank account for 19_8.

(b) A summarised trading and profit and lost account for 19_8, and a balance sheet at 31st December 19_8.

NOTES:

Assume that the forecasts for 19_8 are exactly achieved.
No dividends have been paid, and none are proposed.
Ignore taxation.

(Institute of Bankers)

EXERCISE 24.3

The directors of Gifts Ltd. are reviewing the company's financial estimates. A summary of the company's estimated balance sheet at 31st December 19_1 is shown below:

	£		£	£
Issued Share Capital (£1 ordinary shares)	60,000	Goodwill		8,300
General Reserve	22,000	Freehold property		27,800
Profit and Loss a/c	14,500	Plant at cost	39,900	
Trade creditors	7,500	*Less* accumulated Depreciation	16,600	23,300
		Quoted investments		11,000
		Stocks		17,200
		Trade debtors		10,000
		Cash in hand and bank		6,400
	104,000			104,000

The following information relates to expectations for the year ending 31st December 19_1:

	£
Credit Sales	120,000
Purchases	60,000
Depreciation for the year	4,500
Net profit	7,000

It can be assumed that all transactions will take place at an even rate throughout the year.

The directors are considering making the following amendments to the estimated figures:

1. An issue of 20,000 ordinary shares, at par.
2. A transfer of £5,000 from Profit and Loss account to the general reserve.
3. The average period of credit taken from suppliers to be amended to 2 months.
4. £2,300 to be written off goodwill.
5. Freehold property to be shown in the accounts at £40,000 on the basis of a professional valuation.
6. Depreciation for the year to be increased to £6,000.
7. Quoted investments to be reduced to estimated market value of £10,000.
8. Trade debtors to be reduced by a provision of £1,000 for doubtful debts.
9. The average period of credit allowed to customers to be amended to 2 months.

Required:
A statement showing how *each* of the proposed amendments would affect the cash balance shown in the estimated balance sheet of Gifts Ltd. at 31st December 19_1, compared with the previously estimated position.

Consider each item independently and state your answer in the form:

1. *Increase* £ . . . . . or *decrease* £ . . . . . or *no change*
2. Etc.

You are not required to present an amended balance sheet or to comment on your answers.

NOTE: Ignore taxation.

(Institute of Bankers)

EXERCISE 24.4

Indicate with a tick in the appropriate column what effect each of the following transactions will have on the amount of working capital.

	Effect on Working Capital		
	increase	decrease	none
1. Purchase of stock on credit			
2. Repayments of debentures			

	Effect on Working Capital		
	increase	decrease	none
3. New issue of shares			
4. Receipt of cash from debtors			
5. Profit on sale of stock			
6. Proposed dividend			
7. Sale of fixed asset			
8. Increase in provision for depreciation			
9. Payment made to a creditor			

EXERCISE 24.5

Simon is puzzled by the accounts of Retail Ltd. He says:

> "I have calculated the company's funds generated from operations by adding back depreciation to net profit. The amounts came to £29,000 in 19_5 and £35,000 in 19_6, but, despite modest dividends and fixed asset acquisitions, the company started 19_5 with a bank balance of £5,000 and finished 19_6 with an overdraft of £13,000. Why?"

You are provided with the following figures for Retail Ltd.:

Balance Sheet at 31st December

	19_4	19_5	19_6
	£(thousands)		
Issued share capital	100	100	100
Reserves	33	42	58
Proposed dividends	8	10	8
Trade Creditors	28	36	39
Bank Overdraft	–	5	13
	169	193	218
Fixed assets at cost, at beginning of year	126	137	149
Additions during year	11	12	13
	137	149	162
Less: Depreciation	38	48	59
	99	101	103
Stock	25	32	35
Trade debtors	40	60	80
Bank	5	–	–
	169	193	218

Profit statement for year ended 31st December

		19_5		19_6
		£(thousands)		
Sales: for cash		200		150
on credit		300		400
		500		550
Deductions				
Opening stock	25		32	
Purchases	357		388	
	382		420	
Less: Closing stock	32		35	
Cost of goods sold	350		385	
Sundry Expenses	121		130	
Depreciation	10		11	
		481		526
Net profit		19		24
Proposed dividend		10		8
		9		16

It can be assumed that all sundry expenses were paid in the year in which they were incurred and that trade creditors relate only to purchased goods.

Required:
Numerical statement which will explain the changes in the bank account of Retail Ltd. in 19_5 and 19_6 so far as the information available permits.

NOTE: Ignore taxation.

(Institute of Bankers)

EXERCISE 24.6

Rochford has been in business for many years, and the following series of balance sheets was prepared from his books:

Balance Sheets as at 31st December

	19_7	19_8	19_9
	£	£	£
Assets			
Motor vans	1,900	1,400	2,000
Stock	2,716	2,439	3,129
Debtors	2,018	1,582	2,695
Bank	542	1,729	18
	7,176	7,150	7,842
Sources of finance			
Capital	5,987	3,189	4,766
Creditors	1,189	3,961	3,076
	7,176	7,150	7,842

Rochford's capital account for 19_8 and for 19_9 was as follows:

31.12._8	Drawings	4,760	1. 1._8	Balance	5,987
31.12._8	Balance	3,189	31.12._8	Profit	1,962
		7,949			7,949
31.12._9	Drawings	3,145	1. 1._9	Balance	3,189
31.12._9	Balance	4,766	31.12._9	Profit	4,722
		7,911			7,911

Rochford complains that, despite the high profit in 19_9, his cash position is worse than it was a year earlier.

Required:
A financial statement to explain to Rochford the reason for the variation in his bank balance.

(Institute of Bankers)

EXERCISE 24.7

Solo owns a small retail business selling colour television sets and the following details relate to this business for the periods indicated:

at 31st March	19_0	19_1
	£	£
fixed assets at cost	20,000	22,000
stock	7,400	12,500
cash and balance at bank	4,800	900
loan from bank	2,800	—
creditors	2,000	2,400
provision for depreciation	4,000	5,000

for the year ended 31st March 19_1	£
sales	40,000
purchases	32,000
general expenses (including rates, wages, and electricity)	4,100
cash withdrawn for personal use	3,400

Required:

(a) Trading and profit and loss account for the year ended 31st March 19_1; show net profit as a percentage of turnover.

(b) Calculate the average length of time, in months, that goods remain in stock.

(c) Advise Solo on **two** possible ways, not necessarily quantitative, to increase stock turnover so that profits are increased.

(d) Prepare a statement which illustrates to Solo why his cash resources have fallen to £900 in spite of cash drawings of only £3,400 which are well below the net profit for the year. (Note: there were no sales of fixed assets during the period.)

(A.E.B. "A" level)

EXERCISE 24.8

The following are the balance sheets of J. Taylor as at 31st May 19_7 and 31st May, 19_8.

Balance Sheets

	19_7	19_8		19_7	19_8
	£	£		£	£
Capital	8,400	9,000	Fixed Assets (cost)	11,300	13,300
Add Profit for year	2,100	3,000	Less depreciation	1,700	3,000
	10,500	12,000		9,600	10,300
Less Drawings	1,500	3,600			
	9,000	8,400			
Long Term Loan	3,000	2,000	Stock	2,700	2,100
Bank overdraft	1,000	3,400	Debtors	3,200	3,500
Creditors	2,500	2,100			
	15,500	15,900		15,500	15,900

Taylor is puzzled, because despite his net profit increasing by £900 in 19_8, his bank overdraft is £2,400 greater than it was in 19_7.

Prepare a statement showing him why this has happened.

CHAPTER 25

STATEMENTS OF SOURCE AND APPLICATION OF FUNDS

So far we have looked at Cash Flow Statements as a concise means of showing an overall picture of cash flows in and out of a business during a particular period. We have seen that cash is only a part of working capital as a whole, and we could therefore prepare in addition to our Cash Flow Statement a Working Capital Flow Statement which would show all those things which have increased (sources) and decreased (uses) not just cash, but working capital as a whole. We would be accounting for the change in *working capital* (current assets less current liabilities) over a period of time.

Both types of flow "statements" would, in effect, select certain information from the profit and loss account and balance sheet prepared at the end of a period, and summarise this information – obviously a very useful aid in assessing the financial position of a business.

A statement which combines changes in cash with changes in working capital overall – i.e. accounts for changes in "funds" – is called a "Statement of Source and Application of Funds". This statement shows the profit or loss for the period with adjustments for items not affecting funds (e.g. book entries such as depreciation), the purchase and sale of fixed assets, the issue and repayment of shares and long-term loans, dividends paid, tax paid, and finally the increase and decrease of working capital sub-divided into its individual components.

We do not want a statement showing movements in cash alone (a cash flow statement). We want a statement accounting for movements in working capital *overall.* A Statement of Sources and Applications of Funds will show movements in cash *and* working capital generally over a period of time.

What transactions cause changes in working capital? You already know this from previous reading!

Now study the following example.

Example:

X Ltd. Balance Sheets

	Year 1	*Year 2*		*Year 1*	*Year 2*
	£	£		£	£
Share Capital	40,000	50,000	Fixed Assets (cost)	77,400	102,000
General Reserve	11,000	14,000	Less depreciation	27,400	33,500
Retained Profits	4,500	7,800		———	———
Debentures	7,000	5,000		50,000	68,500

Current Liabilities			*Current Assets*		
Taxation	5,700	6,500	Stock	19,000	21,000
Creditors	6,300	7,200	Debtors	8,000	6,300
Proposed Dividends	4,500	6,000	Bank	2,000	700
	79,000	96,500		79,000	96,500

N.B. No fixed assets were sold during Year 2.

From the above information prepare a Statement of Source and Application of Funds for Year 2:

Answer:

(i) The first step is to determine the funds generated from trading – i.e. the profit before tax. The profit and loss account has increased by £3,300 and this is *after* transferring £3,000 to General Reserve, *after* providing for a proposed dividend of £6,000 and taxation of £6,500. Therefore, the profit *before* any of these appropriations were made must have been – £3,300 + £3,000 + £6,000 + £6,500 = *£18,800*.

(ii) The depreciation charge in year 2 was £6,100 (the difference between Year 1 and Year 2), and our profit of £18,800 was *after* charging for this, so the £6,100 must be added back to show the true inflow of funds from profits.

(iii) Share capital has increased by £10,000 – therefore funds have been increased by £10,000 (source).

(iv) Funds have been applied in paying off £2,000 of debentures (application).

(v) Year *1's* proposed dividend of £4,500 and taxation liability of £5,700 will have been *paid* during Year 2 – i.e. applications of funds.

(vi) Fixed assets were purchased for £24,600 (an application of funds).

X Ltd.
Statement of Source and Application of Funds for the period 1st January to 31st December, Year 2

Source of Funds	£
Profits before tax	18,800
Adjustments for items not involving a movement of funds:	
Depreciation	6,100
	24,900
Issue of shares for cash	10,000
	34,900

Application of Funds	£	
Repayment of Debentures	2,000	
Dividends paid	4,500	
Tax paid	5,700	
Purchase of fixed assets	24,600	
		36,800
	Decrease	(1,900)

What does the above tell us? That funds show a net decrease of £1,900 in the year – but how can we reconcile this?

We finish off the Statement of Source and Application of Funds with a final section, thus:

Increase (Decrease) in Working Capital	£	£
Increase in stocks	2,000	
Decrease in debtors	(1,700)	
Increase in creditors	(900)	
Decrease in Bank	(1,300)	
Decrease		(1,900)

N.B. Both figures have been reconciled (i.e. agreed).

In doing this final "reconciliation" we are looking at each *change* in stock, debtors, bank, cash, creditors (i.e. *all* current assets and liabilities) *in isolation.* For example, if stocks have increased by £2,000 then current assets have increased by £2,000, whilst current liabilities have remained the same – therefore an increase in working capital. Note – it is important, when preparing this reconciliation, to think of *each* change in current assets and liabilities in isolation of all other changes in other current assets and current liabilities. Similarly, a decrease in debtors of £1,700 (in isolation of everything else) indicates a decrease in current assets, while total current liabilities have remained the same, therefore a decrease in working capital overall. An increase in creditors of £900 means *more* current liabilities and the same total of current assets – therefore a decrease in working capital. Finally, a decrease in bank balance of £1,300 means less current assets but the same current liabilities – therefore a decrease in working capital.

The final net result of these changes in working capital should, if you have done everything correctly, agree with the increase or decrease shown in your sources and applications of funds statement. In preparing this reconciliation you are *not* concerned with dividends or taxation and these items are simply a "break-away" element of the Profit and

Loss account balance. Stock, debtors, bank and creditors are not.

Our Statement therefore consists of three main headings:

	£
Source of Funds	
Details	
Less Application of Funds	
Details	
Increase (Decrease)	

	£
Increase (Decrease) in Working Capital	
Increase (Decrease)	

Whenever you are asked to prepare a Statement of Source and Application of Funds I would recommend that you use the above form although variations on this would be acceptable to the examiner.

Remember that only dividends *paid* (i.e. last year's proposed dividend) and tax *paid* (last year's proposed taxation) will show in these statements as applications of funds.

In attempting this type of question deal with it methodically – compare carefully the changes which have taken place in all of the various items shown in the balance sheets given, and think carefully of their effect on working capital, and their effect on your final reconciliation. *Use rough paper* to see what is happening – what is happening within the "circle" of current assets and current liabilities, and what is affecting items outside of the circle? If you do this you can't go wrong!

EXERCISE 25.1

The balance sheets of Albany Ltd. at 31st December 19_8 and 31st December 19_9 are as follows:

	19_8	19_9
	£	£
Share capital	105,000	120,000
Retained profit	44,148	48,972
	149,148	168,972
Debentures	—	45,000
Current liabilities	30,783	40,458
	£179,931	£254,430

	£	£	£	£
Fixed assets				
Plant at cost	127,500		206,250	
less depreciation	51,300	76,200	80,700	125,550
Transport at cost	25,200		35,100	
less depreciation	7,650	17,550	13,110	21,990
		93,750		147,540
Current assets				
Stock	36,351		57,747	
Debtors	27,414		42,348	
Bank	22,416	86,181	6,795	106,890
		£179,931		£254,430

Required:
A flow of funds statement for 19_9 in which you identify changes in working capital.

NOTE: No dividends were paid in 19_9 and none are proposed.

(Royal Society of Arts)

EXERCISE 25.2

From the following balance sheets prepare a Statement of Source and Application of Funds for the period Year 2.

Balance Sheets

	Year 1	*Year 2*		*Year 1*	*Year 2*
	£	£		£	£
Share Capital			*Fixed Assets*		
(£1 shares)	80,000	100,000	Plant & Equipment		
General Reserve	12,000	17,000	(at cost)	51,400	70,300
Retained Earnings	9,500	13,500	*Less* depreciation	8,400	14,300
	101,500	130,500		43,000	56,000
8% Debentures	20,000	25,000	Premises	60,000	60,000
Current liabilities			*Current Assets*		
Corporation tax	13,500	16,000	Stock	44,000	61,000
Creditors	23,000	27,500	Debtors	28,000	32,000
Dividends Proposed	10,500	15,000	Bank	—	5,000
Bank overdraft	6,500	—			
	175,000	214,000		175,000	214,000

EXERCISE 25.3

Balance Sheets of ABC Ltd.

	Year 1	*Year 2*		*Year 1*	*Year 2*
	£	£		£	£
Share Capital	100,000	120,000	Fixed Assets (cost)	140,000	170,000
Share Premium	15,000	18,000	*Less* provision for		
General Reserve	30,000	34,000	depreciation	81,000	87,000
P & L Appropriation a/c*	6,200	8,700		59,000	83,000
Debentures	25,000	20,000	Stock	58,000	65,200
Reserve for Corp. tax	14,000	16,000	Debtors	43,200	55,000
Current Liabilities	30,000	38,500	Bank	60,000	52,000
	220,200	255,200		220,200	255,200

	£
*Net profit in year 2	37,500
Less depreciation for year	6,000
	31,500
Less estimated tax for year (To reserve)	16,000
	15,500
Less Transfer to General Reserve	4,000
	11,500
Less Dividend paid	9,000
	2,500
ADD P & L Appropriation a/c Balance from Year 1	6,200
P & L Appropriation a/c balance c/fwd at end of Year 2	8,700

Prepare a statement showing the sources and applications of funds for Year 2.

(Institute of Bankers)

EXERCISE 25.4

The balance sheets of Boswell Ltd. at 31st March 19_2, and 31st March 19_3, appear below:

	31st March 19_2	*31st March 19_3*		*31st March 19_2*	*31st March 19_3*
	£	£		£	£
Issued Share Capital	30,000	30,000	Freehold property		
Profit and Loss a/c	27,000	33,000	at cost	25,000	25,000
Corporation Tax due:			Equipment (see note)	18,000	22,200
1st January 19_3	6,000	—	Stock in trade	16,400	17,800
1st January 19_4	—	4,000	Debtors	13,600	14,000
Creditors	12,000	13,000	Bank	2,000	1,000
	75,000	80,000		75,000	80,000

NOTE: Equipment movements during the year ended 31st March 19_3, were:

	Cost	*Depreciation*	*Net*
	£	£	£
Balance at 31st March 19_2	30,000	12,000	18,000
Additions during year	9,000		
Depreciation provided during year		3,800	
	39,000	15,800	
Disposals during year	4,000	3,000	
Balance at 31st March 19_3	35,000	12,800	22,200

The company's summarised profit calculation for the year ended 31st March 19_3, revealed:

	£	£
Sales		100,000
Gain on sale of equipment		400
		100,400
Less		
Cost of goods and trading expenses	86,600	
Depreciation	3,800	90,400
Net Profit		10,000
Corporation tax on profits of the year		4,000
Retained profit of the year		6,000

Required:
A Statement of Source and Application of Funds for the year ended 31st March 19_3.

(Institute of Bankers)

EXERCISE 25.5

The following represent (in abbreviated form) the balance sheets of Jingles and Co. on 31st March 19_8 and 31st March 19_9.

			19_8 £'000s			19_9 £'000s
Mr Jingles –						
Capital Account			104			128
Current Account			56			28
			160			210
Long Term Loan			50			40
Long Term Capital Employed			£210			£250
Fixed Assets						
Land and Buildings, at cost			90			95
Plant and Machinery, at cost		60			70	
Accumulated Depreciation		15	45		20	50
Motor vehicles, at cost		25			30	
Accumulated Depreciation		10	15		13	17
			150			162
Trade Investment, at cost			40			38
Current Assets						
Stock		80			50	
Debtors		60			65	
		140			115	
Less: Current Liabilities						
Creditors	60			50		
Tax Payable	20			15		
Bank Overdraft	40	120	20	—	65	50
			£210			£250

For simplicity Income Tax on Mr Jingles' profits is paid through the firm's bank account. No sales of fixed assets took place during the year. Drawings by Mr Jingles were £10,000 in 1978 and £12,000 in 19_9.

You are required to:

(a) Prepare a Funds Flow Statement for the year ended 31st March 19_9.

(b) How could the Statement you have produced be of use to Mr Jingles?

(Association of Accounting Technicians)

EXERCISE 25.6

The summarised balance sheets of the partnership of Small and Large at 30th June 19_8 and 19_9 are as follows:

19_8		19_9	19_8		19_9
£		£	£		£
	Capital accounts		16,000	Freehold properties at cost	5,000
18,000	Small	29,470	–	Freehold properites at valuation	18,000
23,000	Large	27,530			
–	Tiny	2,000	24,500	Other fixed assets at cost	
	Current accounts			less depreciation	38,000
5,400	Small	6,300			
2,800	Large	3,500	12,300	Stock	17,100
			6,100	Debtors	8,300
9,000	Loan from Mrs Small	10,500	4,500	Bank	–
5,200	Trade creditors	5,600			
–	Bank overdraft	1,500			
63,400		86,400	63,400		86,400

The summarised profit and loss account for the year ended 30 June 19_9, appeared as follows:

	£	£
Gross profit		25,900
less rates	900	
staff salaries	9,250	
selling expenses	3,750	
depreciation of fixed assets	4,400	
bad debts written off	500	
profit on sale of property	(1,700)	
general expenses	2,800	
		19,900
Net profit for the year		6,000

You are also given the following information:

(a) After allowing 10% interest on capital account balances at the start of each year, the balance of profit was divided, Small $\frac{2}{5}$; Large $\frac{3}{5}$.

(b) During the year, the partners have taken goods from stock for private purposes as follows, Small £800; Large £600.

(c) During the year a freehold property which cost £2,250 was sold. Following professional advice certain of the other properties were revalued at market value, and one new property was bought for £2,000. Depreciation is not provided on properties.

(d) Some small items included in "other fixed assets" were sold for £1,500 which was £300 less than written down value at 30th June 19_8. This small loss has been included in the depreciation charge for the year.

(e) Small introduced into the business during the year the proceeds of a legacy from his late Aunt. Large did not bring any cash capital into the firm during the year.
(f) On 28th June 19_9 Tiny was admitted as a partner. On that day he paid into the firm's bank account £2,300 to include his capital and share of unrecorded goodwill at that date. It was agreed that Tiny was not entitled to share in any profits arising during the year to 30th June 19_9.

Required:

(i) Partners' Capital and Current accounts for the year ended 30 June 19_9.
(ii) A Statement to show the Sources and Applications of Funds becoming available for the year ended 30 June 19_9.

(A.E.B. "A" level)

EXERCISE 25.7

The following are the summarised balance sheets at 30th April 19_7 and 19_3 of Pincushion Limited, retailers of hardware kitchen goods.

	19_7 £	19_8 £		19_7 £	19_8 £
Capital:			Plant and machinery:		
Ordinary shares	20,000	50,000	at cost	20,000	18,000
6 per cent preference shares	5,000	5,000	Less depreciation to date	8,000	9,000
Share premium account	–	5,000		12,000	9,000
General reserve	3,000	8,000	Freehold buildings at cost	–	46,000
Retained earnings	2,000	7,000			
8 per cent Loan Stock	4,000	4,000	Stocks and work in progress	9,000	13,000
Bank overdraft	–	3,000	Debtors	11,000	20,000
Creditors	3,000	1,000	Balance at bank	7,000	–
Dividends proposed	2,000	5,000			
	39,000	88,000		39,000	88,000

The summarised retained earnings account for the year ended 30th April 19_8, is as follows:

	£	£
Profit for the year		15,000
Transfer to general reserve	5,000	
Proposed dividends	5,000	10,000
		5,000
Balance brought forward		2,000
Balance carried forward		7,000

During the year ended 30th April 19_8 plant and machinery additions amounted to £5,000 at cost and disposals realised £7,000. The depreciation charge for the year on plant and machinery was £3,000.

(a) Prepare sources and applications of funds statement for the year ended 30th April 19_8 to account for the change in working capital.
(b) Comment briefly on whether you consider the working capital to be adequate at 30th April 19_8, giving reasons for your answer.

EXERCISE 25.8

The balance sheets of Rainbow Limited as at 31st December 19_0 and 19_1 are as follows:

		19_0		19_1
	£	£	£	£
Fixed assets at cost		240,000		284,000
less depreciation		100,000		122,000
		140,000		162,000
Current assets:				
Stock	32,000		48,000	
Debtors	26,000		34,000	
Bank balance	14,000		6,000	
		72,000		88,000
		212,000		250,000
Issued Share Capital				
Ordinary shares of £1		90,000		100,000
Retained profits		41,000		81,000
		131,000		181,000
Debentures		45,000		30,000
Current liabilities		36,000		39,000
		212,000		250,000

Included in current liabilities at 31st December 19_0 is a proposed ordinary share dividend of £6,000 for that year subsequently paid. The directors have not decided on the amount of ordinary share dividend for 19_1.

Required:

(a) A source and application of funds statement for the year ended 31st December 19_1, indicating how the reduction in bank balance has arisen.

(b) Computation of the maximum dividend that could be proposed for 19_1, if the working capital ratio in the 19_1 balance sheet is to be identical with that as disclosed in the 19_0 balance sheet.

(I.C.S.A.)

CHAPTER 26

ACCOUNTING RATIOS AND INTERPRETATION

When someone is considering buying an existing business, or is assessing the financial stability of their own business, or is considering investing their money in a business, or is preparing advice for someone already in business, then that person will take into account many varying factors.

Personal knowledge of the situation will obviously play its part, but much of the information regarding the 'financial health" of the business in question will be provided by inspection of the trading and profit and loss accounts and balance sheets of the business over the past few years.

As the buyer, investor or adviser interprets the accounts in front of him, he will obviously be making comparisons – for example he will notice that sales have increased between one year and another, or that profits are "down on last year", etc. It is not sufficient however to note these things in isolation. A weakness in one area may be compensated for by increased strength in another area. He must, therefore, look at the "whole picture" and note relationships between items, particularly changing relationships.

To do this he will employ a technique known as "ratio analysis' whereby he will analyse the relationships between items shown in the accounts.

Before we look closely at ratio analysis let's have a look at the different types of costs involved in business.

FIXED AND VARIABLE COSTS

Manufacturers have many different types of costs to bear, as you will see by looking at all the debit items in a manufacturing and profit and loss account – e.g. cost of raw materials, labour, power, advertising, salaries, rent, etc. If the manufacturer increases production (and therefore sales) he expects his costs to increase; but by how much? If production was doubled would his total costs also double? The answer is "No" – his costs would *increase* but would not double.

This is because certain costs are **FIXED** – that is to say, they are not affected by changes in the volume of production. An example would be rent, which has to be paid whether production is low or high, and the amount of activity going on in the factory or in the office does not affect in the slightest the amount of rent which has to be paid. There are many other examples – think of as many as you can.

If **ALL** costs of a manufacturer were fixed, then he could double production without any increase at all in his total costs; but some of his costs are not fixed – they are **VARIABLE**, i.e. they vary as production varies. The best example is the cost of raw materials – obviously, if production increases by 20%, then the cost of materials must increase by 20%. These are perfectly variable costs, but most variable costs move by different degrees, in sympathy with production. If production increases by 20% it may be necessary to increase the work force (labour) costs by only 2%. (This is where efficient management comes in!). How many other examples can you think of?

We know then that all costs must be either **FIXED** or **VARIABLE**. *Fixed Costs* remain constant despite movements in production or sales. *Variable Costs* move up or down (in varying degrees) with production and sales.

However, in the long run, all costs tend to become variable to some extent; the rapidly expanding firm must eventually reach the point where more premises are needed, and then the rent, etc., cost increases.

What has been said of the manufacturer above applies equally to the pure trader. If he doubles sales he does not expect to double rent, rates, wages, etc. In interpreting *any* business accounts regard must be had for the differences between fixed and variable costs.

ACCOUNTING RATIOS

There are scores of ratios which *can* be calculated and commented on. Many of them however, reveal very little useful information and become merely an academic exercise. We are going to look at a few standard ratios which are regularly employed and which do provide useful "pointers". For the purpose of illustrating these ratios we will use a simple set of accounts and balance sheet as a reference basis:

Trading and Profit & Loss Account

	£		£
Stock	4,000	Sales	60,000
Purchases	38,000		
	42,000		
Less Stock	6,000		
Cost of Goods Sold	36,000		
Gross Profit	24,000		
	60,000		60,000
Various Expenses	11,500	Gross Profit	24,000
Interest on Loan	500		
Depreciation	3,000		
Net Profit	9,000		
	24,000		24,000
Dividend paid	9,000	Balance b/fwd	10,000
Balance c/d	10,000	Net profit	9,000
	19,000		19,000

Balance Sheet

	£		£
Issued Share Capital	30,000	Fixed Assets	39,000
Reserves	10,000	*Current Assets*	
Long Term Loans	5,000	Stock	7,000
		Debtors	4,000
Creditors	6,000	Bank	1,000
	51,000		51,000

RATIOS APPLIED:

GROSS PROFIT MARGIN

Calculation: $\frac{\text{Gross Profit}}{\text{Sales}} \times \frac{100}{1} = \%$

$$= \frac{24,000}{60,000} \times \frac{100}{1} = 40\%$$

This is a key ratio for most types of business, and is simply the gross profit expressed as a percentage of sales. It measures the efficiency of the main area of activity (i.e. buying and selling). Remember that the gross profit has to cover all expenses (in the profit and loss account) and leave something over for final profit (net profit). In types of businesses which naturally have many overheads (e.g. hotel and catering industry) the gross profit needs to form a large percentage of sales in order to cover those overheads – i.e. a large gross profit margin. Other businesses with few expenses can manage with a low profit margin.

The main thing is that the margin should remain at a fairly constant level year by year, and should therefore be compared with previous years. This is because as sales increase (or decrease), cost of goods sold should increase (or decrease) in proportion, so that although the gross profit *amount* changes, its relationship with the changed sales figure is the same.

If there is a significant change in this percentage figure it should be investigated. If it has fallen it could be due to increased costs of supplies not being passed on to selling price, or it could be due to reduced selling prices whilst cost of supplies remains the same. The latter reason is sometimes accompanied by a large increase in the volume of sales (as a result of cut price selling).

Try altering the sales and cost of goods sold figures in the above model and observe the results, with these comments in mind.

NET PROFIT MARGIN

Calculation:

$$\frac{\text{Net profit before tax and dividends}}{\text{Sales}} \times \frac{100}{1} = \%$$

$$= \frac{9{,}000}{60{,}000} \times \frac{100}{1} = 15\%$$

This is an extension of the gross profit margin, i.e. allowing for expenses.

By comparing this return with previous years, attention can be drawn to any disproportionate increases in expenses generally. For example, using the model accounts above, if we increase sales by 100% *and* increase expenses by 100% then the return remains at 15%. Now – if sales have increased, there should have been *some* increase in our net profit return because some of the expenses will be *fixed* (i.e. an increase in sales does not cause a proportionate increase in the expense – e.g. rates), and a doubling of sales should *not* cause a doubling of all expenses.

Again, alter the figures in the model and observe the results first hand.

STOCK TURNOVER

Calculation:

$$\frac{\text{Cost of Goods Sold}}{\text{Average Stock}} = \text{No. of times per year}$$

$$= \frac{36{,}000}{5{,}000 \text{ (average)}} = \underline{\underline{7{\cdot}2}}$$

This ratio shows the speed with which the business "turns over" its stock (i.e. clears the stock room and replaces stock). A turnover of 4 indicates that as stock turns over 4 times in a year, then stock remains in the storeroom for an average of ¼ of a year (3 months) before being sold.

The turnover of 7·2 indicates that stock is held for about 7 weeks, on average, before being sold. Note that where opening and closing stocks are given, the average of these can be taken in your calculation of average stock.

Whether the turnover figure is satisfactory or not depends on the type of business. For a business dealing in very expensive and specialised equipment a turnover of 4 may be considered reasonable, but if the business in question was a fishmonger then something would be very wrong! Obviously, with any business, the faster the turnover, the better, because this is where profits are being made.

A comparison from year to year of this ratio may reveal interesting possibilities. For example, a quickening of turnover may be due to holding smaller stocks on average (and hence a danger of running out of stock!) or, ideally, due to increased sales. A slowing down of turnover could be due to a drop in demand, or holding too much stock (some of this excess stock may in fact be "bad" stock).

In calculating the period that stocks are held before being sold, we are assuming that trade is evenly spread over the year – i.e. the trade is not "seasonal", where sales take place within a confined period of the year.

RETURN ON ORDINARY SHAREHOLDERS' CAPITAL

Calculation:

$$\frac{\text{Net Profit before tax and dividends}}{\text{Ordinary Share Capital plus reserves}} \times \frac{100}{1} = \%$$

$$= \frac{9{,}000}{40{,}000} \times \frac{100}{1} = \underline{\underline{22 \cdot 5\%}}$$

This is sometimes referred to as "return on equity", and shows what has been earned from the ordinary shareholders' provision of funds (i.e. their share capital plus what they have left in the business as reserves). It shows how effectively the ordinary shareholders' funds are being used by the management – in this example, to create a return of 22½% before tax, which is good. If the return had been, say, 5% then the ordinary shareholders might be thinking that their money would be earning more in the bank or building society without the same risk, and this ratio tends therefore to be of more interest to the ordinary shareholders than to others. Note that preference share capital is not counted in this ratio.

RETURN ON LONG TERM CAPITAL EMPLOYED

Calculation:

$$\frac{\text{Net profit before interest, tax and dividends}}{\text{Total Issued Share Capital plus reserves, } \textit{plus} \text{ long term loans}} \times \frac{100}{1} = \%$$

$$= \frac{9{,}500}{45{,}000} \times \frac{100}{1} = \underline{\underline{21\%}} \text{ (approx.)}$$

Whereas the previous ratio showed how effectively the ordinary shareholders' funds were being used in the business, this ratio shows how effectively *all* of the long term capital at the company's disposal is being used. Our model company has £45,000 of long term funds to "play around with", and has generated a return of profits of over 21% which is an indication of pretty efficient management. This is a very useful indicator of how efficiently available funds are being used.

NOTE: The last two ratios we have looked at are sometimes described loosely as "Return on Capital Employed", without distinguishing between shareholders' capital and all long term capital. If you come across this term you should read it as "Return on Long Term Capital Employed" and include long term loans such as debenture stock, and don't forget to include preference shares, if any.

CURRENT RATIO

Calculation: $$\frac{\text{Current Assets}}{\text{Current Liabilities}} = ? \text{ to } 1$$

$$= \frac{12{,}000}{6{,}000} = 2 \text{ to } 1 \text{ (i.e. } 2:1)$$

We have already looked at this particular ratio in Chapter 24 and it should therefore be familiar to you. However, to recap, it is the ratio which gives an indication of the ability of the business to pay its short term debts (creditors, bank overdraft, etc.) without having to resort to selling off fixed assets. In other words it shows the ability to pay debts as they become due, and therefore the degree of solvency.

The *type* of business must be considered in deciding whether the ratio shown is adequate or not. A business which has, by its nature, to rely on large credit facilities (e.g. builders) is going to have to have a substantial current ratio (say, at least 2 to 1) in order to feel "comfortable" at any one time, whereas a business which deals mainly in cash and has no real outlay on materials and labour before receipt of sales income, would be quite "comfortable" with a ratio of 1·5 to 1 (or even slightly less). The *average* type of business in the U.K. has a current ratio of just over 1·5 to 1 so you must decide whether the business in question is average (regarding dependence on credit) or not.

In looking at this current ratio we are assuming that all current assets are fairly liquid – i.e. stock *is* selling and producing debtors, who will pay cash within a fairly short space of time.

Suppose however, that stock is *not* selling and that it forms a substantial proportion of total current assets – in this case the current ratio is going to show a misleading picture. This is why an assessor of any accounts will, after looking at the current ratio of the business, now look at the:

LIQUID (OR "QUICK") RATIO

Calculation: $\dfrac{\text{Current Assets less stocks}}{\text{Current Liabilities}}$

$$\frac{5{,}000}{6{,}000} = \underline{\underline{0{\cdot}83 \text{ to } 1\ (0{\cdot}83:1)}}$$

We are now saying, "suppose stock is not selling quickly – then we cannot rely on this to provide 'quick liquidity'", and we must therefore rely on the other current assets (usually debtors and bank) to provide immediate liquidity to meet any demands from short term creditors.

A very rough "rule of thumb" here is to regard a 1 to 1 ratio as good – in other words, if a business can cover its current liabilities once over by using its debtors and cash only, then it is unlikely to find itself in a position whereby it cannot meet demands for payment of debts. In all probability stock *is* selling and this adds to this ability.

You would normally expect to see a ratio of from 0·75 to 1 to 1·5 to 1, again depending on the *type* of business in question. Too high a ratio could mean that *too much* is being held in debtors (bad debts?) and bank – i.e. funds not being utilised effectively.

This ratio – "Liquid Ratio" is sometimes referred to as the "Quick" or "Acid" ratio.

PERIOD OF CREDIT TAKEN BY DEBTORS

Calculation: $\dfrac{\text{Debtors (per Balance Sheet)}}{\text{Credit Sales for year}} \times \dfrac{365}{1}$ = No. of days
= 24 days.

The above is an indication of how quickly, *on average*, the business collects its debts. The debtors in the calculation must represent *average* debtors and this is why, in examination questions, you are often told to assume that sales occur evenly throughout the year. By taking these debtors as a proportion of total credit sales you can arrive at the proportion of the year taken as credit.

In normal trade, 4/5 weeks credit is usually acceptable, and if the period indicated exceeds this then an investigation is called for, unless there are circumstances to give good reason for excessive periods being granted.

PERIOD OF CREDIT TAKEN FROM CREDITORS

Calculation: $\frac{\text{Trade Creditors (per Balance Sheet)}}{\text{Purchases on credit for year}} \times \frac{365}{1}$ = No. of days
= 58 days.

This gives similar information as in the previous ratio, but refers to creditors rather than debtors – i.e. how quickly the business pays its debts. Remember that when a business is experiencing a shortage of cash it will delay payment to creditors as long as possible, and thus risk possible bankruptcy proceedings.

FINALLY

All of the above ratios can provide useful pointers as to how a business is operating, but a ratio in isolation is meaningless – the overall picture must be looked at, and comparisons made wherever possible – i.e. comparisons with previous years in order to see *the trend*, and comparisons with similar businesses in the same trade. Only by doing this can ratios perform any useful function.

In the examination you may be asked to calculate ratios and comment on the information produced. Do remember, that your comments on the possible significance of your ratios will gain a lot of marks – therefore don't be content with simply working out the ratios. Make your comments brief, but good.

EXERCISE 26.1

Z. Javatt, a businessman, wished to assess the relative merits of the following two businesses. In each case the information provided has been extracted from the final accounts for the year ended 31st December 19_8.

	Business X	*Business Y*
	£	£
Net capital employed in the business	32,500	40,000
Sales	50,000	80,000
Purchases	35,000	75,000
Variable expenses	2,500	6,800
Opening stock	15,000	5,000
Fixed expenses	1,000	1,200
Closing stock	10,000	12,000

Required:

(a) For each business:

(i) gross profit/sales ratio,
(ii) net profit/sales ratio,
(iii) rate of turnover,
(iv) net profit as a percentage of the net capital employed.

(b) Using the results of your calculations in (a), an explanation to Javatt stating which business appears to offer the best prospects for investment.

(A.E.B. "O" level)

EXERCISE 26.2

The following summary refers to the final accounts of Multipurposes Ltd. for the year ended 31st December 19_8:

Trading and Profit & Loss A/c.

	£000	£000
Net sales (all credit)		720
Stock 1/1/_8	27	
Purchases	606	
	633	
Stock 31/12/_8	33	
Cost of goods sold	600	600
Gross Profit		120
Selling and Admin. Expenses		60
Net Profit before Tax		60

Balance Sheet 31.12_8

	£000
Fixed Assets	285
Current Assets	
Stock	33
Debtors	90
Cash	27
	435
Capital and Reserves	
Ordinary shares	300
Revenue reserves	75
Current liabilities	60
	435

Required:
From the above summary, calculate to one decimal place the following ratios and *show your workings.*

1. % Return on total assets employed
2. Ratio of Working Capital (Current Ratio)
3. Rate of stock turnover
4. Debtors' turnover, i.e. average time in months debtors take to pay their debts.

(London Chamber of Commerce)

EXERCISE 26.3

John Beard's Balance Sheets as at 31st December 19_7 and 19_8 are set out below:

	19_7	19_8		19_7	19_8
	£	£		£	£
Capital	40,000	40,000	Fixed assets	35,000	31,000
Creditors	3,750	2,860	Stock	6,000	8,000
			Debtors	2,150	3,350
			Cash	600	510
	43,750	42,860		43,750	42,860

Sales during the year ended 31st December 19_8, £217,000.
Gross profit during the year £42,000.

(a) Find the working capital at the end of each year.
(b) Find the rate of stock turnover for the year ended 31st December 19_8.
(c) What conclusions can be drawn from the figures which show the capital unchanged?
(d) What is the capital employed in the business on 31st December 19_8?
(e) £1,000 has been spent on new fixtures during the year 19_8. How much has been charged for depreciation?
(f) Calculate the value of purchases made during the year ended 31st December 19_8.

(University of London "O" level)

EXERCISE 26.4

Summarised financial information is available from SK (Retailers) Limited for the last three years, and is presented below:

	19_3	*19_4*	*19_5*
	£000's	£000's	£000's
Credit sales	1,200	1,280	1,440
Cost of sales	720	780	892
Gross profit	480	500	548
Net profit	120	130	136

Balance Sheet as at	*19_3*	*19_4*	*19_5*
	£000's	£000's	£000's
CURRENT ASSETS:			
Cash at bank	60	–	–
Debtors	160	200	300
Stock	240	300	440
Prepayments	10	20	20
TOTAL CURRENT ASSETS	470	520	760
FIXED ASSETS:			
Land and buildings	816	1,068	1,744
Furniture, fittings and equipment	314	412	496
	1,130	1,480	2,240
TOTAL ASSETS	1,500	2,000	3,000
CURRENT LIABILITIES:			
Creditors	80	120	280
Bank overdraft	–	40	160
Dividends	60	60	76
Taxation	50	56	60
	190	276	576
Debentures	200	200	200
SHAREHOLDERS' FUNDS:			
Share capital (£1 shares fully paid)	1,200	1,500	2,200
Retained earnings	10	24	24
TOTAL EQUITIES	1,600	2,000	3,000

Required:

Computation of the following performance and solvency business indicators for the three years. End of year figures, rather than average figures, may be used where relevant.

(i) Rate of return on capital employed.
(ii) Net working capital.
(iii) Stock turnover.
(iv) Debtors collection period.

(I.C.S.A.)

EXERCISE 26.5

The following are summaries of revenue accounts of 19_9 and balance sheets at 31st December 19_9.

Revenue Accounts	*Whiz Ltd*	*Bang Ltd.*
	£000's	£000's
Cost of goods sold (materials used)*	840	110
Wages, depreciation, expenses, etc.	120	100
Net profit	40	40
Sales	1,000	250

* Underlining refers to Bang Ltd.

Balance Sheets

	Whiz Ltd.	*Bang Ltd.*
	£000's	£000's
Issued ordinary shares	60	60
Issued 5 per cent preference shares	–	40
Retained profit	40	30
5 per cent debentures	–	40
Bank overdraft	–	20
Creditors	100	40
	200	230
Fixed assets	100	80
Stocks (and work-in-progress)*	70	80
Debtors	9	70
Bank	21	–
	200	230

* underlining refers to Bang Ltd.

Whiz Ltd. is a supermarket firm; Bang Ltd. is engaged in heavy constructional engineering.

Required:

A table completed in the following form:

	Whiz Ltd.	Bang Ltd.
Current ratio		
Liquid ("quick" or "acid") ratio		
Rate of stock turnover per annum		
Net earnings for ordinary shareholders as percentage of equity		
Earnings on long term capital employed (i.e. ordinary and preference shares and debentures)		
Net profit as a percentage of sales		

(Institute of Bankers)

EXERCISE 26.6

Manufacturer Ltd. and Bank Ltd. are two independent companies which have no financial connection with each other.

The following are summaries of balance sheets at 31st December 19_4, and excerpts from the companies' profit and loss accounts for the year ended 31st December 19_4.

	Manufacturer Ltd.	*Bank Ltd.*
	£000's	£000's
Issued share capital	13,000	2,000
Revenue reserves	7,000	5,200
10 per cent. debentures	29,000	800
Current taxation	1,000	1,000
Trade creditors	43,000	–
Overdraft	7,000	–
Current and deposit accounts	–	91,000
	100,000	100,000

	Manufacturer Ltd.	*Bank Ltd.*
	£000's	£000's
Fixed assets, less depreciation	39,000	4,000
Goodwill	6,000	–
Unquoted investments	1,000	9,000
Advances	–	59,000
Stock-in-trade	17,000	–
Trade debtors	37,000	–
Cash and liquid assets	–	28,000
	100,000	100,000
Net profit before taxation	1,800	1,600
after charging depreciation of	1,200	100

The companies' businesses are entirely concerned with the activities which their names suggest.

Required:

(a) A list comparing, in numerical terms, *four* aspects from the accounts which you consider reveal the most important differences or similarities between the two companies. Use ratios where appropriate.

(b) A brief discussion of your figures in part (a), with particular regard to the apparent financial stability of the two companies, and the usefulness or limitations of the comparisons you have made.

(Institute of Bambers)

APPENDIX OF ANSWERS

The following answers are provided by the author. The various examining bodies who have kindly given permission for the use of their questions accept no responsibility whatsoever for the accuracy or method of working in the answers given.

Many of the balance sheets in the answers simply list the assets and liabilities without the headings of "fixed assets", "current assets" or "current liabilities". Although the correct figures are the most important consideration, **DO** remember to write in the relevant headings in an examination.

Answers are only given for the numerical aspects of the questions and where a question demands comments it is hoped that the readers will use their knowledge acquired to think out a suitable answer, coupled ideally with class discussion.

ANSWER 1.1

Balance Sheet as at End of Day 1

	£		£
Capital	60,000	Cash	26,000
		Premises	30,000
		Shop Fittings	4,000
	60,000		60,000

Balance Sheet as at End of Day 2

	£		£
Capital	60,000	Bank	20,000
		Cash	4,000
		Premises	30,000
		Shop Fittings	4,000
		Stock	1,200
		Debtor	800
	60,000		60,000

Balance Sheet as at End of Day 3

	£		£
Capital	60,000	Bank	20,300
Creditor	500	Cash	4,000
		Premises	30,000
		Shop Fittings	4,000
		Stock	1,700
		Debtor	500
	60,500		60,500

Balance Sheet as at End of Day 4

	£		£
Capital	60,000	Bank	19,950
		Cash	3,500
		Premises	30,000
		Shop Fittings	4,000
		Stock	1,100
		Debtors	1,100
		Cash Till	350
	60,000		60,000

ANSWER 1.2

Day 1 (ii) = b; Day 2 (ii) = b; Day 3 (i) = a; Day 3 (ii) = b; Day 4 (iii) = c.

ANSWER 1.3

Balance Sheet as at 30th June

	£		£
Capital	60,000	Cash	1,200
Creditor	1,200	Bank	23,800
		Shop Fittings	4,000
		Stock	900
		Office Furniture	100
		Premises	30,000
		Debtors	1,200
	61,200		61,200

ANSWER 1.4

Balance Sheet as at 31st October

	£		£
Capital	25,000	Premises	30,000
Loan	15,000	Shop Fittings	6,000
Bank Overdraft	7,000	Stock	1,200
Creditors	1,500	Cash	500
		Office Equipment	2,000
		Office Furniture	8,000
		Debtors	800
	48,500		48,500

ANSWER 1.5

Balance Sheet as at 31st May

	£		£
Capital	10,000	Motor Vehicles	17,000
Loans	31,000	Office Furniture	600
Bank Overdraft	5,000	Stock	6,400
Creditor	2,000	Premises	22,000
		Cash	2,000
	48,000		48,000

ANSWER 2.1

Balance Sheet as at 30th June

		£		£
Capital		40,000	Machinery	20,000
Plus profit	1,700		Office Furniture	8,000
Less expenses	860		Stock	3,000
		840	Debtors	2,400
			Bank	5,940
		40,840	Cash	3,700
Creditors		2,200		
		43,040		43,040

ANSWER 2.2

(a) £53,450; (b) Profits or introduction of new capital; (c) Losses or drawings of capital by owner.

ANSWER 2.3

	Capital Exp.	*Revenue Exp.*
Purchase of office furniture	√	
Payment of rates		√
Purchase of delivery van	√	
Tax and insurance for van		√
Repairs to machinery		√
Petrol for van		√
Decoration of office		√
Extension to factory	√	

ANSWER 2.4

(a) Capital; (b) Revenue; (c) Capital; (d) Capital; (e) Revenue; (f) Revenue; (g) Capital.

N.B. Re. (c) Installation costs (and legal fees) are usually regarded as part of the cost of the asset.

ANSWER 2.5

Balance Sheet as at 30th June

		£		£
Capital		40,000	Premises	27,000
Add Profit	750		Shop Fittings	2,500
Less Expenses	330		Office Equipment	150
		420	Stock	1,620
			Debtors	3,000
		40,420	Bank	7,520
Creditors		1,710	Cash	340
		42,130		42,130

ANSWER 3.1

Capital

			May 1	Cash	£40,000

Cash

		£			£
May 1	Capital	40,000	May 1	Shop Fittings	4,000
			May 3	Equipment	700
			May 8	Bank	30,000

Shop Fittings

		£	
May 1	Cash	4,000	
May 20	T.S. Ltd.	900	
May 31	Bank	650	

Equipment

		£	
May 2	T.S. Ltd.	300	
May 3	Cash	700	
May 14	Bank	600	

T.S. Ltd.

		£			£
May 12	Bank	300	May 2	Equipment	300
			May 20	Shop Fittings	900

Bank

		£			£
May 8	Cash	30,000	May 12	T.S. Ltd.	300
			May 14	Equipment	600
			May 31	Shop Fittings	650

Balance Sheet as at 31st May

	£		£
Capital	40,000	Equipment	1,600
Creditors	900	Shop Fittings	5,550
		Bank	28,450
		Cash	5,300
	40,900		40,900

ANSWER 3.2

Capital

					£
			Oct. 1	Cash	70,000
			Oct. 1	Motor Vans	5,000

Cash

		£			£
Oct. 1	Capital	70,000	Oct. 3	Equipment	8,000
Oct. 31	Bank	3,000	Oct. 5	Bank	60,000

Equipment

		£
Oct. 3	Cash	8,000
Oct. 28	Bank	22,000

Motor Vans

Oct. 1	Capital	£5,000

Bank

		£			£
Oct. 5	Cash	£60,000	Oct. 9	Land	20,000
			Oct. 14	Mobile Office	4,500
			Oct. 20	XYZ Ltd.	800
			Oct. 28	Equipment	22,000
			Oct. 31	Cash	3,000

Loose Tools

Oct. 7	XYZ Ltd.	£1,400

XYZ Ltd.

Oct. 20	Bank	£800	Oct. 7	Loose Tools	£1,400

Land

Oct. 8	Bank	£20,000

Office Fittings

Oct. 18	O.S. Ltd.	£850

Mobile Office

Oct. 14	Bank	£4,500

O.S. Ltd.

Oct. 18	Office Fittings	£850

Balance Sheet as at 31st October

	£		£
Capital	75,000	Equipment	30,000
Creditors	1,450	Motor Vans	5,000
		Land	20,000
		Mobile Office	4,500
		Loose Tools	1,400
		Office Fittings	850
		Bank	9,700
		Cash	5,000
	76,450		76,450

ANSWER 3.3

Capital

					£
			Dec. 1	Cash	20,000
			Dec. 1	Motors	4,300
			Dec. 1	Office Furniture	100
			Dec. 16	Equipment	300
			Dec. 26	Cash	2,000

Cash

		£			£
Dec. 1	Capital	20,000	Dec. 2	Bank	15,000
Dec. 26	Capital	2,000	Dec. 4	Machinery	2,000
			Dec. 5	Fixtures & fittings	400
			Dec. 27	Bank	4,400

Motor Vehicles

Dec. 1	Capital	£4,300	

Office Furniture

		£	
Dec. 1	Capital	100	
Dec. 20	Bank	500	

Bank

		£			£
Dec. 2	Cash	15,000	Dec. 10	Premises	18,000
Dec. 6	ABC Ltd.	10,000	Dec. 20	Furniture	500
Dec. 27	Cash	4,400	Dec. 25	Machinery	7,000

Machinery

		£	
Dec. 4	Cash	2,000	
Dec. 25	Bank	7,000	

Fixtures and Fittings

Dec. 5	Cash	£400	

ABC Finance Ltd.

	Dec. 6	Bank	£10,000

Office Equipment

Dec. 16	Capital	£300	

Premises

Dec. 10	Bank	£18,000	

Balance Sheet as at 31st December

	£		£
Capital	26,700	Premises	18,000
Loan – ABC Ltd.	10,000	Machinery	9,000
		Motor Vehicles	4,300
		Equipment	300
		Fixtures and Fittings	400
		Office Furniture	600
		Bank	3,900
		Cash	200
	36,700		36,700

ANSWER 3.4

Cash

		£			£
Sept. 1	Capital	10,000	Sept. 3	Office Furniture	600
Sept. 25	Capital	1,000	Sept. 7	Machinery	2,000
			Sept. 16	Office Furniture	200
			Sept. 16	LTS Ltd.	450
			Sept. 28	Bank	5,000
			Sept. 30	Machinery	1,500

Capital

					£
			Sept. 1	Cash	10,000
			Sept. 25	Cash	1,000

Office Furniture

		£			
Sept. 3	Cash	600			
Sept. 16	Cash	200			

Machinery

		£			
Sept. 7	Cash	2,000			
Sept. 30	Cash	1,500			

LTS Ltd.

Sept. 16	Cash	£450	Sept. 12	Loose Tools	£900

Loose Tools

Sept. 12	LTS Ltd.	£900			

Bank

Sept. 28	Cash	£5,000			

Balance Sheet as at 30th September

	£		£
Capital	11,000	Machinery	3,500
Creditors	450	Office Furniture	800
		Loose Tools	900
		Bank	5,000
		Cash	1,250
	11,450		11,450

ANSWER 4.1

Real Accounts

Capital

			March 1	Cash	£45,000

Premises

March 3	Cash	£28,000			

Cash

		£			£
March 1	Capital	45,000	March 3	Premises	28,000
March 10	Sales	1,600	March 4	Bank	15,000
March 20	Sales	4,120	March 7	Wages	60
			March 12	Stationery	48
			March 21	Wages	270
			March 23	Advertising	140
			March 28	Bank	4,000

Bank

		£			£
March 4	Cash	15,000	March 6	Shop Fittings	£1,200
March 24	PTS Ltd.	700	March 8	Office Furniture	600
March 28	Cash	4,000	March 12	Insurance	65
			March 18	Rates	280
			March 22	Purchases	3,000
			March 25	VS Ltd.	4,000
			March 27	Wages	310
			March 31	Electric	214

VS Ltd

March 25	Bank	£4,000	March 5	Purchases	£8,000

Shop Fittings

March 6	Bank	£1,200	

Office Furniture

March 8	Bank	£600	

PTS Ltd.

		£			£
March 14	Sales	1,930	March 24	Bank	700
March 26	Sales	7,940			

Nominal Accounts

Purchases

		£			
March 5	VS Ltd	8,000			
March 22	Bank	3,000			

Sales

					£
			March 10	Cash	1,600
			March 14	PTS Ltd.	1,930
			March 20	Cash	4,120
			March 26	PTS Ltd.	7.940

Wages

		£	
March 7	Cash	60	
March 21	Cash	270	
March 27	Bank	310	

Stationery

March 12	Cash	£48	

Insurance

March 12	Bank	£65	

Rates

March 18	Bank	£280	

Advertising			
March 23	Cash	£140	

Electricity			
March 31	Bank	£214	

ANSWER 4.2

Real Accounts

Capital

			May 1	Cash	£40,000

Cash

		£			£
May 1	Capital	40,000	May 2	Bank	30,000
May 12	Sales	180	May 7	Wages	80
May 26	Sales	450	May 24	Purchases	2,200
May 27	Spiro	100	May 26	Wages	210
May 28	Sales	4,600			

Bank

		£			£
May 2	Cash	30,000	May 6	Purchases	4,000
			May 10	Rent	60
			May 16	Fixtures & fittings	1,000
			May 18	Mortimer	1,200
			May 25	Fittings	600
			May 28	Advertising	30

P. Spiro

May 20	Sales	£480	May 27	Cash	£100

Fixtures & Fittings

		£	
May 16	Bank	1,000	
May 25	Bank	600	

J. Mortimer

May 18	Bank	£1,200	May 4	Purchases	£3,000

Dickens School of Music

May 25	Sales	£4,400	

Job Lots Ltd.

May 30	Sales	£6,800	

Nominal Accounts

Purchases

		£	
May 4	Mortimer	3,000	
May 6	Bank	4,000	
May 24	Cash	2,200	

Sales

			£
	May 12	Cash	180
	May 20	Spiro	480
	May 25	Dickens	4,400
	May 26	Cash	450
	May 28	Cash	4,600
	May 30	Job Lots	6,800

Wages

		£	
May 7	Cash	80	
May 26	Cash	210	

Rent

May 10	Bank	£60			

Advertising

May 28	Bank	£30			

ANSWER 4.3

Capital

			June 1	Cash	£80,000

Cash

		£			£
June 1	Capital	80,000	June 2	Premises	40,000
June 6	Sales	2,400	June 4	Bank	30,000
			June 4	Bank Deposit	5,000
			June 12	Van Expenses	18
			June 16	Wages	310
			June 27	Wages	280
			June 30	Gen. Expenses	800

Premises

June 2	Cash	£40,000			

ABC Supplies

					£
			June 3	Purchases	7,000
			June 22	Purchases	3,000

Bank

		£			£
June 4	Cash	30,000	June 7	Rates	620
			June 10	Motors	3,500
			June 12	Van Expenses	85
			June 12	Van Expenses	150
			June 18	Machinery	400
			June 24	Telephone	80

Bank Deposit account

June 4	Cash	£5,000			

Motor Vans

June 10	Bank	£3,500			

Machinery

June 18	Bank	£400			

Jaynes

June 28	Sales	£7,500			

Ames and Co.

June 20	Sales	£2,400			

Purchases

		£			
June 3	ABC	7,000			
June 22	ABC	3,000			

Sales

					£
			June 6	Cash	2,400
			June 20	Ames	2,400
			June 28	Jaynes	7,500

Rates

June 7	Bank	£620			

Van Expenses

		£			
June 12	Cash	18			
June 12	Bank	85			
June 12	Bank	150			

Wages

		£			
June 16	Cash	310			
June 27	Cash	280			

Telephone

June 24	Bank	£80			

General Expenses

June 30	Cash	£800			

ANSWER 4.4

Capital

			Nov. 1	Cash	£2,000

Cash

		£			£
Nov. 1	Capital	2,000	Nov. 2	Equipment	70
Nov. 16	Sales	200	Nov. 4	Equipment	40
			Nov. 6	Insurance	60
			Nov. 7	Bank	1,500
			Nov. 18	Wages	40

Equipment

		£			
Nov. 2	Cash	70			
Nov. 4	Cash	40			

Bank

		£			£
Nov. 7	Cash	1,500	Nov. 20	Purchases	160
			Nov. 27	Vans	800
			Nov. 29	WPS Ltd.	90

W.P.S. Ltd.

Nov. 29	Bank	£90	Nov. 10	Purchases	£90

J. Dodd

Nov. 26	Sales	£540			

Motor Vans

Nov. 27	Bank	£800			

Insurance

Nov. 6	Cash	£60			

Purchases

		£			
Nov. 10	W.P.S. Ltd.	90			
Nov. 20	Bank	160			

Wages

Nov. 18	Cash	£40			

Sales

					£
			Nov. 16	Cash	200
			Nov. 26	Dodd	540

ANSWER 4.5

Capital

			Feb. 1	Cash	£500

Cash

		£			£
Feb. 1	Capital	500	Feb. 3	Office furniture	70
Feb. 6	Sales	180	Feb. 26	Wages	30
Feb. 10	Sales	260			
Feb. 25	Sales	420			
Feb. 28	Sales	700			

AB Supplies Ltd.

		£			£
Feb. 27	Bank	1,000	Feb. 1	Purchases	200
			Feb. 8	Purchases	600
			Feb. 15	Purchases	800

Office Furniture

Feb. 3	Cash	£70			

Motor Vans

Feb. 4	XYZ	£900			

Bank

		£			£
Feb. 16	Williams	5,000	Feb. 18	Rent	60
			Feb. 24	Van Expenses	160
			Feb. 27	AB Ltd.	1,000

XYZ Garages Ltd.

			Feb. 4	Vans	£900

Williams – Loan

			Feb. 16	Bank	£5,000

J. Stone

Feb. 20	Sales	£700			

Purchases

		£			
Feb. 1	AB Ltd.	200			
Feb. 8	AB Ltd.	600			
Feb. 15	AB Ltd.	800			

Sales

					£
			Feb. 6	Cash	180
			Feb. 10	Cash	260
			Feb. 20	Stone	700
			Feb. 25	Cash	420
			Feb. 28	Cash	700

Rent

Feb. 18	Bank	£60			

Van Expenses

Feb. 24	Bank	£160			

Wages

Feb. 26	Cash	£30			

ANSWER 5.1

GREEN

Capital

		£			£
June 30	Net Loss	43	June 1	Cash	80,000
June 30	Balance c/d	79,957			
		80,000			80,000
			June 30	Balance b/d	79,957

Cash

		£			£
June 1	Capital	80,000	June 2	Premises	40,000
June 6	Sales	2,400	June 4	Bank	30,000
			June 4	Bank Deposit	5,000
			June 12	Van Expenses	18
			June 16	Wages	310
			June 27	Wages	280
			June 30	Gen. Expenses	800
			June 30	Balance c/d	5,992
		82,400			82,400
June 30	Balance b/d	5,992			

Premises

June 2	Cash	£40,000			

ABC Supplies

		£			£
June 30	Balance c/d	10,000	June 3	Purchases	7,000
			June 22	Purchases	3,000
		10,000			10,000
			June 30	Balance b/d	10,000

Bank Deposit a/c

June 4	Cash	£5,000			

Bank

		£			£
June 4	Cash	30,000	June 7	Rates	620
			June 10	Motors	3,500
			June 12	Van Expenses	85
			June 12	Van Expenses	150
			June 18	Machinery	400
			June 24	Telephone	80
			June 30	Balance c/d	25,165
		30,000			30,000
June 30	Balance b/d	25,165			

Motor Vans

June 10	Bank	£3,500	

Machinery

June 18	Bank	£400	

Ames and Co.

June 20	Sales	£2,400	

Jaynes

June 28	Sales	£7,500	

Purchases

		£			£
June 3	ABC	7,000	June 30	Trading a/c	10,000
June 22	ABC	3,000			
		10,000			10,000

Sales

		£			£
June 30	Trading a/c	12,300	June 6	Cash	2,400
			June 20	Ames	2,400
			June 28	Jaynes	7,500
		12,300			12,300

Rates

		£			£
June 7	Bank	620	June 30	P & L a/c	620
		620			620

Van Expenses

		£			£
June 12	Cash	18	June 30	P & L a/c	253
June 12	Bank	85			
June 12	Bank	150			
		253			253

Wages

		£			£
June 16	Cash	310	June 30	P & L a/c	590
June 27	Cash	280			
		590			590

Telephone

		£			£
June 24	Bank	80	June 30	P & L a/c	80
		80			80

General Expenses

		£			£
June 30	Cash	800	June 30	P & L a/c	800
		800			800

Trading and Profit and Loss Account for month of June

	£		£
Purchases	10,000	Sales	12,300
Gross Profit	2,300		
	12,300		12,300
Rates	620	Gross Profit	2,300
Van Expenses	253	Net Loss	43
Wages	590		
Telephone	80		
General Expenses	800		
	2,343		2,343

Balance Sheet as at 30th June

	£		£
Capital	80,000	Premises	40,000
Less Net Loss	43	Machinery	400
		Motor Vans	3,500
	79,957	Debtors	9,900
		Bank	25,165
Creditors	10,000	Bank Deposit	5,000
		Cash	5,992
	89,957		89,957

DENVER

Capital

		£			£
Nov. 30	Balance c/d	2,390	Nov. 1	Cash	2,000
			Nov. 30	Net Profit	390
		2,390			2,390
			Nov. 30	Balance b/d	2,390

Cash

		£			£
Nov. 1	Capital	2,000	Nov. 2	Equipment	70
Nov. 16	Sales	200	Nov. 4	Equipment	40
			Nov. 6	Insurance	60
			Nov. 7	Bank	1,500
			Nov. 18	Wages	40
			Nov. 30	Balance c/d	490
		2,200			2,200
Nov. 30	Balance b/d	490			

Equipment

		£			£
Nov. 2	Cash	70	Nov. 30	Balance c/d	110
Nov. 4	Cash	40			
		110			110
Nov. 30	Balance b/d	110			

Bank

		£			£
Nov. 7	Cash	1,500	Nov. 20	Purchases	160
			Nov. 27	Vans	800
			Nov. 29	WPS Ltd.	90
			Nov. 30	Balance c/d	450
		1,500			1,500

W.P.S. Ltd.

		£			£
Nov. 29	Bank	90	Nov. 10	Purchases	90
		90			90

J. Dodd

Nov. 26	Sales	£540			

Motor Vans

Nov. 27	Bank	£800			

Insurance

		£			£
Nov. 6	Cash	60	Nov. 30	P & L a/c	60
		60			60

Purchases

		£			£
Nov. 10	W.P.S. Ltd.	90	Nov. 30	Trading a/c	250
Nov. 20	Bank	160			
		250			250

Wages

		£			£
Nov. 18	Cash	40	Nov. 30	P & L a/c	40
		40			40

Sales

		£			£
Nov. 30	Trading a/c	740	Nov. 16	Cash	200
			Nov. 26	Dodd	540
		740			740

Trading and Profit & Loss Account for month of November

	£		£
Purchases	250	Sales	740
Gross Profit c/d	490		
	740		740
Insurances	60	Gross Profit b/d	490
Wages	40		
Net Profit	390		
	490		490

Balance Sheet as at 30th November

	£		£
Capital	2,000	Equipment	110
Net Profit	390	Motor Vans	800
		Debtors	540
	2,390	Bank	450
		Cash	490
	2,390		2,390

BRAGG

Capital

		£			£
Feb. 28	Balance c/d	910	Feb. 1	Cash	500
			Feb. 28	Net Profit	410
		910			910
			Feb. 28	Balance b/d	910

Cash

		£			£
Feb. 1	Capital	500	Feb. 3	Office Furniture	70
Feb. 6	Sales	180	Feb. 26	Wages	30
Feb. 10	Sales	260	Feb. 28	Balance c/d	1,960
Feb. 25	Sales	420			
Feb. 28	Sales	700			
		2,060			2,060
Feb. 28	Balance b/d	1,960			

AB SUPPLIERS LTD.

		£			£
Feb. 27	Bank	1,000	Feb. 1	Purchases	200
Feb. 28	Balance c/d	600	Feb. 8	Purchases	600
			Feb. 15	Purchases	800
		1,600			1,600
			Feb. 28	Balance b/d	600

Office Furniture

Feb. 3	Cash	£70	

Motor Vans

Feb. 4	XYZ	£900	

Bank

		£			£
Feb. 16	Williams	5,000	Feb. 18	Rent	60
			Feb. 24	Van Expenses	160
			Feb. 27	AB Ltd.	1,000
			Feb. 28	Balance c/d	3,780
		5,000			5,000
Feb. 28	Balance b/d	3,780			

XYZ Garage Ltd.

	Feb. 4	Vans	£900

Williams – Loan

	Feb. 16	Bank	£5,000

J. Stone

Feb. 20	Sales	£700	

Purchases

		£			£
Feb. 1	AB Ltd.	200	Feb. 28	Trading a/c	1,600
Feb. 8	AB Ltd.	600			
Feb. 15	AB Ltd.	800			
		1,600			1,600

Sales

		£			£
Feb. 28	Trading a/c	2,260	Feb. 6	Cash	180
			Feb. 10	Cash	260
			Feb. 20	Stone	700
			Feb. 25	Cash	420
			Feb. 28	Cach	700
		2,260			2,260

Rent

		£			£
Feb. 18	Bank	60	Feb. 28	P & L a/c	60
		60			60

Van Expenses

		£			£
Feb. 24	Bank	160	Feb. 28	P & L a/c	160
		160			160

Wages

		£			£
Feb. 26	Cash	30	Feb. 28	P & L a/c	30
		30			30

Trading and Profit & Loss Account for month of February

	£		£
Purchases	1,600	Sales	2,260
Gross Profit c/d	660		
	2,260		2,260
Rent	60	Gross Profit b/d	660
Van Expenses	160		
Wages	30		
Net Profit	410		
	660		660

Balance Sheet as at 28th February

	£		£
Capital	500	Motor Vans	900
Net Profit	410	Office Furniture	70
		Debtors	700
	910	Bank	3,780
		Cash	1,960
Creditors	6,500		
	7,410		7,410

ANSWER 5.2

Capital

		£			£
May 31	Balance c/d	11,960	May 1	Bank	10,000
			May 31	Net Profit	1,960
		11,960			11,960
			May 31	Balance b/d	11,960

Bank

		£			£
May 1	Capital	10,000	May 5	Rent	70
			May 7	Furniture	2,400
			May 10	Vans	3,100
			May 12	Tomkins	1,600
			May 16	Purchases	1,500
			May 26	Furniture	140
			May 27	Van Expenses	80
May 31	Balance c/d	990	May 30	Smith	2,100
		10,990			10,990
			May 31	Balance b/d	990

Smith

		£			£
May 30	Bank	2,100	May 2	Purchases	1,200
			May 31	Balance c/d	900
		2,100			2,100
May 31	Balance b/d	900			

Cash

		£			£
May 4	Sales	450	May 14	Van Expenses	270
May 28	Sales	1,700	May 23	Wages	120
			May 31	Balance c/d	1,760
		2,150			2,150
May 31	Balance b/d	1,760			

Tomkins

		£			£
May 12	Bank	1,600	May 2	Purchases	1,600
		1,600			1,600

Vans

		£			
May 10	Bank	3,100			

Office Furniture

		£			£
May 7	Bank	2,400	May 31	Balance c/d	2,540
May 26	Bank	140			
		2,540			2,540
May 31	Balance b/d	2,540			

P. Sherriff

May 18	Sales	£2,900			

Appleby

May 25	Sales	£950			

Braintree

May 25	Sales	£800			

Purchases

		£			£
May 2	Smith	1,200	May 31	Trading a/c	4,300
May 2	Tomkins	1,600			
May 16	Bank	1,500			
		4,300			4,300

Sales

		£			£
May 31	Trading a/c	6,800	May 4	Cash	450
			May 18	Sherriff	2,900
			May 25	Braintree	800
			May 25	Appleby	950
			May 28	Cash	1,700
		6,800			6,800

Rent

		£			£
May 5	Bank	70	May 31	P & L a/c	70
		70			70

Van Expenses

		£			£
May 14	Cash	270	May 31	P & L a/c	350
May 27	Bank	80			
		350			350

Wages

		£			£
May 23	Cash	120	May 31	P & L a/c	120
		120			120

Trading and Profit & Loss Account for month ending 31st May

	£		£
Purchases	4,300	Sales	6,800
Gross Profit c/d	2,500		
	6,800		6,800
Rent	70	Gross Profit b/d	2,500
Van Expenses	350		
Wages	120		
Net Profit to Capital a/c	1,960		
	2,500		2,500

Balance Sheet as at 31st May

	£		£
Capital	10,000	Motor Vans	3,100
Net Profit	1,960	Office Furniture	2,540
		Debtors	5,550
	11,960	Cash	1,760
Bank overdraft	990		
	12,950		12,950

ANSWER 5.3

Trading and Profit & Loss Account for year 19_7

	£		£
Purchases	2,600	Sales	3,600
Gross Profit c/d	1,000		
	3,600		3,600
Interest on Loans	50	Gross Profit b/d	1,000
Rent and Rates	400	Net Loss to Capital a/c	1,190
Wages	900		
Insurance	60		
Light and Heat	280		
Telephone	110		
Van Expenses	340		
Stationery and Postage	40		
Loss from theft	10		
	2,190		2,190

Balance Sheet as at end of 19_7

	£		£
Capital	1,600	Office Furniture	900
Less Net Loss	1,190	Motor Vans	2,600
		Debtors	830
	410		
Loans	2,000		
Creditors	620		
Bank overdraft	1,300		
	4,330		4,330

ANSWER 5.4

Capital

	£		£
June 30 Balance c/d	50,620	June 1 Bank	50,000
		June 30 Net Profit	620
	50,620		50,620
		June 30 Balance b/d	50,620

Bank

	£		£
June 1 Capital	50,000	June 3 Premises	40,000
		June 4 Fittings	3,500
		June 10 Vans	4,200
		June 14 Rates	370
		June 16 Wages	90
		June 27 Meat S. Ltd.	1,400
		June 30 Balance c/d	440
	50,000		50,000
June 30 Balance b/d	440		

Premises

June 3	Bank	£40,000			

Cash

		£			£
June 8	Sales	650	June 24	Purchases	500
June 12	Sales	800	June 26	Wages	70
			June 30	Balance c/d	880
		1,450			1,450
June 30	Balance b/d	880			

Shop Fittings

June 4	Bank	£3,500			

Meat Suppliers Ltd.

		£			£
June 27	Bank	1,400	June 6	Purchases	2,800
June 30	Balance c/d	1,400			
		2,800			2,800
			June 30	Balance b/d	1,400

Motor Vans

June 10	Bank	£4,200			

Rowland

		£			£
June 27	Sales	1,900	June 30	Balance c/d	3,000
June 28	Sales	1,100			
		3,000			3,000
June 30	Balance b/d	3,000			

Purchases

		£			£
June 6	Meat Supp. Ltd.	2,800	June 30	Trading a/c	3,300
June 24	Cash	500			
		3,300			3,300

Sales

		£			£
June 30	Trading a/c	4,450	June 8	Cash	650
			June 12	Cash	800
			June 27	Rowland	1,900
			June 28	Rowland	1,100
		4,450			4,450

Rates

		£			£
June 14	Bank	370	June 30	P & L a/c	370
		370			370

Wages

		£			£
June 16	Bank	90	June 30	P & L a/c	160
June 26	Cash	70			
		160			160

Trading and Profit & Loss Account for month ended 30th June

	£		£
Purchases	3,300	Sales	4,450
Gross Profit c/d	1,150		
	4,450		4,450
Rates	370	Gross Profit b/d	1,150
Wages	160		
Net Profit to Capital a/c	620		
	1,150		1,150

Balance Sheet as at 30th June

	£		£
Capital	50,000	Premises	40,000
Add Net Profit	620	Shop Fittings	3,500
		Motor Vans	4,200
	50,620	Debtors	3,000
Creditors	1,400	Bank	440
		Cash	880
	52,020		52,020

ANSWER 6.1

Trading and Profit & Loss Account for year ended 31st December 19_7

	£		£
Purchases	60,000	Sales	82,000
Gross Profit c/d	22,000		
	82,000		82,000
Salaries	9,100	Gross Profit b/d	22,000
Rates	650		
Insurances	150		
Telephone	100		
Net Profit	12,000		
	22,000		22,000

Balance Sheet as at 31st December 19_7

	£		£
Capital	21,900	Land and Buildings	28,000
Add Net Profit	12,000	Fixtures and Fittings	1,800
		Motor Van	2,200
	33,900	Debtors	2,400
Creditors	1,800	Bank	700
		Cash	600
	35,700		35,700

ANSWER 6.2

Capital

		April 1 Bank	£6,000

Bank

	£		£
April 1 Capital	6,000	April 2 Fixtures	400
April 18 Swan	440	April 5 Rent	420
		April 8 Insurance	74
		April 12 Teal Ltd.	1,440
		April 30 Balance c/d	4,106
	6,440		6,440
April 30 Balance b/d	4,106		

Fixtures

April 2 Bank	£400		

Cash

	£		£
April 8 Sales	400	April 9 Wages	45
April 15 Sales	210	April 10 Purchases	200
		April 16 Wages	45
		April 30 Balance c/d	320
	610		610
April 30 Balance b/d	320		

Teal Ltd.

	£		£
April 12 Bank	1,440	April 3 Purchases	840
		April 11 Purchases	600
	1,440		1,440

P. Swan

	£		£
April 15 Sales	440	April 18 Bank	440
	440		440

Purchases

		£			£
April 3	Teal Ltd.	840	April 30	Balance c/d	1,640
April 10	Cash	200			
April 11	Teal	600			
		1,640			1,640
April 30	Balance b/d	1,640			

Sales

		£			£
April 30	Balance c/d	1,050	April 8	Cash	400
			April 15	Cash	210
			April 15	Swan	440
		1,050			1,050
			April 30	Balance b/d	1,050

Rent

April 5	Bank	£420			

Wages

		£			£
April 9	Cash	45	April 30	Balance c/d	90
April 16	Cash	45			
		90			90
April 30	Balance b/d	90			

Insurance

April 8	Bank	£74			

Trial Balance as at 30th April

	DR	CR
	£	£
Capital		6,000
Bank	4,106	
Cash	320	
Fixtures	400	
Purchases	1,640	
Sales		1,050
Rent	420	
Insurance	74	
Wages	90	
	7,050	7,050

ANSWER 6.3

Trading and Profit & Loss Accounts for year ended 31st December 19_5

	£		£
Purchases	9,510	Sales	14,790
Gross Profit c/d	5,280		
	14,790		14,790
Wages and Salaries	1,050	Gross Profit b/d	5,280
Rent and Rates	480		
General Expenses	270		
Net Profit	3,480		
	5,280		5,280

Balance Sheet as at 31st December 19_5

	£		£
Capital	4,800	Office Furniture	1,840
Add Net Profit	3,480	Van	2,600
		Debtors	3,110
	8,280	Bank	3,330
Creditors	2,670	Cash	70
	10,950		10,950

ANSWER 6.4

Trading and Profit & Loss Accounts for year ended 30th June 19_2

	£		£
Purchases	24,300	Sales	33,400
Gross Profit c/d	9,100		
	33,400		33,400
Rent	1,200	Gross Profit b/d	9,100
Rates	1,100	Net Loss	3,900
Wages	8,600		
Insurances	400		
General Expenses	1,700		
	13,000		13,000

Balance Sheet as at 30th June 19_2

	£		£
Capital	68,500	Premises	40,000
Less Net Loss	3,900	Furniture & Fittings	9,000
		Equipment	3,000
	64,600	Motor Vehicles	6,000
		Debtors	11,000
Creditors	6,500	Bank	1,500
		Cash	600
	71,100		71,100

ANSWER 6.5

Trading and Profit & Loss Accounts for year ended 30th April 19_8

	£		£
Purchases	170,400	Sales	289,600
Gross Profit c/d	119,200		
	289,600		289,600
Wages	80,900	Gross Profit b/d	119,200
Light and Heat	11,000		
General Expenses	6,200		
Insurances	1,800		
Net Profit	19,300		
	119,200		119,200

Balance Sheet as at 30th April 19_8

	£		£
Capital	83,000	Premises	80,000
Add Net Profit	19,300	Fixtures & Fittings	15,600
		Debtors	34,300
	102,300		
Creditors	27,600		
	129,900		129,900

ANSWER 6.6

Trial Balance

	DR	CR
	£	£
Capital		51,300
Premises	37,000	
Motor Vehicles	8,000	
Office Equipment	4,000	
Sales		16,400
Purchases	9,800	
Rates	1,100	
Wages and Salaries	4,100	
Insurances	500	
General Expenses	1,400	
Debtors	6,700	
Creditors		5,600
Advertising	700	
	73,300	73,300

ANSWER 6.7

Trial Balance as at 30th April 19_6

	DR	CR
	£	£
Capital		1,070
Debtors	6,310	
Creditors		1,760
Purchases	6,280	
Sales		11,640
Wages and Salaries	2,080	
Cash	140	
Office Furniture	650	
Bank Overdraft		1,480
General Expenses	490	
	15,950	15,950

ANSWER 6.9

Bank

		£			£
Dec. 1	Capital	5,000	Dec. 1	Furniture	1,000
Dec. 29	Pike	1,000	Dec. 8	Rent	40
Dec. 31	Sales	900	Dec. 19	Electricity	130
			Dec. 19	Van	1,000
			Dec. 20	Pack Mat.	140
			Dec. 29	Smith	400
			Dec. 29	Gray	300
			Dec. 29	Coals	140
			Dec. 31	Balance c/d	3,750
		6,900			6,900
Dec. 31	Balance b/d	3,750			

Capital

			Dec. 1	Bank	5,000

Furniture and Fittings

		£			£
Dec. 1	Bank	1,000	Dec. 31	Balance c/d	1,500
Dec. 29	Office Supplies	500			
		1,500			1,500
Dec. 31	Balance b/d	1,500			

R. Pike

		£			£
Dec. 8	Sales	600	Dec. 29	Bank	1,000
Dec. 29	Sales	400			
		1,000			1,000

T. Smith

		£			£
Dec. 29	Bank	400	Dec. 8	Purchases	400
		400			400

T. Trout

Dec. 20	Sales	700			

R. Gray

		£			£
Dec. 29	Bank	300	Dec. 12	Purchases	300
		300			300

Motor Vans

Dec. 19	Bank	£1,000			

B. Coals

		£			£
Dec. 29	Bank	140	Dec. 19	Purchases	140
		140			140

Office Supplies Ltd.

			Dec. 29	Furniture	£500

Purchases

		£			
Dec. 8	Smith	400			
Dec. 12	Gray	300			
Dec. 19	Coals	140			

Sales

					£
			Dec. 8	Pike	600
			Dec. 20	Trout	700
			Dec. 29	Pike	400
			Dec. 31	Bank	900

Rent

Dec. 8	Bank	£40			

Electricity

Dec. 19	Bank	£130			

Packing Materials

Dec. 20	Bank	£140			

Trial Balance as at 31st December 19_8

	DR	CR
	£	£
Capital		5,000
Bank	3,750	
Furniture and Fittings	1,500	
Motor Vans	1,000	
Debtors	700	
Creditors		500
Purchases	840	
Sales		2,600
Rent	40	
Electricity	130	
Packing Materials	140	
	8,100	8,100

ANSWER 7.1

Trading and Profit & Loss Account for year ended 31st March 19_9

	£		£
Purchases	7,620	Sales	13,990
Less Returns	190	*Less* Returns	270
	7,430		13,720
Gross Profit c/d	6,290		
	13,720		13,720
Discounts Allowed	480	Gross Profit b/d	6,290
Rent, Rates, Insurance	580	Discounts Received	310
Wages and Salaries	2,980		
General Expenses	150		
Net Profit	2,410		
	6,600		6,600

Balance Sheet as at 31st March 19_9

	£		£
Capital	2,400	Fixtures and Fittings	3,800
Add Net Profit	2,410	Delivery Van	700
		Debtors	3,970
	4,810	Cash	30
Bank overdraft	1,450		
Creditors	2,240		
	8,500		8,500

ANSWER 7.2

Textiles Ltd.

			£
	Oct. 3	Purchases	45
	Oct. 13	Purchases	76

H. Church

		£	
Oct. 6	Sales	38	
Oct. 25	Sales	38	

Newtown Warehouse Ltd.				A. Richards			
				Oct. 3 Purchases	£65	Oct. 19 Sales	27

ANSWER 7.3

Trading and Profit & Loss Account for year ended 30th April 19_1

	£		£
Purchases	22,000	Sales	44,000
Less returns	150	*Less* returns	300
Cost of Goods Sold	21,850		43,700
Gross Profit c/d	21,850		
	43,700		43,700
Telephone	250	Gross Profit b/d	21,850
Wages	2,650	Discounts Received	200
Salaries	6,000		
Motor Expenses	2,350		
Office Expenses	2,500		
Light and Heat	1,700		
Rates	600		
Discounts Allowed	250		
Net Profit	5,750		
	22,050		22,050

Balance Sheet as at 30th April 19_1

	£		£
Capital	16,850	Premises	17,000
Add Net Profit	5,750	Fixtures and Fittings	1,800
		Vehicles	2,000
	22,600	Debtors	6,000
Loan	5,000	Bank and Cash	8,800
Creditors	8,000		
	35,600		35,600

ANSWER 7.4

Trading and Profit and Loss Account for year ended 30th September 19_2

	£		£
Purchases	6,580	Sales	10,670
Less returns	280	*Less* returns	410
	6,300		10,260
Gross Profit c/d	3,960		
	10,260		10,260
Wages and Salaries	1,980	Gross Profit b/d	3,960
Rent, Rates, Insurance	330	Discounts Received	370
General Expenses	200		
Discounts Allowed	520		
Net Profit	1,300		
	4,330		4,330

Balance Sheet as at 30th September 19_2

	£		£
Capital	4,570	Equipment	2,000
Net Profit	1,300	Motor Vans	1,380
	——	Fixtures and Fittings	550
	5,870	Debtors	2,900
Creditors	1,580	Bank	580
		Cash	40
	——		——
	7,450		7,450
	====		====

ANSWER 7.6

Capital

		Feb. 21 Balance	£5,200

Bank

	£		£
Feb. 21 Balance	2,000	Feb. 25 Returns	40
Feb. 23 Cann	300	Feb. 28 Barker	420
Feb. 28 Sales	300	Feb. 28 Balance c/d	2,140
	——		——
	2,600		2,600
	====		====
Feb. 28 Balance b/d	2,140		

Fixed Assets

Feb. 21 Balance	£3,500		

L. Cann

	£		£
Feb. 21 Balance	500	Feb. 23 Bank	300
Feb. 28 Sales	352	Feb. 28 Balance c/d	552
	——		——
	852		852
	====		====
Feb. 28 Balance b/d	552		

B. Barker

	£		£
Feb. 28 Bank	420	Feb. 21 Balance	420
Feb. 28 Balance c/d	330	Feb. 28 Purchases	330
	——		——
	750		750
	====		====
		Feb. 28 Balance b/d	330

Purchases

	£		£
Feb. 21 Balance	420	Feb. 28 Balance c/d	750
Feb. 24 Barker	330		
	——		——
	750		750
	====		====
Feb. 28 Balance b/d	750		

D. Smythe

		£			£
Feb. 23	Sales	176	Feb. 28	Returns	55
Feb. 26	Sales	198	Feb. 28	Balance c/d	319
		374			374
Feb. 28	Balance b/d	319			

Sales

		£			£
Feb. 28	Balance c/d	1,926	Feb. 21	Balance	900
			Feb. 23	Smythe	176
			Feb. 26	Smythe	198
			Feb. 28	Cann	352
			Feb. 28	Bank	300
		1,926			1,926
			Feb. 28	Balance b/d	1,926

Returns Inwards

		£			£
Feb. 21	Balance	100	Feb. 28	Balance c/d	195
Feb. 25	Bank	40			
Feb. 28	Smythe	55			
		195			195
Feb. 28	Balance b/d	195			

Trial Balance as at 28th February

	DR £	CR £
Capital		5,200
Fixed Assets	3,500	
Bank	2,140	
Debtors	871	
Creditors		330
Purchases	750	
Sales		1,926
Returns Inwards	195	
	7,456	7,456

ANSWER 7.7

J. Daniels

		£			£
Oct. 15	Bank	51·30	Oct. 4	Purchases	54·00
Oct. 15	Discount Rec'd	2·70			

W. Wallis

Oct. 16	Returns	£5·25	Oct. 6	Purchases	£52·50

D. Cox

Oct. 14	Sales	£444·0	Oct. 20	Allowances	£15·00

Bank

			Oct. 15	Daniels	£51·30

Purchases

		£			
Oct. 4	Daniels	54·00			
Oct. 6	Wallis	52·50			

Sales

			Oct. 14	Cox	£444·00

Discounts Received

			Oct. 15	Daniels	£2·70

Purchases Returns

			Oct. 16	Wallis	£5·25

Sales Returns and Allowances

Oct. 20	Cox	£15·00			

ANSWER 8.1

Trading and Profit & Loss Account for year ended 31st December, 19_7

		£		£
Opening Stock		5,000	Sales	70,300
	£			
Purchases	50,000			
Less returns	200	49,800		
		54,800		
Less Closing Stock		6,000		
		48,800		
Gross Profit c/d		21,500		
		70,300		70,300
Vehicle Expenses		400	Gross Profit b/d	21,500
General Expenses		800	Discounts Received	100
Prop' Expenses		1,200		
Wages and Salaries		9,000		
Net Profit		10,200		
		21,600		21,600

Balance Sheet as at 31st December, 19_7

	£		£
Capital	22,000	Land and Buildings	17,000
Add Net Profit	10,200	Furniture & Fittings	1,000
		Motor Vehicles	2,500
	32,200	Stock	6,000
Creditors	5,000	Debtors	8,000
		Cash and Bank	2,700
	37,200		37,200

ANSWER 8.2

Trading and Profit & Loss Account for year ended 31st October, 19_2

	£	£		£
Stock		2,040	Sales	15,530
	£		*Less* returns	390
Purchases	8,760			
Less returns	220	8,540		15,140
		10,580		
Less Stock		2,520		
Cost of Goods Sold		8,060		
Gross Profit		7,080		
				15,140
		15,140		
			Gross Profit	7,080
Wages and Salaries		3,930		
Rent and Rates		720	Discounts Received	120
General Expenses		80		
Discounts Allowed		100		
Travelling Expenses		480		
Net Profit		1,890		
		7,200		7,200

Balance Sheet as at 31st October, 19_2

	£		£
Capital	6,490	Office Furniture	600
Net Profit	1,890	Stock	2,520
		Debtors	3,910
	8,380	Bank	3,390
Creditors	2,090	Cash	50
	10,470		10,470

ANSWER 8.3

	£
Value of stock at 5th March (cost)	1,970
Add sales of £144 – cost price =	108
	2,078
Less purchases (cost price)	75
Value of Stock at 28th February	2,003

ANSWER 8.4

Trading Account for period 1st January – 20th February, 19_2

	£		£
Stock at Jan. 1	2,880	Sales	2,580
Purchases	1,510		
	4,390		
Less Stock at Feb. 20	2,240*		
Cost of Goods Sold	2,150		
Gross Profit ($\frac{1}{6}$ of sales)	430		
	2,580		2,580

* Balancing figure.

Therefore stock destroyed = Stock of £2,240 less £120 of goods still in transit = £2,120.

ANSWER 8.5

(a) *Book Value of Stock at 31st December*

19_5	19_6	19_7	19_8	19_9
£	£	£	£	£
12,000	9,000	13,500	25,500	40,500

(b) *Trading and Profit & Loss Accounts to 31st December*

	19_5	19_6	19_7	19_8	19_9		19_5	19_6	19_7	19_8	19_9
	£	£	£	£	£		£	£	£	£	
Stock	—	12,000	9,000	13,500	25,500	Sales	36,000	54,000	78,000	120,000	
Purchases	39,000	37,500	63,000	108,000	135,000						
	39,000	49,500	72,000	121,500	160,500						
Less stock	12,000	9,000	13,500	25,500	40,500						
	27,000	40,500	58,500	96,000	120,000						
Gross Profit	9,000	13,500	19,500	24,000	30,000						
	36,000	54,000	78,000	120,000	150,000		36,000	54,000	78,000		
Selling Expenses	900	1,350	1,950	3,600	5,250	Gross Profit	9,000	13,500	19,500		
Rent	3,000	3,000	3,000	6,000	6,000						
Gen. Expenses	4,500	5,250	6,000	9,000	11,250						
Net Profit	600	3,900	8,550	5,400	7,500						
	9,000	13,500	19,500	24,000	30,000		9,000	13,500	19,500		

ANSWER 8.6

(a)	*Stock at 31st March*	*Net Profit*
	£	£
19_5	35,000	11,000
19_6	27,000	13,600
19_7	37,600	15,200
19_8	32,700	16,600

ANSWER 8.7

Trading and Profit & Loss Account for year ended 31st December 19_4

	£		£
Stock	6,300	Sales	60,900
Purchases	48,500		
	54,800		
Less Stock	8,800		
	46,000		
Gross Profit	14,900		
	60,900		60,900
Repairs	848	Gross Profit	14,900
Car Expenses	318		
Wages and Salaries	8,606	Discounts Received	854
Discounts Allowed	1,061		
Rates and Insurance	248		
Bank Charges & Interest	759		
General Expenses	1,586		
Net Profit	2,328		
	15,754		15,754

Balance Sheet as at 31st December 19_4

	£		£
Capital	20,600	Land and Buildings	10,000
Net Profit	2,328	Motor Vehicles	950
		Furniture and Fittings	1,460
	22,928	Stock	8,800
Creditors	4,035	Debtors	5,213
		Bank	540
	26,963		26,963

ANSWER 8.8

(a) Trading and Profit & Loss Accounts for years ending 31st December

	19_4	19_5	19_6		19_4	19_5	19_6
	£	£	£		£	£	£
Stock	1,000	3,000	5,000	Sales	22,000	26,000	40,000
Purchases	14,000	17,000	21,000				
Carriage Inwards	400	600	800				
	15,400	20,600	26,800				
Less Stock	3,000	5,000	7,000				
	12,400	15,600	19,800				
Gross Profit	9,600	10,400	20,200				
	22,000	26,000	40,000		22,000	26,000	40,000

(b) Stock Account

		£			£
19_3			*19_4*		
Dec. 31	Trading a/c	1,000	Dec. 31	Trading a/c	1,000
19_4			*19_5*		
Dec. 31	Trading a/c	3,000	Dec. 31	Trading a/c	3,000
19_5			*19_6*		
Dec. 31	Trading a/c	5,000	Dec. 31	Trading a/c	5,000
19_6					
Dec. 31	Trading a/c	7,000			

ANSWER 8.9

Profit for week 1 = £12: Profit for week 2 = £27.
Workings:

Trading Account for Weeks 1 and 2

	Week 1	*Week 2*		*Week 1*	*Week 2*
	£	£		£	£
Stock	—	16	Sales	28	63
Purchases	32	40			
	32	56			
Less Stock	16	20			
Cost of Goods Sold	16	36			
Gross Profit	12	27			
	28	63		28	63

ANSWER 9.1

Trading and Profit & Loss Accounts for year ended 30th September 19_2

	£		£
Stock	4,400	Sales	31,219
Purchases	21,435		
	25,835		
Less stock	7,200		
Cost of Goods Sold	18,635		
Gross Profit	12,584		
	31,219		31,219
Wages	4,399	Gross Profit	12,584
Rates and Insurance	242	Rents Received	500
Light and Heat	185		
Sundry Expenses	319		
Selling Expenses	532		
Net Profit	7,407		
	13,084		13,084

Balance Sheet as at 30th September 19_2

	£		£
Capital	12,920	Land and Buildings	7,700
Net Profit	7,407	Equipment	1,400
		Vehicles	1,500
	20,327	Office Furniture	2,816
Creditors	2,829	Stock	7,200
Wages owing	95	Debtors	2,926
Bank overdraft	323	Insurance prepayment	32
	23,574		23,574

ANSWER 9.2

Trading and Profit & Loss Account for year ended 31st December 19_7

	£		£
Stock	9,274	Sales	81,742
Purchases	62,101		
	71,375		
Less Stock	9,884		
Cost of Goods Sold	61,491		
Gross Profit	20,251		
	81,742		81,742
Rent and Rates	840	Gross Profit	20,251
Light and Heat	331		
Salaries and Wages	8,268	Rent Received	1,000
Insurances	90		
Motor Expenses	1,190		
General Expenses	933		
Net Profit	9,599		
	21,251		21,251

Balance Sheet as at 31st December 19_7

	£		£
Capital	24,447	Premises	10,000
Net Profit	9,599	Motor Vans	8,000
		Office Furniture	2,148
	34,046	Stock	9,884
Creditors	5,462	Debtors	7,689
Light and Heat due	85	Bank	1,582
		Rates in advance	40
		Rent due	250
	39,593		39,593

ANSWER 9.3

Interest Account

		£			£
19_4			*19_4*		
Oct. 31	Bank	600	Dec. 31	P & L a/c	600
19_5					
April 30	Bank	600	*19_5*		
Oct. 31	Bank	600	Dec. 31	P & L a/c	1,200
		1,200			1,200
19_6					
April 30	Bank	600	*19_6*		
Dec. 31	Balance c/d	600	Dec. 31	P & L a/c	1,200
		1,200			1,200
19_7					
Jan. 10	Bank	600	*19_6*		
April 30	Bank	600	Dec. 31	Balance b/d	600
Oct. 31	Bank	600	*19_7*		
			Dec. 31	P & L a/c	1,200
		1,800			1,800
19_8					
April 30	Bank	600			
Oct. 31	Bank	600	*19_8*		
			Dec. 31	P & L a/c	1,200
		1,200			1,200

ANSWER 9.4

Rent

		£			£
19_1			*19_1*		
	Cash	300	Dec. 31	P & L a/c	400
Dec. 31	Balance c/d	100			
		400			400
			Dec. 31	Balance b/d	100

Rates

		£			£
19_1			*19_1*		
Jan. 1	Balance b/d	80	Dec. 31	P & L a/c	350
19_1	Cash	360	Dec. 31	Balance c/d	90
		440			440
Dec. 31	Balance b/d	90			

Sections of Balance Sheet at 31st December 19_1

	£		£
Current Liabilities		*Current Assets*	
Rent owing	100	Rates Paid in advance	90

ANSWER 9.5

(b) Rent and Rates Account

		£			£
			19_8		
19_9	Cash (Rent)	2,500	Dec. 31	Balance b/d (Rent)	750
19_9	Cash (Rates)	1,800	Dec. 31	Balance b/d (Rates)	300
			Dec. 31	P & L a/c	4,200
19_9			*19_9*		
Dec. 31	Balance c/d (Rent)	1,250	Dec. 31	Balance c/d (Rates)	300
		5,550			5,550
19_9					
Dec. 31	Balance b/d (Rates)	300			
			19_9		
			Dec. 31	Balance b/d (Rent)	1,250

Section of Balance Sheet at 31st December 19_9

	£		£
Current Liabilities		*Current Assets*	
Rent owing	1,250	Rates in advance	300

ANSWER 9.6

Trading and Profit & Loss Account for year ended 31st October, 19_9

	£		£
Stock	960	Sales	12,060
Purchases	5,180		
	6,140		
Less stock	1,080		
Cost of Goods Sold	5,060		
Gross Profit	7,000		
	12,060		12,060
Wages and salaries	1,710	Gross Profit	7,000
Rent and Rates	550	Discounts Received	310
Discounts Allowed	470		
Insurance	100		
Light and Heat	490		
General Expenses	110		
Net Profit	3,880		
	7,310		7,310

Balance Sheet as at 31st October 19_9

	£		£
Capital	5,970	Office Furniture	800
Net Profit	3,880	Equipment	1,200
		Motor Vehicles	3,000
	9,850	Loose Tools	1,100
Creditors	1,480	Stock	1,080
Wages due	240	Debtors	2,950
		Bank	1,330
		Cash	40
		Prepayments	70
	11,570		11,570

ANSWER 9.7

Rent Payable

		£			£
19_2					
May 30	Cash	150	*19_3*		
Aug. 25	Cash	300	April 30	P & L a/c	630
19_3			*19_3*		
Feb. 12	Cash	360	April 30	Balance c/d	180
		810			810
19_3					
April 30	Balance b/d	180			

Rent Receivable

		£			£
19_3			*19_2*		
April 30	P & L a/c	360	July 31	Cash	90
			Nov. 30	Cash	90
			19_3		
			Feb. 28	Cash	90
			April 30	Balance c/d	90
		360			360
19_3					
April 30	Balance b/d	90			

ANSWER 9.8

(a) Rent Payable

		£			£
			19_7		
19_7	Cash	730	Jan. 1	Balance b/d	40
Dec. 31	Balance c/d	60	Dec. 31	P & L a/c	750
		790			790
			Dec. 31	Balance b/d	60

(b) Rates

		£			£
19_9	Cash	1,040	*19_9*		
			Jan. 1	Balance b/d	120
			Dec. 31	P & L a/c	850
			Dec. 31	Balance c/d	70
		1,040			1,040
Dec. 31	Balance b/d	70			

(c) Rates

		£			£
19_5			*19_5*		
Jan. 1	Balance b/d	120	Dec. 31	P & L a/c	1,200
19_5	Cash	900			
Dec. 31	Balance c/d	180			
		1,200			1,200
			Dec. 31	Balance b/d	180

(d) Rent Receivable

		£			£
19_2					
Jan. 1	Balance b/d	30	19_2	Cash	1,420
Dec. 31	P & L a/c	1,440	Dec. 31	Balance c/d	50
		1,470			1,470
Dec. 31	Balance b/d	50			

(e) Rent Receivable

		£			£
19_1			*19_1*		
Dec. 31	P & L a/c	950	Jan. 1	Balance b/d	100
			19_1	Cash	725
			Dec. 31	Balance c/d	125
		950			950
Dec. 31	Balance b/d	125			

ANSWER 10.1

(a) Delivery Van Account

		£			£
Year 1	Bank	1,500	Year 1		
			Dec. 31	Depreciation (P & L a/c)	150
			Dec. 31	Balance c/d	1,350
		1,500			1,500
Dec. 31	Balance b/d	1,350	Year 2		
			Dec. 31	Dep'n (P & L a/c)	150
			Dec. 31	Balance c/d	1,200
		1,350			1,350
			Year 3		
			Dec. 31	Dep'n (P & L a/c)	150
Dec. 31	Balance b/d	1,200	Dec. 31	Balance c/d	1,050
		1,200			1,200
Dec. 31	Balance b/d	1,050			

(b) Delivery Van Account

		£			£
Year 1	Bank	1,500	Year 1		
			Dec. 31	Dep'n (P & L a/c)	150
			Dec. 31	Balance c/d	1,350
		1,500			1,500
Dec. 31	Balance b/d	1,350	Year 2		
			Dec. 31	Dep'n (P & L a/c)	135
				Balance c/d	1,215
		1,350			1,350
			Year 3		
Dec. 31	Balance b/d	1,215	Dec. 31	Dep'n (P & L a/c)	121
				Balance c/d	1,094
		1,215			1,215
	Balance b/d	1,094			

NOTE: Depreciation would not normally be credited to the actual asset account, but to a Provision for Depreciation of Vans Account.

ANSWER 10.2

(a) £3,300 (net profit plus non-cash debit "depreciation")
(b) (i) Reduce profit by £630 (ii) No effect.

ANSWER 10.3

Trading and Profit and Loss Account for year ended 31st March 19_9

		£		£
Stock		1,800	Sales	12,940
Purchases	7,400		*Less* returns	170
Less returns	90	7,310		12,770
		9,110		
Less stock		2,100		
Cost of Goods Sold		7,010		
Gross Profit		5,760		
		12,770		12,770
Discounts Allowed		320	Gross Profit	5,760
Rent and Rates		590	Discounts Received	110
Wages and Salaries		3,260		
General Expenses		170		
Depreciation on:				
Motor Vehicles		750		
Fixtures & Fittings		70		
Net Profit		710		
		5,870		5,870

Balance Sheet as at 31st March 19_9

	£		£	£
Capital	2,060	Motor Vehicles (cost)	3,000	
Net profit	710	*Less* prov. for dep'n	3,000	—
	2,770	Fixtures & Fittings (cost)	1,500	
Creditors	3,300	*Less* prov. for Dep'n	870	630
Wages accrued	150			
General Expenses accrued	40	Stock		2,100
Bank overdraft	830	Debtors		4,200
		Cash		100
		Rates prepaid		60
	7,090			7,090

ANSWER 11.1

Machinery and Plant

		£			£
19_1			*19_7*		
Jan. 1	Bank	500,000	Dec. 31	Disposals	250,000
19_8			*19_8*		
Feb. 15	Cash	700,000	May 31	Balance c/d	950,000
		1,200,000			1,200,000
19_8					
May 31	Balance b/d	950,000			

Machinery Disposals

		£			£
19_7			*19_7*		
Dec. 31	Mach. & Plant	250,000	Dec. 31	Cash	150,000
	Gain on Sale	75,000	Dec. 31	Prov. for Dep'n	175,000
		325,000			325,000

Provision for Depreciation – Plant and Machinery

		£			£
19_7			*19_7*		
Dec. 31	Disposals	175,000	May 31	Balance b/d	300,000
19_8			*19_8*		
May 31	Balance c/d	220,000	May 31	P & L a/c (Dep'n)	95,000
		395,000			395,000
			May 31	Balance b/d	220,000

Balance Sheet extract

		£
	Machinery & Plant (cost)	950,000
	Less prov. for dep'n	220,000
		730,000

ANSWER 11.2

Machinery

		£			£
19_8			*19_0*		
Jan. 1	Bank	3,000	Jan. 1	Disposals	1,000
			Dec. 31	Balance c/d	2,000
		3,000			3,000
19_0					
Dec. 31	Balance b/d	2,000			

Machinery Disposals

		£			£
19_0			*19_0*		
Jan. 1	Machinery	1,000	Jan. 1	Cash	762
			Jan. 1	Prov. for dep'n	200
			Jan. 1	Loss on Sale	38
		1,000			1,000

Provision for Depreciation – Machinery

		£			£
19_0			*19_8*		
Jan. 1	Disposals	200	Dec. 31	P & L a/c	300
Dec. 31	Balance c/d	600	*19_9*		
			Dec. 31	P & L a/c	300
			19_0		
			Dec. 31	P & L a/c	200
		800			800
			Dec. 31	Balance b/d	600

ANSWER 11.3

Van A Account

19_6					
March 1	Balance b/d	£1,550			

Van B Account

19_6			19_6		
March 1	Balance b/d	£1,500	Dec.	Disposals	£1,500

Office Equipment Account

19_6					
March 1	Balance b/d	£2,100			

Provision for Depreciation – Van A

			19_6		£
			March 1	Balance b/d	1,388
			19_7		
			Feb. 28	P & L a/c	65

Provision for Depreciation – Van B

19_6		£	19_6		£
Dec.	Disposals	960	March 1	Balance b/d	960

Provision for Depreciation – Equipment

			19_6		£
			March 1	Balance b/d	780
			Feb. 28	P & L a/c	210

Disposals Account – Van B

		£			£
Dec.	Van a/c	1,500	Dec.	Cash	230
			Dec.	Depreciation	960
			Dec.	Loss on Sale	310
		1,500			1,500

Van C Account

Dec.	Bank	£1,620	

Provision for Depreciation – Van C

			Feb. 28	P & L a/c	£648

ANSWER 11.4

(b)

Vehicles Account

19_8		£	*19_9*		£
Dec. 31	Balance b/d	30,300	Dec. 31	Disposals	3,500
19_9			Dec. 31	Disposals	950
March 31	Bank	6,500	Dec. 31	Disposals	4,000
April 30	Bank	8,400	Dec. 31	Balance c/d	43,250
Aug. 31	Bank	6,500			
		51,700			51,700
Dec. 31	Balance b/d	43,250			

Vehicles Disposal Account

19_9		£	19_9		£
Dec. 31	Truck	3,500	Dec. 31	Prov. for dep'n	1,225
Dec. 31	Car	950	Dec. 31	Cash	450
Dec. 31	Dumper	4,000	Dec. 31	Loss on Sale	1,825
Dec. 31	Gain on Sale of Dumper	250	Dec. 31	Prov. for dep'n	665
			Dec. 31	Cash	75
			Dec. 31	Loss on Sale	210
			Dec. 31	Prov. for dep'n	4,000
			Dec. 31	Cash	250
		8,700			8,700

Provision for Depreciation Account

19_9		£	19_8		£
Dec. 31	Disposals – Truck	1,225	Dec. 31	Balance b/d	7,100
Dec. 31	Disposals – Car	665	19_9		
Dec. 31	Disposals – Dumper	4,000	Dec. 31	P & L a/c	6,898
Dec. 31	Balance c/d	8,108			
		13,998			13,998
			Dec. 31	Balance b/d	8,108

ANSWER 11.5

Trading and Profit & Loss Account for year ending 31st December 19_2

	£		£
Stock	4,700	Sales	62,220
Purchases	48,360		
	53,060		
Less Stock	6,465		
Cost of Goods Sold	46,595		
Gross Profit	15,625		
	62,220		62,220
General Expenses	1,469	Gross Profit	15,625
Motor Expenses	418	Discounts Received	871
Rent and Rates	646		
Discounts Allowed	1,126		
Wages and Salaries	7,462		
Light and Heat	97		
Loss on Sale of Van	68		
Depreciation of Vans	240		
Net Profit	4,970		
	16,496		16,496

Balance Sheet as at 31st December 19_2

	£			£
Capital	9,600	Furniture & Fittings		800
Net Profit	4,970	Equipment		3,750
		Motor Vans	1,200	
	14,570	*Less* depreciation	240	
Creditors	4,116			960
Accruals	12	Stock		6,465
		Debtors		5,280
		Bank		1,415
		Prepayments		28
	18,698			18,698

ANSWER 11.6

(a)

Plant Account

		£			£
19_7			19_7		
Sept. 30	Balance b/d	410,100	Dec. 4.	Disposals a/c	46,800
19_8			19_8		
May 15	Bank	81,400	Sept. 30	Balance c/d	444,700
		491,500			491,500
Sept. 30	Balance b/d	444,700			

Plant Disposals Account

		£			£
19_7			19_7		
Dec. 4	Plant	46,800	Dec. 4	Bank	16,212
			Dec. 4	Depreciation	27,630
			Dec. 4	Loss on Sale	2,958
		46,800			46,800

Provision for Depreciation of Plant

		£			£
19_7			19_7		
Dec. 4	Disposals	27,630	Sept. 30	Balance b/d	159,180
19_8			19_8		
Sept. 30	Balance c/d	194,180	Sept. 30	P & L a/c	62,630
		221,810			221,810
			Sept. 30	Balance b/d	194,180

ANSWER 11.7

Plant and Machinery

		£			£
1.3._2	Bank (M5)	12,000	1.9._4	Disposals	12,000
1.1._3	Bank (M6)	18,700	31.12._4	Balance c/d	38,700
1.9._4	Disposal a/c (M7)	4,000			
1.9._4	Bank (M7)	16,000			
		50,700			50,700
31.12._4	Balance b/d	38,700			

Provision for Depreciation – Plant and Machinery

		£			£
1.9._4	Disposals (M5)	4,000	31.12._2	Profit & Loss a/c	2,000
31.12._4	Balance c/d	5,600	31.12._3	Profit & Loss a/c	4,100
			31.12._4	Profit & Loss a/c	3,500
		9,600			9,600
			31.12._4	Balance b/d	5,600

Disposals Account – Plant and Machinery (M5)

		£			£
1.9._4	Plant & Machinery	12,000	1.9._4	Plant & Machinery	4,000
			1.9._4	Depreciation	4,000
			1.9._4	Loss on Sale	4,000
		12,000			12,000

ANSWER 11.8

Machinery Account

		£			£
19_8			*19_9*		
Dec. 31	Balance b/d	36,000		Disposals	6,000
19_9	Bank	9,000		Disposals	10,000
	Disposals } (F)	2,000		Disposals	8,000
	Cash } (F)	12,000	Dec. 31	Balance c/d	35,000
		59,000			59,000
Dec. 31	Balance b/d	35,000			

Machinery Disposals Account

19_9		£	19–9		£
	Machinery (B)	6,000		Cash	3,000
	Machinery (C)	10,000		Prov. for Dep'n	2,400
	Gain on Sale (C)	500		Loss on Sale	600
	Machinery (A)	8,000		Cash	8,500
				Prov. for Dep'n	2,000
				Machinery	2,000
				Prov. for Dep'n	4,800
				Loss on Sale	1,200
		24,500			24,500

Provision for Depreciation

19_9		£	19_8		£
	Disposals (B)	2,400	Dec. 31	Balance b/d	10,400
	Disposals (C)	2,000	19_9		
	Disposals (A)	4,800	Dec. 31	P & L a/c	3,500
Dec. 31	Balance c/d	4,700			
		13,900			13,900
			Dec. 31	Balance b/d	4,700

ANSWER 12.1

Bad Debts

	£	19_2		£
Smith	25	May 31	P & L a/c	169
Edwards	31			
Williams	18			
Frost	43			
Parsons	52			
	169			169

Provision for Bad Debts

19_2		£	19_1		£
May 31	Balance c/d	192	May 31	Balance b/d	130
			19_2		
			May 31	P & L a/c	62
		192			192
			May 31	Balance b/d	192

ANSWER 12.2

Balance Sheet as at 31st May 19_2

		£			£
Capital		124,000	*Fixed Assets*		
Net Profit		13,800	Premises		110,000
			Current Assets	£	
		137,800	Stock	25,000	
Less Drawings		10,000	Debtors	2,600	
			Bank	1,400	
		127,800	Cash	20	
Long Term Loan		9,500	Prepayments	500	
Current Liabilities					29,520
Trade Creditors	1,950				
Expense Creditors	270				
		2,220			
		139,520			139,520

(b) Capital Account

		£			£
19_2			*19_1*		
May 31	Drawings	10,000	May 31	Balance	124,000
May 31	Balance c/d	127,800	*19_2*		
			May 31	Net Profit	13,800
		137,800			137,800
			May 31	Balance b/d	127,800

ANSWER 12.3

(a) Machinery

		£			£
19_8			*19_8*		
Jan. 1	Balance b/d	120,000	Dec. 31	Disposals	4,000
Jan. 1	Bank	50,000	Dec. 31	Balance c/d	166,000
		170,000			170,000
Dec. 31	Balance b/d	166,000			

(b) Machinery Disposals

		£			£
19_8			*19_8*		
Dec. 31	Machinery	4,000	Dec. 13	Cash	2,000
Dec. 31	Gain on sale to P & L a/c	400	Dec. 31	Prov. for dep'n	2,400
		4,400			4,400

(c) Provision for Depreciation – Machinery

		£			£
19_8			*19_8*		
Dec. 31	Disposals	2,400	Jan. 1	Balance b/d	50,000
Dec. 31	Balance c/d	80,800	Dec. 31	P & L a/c	33,200
		83,200			83,200
			Dec. 31	Balance b/d	80,800

(d) Provision for Doubtful Debts

		£			£
19_8			*19_8*		
Dec. 31	P & L a/c	300	Jan. 1	Balance b/d	4,500
Dec. 31	Balance c/d	4,200			
		4,500			4,500
				Balance b/d	4,200

(e) Profit and Loss Account Extract

	£		£
Provision for Depreciation of Machinery	33,200	Gain on Sale	400
		Decrease in Provision for Doubtful Debts	300

ANSWER 12.4

Trading and Profit and Loss Account for year ending 31st December 19_4

	£		£
Stock (Jan. 1)	6,300	Sales	60,900
Purchases	46,300		
	52,600		
Less Stock (Dec. 31)	8,800		
	43,800		
Gross profit c/d	17,100		
	60,900		60,900
Rates & Insurance	203	Gross profit b/d	17,100
Wages & Salaries	8,924	Provision for bad debts	40
Bad debts	359	Discounts received	814
Repairs to buildings	198		
Car expenses	212		
General expenses	1,586		
Discounts allowed	1,061		
Net profit to Capital a/c	5,411		
	17,954		17,954

Balance Sheet as at 31st December 19_4

	£	£			£	£
Capital (Jan. 1)	20,500		Freehold land			
Add net profit	5,411		& buildings		10,000	
			Add additions		650	
	25,911					
Less drawings	2,706				10,650	
		23,205	Furniture &			
Trade Creditors	4,035		fittings		1,460	
Wages & Salaries due	318		Motor car		950	
		4,353				13,060
			Stock		8,800	
			Debtors	5,213		
			Less Prov.	100		
					5,113	
			Rates & Insurance			
			pre-paid		45	
			Balance at Bank		540	
						14,498
		27,558				27,558

ANSWER 12.5

Trading and Profit and Loss Account for year ending 31st December 19_6

	£	£		£
Stock		8,495	Sales	93,140
Purchases	71,420		*Less* Returns	811
Less Returns	432	70,988		
				92,329
		79,483		
Less Stock		8,869		
		70,614		
Gross profit c/d		21,715		
		92,329		92,329
Rates and insurance		368	Gross profit b/d	21,715
Rent		600		
Salaries		11,084		
Motor expenses		378		
General expenses		1,424		
Bank Charges		16		
Bad Debts		440		
Prov. for bad debts		62		
Prov. for Depreciation:				
Motor Vehicles		468		
Net profit to Capital a/c		6,875		
		21,715		21,715

Balance Sheet as at 31st December 19_6

	£	£			£	£
Capital (Jan. 1)	17,400		Premises (cost)			9,500
Add net profit	6,875		Motor vehicles (cost)		2,600	
			Less prov. for			
	24,275		Depreciation		1,720	880
Less drawings	3,655					
		20,620				10,380
Creditors	6,105		Stock		8,869	
Rent owing	150		Debtors	7 266		
		6,255	*Less* prov.			
			for bad debts	442	6,824	
			Insurance prepaid		20	
			Bank Balance		782	
						16,495
		26,875				26,875

ANSWER 12.6

(c) Provision for Doubtful Debts

		£			£
19_5			19_4		
Dec. 31	P & L a/c	100	Dec. 31	P & L a/c	400
19_7			19_6		
Dec. 31	Balance c/d	450	Dec. 31	P & L a/c	150
		550			550
			19_7		
			Dec. 31	Balance b/d	450

ANSWER 13.1

Cash Book

		Cash	Bank			Cash	Bank
		£	£			£	£
June 1	Balances	610	1,470	June 2	Brown		690
June 10	Briggs	470		June 4	Wages	320	
June 12	Rent Received	60		June 6	Equipment		750
June 18	Office Furniture			June 16	Bank Charges		120
	Disposals	2,000		June 20	Bank	1,600	
June 20	Cash		1,600	June 27	Fixtures &		
June 30	Balance c/d		4,990		Fittings		6,500
				June 30	Wages	410	
				June 30	Balance c/d	810	
		3,140	8,060			3,140	8,060
June 30	Balance b/d	810		June 30	Balance b/d		4,990

ANSWER 13.2

Cash Book (Bank)

		£			£
	Credit Transfer	900	May 31	Balance b/d	4,000
	Dividends	1,500		Bank Charges	400
	Balance c/d	2,000			
		4,400			4,400
				Balance b/d	2,000

Bank Reconciliation Statement

	£
Balance as per Bank Statement	1,500
Less unpresented cheques	10,000
	(8,500)
Add credit not yet entered	3,500
	(5,000)
Add transfer from Deposit a/c	3,000
Overdraft as per Cash Book	(2,000)

ANSWER 13.3

Cash Book (Bank)

		£		£
March 31	Balance b/d	787	Standing Order	25
March 31	Credit Transfer	73	Balance c/d	835
		860		860
March 31	Balance b/d	835		

Bank Reconciliation Statement

	£
Balance as per Bank Statement*	850
Less unpresented cheques, £34, £41, and £52.	127
	723
Add credit not yet entered	112
Balance as per Cash Book	835

* Balancing figure.

ANSWER 13.4

Bank Reconciliation Statement

	£	£
Balance as per Cash Book		625
Add Credit Transfer	42	
Interest	54	96
		721
Less Standing Order	75	
Dishonoured Cheque	44	119
		602
Add unpresented cheques, £21, £17, £57, £61		156
Balance as per Bank Statement		758

NOTE: The above method would not be used in practice but we must always do exactly what the examiner asks.

ANSWER 13.5

Cash Book (Bank)

	£		£
Adjust re Interest	40	Balance b/d	490
Adjust re error	70	Adjust re error	90
Dividend	1,000	Adjust re error (2 × £319)	638
		Dishonoured Cheque	143
		Rent	120
Balance c/d	469	Adjust re error	98
	1,579		1,579
		Balance b/d	469

Bank Reconciliation Statement

	£
Overdraft as per Bank Statement	(873)
Add unpresented cheques	376
	(1,249)
Less credit not entered	780
Balance as per Cash Book	(469)

ANSWER 13.6

(a) Cash Book (Bank)

	£		£
Balance b/d	3,856	Dishonoured Cheque	48
Error	100	Interest	10
		Balance c/d	3,898
	3,956		3,956
Balance b/d	3,898		

(b) *Bank Reconciliation Statement*

	£	£
Balance per Bank Statement		4,161
Less unpresented cheques	218	
wrong credit	95	313
		3,848
Add credit not yet banked		50
Balance per Cash Book		3,898

ANSWER 13.7

Cash Book (Bank)

		£		£
April 30	Balance	1,310·40	Bank Charges	12·80
	To correct (No. 130)	9·90	Standing Order	32·52
	Giro Credit	21·47	Balance c/d	1,296·45
		1,341·77		1,341·77
April 30	Balance b/d	1,296·45		

Bank Reconciliation Statement at 30th April

		£
Balance per Bank Statement		1,166·45
Less unpresented cheques:		
236131	£30·00	
236134	£52·27	82·27
		1,084·18
Add credit not yet entered		192·80
		1,276·98
Add wrong debit (427519) until confirmed with bank		19·47
Balance per Cash Book		1,296·45

ANSWER 14.1

(a) Cash Book

		Discounts Allowed	Cash	Bank			Discounts Received	Cash	Bank
		£	£	£			£	£	£
May 1	Balances b/d		27	495	May 3	Johnson	3		47
May 12	Holt	5		60	May 9	Wages			32
May 17	Layton	2	23		May 24	Bank		10	
May 24	Cash			10	May 26	Parsons	3	32	
May 29	Bank		25		May 29	Cash			25
					May 31	Balances c/d		33	461
		7	75	565			6	75	565
May 31	Balances b/d		33	461					

(b) Debit £7 to Discounts Allowed; Credit £6 to Discounts Received.

ANSWER 14.2

Journal

(a)	DR	CR
	£	£
Office Furniture	240	
Bank		170
Office Furniture		70
Being purchase of new furniture		
Loss on Sale of Furniture a/c	15	
Office Furniture		15
Being loss on exchange of furniture		
(b)		
Gordon	307	
Bills accepted		307
Being acceptance of Bill No.		
Gordon	13	
Discounts Received		13
Being discount received on Acceptance of Bill		
(c)		
Wilson	27	
Sales		27
Being correction of error		
(d)		
Cash	150	
Loss on sale of van	16	
Delivery Vans		166
Being sale of van		

ANSWER 14.3

(a) Cash Book (Bank)

		Discounts Allowed	Cash	Bank			Discounts Received	Cash	Bank
		£	£	£			£	£	£
April 1	Balances b/d		43	449	April 9	Thompson	3		37
April 6	Jones	5		55	April 16	Jones			55
April 14	Wilson	4	56		April 19	Bank		80	
April 19	Cash			80	April 23	Gibson	7		68
					April 26	Salaries			88
					April 30	Balances c/d		19	336
		9	99	584			10	99	584
April 30	Balances b/d		19	336					

(b) Debit Discounts Allowed £9; Credit Discounts Received £10.

(c) A debit of £55 to Jones' account.

ANSWER 14.4

(i)

Purchases Day Book

Date	*Details*	*Inv. No.*	*Amount*
			£
Oct. 3	A. Wise	1	46·80
Oct. 11	W. Smith	2	75·00
Oct. 22	F. Jones	3	80·00
Oct. 31	Total to Purchases a/c		201·80

Sales Day Book

Date	*Details*	*Copy Inv. No.*	*Amount*
			£
Oct. 7	C. Jackson	101	57·00
Oct. 15	J. Shipley	102	48·60
Oct. 29	S. Nichols	103	40·00
Oct. 31	Total to Sales a/c		145·60

(ii)

A. Wise

			Oct. 3	Purchases	£46·80

W. Smith

			Oct. 11	Purchases	£75·00

F. Jones

			Oct. 22	Purchases	£80·00

C. Jackson

Oct. 7	Sales	£57·00	

J. Shipley

Oct. 15	Sales	£48·60	

S. Nichols

Oct. 29	Sales	£40·00			

(iii)

Purchases

Oct. 31	Month's Purchases	£201·80			

Sales

			Oct. 31	Month's Sales	£145·60

ANSWER 14.5

Journal

(a)	DR	CR
	£	£
Cash	320	
Loss on Sale of Van	40	
Delivery Vans		360
Being sale of delivery van		
(b)		
Bills Receivable	287	
Discounts Allowed	3	
Smith		290
Being acceptance of Bill of Exchange		
(c)		
Bank	92	
Bad Debts	68	
Harrison		160
Being dividend on bankruptcy and resultant bad debt written off		
(d)		
Rent	60	
Drawings	30	90
Bank		
Being payment of rent for period		

ANSWER 14.6

Journal

(1)	DR	CR
	£	£
W. Jones	37	
A. Jones		37
Being correction of errors		
(2)		
M. Ives	30	
Office Furniture		28
Discounts Received		2
Being desk used to settle debt		
Loss on Sale of Furniture	5	
Office Furniture		5
Being loss on desk to settle debt		
(3)		
Motor Vans	1,460	
Motor Expenses	130	
Bank		1,590
Being payment for new Motor Van and Tax and Insurance		
Motor Vans	500	
Motor Vans		500
Contra entry re part exchange		
(4)		
Dawson	45	
Sales		45
Being correction of error		

ANSWER 14.7

(i) Cash Book

	Discounts Allowed	Cash	Bank		Discounts Received	Cash	Bank
	£	£	£		£	£	£
May 1 Balances b/d		31	537	May 11 Johnson	4		56
May 5 Gordon	2		38	May 12 Cash			40
May 12 Cash		40		May 13 Wages		37	
May 16 Layton	5	39		May 25 Gill	2	18	
May 29 Cash			30	May 29 Bank		30	
				May 29 Salaries			58
				May 31 Balances c/d		25	451
	7	110	605		6	110	605
May 31 Balances b/d		25	451				

(iii) Debit Discounts Allowed £7; Credit Discounts Received £6.

ANSWER 14.8

(i) *Purchases Day Book*

Date	*Details*	*Inv. No.*	*Amount*
			£
March 3	W. Jones	1	57·00
March 7	A. Wills	2	38·00
March 21	W. Jones	3	40·00
March 31	Totals to Purchases a/c		135·00

Sales Day Book

Date	*Details*	*Copy Inv. No.*	*Amount*
			£
March 11	J. Adams	25	54·00
March 17	F. Moore	26	18·00
March 26	J. Adams	27	45·00
March 31	Totals to Sales a/c		117·00

W. Jones

			£
			£
		March 3 Purchases	57
		March 21 Purchases	40

A. Wills

		March 7 Purchases	£38

J. Adams

	£		
March 11 Sales	54		
March 26 Sales	45		

F. Moore

March 17 Sales	£18		

(ii) Purchases

March 31 Totals for month	£135		

Sales

		March 31 Totals for month	£117

ANSWER 15.1

(a) Suspense a/c

	£		£
Purchases	500	Balance	2,500
Jitsum	700	Sales Returns	350
Bank	1,500		
Creditors	150		
	2,850		2,850

(b) Profit & Loss account for year ended 31st March, 19_0

	£		£
Heat and Light	1,640	Gross Profit b/d	20,400
Wages and Salaries	7,700		
Advertising	800		
Carriage Outwards	700		
Motor Expenses	1,750		
Rent and Rates	2,500		
Depreciation on:			
Fixtures & Fittings	780		
Motor Vehicles	860		
Net Profit	3,670		
	20,400		20,400

(c) Balance Sheet as at 31st March 19_0

	£		£	£
Capital	53,800	*Fixed Assets*		
Net Profit	3,670	Freehold Premises (cost)		26,000
		Fixtures & Fittings (cost)	7,800	
	57,470	*Less* prov. for dep'n	4,280	
Less Drawings	9,750			3,520
		Motor Vehicles (cost)	4,300	
	47,720	*Less* prov. for dep'n	3,260	
Current Liabilities				1,040
Trade Creditors	11,450			
Accruals	540			30,560
		Current Assets		
		Stock	13,800	
		Debtors	8,500	
		Bank	5,000	
		Cash	1,750	
		Prepayments	100	
				29,150
	59,710			59,710

ANSWER 15.2

(a) (i) *Journal*

	DR	CR
	£	£
Suspense a/c	124	
Returns Outwards		124
Being correction of error		
Purchases	100	
Dawson		100
Being Invoice No......		
Vehicle Repairs	6	
Suspense a/c		6
Being correction of error		
R. Race	36	
Suspense a/c		36
Being correction of error		

(ii) Suspense a/c

	£		£
Returns	124	Repairs	6
		R. Race	36
		Original Difference i.e. Balance	82
	124		124

(iii) £9,918

ANSWER 15.3

(1) *Journal*

	DR	CR
	£	£
Motor Vehicles	1,100	
Material Purchases		1,100
Profit and Loss a/c	220	
Provision for Depreciation – M.V.		220
Wages	100	
Drawings		100
Drawings	75	
Purchases		75
A. Smythe	150	
A. Smith		150
Suspense a/c	950	
Sales		950
Rates	450	
Suspense a/c		450

(2) *Capital Account Details*

	£
Opening Balance	11,500
Net Profit	7,105
	18,605
Less Drawings	4,875
New Balance	13,730

ANSWER 15.4

Journal

	DR £	CR £
Motor Vehicles	90	
Suspense		90
Being correction of error		
W. Jones	5	
Suspense		5
Property Repairs	100	
Freehold Premises		100
Interest on Loan	200	
Suspense		200
Suspense	50	
Machinery		50

Suspense Account

	£		£
Machinery	50	Motor Vehicles	90
Balance c/d	245	Jones	5
		Interest	200
	295		295
		Balance b/d	245

ANSWER 15.5

(a) *Journal*

	DR £	CR £
R. Williams	170·64	
G. Williams		170·64
Being correction of error		
Machinery Repairs	145·00	
Machinery		145·00
Suspense a/c	400·00	
Sales		400·00
Suspense a/c	18·26	
Telephone a/c		18·26

(b) Suspense Account

	£		£
Sales	400·00	Trial Balance	418·26
Telephone	18·26		
	418·26		418·26

ANSWER 15.6

(a) Suspense Account

	£		£
Balance	210	Bank	35
Discounts Received	426	Smith	94
		Discounts Allowed	396
		Bank Interest	111
	636		636

Re error (ii) Debit Drawings £69; Credit Purchases £69
(vi) Debit A. Able, £211; Credit B. Able £211.

ANSWER 15.7

(a) Suspense Account

	£		£
Balance	1,465	Trial Balance	2,500
Purchases	90	(Investment)	
Cash	495		
Creditors	250		
Debtors	200		
	2,500		2,500

(b) Balance Sheet as at 31st December 19_9

	£		£
Capital Account	50,000	Fixed Assets	87,214
Current Account	209	Investment	2,500
		Current Assets	
	50,209	Stock	11,595
Net Profit	23,703	Debtors	27,295
		Cash	55
	73,912		
Less Drawings	4,650		
	69,262		
Long Term Loan	20,000		
Current Liabilities			
Trade Creditors	25,141		
Bank Overdraft	12,256		
Interest owing	2,000		
	128,659		128,659

ANSWER 15.8

Effect of Corrections on Net Profit

	Increase (£)	*Decrease* (£)
Item i		23
ii	170	
iii	–	–
iv	100	
v	–	–
vi	175	
	445	23

The corrections have resulted in an increase in profit of £422 – the true net profit was therefore *£3,522.*

Corrected Balance Sheet

		£		£
	Capital	6,300	Machinery *less* Dep'n	4,250
	Net Profit	3,522	Office Furniture *less* Depreciation	975
		9,822	Stock	3,170
	Less drawings	2,200	Debtors	2,520
		7,622		
	Creditors	2,640		
Bank overdraft		653		
		10,915		10,915

ANSWER 15.9

(a)

Corrected Trial Balance

	DR £	CR £
Provision for Doubtful Debts		200
Bank overdraft		1,654
Capital		4,591
Creditors		1,637
Debtors	2,983	
Discounts Received		252
Discounts Allowed	733	
Drawings	1,200	
Office Furniture	2,155	
Provision for Depreciation of Furniture		364
General Expenses	829	
Purchases	10,923	
Returns Inwards	330	
Rent and Rates	314	
Salaries	2,520	
Sales		16,882
Stock	2,418	
Suspense account	1,175	
	25,580	25,580

(b)

Journal

	DR £	CR £
Jones	20	
Suspense		20
Being correction of error		
Furniture	173	
General Expenses		173
Purchases	370	
Suspense		370
A. Hope Ltd.	450	
Suspense		450
Capital	300	
Suspense		300
Sales	86	
A. Blunt		86
Discounts Allowed	35	
Suspense		35

Suspense Account

	£		£
Trial Balance	1,175	Jones	20
		Purchases	370
		Hope Ltd.	450
		Capital	300
		Discounts	35
	1,175		1,175

ANSWER 15.10

(a) Trading and Profit and Loss Account for year ending 31st December 19_3

	£		£
Stock (1st Jan.)	1,536	Sales	30,173
Purchases	21,906		
	23,442		
Less stock (31st Dec.)	1,418		
	22,024		
Gross Profit c/d	8,149		
	30,173		30,173
Wages	4,659	Gross profit b/d	8,149
Repairs	205		
Discounts allowed	467		
General expenses	894		
Net Profit to Capital a/c	1,924		
	8,149		8,149

Balance Sheet as at 31st December 19_3

	£		£
Capital (1st Jan.)	339	Furniture	908
Add Net Profit	1,924	Stock	1,418
	2,263	Debtors	1,548
Creditors	1,466		
Bank overdraft	145		
	3,874		3,874

(b) General Expenses

	£		£
Total Payments therefore =	894	Original "Suspense"	290
		Profit & Loss a/c	604
	894		894

ANSWER 15.11

(i)

		£
Error (1)	Credit overstated or Debit understated	450
(2)	Credit understated or Debit overstated	168
(3)	No effect	
(4)	Credit overstated or Debit understated	27

(ii)

Effect of Corrections on Net Profit of £2,770

	Increase	*Decrease*
	£	£
Item (1)		450
(2)	168	
(3)		66
(4)	–	–
	168	516
		168
Net Decrease =		348
Therefore correct net profit =		2,422

ANSWER 16.1

Sales Ledger Control Account

	£		£
Balance b/d	97,550	Balance b/d	48
Credit Sales	248,620	Bank	260,090
Interest	150	Bad debts	1,260
Dishonoured Cheque	250	Discounts Allowed	5,860
Refund	370	Balance c/d	79,912
Balance c/d	230		
	347,170		347,170
Balance b/d	79,912	Balance b/d	230

Purchases Ledger Control Account

	£		£
Balance b/d	96	Balance b/d	56,900
Bank	216,100	Purchases	194,720
Allowances	2,880	Balance c/d	150
Discount Received	2,520		
Balance c/d	30,174		
	251,770		251,770
Balance b/d	150	Balance b/d	30,174

ANSWER 16.2

Sales Ledger Control Account

	£		£
Balance b/d	2,190	Bank	16,840
Sales	19,830	Discounts Allowed	921
		Sales Returns	320
		Bad Debts	110
		Transfer	65
		Balance c/d	3,764
	22,020		22,020
Balance b/d	3,764		

Purchases Ledger Control Account

	£		£
Cash	25,670	Balance b/d	6,200
Discounts Received	835	Purchases	27,310
Purchases Returns	290		
Transfer	65		
Balance c/d	6,650		
	33,510		33,510
		Balance b/d	6,650

ANSWER 16.3

Sales Ledger Control Account

		£			£
Dec. 1	Balance b/d	19,510	Dec. 1	Balance b/d	24
Dec. 31	Sales	49,382	Dec. 31	Cash	52,018
Dec. 31	Interest	30	Dec. 31	Bad debts	252
Dec. 31	Dishonoured Cheque	50	Dec. 31	Discounts allowed	1,172
Dec. 31	Refund of over-Payment	74	Dec. 31	Balance c/d	15,620
Dec. 31	Balance c/d	40			
		69,086			69,086
Dec. 31	Balances b/d	15,620	Dec. 31	Balance b/d	40

Purchases Ledger Control Account

		£			£
Dec. 1	Balance b/d	48	Dec. 1	Balance b/d	11,380
Dec. 31	Cash	43,220	Dec. 31	Purchases	38,944
Dec. 31	Rebates	576	Dec. 31	Balance c/d	30
Dec. 31	Discounts Received	904			
Dec. 31	Balance c/d	5,606			
		50,354			50,354
Dec. 31	Balance b/d	30	Dec. 31	Balance b/d	5,606

ANSWER 16.4

(a) Purchases Ledger Control Account

	£		£
Mahoney	210	Balance b/d	4,120
Balance c/d	4,490	Purchases	130
		Kennedy	450
	4,700		4,700
		Balance b/d	4,490

(b)

		£
Correct balances	=	4,490
Less error (iii)		450
		4040
Add error (iv)		40
Original Balances	=	4,080

ANSWER 16.5

Purchases Ledger Control Account

	£		£
Balance b/d	256	Balance b/d	25,038
Returns – Street	160	Balance c/d	256
King	420		
Balance c/d	24,458		
	25,294		25,294
Balance b/d	256	Balance b/d	24,458

Sales Ledger Control Account

	£		£
Balance b/d	38,910	Balance b/d	1,556
Balance c/d	914	Overcasting of Sales	1,500
		Bad Debts – Wood	600
		Balance c/d	36,168
	39,824		39,824
Balance b/d	36,168	Balance b/d	914

ANSWER 16.6

(a) Debtors' Ledger Control Account

		£			£
April 1	Balance b/d	65,200	April 1	Balance b/d	900
	Sales	213,500		Cash/Bank	179,800
April 30	Balance c/d	700		Returns	2,300
				Bad Debts	700
				Bills Accepted	3,300
				Discounts Allowed	3,400
				Creditors' Ledger	1,200
			April 30	Balance c/d	87,800
		279,400			279,400
April 30	Balance b/d	87,800	April 30	Balance b/d	700

Creditors' Ledger Control Account

		£			£
April 1	Balance b/d	100	April 1	Balance b/d	37,400
	Cash/Bank	87,100		Purchases	106,700
	Returns	1,500	April 30	Balance c/d	150
	Discounts Rec'd	2,050			
	Debtors' Ledger	1,200			
April 30	Balance c/d	52,300			
		144,250			144,250
April 30	Balance b/d	150	April 30	Balance b/d	52,300

ANSWER 16.7

(b) Sales Ledger Control Account

		£			£
19_8	Balance b/d	27,124	19_8	Balance b/d	222
	Sales	237,548		Bank	228,413
	Refunds	97		Discounts	1,352
19_9	Balance c/d	305		Bad Debts	2,018
			19_9	Balance c/d	33,069
		265,074			265,074
19_9	Balance b/d	33,069	19_9	Balance b/d	305

Purchases Ledger Control Account

		£			£
19_8	Balance b/d	375	19_8	Balance b/d	19,763
	Bank	139,276		Purchases	144,137
	Discounts Rec'd	1,097		Balance c/d	164
	Balance c/d	23,316			
		164,064			164,064
	Balance b/d	164		Balance b/d	23,316

ANSWER 17.1

(1) Statement of Affairs at 1st April 19_8

Capital	£	*Assets*	£
(Balancing figure)	31,148	Debtors	2,400
Creditors	2,362	Bank	7,709
		Cash	401
		Fixtures	2,500
		Premises	15,500
		Stock	5,000
	33,510		33,510

(2) Cash £1,221; Bank £8,962.

(3) Trading and Profit & Loss Account for year ended 31st March 19_9

	£		£
Stock	5,000	Sales	30,000
Purchases	19,700		
	24,700		
Less Stock	4,700		
Cost of Goods Sold	20,000		
Gross Profit c/d	10,000		
	30,000		30,000
Wages and Salaries	3,050	Gross Profit b/d	10,000
Rates	590		
Advertising	140		
Insurance	100		
Repairs, etc.	385		
Carriage Outwards	170		
Discounts Allowed	1,564		
Depreciation of Fixtures	250		
Net Profit	3,751		
	10,000		10,000

Balance Sheet as at 31st March 19_9

	£			£
Capital	31,148	*Fixed Assets*		
New Capital	108	Freehold Premises		15,500
Net Profit	3,751	Fixtures & Fittings	2,500	
		Less depreciation	250	
	35,007			2,250
Less Drawings	4,650			
				17,750
	30,357	*Current Assets*		
Current Liabilities		Stock	4,700	
Creditors	4,562	Debtors	2,386	
Wages due	150	Insurance Prepaid	50	
		Bank	8,962	
		Cash	1,221	
				17,319
	35,069			35,069

ANSWER 17.2

Trading and Profit & Loss Account for year ended 30th April 19_7

	£		£
Stock	5,120	Sales	24,519
Purchases	19,508		
	24,628		
Less Stock	4,259		
	20,369		
Gross Profit	4,150		
	24,519		24,519
Trade Expenses	1,630	Gross Profit	4,150
Depreciation on:			
Fixtures & Fittings 1	140		
Motor Van	175		
Net Profit	2,205		
	4,150		4,150

Balance Sheet as at 30th April 19_7

	£		£
Capital	6,745	Fixtures and Fittings	1,260
Net Profit	2,205	Motor Van	525
		Stock	4,259
	8,950	Debtors	40
Less Drawings	2,033	Bank	1,660
	6,917		
Creditors	827		
	7,744		7,744

ANSWER 17.3

(a) Statement of Affairs as at 1st June 19_6

	£		£
Capital		Furniture	200
(Balancing figure)	570	Stock	1,000
Creditors	800	Bank	240
Accruals	70		
	1,440		1,440

(b) Creditors' Control Account

		£			£
	Bank	12,400	19_6	Balance b/d	800
19_7	Balance c/d	900		*Purchases*	12,500
		13,300			13,300

(c) Sales = £15,780

(d)

Expenses

		£			£
	Bank	1,262	19_6	Balance b/d	70
19_7	Balance c/d	100	19_7	*P & L a/c*	1,292
		1,362			1,362

Trading and Profit & Loss Account for year 19_7

	£		£
Stock	1,000	Sales	15,780
Purchases	12,500		
	13,500		
Less Stock	900		
	12,600		
Gross Profit	3,180		
	15,780		15,780
Expenses	1,292	Gross Profit	3,180
Rent	150		
Depreciation	20		
Net Profit	1,718		
	3,180		3,180

Balance Sheet as at 31st May 19_7

	£		£
Capital	570	Furniture	180
Net Profit	1,718	Stock	900
		Bank	408
	2,288		
Less Drawings	1,800		
	488		
Creditors	900		
Accruals	100		
	1,488		1,488

ANSWER 17.4

Trading and Profit & Loss Account for year 19_9

	£		£
Stock	4,725	Sales	41,526
Purchases	29,426		
	34,151		
Less Stock	5,600		
	28,551		
Gross Profit	12,975		
	41,526		41,526
Expenses	1,750	Gross Profit	12,975
Rates	2,375	Discounts Rec'd	400
Interest	400		
Depreciation of Van	900		
Net Profit	7,950		
	13,375		13,375

Balance Sheet as at 31st December 19_9

	£		£
Capital	50,500	Premises	45,000
Net Profit	7,950	Delivery Vans	1,500
		Stock	5,600
	58,450	Rates in advance	625
Less Drawings	8,000	Bank	4,825
	50,450		
Mortgage Loan	4,800		
Creditors	2,300		
	57,550		57,550

ANSWER 17.5

Trading and Profit & Loss Account for year ending 31st December 19_9

	£		£
Stock (1st Jan.)	2,729	Sales	20,402
Purchases	14,040		
	16,769		
Less stock (31st Dec.)	3,018		
	13,751		
Gross Profit c/d	6,651		
	20,402		20,402
Rent and rates	510	Gross Profit b/d	6,651
Wages	1,250		
General Expenses	2,209		
Net profit to capital a/c	2,682		
	6,651		6,651

Balance Sheet as at 31st December 19_9

	£	£		£	£
Capital (1st Jan.)	4,172		Furniture & Fittings		650
Add net profit	2,682		Stock	3,018	
			Trade debtors	1,641	
	6,854		Rates prepaid	32	
Less drawings	3,359		Cash in hand	51	
		3,495			4,742
Trade creditors	1,595				
Bank overdraft	77				
Expenses owing	135				
Rent owing	90				
		1,897			
		5,392			5,392

ANSWER 17.6

(a)

	£	£
Bank Balance at 30th Sept. 19_9		8,500
Cash banked in 19_0 – Cash Sales		82,000
From Debtors		77,500
		168,000
Less Payments in 19_0 – Purchases	110,700	
Administration Expenses	11,200	
Establishment Expenses	9,400	
Fixed Assets	20,000	
Drawings	10,000	161,300
Correct bank balance		6,700
Actual bank balance (overdraft)		(5,000)
Amount misappropriated in 19_0		11,700

(b) Trading and Profit & Loss Account for 19_0

	£		£
Stock	17,000	Sales	160,000
Purchases	114,000		
	131,000		
Less Stock	11,000		
Cost of Sales	120,000		
Gross Profit	40,000		
	160,000		160,000
Establishment Expenses	9,000	Gross Profit	40,000
Admin' Expenses	11,000		
Cash Misappropriated	11,700		
Depreciation	8,000		
Net Profit	300		
	40,000		40,000

Balance Sheet as at 30th September 19_0

	£	£		£	£
Capital Account:			Fixed Assets:		
At 30th Sept. 19_9		69,000	At cost		160,000
Add: Net profit			*Less:* Depreciation to date		104,000
		300			56,000
		69,300	Current Assets:		
Less: Drawings		10,000	Stock	11,000	
			Trade debtors	6,500	
		59,300	Amounts prepaid	800	18,300
Current Liabilities:					
Bank overdraft	5,000				
Trade creditors	9,500				
Accrued charges	500	15,000			
		£74,300			£74,300

ANSWER 17.7

Trading and Profit & Loss Account for year ended 31st March 19_2

	£		£
Stock	18,000	Sales	130,000
Purchases	80,000		
	98,000		
Less Stock	70,000		
	91,000		
Gross Profit	39,000		
	130,000		130,000
Misc. Expenses	9,974	Gross Profit	39,000
Rent	3,050		
Rates	680		
Dep'n of Equipment	900		
Lost through theft	5,000		
Net Profit	19,396		
	39,000		39,000

Balance Sheet as at 31st March 19_2

	£		£
Capital	36,620	Equipment	14,100
Net Profit	19,396	Stock	7,000
		Debtors	13,500
	56,016	Bank	25,866
Less Drawings	5,000	Rent prepaid	1,200
	51,016		
Creditors	10,650		
	61,666		61,666

ANSWER 17.8

(a) Profit Statement to 30th June 19_0

	£		£
Wages	2,080	Gross Profit	8,090
Insurance	80		
Expenses	600		
Depreciation – Shop	600		
,, Fixtures	300		
Net Profit	4,430		
	8,090		8,090

(b) Statement of Affairs at 30th June 19_0

	£			£
Capital	9,515	Shop Premises (cost)		12,000
New Capital	600	*Less* depreciation		3,000
Net Profit *	4,430			
				9,000
	14,545	Fixtures (cost)	3,000	
Less Drawings	3,380	*Less* Depreciation	1,500	
				1,500
	11,165	Stock		4,600
Loan	1,500	Debtors		2,540
Creditors	3,730	Cash		105
Bank overdraft	1,350			
	17,745			17,745

* Balancing figure.

ANSWER 17.9

Trading and Profit & Loss Account for year ended 31st May 19_4

	£		£
Stock	3,220	Sales	14,200
Purchases	9,200		
	12,420		
Less Stock	1,060		
	11,360		
Gross Profit	2,840		
	14,200		14,200
Sundry Expenses	400	Gross Profit	2,840
Rent and Rates	500		
Light and Heat	300		
Depreciation of Fixtures	200		
Depreciation of Vehicles	100		
Net Profit	1,340		
	2,840		2,840

Balance Sheet as at 31st May 19_4

	£		£
Capital	7,120	Fixtures & Fittings	2,800
Net Profit	1,340	Motor Vehicles	1,100
		Stock	1,060
	8,460	Debtors	1,400
Less Drawings	3,000	Bank	1,300
	5,460		
Creditors	2,200		
	7,660		7,660

ANSWER 18.1

Income and Expenditure Account for year ended 31st December 19_9

	£		£
Transport	840	Subscriptions	570
Upkeep of Uniform	110	Fees received	3,230
Rent of Hall	480	Investment Income	270
Repairs to instruments	320		
Expenses of members	585		
Sheet music	95		
Insurance	100		
Secretary's expenses	230		
Depreciation of Instruments	270		
Surplus:			
Instrument Fund	500		
Accumulated Fund	540		
	4,070		4,070

Balance Sheet as at 31st December 19_9

		£		£
Accumulated Fund		5,000	Instruments	4,760
Add Surplus		540	Music Stands	250
			Investments	3,700
		5,540	Subs due	210
Instrument Fund	3,500		Bank	810
Add Surplus	500			
		4,000		
Rent owing		40		
Expenses to members		60		
Subs in advance		90		
		9,730		9,730

ANSWER 18.2

(a) Assets at 1st April 19_9 = £99,490; Liabilities = £170;
Capital therefore = £99,320.

(b) Income and Expenditure Account as at 31st March 19_0

	£		£
Loss on Dinner Dance	280	Profit on Bingo	3,620
Light and Heat	1,330	Subscriptions	8,030
Maintenance Costs	3,500	Sales of Fish	5,700
Insurance	1,100		
Misc. Expenses	170		
Diesel Oil Used	8,475		
Loss on boat	800		
Surplus	1,695		
	17,350		17,350

(c) Balance Sheet as at 31st March 19_0

	£		£
Capital	99,320	Boats	40,150
Surplus	1,695	Equipment	5,500
		Boatyard Premises	25,000
	101,015	Club House	20,000
Heat and Light due	350	Stock of Oil	1,700
Diesel Oil owing	375	Bank	9,390
	101,740		101,740

ANSWER 18.3

Bar Trading Account for year ended 31st May 19_1

	£		£
Stocks	640	Sales	4,760
Purchases	2,950		
	3,590		
Less Stocks	810		
	2,780		
Wages (1/3)	730		
Light and Heat (1/3)	150		
Profit on Bar	1,100		
	4,760		4,760

Income and Expenditure Account for year ended 31st May 19_1

	£		£
Secretary's salary	700	Subscriptions	3,790
Staff wages (2/3)	1,460	Income from Socials	310
Rates and Insurance	580	Profit on Bar	1,100
Post and Telephone	230		
Sundry expenses	270		
Light and Heat (2/3)	300		
Dep'n of Furniture	60		
Surplus	1,600		
	5,200		5,200

Balance Sheet as at 31st May 19_1

	£		£
Accumulated Fund	5,680	Premises	5,200
Surplus	1,600	Furniture and Fittings	800
		Bar stocks	810
	7,280	Subscriptions due	20
		Bank	420
		Cash	30
	7,280		7,280

ANSWER 18.4

(a) Receipts and Payments Account

Receipts	£	*Payments*	£
Balance b/d	850	Rent of Hall	220
Subscriptions	1,200	Games Equipment	210
Proceeds of Whist and Dances	175	Cleaner's Wages	520
Refreshments	410	Heat and Light	175
		Secretarial Expenses	500
		Furniture	400
		May 31 Balance c/d	610
	2,635		2,635
May 31 Balance b/d	610		

(b) Income and Expenditure Account for year ended 31st May 19_1

	£		£
Rent of Hall	240	Subscriptions	1,200
New games equipment	210	Profit on Refreshments	410
Cleaner's Wages	520	Proceeds of events	175
Heat and Light	200		
Secretarial Expenses	500		
Surplus	115		
	1,785		1,785

ANSWER 18.5

(a) Bar Trading Account for year ended 31st October 19_0

	£	£		£
Opening stock	1,840		Sales	13,800
Purchases	8,700			
	10,540			
Less Closing stock	2,360			
		8,180		
Warden's salary (proportion)		1,175		
Clubhouse costs, including depreciation (proportion)		1,395		
		10,750		
Net profit for year		3,050		
		13,800		13,800

(b) Income and Expenditure Account for the year ended 31st October 19_0

	£		£
Clubhouse costs, including depreciation (proportion)	1,395	Subscriptions	8,450
Warden's salary (proportion)	3,525	Net profit on bar	3,050
Annual dinner	180	Deposit account interest	130
Sports equipment depreciation	821		
Hire of films	89		
Stationery and printing	248		
Postages	114		
	6,372		
Excess of income over expenditure for year	5,258		
	11,630		11,630

Balance Sheet as at 31st October 19_0

	£			£
Capital a/c (19_9)	16,560	Clubhouse at cost		15,000
Add surplus	5,258	*Less* Depreciation		1,500
	21,818			13,500
Coaching Bursary Fund	1,168	Sports Equipment at cost	2,463	
		Less Depreciation	821	
	22,986			1,642
Creditors	1,900			
Subs in advance	360			15,142
		Bar Stocks		2,360
		Bank Current a/c		7,004
		Bank Deposit a/c		730
		Cash		10
	25,246			25,246

ANSWERS 18.6

(a) Bar Trading Account

	£		£
Stock	1,250	Sales	15,510
Purchases	12,790		
	14,040		
Less Stock	960		
	13,080		
Profit	2,430		
	15,510		15,510

(b) Income and Expenditure Account for year ended 31st August 19_8

	£		£
Salaries	2,700	Profit on Bar	2,430
Rent, Rates, Insurance	1,840	Subscriptions	9,475
Repairs	425	Collections	1,280
Travelling Expenses	2,870	Bank Interest	480
Printing & Stationery	560		
Depreciation – Pavilion	800		
Depreciation – Cash Register	100		
Rugby Equipment	500		
Post Expenses	90		
Surplus	3,780		
	13,665		13,665

(c) Balance sheet as at 31st August 19_8

	£			£
Capital	6,800	Pavilion at cost		16,000
Surplus	3,780	*Less* depreciation		12,000
Appeal Fund	5,000			
				4,000
	15,580	Cash Register	400	
Creditors for bar	1,910	*Less* Depreciation	100	300
Subscriptions in advance	55			
		Bar Stocks		960
		Subscriptions due		720
		Bank Current a/c		4,250
		Bank Deposit a/c		7,300
		Petty Cash		15
	17,545			17,545

ANSWER 18.7

Subscriptions Account

	£		£
Balance b/d	164	Balance b/d	324
Year's subscriptions	1,642	Cash	1,647
Balance c/d	248	Balance c/d	83
	2,054		2,054

Trading Account

	£		£
Stock	261	Sales	2,132
Purchases	1,383		
	1,644		
Less Stock	390		
	1,254		
Profit	878		
	2,132		2,132

Subscription income + Profit = £2,520. 5% = £126

ANSWER 18.8

(a) Income and Expenditure Account for year ended 30th September 19_1

	£		£
General Expenses	4,790	Profit on Bar	1,500
Groundsman's Salary	5,700	Profit on Dance	2,100
Repairs	370	Subscriptions	4,460
Depreciation of Equipment	860	Misc. Receipts	1,450
		Deficit	2,210
	11,720		11,720

(b) Balance Sheet as at 30th September 19_1

	£		£
Capital	22,960	Premises	15,000
Less Deficit	2,210	Equipment	2,940
		Stock in Bar	550
	20,750	Subscriptions due	100
Bar Creditors	420	Bank	2,870
Subscriptions in advance	80		
General Expenses due	210		
	21,460		21,460

ANSWER 18.9

(1) Bingo Profit and Loss Account

	£		£
Caller's Wages	2,500	Receipts	20,000
Rent	450	Donations	800
Printing	750		
Prizes	7,500		
Profit	9,600		
	20,800		20,800

(2) Income and Expenditure Account for year ended 30th September 19_0

	£		£
Travelling Expenses	805	Profit on Bingo	9,600
Ground Rent	1,250	Profit on Bar	8,410
Heat and Light	350	Subscriptions	5,540
Post and Stationery	59		
Loss on Premises	10,000		
Loss on Equipment	3,000		
Surplus	8,086		
	23,550		23,550

(3) Balance Sheet as at 30th September 19_0

	£		£
Capital	28,025	Premises	27,000
Surplus	8,086	Equipment	15,000
		Bar Stocks	1,300
	36,111		
Creditors	4,000		
Subscriptions in advance	250		
Bank overdraft	2,939		
	43,300		43,300

ANSWER 19.1

Manufacturing, Trading and Profit & Loss Accounts for year ended 30th June 19_1

	£		£
Stock of Raw Materials	5,900	Cost of Manufacture of Finished Goods	195,900
Purchase of Raw Materials	129,500		
	135,400		
Less Stock of Raw Materials	8,300		
Raw Materials Used	127,100		
Direct Wages	40,300		
PRIME COST	167,400		
Indirect Costs			
Materials	4,100		
Fuel and Power	2,800		
Heat and Light	1,200		
Fire Insurance	900		
Rent and Rates	4,500		
Salaries	7,000		
Depreciation – Machinery	8,000		
	195,900		195,900
Stock of Finished Goods	5,400	Sales	265,000
Cost of Manufacture	195,900		
	201,300		
Less Stock of Finished Goods	5,600		
	195,700		
Gross Profit	69,300		
	265,000		265,000
Heat and Light	400	Gross Profit	69,300
Fire Insurance	900		
Rent and Rates	1,850		
Sundry and Advertising	5,200		
Office Salaries	4,000		
Provision for Bad Debts	100		
Depreciation – Furniture	700		
Net Profit	56,150		
	69,300		69,300

ANSWER 19.2

(a) Manufacturing and Trading Accounts for year ended 31st March 19_2

		5 star	*3 star*		*5 star*	*3 star*
	£	£	£		£	£
Stocks of Raw Materials	3,860			Cost of Manufacture	67,869	126,925
Purchases	124,514					
Carriage Inwards	320					
	128,694					
Less returns	480					
	128,214					
Less Stocks of Raw Materials	1,320					
	126,894					
Raw Materials Used		50,894	76,000			
Wages		16,000	48,000			
PRIME COST		66,894	124,000			
Light and Heat		325	975			
General Expenses		200	600			
Rent and Rates		450	1,350			
		67,869	126,925		67,869	126,925
(b)						
Stock of Finished Goods		1,225	3,200	Sales	100,000	200,000
Cost of Manufacture		67,869	126,925			
		69,094	130,125			
Less Stock of Finished Goods		594	2,125			
Cost of Goods Sold		68,500	128,000			
Gross Profit c/d		31,500	72,000			
		100,000	200,000		100,000	200,000

ANSWER 19.3

(a) Manufacturing and Trading Account for year ended 30th June 19_9

	£		£
Purchases of Raw Materials	65,000	Factory Cost of Finished Goods	124,000
Less Closing Stock (1/10)	6,500		
Raw Materials Consumed	58,500		
Direct Expenses	4,000		
Wages	31,500		
PRIME COST	94,000		
Heat and Light	2,500		
Maintenance Wages	11,000		
Rent and Rates	2,000		
Repairs to Machinery	5,000		
Depreciation – Machinery	9,500		
	124,000		124,000

(b)

	£		£
Stocks of Finished Goods	27,000	Sales	194,000
Cost of Manufacture	124,000		
	151,000		
Less Stocks of Finished Goods	31,000		
Cost of Goods Sold	120,000		
Gross Profit c/d	74,000		
	194,000		194,000

ANSWER 19.4

Manufacturing, Trading and Profit & Loss Accounts for year ended 31st December 19_7

	Barrows	*Ladders*		*Barrows*	*Ladders*
	£	£		£	£
Materials Used	7,000	3,500	Cost of Production	28,150	14,200
Materials Used	150	200			
	7,150	3,700			
Direct Wages	14,000	7,000			
	21,150	10,700			
Factory Power	4,000	2,000			
Indirect Wages	1,000	500			
Rates	2,000	1,000			
	28,150	14,200		28,150	14,200
Cost of Production	28,150	14,200	Sales	44,000	33,000
Gross Profit	15,850	18,800			
	44,000	33,000		44,000	33,000
Admin' Expenses	8,000	6,000	Gross Profit	15,850	18,800
Selling Expenses	4,000	3,000			
Net Profit	3,850	9,800			
	15,850	18,800		15,850	18,800

ANSWER 19.5

Manufacturing, Trading and Profit & Loss Accounts for year ended 31st March 19_8

	£'000		£'000
Stock of Raw Materials	5	Cost of Production	78
Purchases	44		
	49		
Less Stock of Raw Materials	4		
Raw Materials Used	45		
Direct Wages	20		
PRIME COST	65		
Indirect Wages	4		
Rates (Factory)	3		
Cleaning (Factory)	3		
Plant Maintenance	2		
Depreciation – Plant	2		
	79		
Less Work in Progress (19_8)	1		
	78		78
Stock of Finished Goods	6	Sales	100
Cost of Production	78		
	84		
Less Stock of Finished Goods	7		
Cost of Goods Sold	77		
Gross Profit	23		
	100		100
Office Salaries	3	Gross Profit	23
Office Expenses	2		
Rates (Office)	1		
Cleaning (Office)	1		
Depreciation – Furniture	1		
Interest on Loan	2		
Net Profit	13		
	23		23

Balance Sheet as at 31st March 19_8

	£'000			£'000
Capital	50	Premises		50
Net Profit	13	Machinery & Plant	20	
		Less Depreciation	12	
	63			8
Less Drawings	10	Furniture & Fittings	4	
		Less Depreciation	4	
	53			–
Loan	20	Stocks – Raw Materials		4
Creditors	6	Stocks – W.I.P.		1
Interest unpaid	2	Stocks – Finished Goods		7
		Debtors		8
		Bank and Cash		3
	81			81

ANSWER 20.1

(a) Profit & Loss Appropriation Account for year ended 31st May 19_0

	£		£
Salaries – M	6,000	Net Profit b/d	25,000
P	5,000		
Interest on Capital – M	2,400		
P	1,000		
Share of Profits – M	5,300		
P	5,300		
	25,000		25,000

(b) Balance Sheet as at 31st May 19_0

	£	£			£
CAPITAL ACCOUNTS			*FIXED ASSETS*		
M		24,000	Premises		23,000
P		10,000	Motor Vehicles	7,400	
			Less Provision for depreciation	2,000	
		34,000			5,400
CURRENT ACCOUNTS	£				
M – Balance at 19_9	3,500				28,400
Salary	6,000		*CURRENT ASSETS*		
Interest on Capital	2,400		Stock	11,700	
Share of Profits	5,300		Debtors	6,310	
			Bank	8,100	
	17,200		Cash	3,490	
Less Drawings	6,240				29,600
		10,960			
P – Balance at 19_9	2,520				
Salary	5,000				
Interest on Capital	1,000				
Share of Profits	5,300				
	13,820				
Less Drawings	4,800				
		9,020			
		53,980			
CURRENT LIABILITIES					
Trade Creditors		4,020			
		58,000			58,000

ANSWER 20.2

Trading and Profit & Loss Account for year ended 31st December 19_8

	£		£
Stock	8,000	Sales	115,100
Purchases	71,550	*Less* returns	3,100
Carriage In	2,700		
			112,000
	82,250		
Less Stock	14,540		
	67,710		
Gross Profit	44,290		
	112,000		112,000
Advertising	750	Gross Profit	44,290
Rent and Rates	1,200		
Heat and Light	425		
Wages	7,500		
Financial Charges	395		
Depreciation – Vehicles	1,500		
Depreciation – Fixtures	200		
Net Profit	32,320		
	44,290		44,290
Commission – A	6,600	Net Profit	32,320
B	4,600		
Share of Profits – A	10,560		
B	10,560		
	32,320		32,320

Balance Sheet as at 31st December 19_8

	£		£
Capital Accounts – A	32,000	Premises	15,000
B	16,500	Fixtures *less* depreciation	1,800
Current Accounts – A	2,160	Motor Vehicles *less* depreciation	6,000
B	4,160	Stock	14,540
		Debtors	17,510
	54,820	Bank	8,300
Creditors	11,750	Cash	3,145
Heat and Light owing	75	Rent and Rates prepaid	350
	66,645		66,645

ANSWER 20.3

Profit and Loss Appropriation Account for year 19_4

	£		£
Interest on Capital			
Smith	630	Net Profit	8,400
Jones	420	*Interest on Drawings*	
White	390	Smith	63
Salary – Jones	900	Jones	57
Share of Profits		White	45
Smith	2,490		
Jones	2,490		
White	1,245		
	8,565		8,565

Capital Account Smith

		£			£
July 1	Bank	1,000	Jan. 1	Balance	11,000
Dec. 31	Balance c/d	10,000			
		11,000			11,000
			Dec. 31	Balance b/d	10,000

Capital Account Jones

			Jan. 1	Balance	£7,000

Capital Account White

		£			£
Dec. 31	Balance c/d	7,000	Jan. 1	Balance	6,000
			July 1	Bank	1,000
		7,000			7,000
			Dec. 1	Balance b/d	7,000

Current Account Smith

		£			£
Dec. 31	Interest on Drawings	63	Jan. 1	Balance	600
Dec. 31	Drawings	2,000	Dec. 31	Interest	630
Dec. 31	Balance c/d	1,657	Dec. 31	Share of Profits	2,490
		3,720			3,720
			Dec. 31	Balance b/d	1,657

Current Account Jones

		£			£
Jan. 1	Balance	400	Dec. 31	Interest	420
Dec. 31	Interest on Drawings	57	Dec. 31	Salary	900
Dec. 31	Drawings	1,900	Dec. 31	Share of Profits	2,490
Dec. 31	Balance c/d	1,453			
		3,810			3,810
			Dec. 31	Balance b/d	1,453

Current Account White

		£			£
Jan. 1	Balance	300	Dec. 31	Interest	390
Dec. 31	Interest on Drawings	45	Dec. 31	Share of Profits	1,245
Dec. 31	Drawings	1,500	Dec. 31	Balance c/d	210
		1,845			1,845
Dec. 31	Balance b/d	210			

ANSWER 20.4

(1) Total assets at 1st May 19_7 = £63,750. Total liabilities = £21,750.
Therefore total Capital = *£42,000*.
Capital ($\frac{2}{3}$) = *£28,000*. B's Capital ($\frac{1}{3}$) *£14,000*.

(2) Trading and Profit & Loss Account for year ended 30th April 19_8

	£		£
Stock of Finished Goods	7,500	Sales	150,000
Cost of Manufacture	124,500		
	132,000		
Less Stock of Finished Goods	12,000		
Cost of Sales	120,000		
Gross Profit	30,000		
	150,000		150,000
Vehicle Expenses	1,250	Gross Profit	30,000
Advertising	350		
Bank Interest	520		
Printing & Stationery	180		
Office Rent & Rates	1,500		
Office Salaries	2,600		
Distribution Salaries	6,000		
Depreciation – Motors	3,000		
Net Profit	14,600		
	30,000		30,000
Salary – B	4,600	Net Profit	14,600
Share of Profits – A	7,500		
Share of Profits – B	2,500		
	14,600		14,600

(3) Balance Sheet as at 30th April 19_8

	£		£
Capital Accounts – A	28,000	Land & Buildings	20,000
B	14,000	Plant & Machinery – *Less* Depreciation	5,000
Current Accounts – A	(2,100)	Motor Vehicles – *Less* Depreciation	2,500
B	1,100	Stocks – Raw Materials	8,400
		Finished Goods	12,000
	41,000	Debtors	5,000
Creditors	4,700	Cash	1,210
Bank Overdraft	7,600	Prepayments	150
Accruals	960		
	54,260		54,260

ANSWER 20.5

(a) Profit & Loss Appropriation Account

	Oct./March	April/Sept.		Oct./March	April/Sept.
	£	£		£	£
Bonus – Paul		305	Net Profit	7,970	7,970
Bonus – Mark		315			
Int. on Capital – Paul		1,000			
Int. on Dapital – Mark		1,390			
Salary – Mark		3,000			
Share of Profits – Paul	3,985	1,176			
Share of Profits –Mark	3,985	784			
	7,970	7,970		7,970	7,970

(b) Paul – Current Account

	£		£
Drawings	6,000	Balance b/d	2,100
Balance c/d	2,726	Loan Interest (5%)	160
		Bonus	305
		Interest on Capital	1,000
		Share of Profit	5,161
	8,726		8,726

Mark – Current Account

	£		£
Drawings	7,600	Balance b/d	2,700
Balance c/d	4,574	Bonus	315
		Interest on Capital	1,390
		Salary	3,000
		Share of Profit	4,769
	12,174		12,174

(c)

Balance Sheet as at 30th September 19_3

	£		£
Capital Account – Paul	20,000	Fixed Assets at cost	43,000
Mark	27,800	*Less* Depreciation	8,000
Current Account – Paul	2,726		
Mark	4,574		35,000
		Stock	7,600
	55,100	Debtors	12,000
Loan – Paul	3,200	Bank	9,200
Creditors	5,500		
	63,800		63,800

ANSWER 20.6

Trading and Profit & Loss Accounts for year ended 30th April 19_2

	£		£
Stock	1,180	Sales	8,330
Purchases	4,170		
	5,350		
Less Stock	1,020		
	4,330		
Gross Profit	4,000		
	8,330		8,330
Discounts Allowed	240	Gross Profit	4,000
Rent and Rates	490	Discounts Received	190
Wages and Salaries	1,040		
Bad Debts	110		
General Expenses	250		
Depreciation – Furniture	60		
Net Profit c/d	2,000		
	4,190		4,190
Salary – Chester	500	Net Profit b/d	2,000
Share of Profits			
Bidmead	900		
Chester	600		
	2,000		2,000

Balance Sheet as at 30th April 19_2

	£		£
Capital Accounts			
Bidmead	2,000	Office Furniture	540
Chester	1,400	Stock	1,020
Current Accounts		Debtors	1,860
Bidmead	290	Bank	1,590
Chester	510	Cash	80
		Rent prepaid	30
	4,200		
Creditors	920		
	5,120		5,120

ANSWER 20.7

Trading and Profit & Loss Accounts for year ending 31st October 19_2

		£		£
Stock		2,140	Sales	15,530
Purchase	8,760		*Less* Returns	390
Less Returns	240			
		8,520		15,140
		10,660		
Less Stock		2,520		
		8,140		
Gross Profit		7,000		
		15,140		15,140
Wages and Salaries		3,970	Gross Profit	7,000
Rent and Rates		720		
General Expenses		80		
Travelling Expenses		480		
Net Profit c/d		1,750		
		7,000		7,000
Interest on Capital			Net Profit b/d	1,750
Gilmore		200		
Hall		150		
Share of Profits				
Gilmore		700		
Hall		700		
		1,750		1,750

Balance Sheet as at 31st October 19_2

	£		£
Capital Accounts			
Gilmore	4,000	Office Furniture	600
Hall	3,000	Stock	2,520
Current Accounts		Debtors	3,910
Gilmore	640	Bank	3,390
Hall	600	Cash	50
Creditors	2,190		
Wages accrued	40		
	10,470		10,470

ANSWER 20.8

Profit & Loss Appropriation Account for year ended 31st May 19_9

	£		£
Salaries – Robinson	1,200	Net Profit	10,740
Brown	1,500		
Interest on Capital – Smith	300		
Robinson	240		
Brown	120		
Interest on Loan – Robinson	180		
Share of Profits – Smith	3,600		
Robinson	2,400		
Brown	1,200		
	10,740		10,740

ANSWER 20.9

Trading and Profit & Loss Account for year ended 28th February19_9

	£		£
Stock	2,760	Sales	18,280
Purchases	9,180		
	11,940		
Less Stock	2,660		
	9,280		
Gross Profit	9,000		
	18,280		18,280
Rent, Rates, Insurance	420	Gross Profit	9,000
Discounts Allowed	830	Discounts Received	510
Bad Debts	320		
Wages and Salaries	3,150		
General Expenses	590		
Net Profit c/d	4,200		
	9,510		9,510
Salary – Brown	1,200	Net Profit b/d	4,200
Share of Profits – Amos	2,000		
Brown	1,000		
	4,200		4,200

Balance Sheet as at 28th February 19_9

	£		£
Capital Accounts			
Amos	3,500	Office Furniture	720
Brown	2,000	Stock	2,660
Current Accounts		Debtors	3,040
Amos	230	Bank	1,610
Brown	120	Cash	70
Creditors	2,210	Rates prepaid	40
Wages and Salaries due	80		
	8,140		8,140

ANSWER 20.10

(i) Trading and Profit & Loss Account for year 19_9

	£	£		£
Stock		3,544	Sales	23,538
Purchases	14,090		*Less* Returns	458
Carriage Inwards	140			
				23,080
	14,230			
Less Returns	234			
		13,996		
		17,540		
Less Stock		5,240		
		12,300		
Wages		3,740		
Gross Profit		7,040		
		23,080		23,080
Discounts Allowed		224	Gross Profit	7,040
Carriage Outwards		322	Bank Interest	136
General Expenses		987	Discounts Received	196
Wages and Salaries		1,870		
Insurance		95		
Bad Debts		38		
Depreciation – Fixtures & Fittings		126		
Net Profit		3,710		
		7,372		7,372
Salary – Wallace		1,000	Net Profit	3,710
Interest on Capital – Wallace		600		
Turner		480		
Share of Profits				
Wallace		815		
Turner		815		
		3,710		3,710

(ii) Current Account – Wallace

		£			£
Dec. 31	Drawings	1,960	Dec. 31	Salary	1,000
Dec. 31	Balance c/d	455	Dec. 31	Interest on Capital	600
			Dec. 31	Share of Profits	815
		2,415			2,415
			Dec. 31	Balance b/d	455

ANSWER 21.1

(1)

Journal

	DR	CR
	£	£
Premises	35,000	
Plant	6,000	
Stock	8,000	
Debtors	6,000	
Goodwill	4,000	
Creditors		9,000
A. Swing		50,000
Being purchase of A. Swing's business		
A. Swing	50,000	
Bank		50,000
Being payment of purchase price for Swing's business		

(2)

Balance Sheet as at 1st January 19_9

	£		£
Capital	87,000	Goodwill	4,000
New Capital	25,000	Premises	90,000
		Plant and Machinery	
	112,000	*less* depreciation	30,000
Less loss on plant	700	Fixtures & Fittings	
		less depreciation	4,000
	111,300	Stock	25,000
Bank Loan	25,000	Debtors	15,500
Bank overdraft	15,800	Cash	800
Creditors	17,000		
Expenses owing	200		
	169,300		169,300

ANSWER 21.2

(i)

	Assets	£	*Liabilities*	£
Price –	Office Furniture	650	Creditors	1,240
	Stock	1,490	*Capital*	3,280
	Debtors	1,620		
	Bank	760		
		4,520		4,520
Wilson –	Van	750	Creditors	910
	Stock	2,060	*Capital*	3,330
	Debtors	1,430		
		4,240		4,240

(ii)

Balance Sheet

	£		£
Capital – Price	3,280	Office Furniture	650
Wilson	3,330	Delivery Van	750
Creditors	2,150	Stock	3,550
		Debtors	3,050
		Bank	760
	8,760		8,760

ANSWER 21.3

Journal of Y

	DR	CR
	£	£
Freehold Property	9,500	
Motor Vehicles	3,250	
Stock	4,500	
Goodwill	3,500	
Henderson		20,750
Being purchase of business		
Henderson	20,750	
Cash		20,000
Bank		750
Being payment of purchase price		

ANSWER 21.4

Journal

(a)	DR	CR
	£	
Fixed Assets	4,000	
Stock	2,816	
Debtors	891	
Goodwill	1,574	
Creditors		1,481
Bardfield		7,800
Being purchase of business		
Bardfield	7,800	
Bank		7,800
Being payment of purchase price		
(b)		
Realisation a/c	7,707	
Fixed Assets		4,000
Stock		2,816
Debtors		891
Being sale of business assets		
Creditors	1,481	
Realisation a/c		1,481
Being sale of liabilities		
Halstead	7,800	
Realisation a/c		7,800
Being purchase price of business		
Realisation a/c	1,574	
Capital a/c		1,574
Being profit on realisation		
	£	£
Bank	7,800	
Halstead		7,800
Being receipt of purchase price		
Capital a/c	7,734	
Bank		7,734
Being settlement of Capital a/c		

(c) Balance Sheet

	£		£
Capital	14,448	Goodwill	1,574
Creditors	5,765	Fixed Assets	12,000
Bank overdraft	5,176	Stock	7,077
		Debtors	4,738
	25,389		25,389

ANSWER 21.5

(1) *Journal*

	DR	CR
	£	
Premises	7,000	
Fixtures	1,600	
Stock	2,400	
Debtors	1,020	
Goodwill	2,824	
Creditors		1,500
Provision for Doubtful Debts		51
Robinson		13,293
Being purchase of business		
Robinson	13,293	
Bank		13,293
Being payment of purchase price of Robinson		

Balance Sheet as at 1 January 19_5

	£			£
Capital	15,000	Goodwill		2,824
Loan – XYZ	2,000	Premises		7,000
Creditors	1,500	Fixtures		1,600
		Stock		2,400
		Debtors	1,020	
		Less provision	51	
				969
		Bank		3,707
	18,500			18,500

(2)

Journal

	DR	CR
	£	£
Realisation a/c	11,420	
Premises		6,000
Fixtures		2,000
Debtors		1,020
Stock		2,400
Being transfer of assets to be sold		
Creditors	1,500	
Realisation a/c		1,500
Being transfer of liabilities to be sold		
Todd	13,293	
Realisation a/c		13,293
Being purchase price of business		
Realisation a/c	3,373	
Capital a/c		3,373
Being profit on realisation		
Bank	13,293	
Todd		13,293
Being receipt of purchase price		
Capital a/c	14,149	
Bank		14,149
Being repayment of capital		

ANSWER 22.1

	£	£
Bank	5,000	
C – Capital Account		5,000
Being new capital		
C – Capital Account	2,000	
A – Capital Account		2,000
Being adjustment for goodwill		

ANSWER 22.2

(1) Profit & Loss Appropriation Account

	Jan.–Oct.	Oct.–Dec.		Jan.–Oct.	Oct.–Dec.
	£	£		£	£
Interest on Capital – Jack	900	300	Net Profit b/d	12,000	4,000
Tom	600	200	Adjust Salary – Harry	—	1,000
Harry	—	150	Adjust Rent – Harry	—	250
Salary – Tom	2,250	—			
Share Profits – Jack	4,950	2,300			
Tom	3,300	1,380			
Harry	—	920			
	12,000	5,250		12,000	5,250

(2) Capital Accounts

	JACK	TOM	HARRY		JACK	TOM	HARRY
	£	£	£		£	£	£
Balances c/d	12,000	8,000	6,000	Balances b/d	12,000	8,000	—
				Property			6,000
	12,000	8,000	6,000		12,000	8,000	6,000

(3) Current Accounts

	JACK	TOM	HARRY		JACK	TOM	HARRY
	£	£	£		£	£	£
Adjustment – Salary	—	—	1,000	Balances b/d	1,000	700	—
Adjustment – Rent	—	—	250	Interest on Capital	1,200	800	150
Drawings	5,000	6,000	—	Salary	—	2,250	—
Balances c/d	4,450	2,430	—	Share Profits	4,950	3,300	—
				Share Profits	2,300	1,380	920
				Balance c/d	—	—	180
	9,450	8,430	1,250		9,450	8,430	1,250

ANSWER 22.3

(i) Average of last four year's profits = £2,500 × 3 = £7,500.

(ii) Goodwill

	£		£
Peter – Capital a/c	3,000	Balance c/d	7,500
James – Capital a/c	3,750		
John – Capital a/c	750		
	7,500		7,500

(iii) Balance Sheet

	£		£
Capital – Peter	11,000	Goodwill	7,500
John	2,750	Sundry Assets	8,000
		Cash	2,250
	13,750		
Creditors	4,000		
	17,750		17,750

ANSWER 22.4

Capital Account – A

	£		£
Adjust Goodwill (B)	1,800	Balance b/d	36,000
Balance c/d	34,200		
	36,000		36,000
		Balance b/d	34,200

Capital Account – B

	£		£
Current a/c	16,000	Balance b/d	24,000
Loan a/c	14,200	Adjust Goodwill (A & C)	6,000
Cash	14,200		
	30,000		30,000

Capital Account – C

	£		£
Adjust Goodwill (B)	4,200	Balance b/d	12,000
Balance c/d	7,800		
	12,000		12,000
		Balance b/d	7,800

Loan Account – B

		Capital a/c – B	£14,200

ANSWERS 22.5

Realisation Account

	£		£
Premises	6,000	Creditors	3,400
Plant and Machinery	4,500	Laws Ltd.	25,000
Fixtures and Fittings	1,200		
Stock	5,000		
Debtors	6,000		
Profit – Ward	3,420		
Grant	2,280		
	28,400		28,400

Bank Account

	£		£
Balance b/d	1,250	Ward	4,820
Laws Ltd.	7,000	Grant	3,430
	8,250		8,250

Capital Account – Ward

	£		£
Shares in Law	10,800	Balance b/d	12,000
Cash	4,820	Current a/c	200
		Profit on Realisation	3,420
	15,620		15,620

Capital Account – Grant

	£		£
Shares in Law	7,200	Balance b/d	8,000
Cash	3,430	Current a/c	350
		Profit on Realisation	2,280
	10,630		10,630

ANSWER 22.6

Realisation Account

	£		£
Premises	20,000	Almond – Capital a/c (Premises)	24,000
Machinery	9,200	Almond – Capital a/c (Machinery)	4,000
Vehicles	2,200	Almond – Capital a/c (Debtors)	2,150
Debtors	3,540	Beet – Capital a/c (Vehicles)	1,760
Stock	3,260	Beet – Capital a/c (Machinery)	4,140
Expenses	72	Cherry – Capital a/c (Stock)	3,510
Profit on Realisation:		Remaining Debtors (Bank)	600
Almond	944		
Beet	472		
Cherry	472		
	40,160		40,160

Bank Account

	£		£
Debt Agency	600	Dec. 31 Balance b/d	150
Almond	1,606	Dec. 31 Loan	2,000
Beet	428	Dec. 31 Expenses	72
		Dec. 31 Cherry	412
	2,634		2,634

Almond – Capital Account

	£		£
Premises	24,000	Balance	13,000
Machinery	4,000	Mortgage	12,000
Debtors	2,150	Creditors	2,600
		Profit on Realisation	944
		Bank	1,606
	30,150		30,150

Beet – Capital Account

	£		£
Vehicles	1,760	Balance	5,000
Machinery	4,140	Profit on Realisation	472
		Bank	428
	5,900		5,900

Cherry – Capital Account

	£		£
Stock	3,510	Balance	3,450
Bank	412	Profit on Realisation	472
	3,922		3,922

ANSWER 22.7

(a) Bank Account

	£		£
(Stock) Realisation a/c	2,400	Balance b/d	3,700
(Debtors) Realisation a/c	3,000	(Expenses) Realisation a/c	1,000
Expanders Ltd.	30,000	Creditors	1,700
		A – Capital	9,300
		B – Capital	12,600
		C – Capital	7,100
	35,400		35,400

(b) Realisation Account

	£		£
Premises	25,000	Expanders Ltd.	45,000
Equipment	6,000	A – Capital (Vehicle)	1,200
Fixtures and Fittings	2,000	C – Capital (Vehicle)	1,200
Motor Vehicles	4,000	Bank (Stock)	2,400
Stock	3,000	Bank (Debtors)	3,000
Debtors	4,000	Discount Received	300
Bank (Expenses)	1,000		
Profit – A	2,700		
B	2,700		
C	2,700		
	53,100		53,100

(Note: Partnership Act dictates profit sharing ratios.)

(c) Capital Account – A

	£		£
Realisation a/c	1,200	Balance b/d	10,000
Shares in Expanders Ltd.	5,000	Current a/c	2,800
Bank	9,300	Profit on Realisation	2,700
	15,500		15,500

Capital Account – B

	£		£
Realisation a/c	1,200	Balance b/d	12,000
Shares in Expanders Ltd.	5,000	Current a/c	4,100
Bank	12,600	Profit on Realisation	2,700
	18,800		18,800

Capital Account – C

	£		£
Current a/c	2,600	Balance b/d	12,000
Shares in Expanders Ltd.	5,000	Profit on Realisation	2,700
Bank	7,100		
	14,700		14,700

ANSWER 22.8

Capital Accounts

	A	B	C	D		A	B	C	D
	£	£	£	£		£	£	£	
Loan Interest – 19_7	150		450		Balances b/d	95,000	69,000	38,000	
Loan Interest – 19_8	300				Loan Interest 19_7		600		
Motor Cars			1,200		Loan Interest 19_8		300		
Goodwill				6,000	Profit on car	75	50	25	
Drawings	21,500	17,800	7,400		Goodwill (D)	3,000	2,000	1,000	
Balances c/d	109,860	77,340	40,820	7,230	Interest on Loan	1,200	1,500		
					Share of profits	32,535	21,690	10,845	7,230
					Bank				6,000
	131,810	95,140	49,870	13,230		131,810	95,140	49,870	13,230

ANSWER 22.9

(a)

Capital Account – Ash

		£			£
Dec. 31	Drawings	2,632	Jan. 1	Balance b/d	4,500
Dec. 31	Balance	6,228	Jan. 1	Adjust for goodwill	1,400
			Dec. 31	Stock (re 19_9)	460
			Dec. 31	Share of profits	2,500
		8,860			8,860
			Dec. 31	Balance b/d	6,228

Capital Account – Beech

		£			£
Dec. 31	Drawings	1,598	Jan. 1	Balance b/d	2,800
Dec. 31	Balance c/d	3,382	Jan. 1	Adjust for goodwill	700
			Dec. 31	Stock (re 19_9)	230
			Dec. 31	Share of profits	1,250
		4,980			4,980
			Dec. 31	Balance b/d	3,382

Capital Account – Oak

		£			£
Jan. 1	Adjust for goodwill	2,100	Jan. 1	Bank	4,650
Dec. 31	Drawings	1,390	Dec. 31	Share of profits	1,250
Dec. 31	Balance c/d	2,454	Dec. 31	General Expenses	44
		5,944			5,944
			Dec. 31	Balance b/d	2,454

(b) Trading and Profit & Loss Account for Year Ending 31st December 19_0

	£		£
Stock (Jan. 1)	2,565	Sales	30,416
Purchases	21,132		
	23,697		
Less stock (Dec. 31)	2,168		
	21,529		
Gross Profit c/d	8,887		
	30,416		30,416
Wages and salaries	3,025	Gross Profit b/d	8,887
General expenses	862		
Net profit c/d	5,000		
	8,887		8,887
Share of Profits		Net profit b/d	5,000
Ash capital a/c	2,500		
Beech capital a/c	1,250		
Oak capital a/c	1,250		
	5,000		5,000

Balance Sheet as at 31st December 19_0

	£		£
Capital Account – Ash	6,228	Fixed Assets	9,700
Beech	3,382	Stock	2,168
Oak	2,454	Debtors	1,476
		Bank	140
	12,064		
Creditors	1,420		
	13,484		13,484

ANSWER 23.1

Profit & Loss Appropriation Account

	£		£
Interim Ordinary Dividend	6,000	Net Profit b/d	75,000
Interim Preference Dividend	4,000	Balance b/d	50,000
Proposed Preference Dividend	4,000		
Proposed Ordinary Dividend	30,000		
Transfer to General Reserve	30,000		
Balance c/d	51,000		
	125,000		125,000
		Balance b/d	51,000

Balance Sheet Extract

	£		
Issued Share Capital			
100,000 8% £1 Preference Shares	100,000		
300,000 £1 Ordinary Shares	300,000		
Share Premium	100,000		
General Reserve	65,000		
Retained Profits (P & L)	51,000		
Shareholders' Funds	616,000		

ANSWER 23.2

Trading and Profit & Loss Account for year ended 30th September 19_7

	£		£
Stock	14,248	Sales	80,000
Purchases	43,856	*Less* Returns	372
	58,104		79,628
Less Stock	15,546		
Cost of Sales	42,558		
Gross Profit	37,070		
	79,628		79,628
Rates	2,124	Gross Profit	37,070
Wages & Salaries	8,280	Discounts Received	1,764
Insurance	1,796	Reduction in Provision for Doubtful Debts	184
General Expenses	436		
Bad Debts	676		
Depreciation – Buildings	3,800		
Fixtures	2,400		
Debenture Interest	800		
Net Profit	18,706		
	39,018		39,018
Interim Dividend (Pref)	600	Net Profit	18,706
Dividend Proposed (Pref)	600	Balance b/d	2,000
Dividend Proposed (Ord)	1,000		
General Reserve	8,000		
Balance c/d	10,506		
	20,706		20,706

Balance Sheet as at 30th September 19_7

		£			£
Issued Share Capital		£	*Fixed Assets*		£
20,000 Ord. Shares £1 each fully paid		20,000	Goodwill		16,400
20,000 6% Pref. Shares £1 each fully paid		20,000	Land @ cost		18,000
Share Premium		1,000	Buildings @ cost	38,000	
General Reserve		18,000	*Less* depreciation	9,800	
Profit & Loss a/c		10,506			28,200
			Furniture & Fittings @ cost	22,000	
		69,506	*Less* depreciation	12,400	
Long Term Liabilities					9,600
5% Debentures		16,000			
Current Liabilities					72,200
Creditors		6,300	*Current Assets*		
Accruals		680	Stock	15,546	
Dividends Proposed		1,600	Debtors		
Bank overdraft		6,000	*Less* provision	12,008	
			Prepayments	100	
			Cash	232	
					27,886
		100,086			100,086

ANSWER 23.3

(b) Profit & Loss Appropriation Account for year ended 31st March 19_9

	£		£
Interim Pref. Dividend Paid	3,200	Net Profit b/d	95,000
Proposed Pref. Dividend	3,200	Balance b/d	355,000
Proposed Ordinary Dividend	37,500		
Transfer to General Reserve	150,000		
Balance c/d	256,100		
	450,000		450,000

ANSWER 23.4

Trading and Profit & Loss Account for year ended 31st March 19_9

		£		£
Stock		21,000	Sales	240,000
Purchases	211,000			
Less Returns	4,000			
		207,000		
		228,000		
Less Stock		28,000		
Cost of Sales		200,000		
Gross Profit (16⅔%)		40,000		
		240,000		240,000
Establishment Expenses		6,300	Gross Profit	40,000
Admin' Expenses		3,150	Discounts Received	650
Selling & Dist' Expenses		8,350	Reduction in Provision for Doubtful Debts	100
Discounts Allowed		250		
Loan Interest		300		
Bad Debts		700		
Depreciation – Buildings		500		
Depreciation – Fixtures		3,200		
Net Profit c/d		18,000		
		40,750		40,750
Proposed Dividends – Ord		3,000	Net Profit b/d	18,000
Proposed Dividends – Pref		400	Balance b/d	18,100
Balance c/d		32,700		
		36,100		36,100

Balance Sheet as at 31 March 19_9

Share Capital:		£	£
Ordinary shares of £1 each, fully paid		30,000	
8% Preference shares of £1 each, fully paid		5,000	35,000
Share Premium Account			4,000
Profit & Loss Account			32,700
Long Term Liabilities:			
6% Loan stock			5,000
			76,700
Represented by:	*Cost*	*depreciation*	
Fixed Assets:	£	£	£
Freehold buildings	25,000	3,000	22,000
Fixtures and fittings	32,000	16,000	16,000
	57,000	19,000	38,000
Goodwill			8,000
Current Assets:			
Stock		28,000	
Trade debtors		15,200	
Amounts prepaid		200	
		43,400	
Less: Current Liabilities:			
Creditors and accurals	8,050		
Bank overdraft	1,250		
Proposed dividends	3,400	12,700	30,700
			76,700

ANSWER 23.5

Trading and Profit & Loss Account for year ended 31st December 19_7

	£		£
Stock	42,618	Sales	297,462
Purchases	189,273		
	231,891		
Less Stock	47,288		
	184,603		
Gross Profit	112,859		
	297,462		297,462
Rent and Rates	3,600	Gross Profit	112,859
General Expenses	9,741		
Wages	35,043		
Bad Debts	948		
Provision for Doubtful Debts	124		
Directors' Salaries	25,000		
Depreciation – Vans	11,000		
Net Profit c/d	27,403		
	112,859		112,859
Proposed Dividend	8,000	Net Profit b/d	27,403
Balance c/d	37,800	Balance b/d	18,397
	45,800		45,800

Balance Sheet as at 31st December 19_7

Authorised and Issued Share Capital		£	*Fixed Assets*	£	£
200,000 Shares of £1 each, fully paid		200,000	Freehold Premises		142,000
Share Premium		40,000	Motor Vans	55,000	
Retained Profits		37,800	*Less* depreciation	32,800	
					22,200
Shareholders' Stake		277,800			
Current Liabilities	£				164,200
Creditors	16,974		*Current Assets*		
Wages owing	354		Stock	47,288	
Proposed dividend	8,000		Debtors *less* provision	25,282	
		25,328	Bank	65,958	
			Rent prepaid	400	
					138,928
		303,128			303,128

ANSWER 23.6

Balance Sheet as at 31st December 19_9

CAPITAL EMPLOYED			
Authorised and Issued Share Capital			£
70,000 Ordinary Shares of £1 each, fully paid			70,000
Retained Earnings			35,300
			105,300
UTILISATION OF CAPITAL			
Fixed Assets		£	£
Freehold Land and Buildings at cost			65,000
Motor Vans at cost		9,450	
Less provision for depreciation		6,290	
			3,160
			68,160
Current Assets			
Stock		17,160	
Debtors		22,570	
Bank and Cash		24,930	
		64,660	
Less *Current Liabilities*	£		
Trade Creditors	27,400		
Rates owing	120		
		27,520	
			37,140
			105,300

ANSWER 23.7

(a) Working Capital Ratio in December 19_9 $= \frac{\text{Current Assets (60)}}{\text{Current Liabilities (30)}} = 2$

Working Capital Ratio in December 19_0 $= \frac{\text{C.A. (80)}}{\text{C.L. (40)}} = 2$

Current Liabilities must therefore = £40,000
Dividend proposed should therefore = £3,000

ANSWER 23.8

Trading and Profit & Loss Account for year ended 31st December 19_9

	£		£
Stock	28,572	Sales	179,422
Purchases	129,938		
	158,510		
Less Stock	38,292		
	120,218		
Gross Profit	59,204		
	179,422		179,422
Rent and Rates	2,200	Gross Profit	59,204
General Expenses	5,842		
Wages	20,140		
Bad Debts	542		
Provision for Doubtful Debts	102		
Directors' Salaries	16,000		
Depreciation – Vans	8,000		
Net Profit c/d	6,378		
	59,204		59,204
Proposed Dividend	5,000	Net Profit b/d	6,378
Balance c/d	22,433	Balance b/d	21,055
	27,433		27,433

Balance Sheet as at 31st December 19_9

		£			£
Authorised and Issued Share Capital			*Fixed Assets*		
120,000 Shares of £1 each, fully paid		120,000	Freehold Land & Buildings (cost)		87,000
Share Premium		25,000	Motor Vans (cost)	40,000	
Profit & Loss Account		22,433	*Less* depreciation	22,800	
					17,200
		167,433			
Current Liabilities					104,200
Creditors	11,171		*Current Assets*		
Wages owing	264		Stock	38,292	
Proposed Dividend	5,000		Debtors *less* provision	16,155	
		16,435	Bank	24,921	
			Prepayments	300	
					79,668
		183,868			183,868

ANSWER 23.9

Balance Sheet as at 31st December 19_7

	£			£	£	£
Issued Share Capital		*Fixed Assets*				
45,000 Shares of £1 each, fully paid	45,000	Premises at cost			50,000	
Retained Profits	14,400	*Less* prov. for depreciation			5,000	
						45,000
Net Worth	59,400	Furniture & Fittings				
		at cost			4,000	
		Less prov. for depreciation			2,000	
						2,000
						47,000
		Current Assets		£		
		Stock			7,000	
		Debtors		3,500		
		Less provision		400	3,100	
		Cash and Bank			8,000	
					18,100	
		Less Current Liabilities				
		Creditors		700		
		Proposed Dividend		5,000		
					5,700	
		Working Capital				12,400
	59,400					59,400

ANSWER 24.1

Points to consider – purchase of vans, carrying of more stocks and debtors and less reliance on creditors, i.e.:

Cash Flow Statement for 19_9

	£		£
Sources of Cash		*Uses of Cash*	
Profits	13,074	Purchase of Vans	1,400
		Increase in Stocks	1,352
		Increase in Debtors	2,194
		Decrease in Creditors	2,910
		Drawings	9,432
	13,074		17,288

Decrease in cash = £4,214.

ANSWER 24.2

(a) Summary Bank Account

		£		£
19_7	Balance	2,540	Premises	20,000
	Loan	15,000	Plant	24,000
	Debtors	85,368	Creditors (Materials)	36,820
			Wages	25,090
			Interest on Loan	1,500
	Balance c/d	10,843	Expenses	6,341
		113,751		113,751

(b) Trading and Profit & Loss Account for year ended 31st December 19_8

	£		£
Materials Consumed	37,842	Sales	88,240
Wages	25,090		
Depreciation	6,830		
Gross Profit	18,478		
	88,240		88,240
Expenses	6,521	Gross Profit	18,478
Loan Interest	1,500		
Net Profit c/d	10,457		
	18,478		18,478
		Net Profit b/d	10,457
Balance c/d	18,877	Balance b/d	8,420
	18,877		18,877
		Balance b/d	18,877

Balance Sheet as at 31st December 19_8

	£		£	£
Share Capital	36,000	Buildings at cost		40,000
Retained Profit	18,877	Plant (cost)	54,640	
		Less depreciation	18,320	
	54,877			
Loan	15,000			36,320
Creditors	10,250	Stock		8,900
Expenses due	450	Debtors		6,200
Bank overdraft	10,843			
	91,420			91,420

ANSWER 24.3

Item 1 – Increase £20,000; Item 2 – No Change;
Item 3 – Increase £2,500; Item 4 – No change;
Item 5 – No change; Item 6 – No change; Item 7 – No change; Item 8 – No change;
Item 9 – Decrease £10,000

ANSWER 24.4

Item 1 – None; Item 2 – Decrease; Item 3 – Increase; Item 4 – None
Item 5 – Increase; Item 6 – Decrease; Item 7 – Increase; Item 8 – None; Item 9 – None.

ANSWER 24.5

Cash Flow Statements for 19_5 and 19_6

	19_5 £'000	*19_6* £'000		*19_5* £'000	*19_6* £'000
Sources			*Uses*		
Profits	19	24	Purchase of Fixed Assets	12	13
Add Depreciation	10	11	Increase in Stock	7	3
	—	—	Increase in Debtors	20	20
	29	35	Dividend paid	8	10
Increase in Creditors	8	3			
	—	—		—	—
	37	38		47	46
	=	=		=	=
Increase (Decrease) in Cash	(10)	(8)			

ANSWER 24.6

Cash Flow Statement for 19_9

	£		£
Sources		*Uses*	
Profits	4,722	Purchase of Vans	600
		Increase in Stock	690
		Increase in Debtors	1,113
		Decrease in Creditors	885
		Drawings	3,145
	4,722		6,433

= Decrease in cash of £1,711

ANSWER 24.7

(a) Trading and Profit & Loss Account for year ended 31st March 19_1

	£		£
Stock	7,400	Sales	40,000
Purchases	32,000		
	39,400		
Less Stock	12,500		
Cost of Goods Sold	26,900		
Gross Profit	13,100		
	40,000		40,000
Depreciation	1,000	Gross Profit	13,100
General Expenses	4,100		
Net Profit (20%)	8,000		
	13,100		13,100

(b) $$\frac{\text{(Average Stock) } 9{,}950}{\text{(Cost of Goods Sold) } 26{,}900} \times \frac{12}{1}\text{(months)} = \underline{\underline{4.}}$$

(d) Cash Flow Statement for 19_1

	£		£
Sources		*Uses*	
Profits	8,000	Purchase fixed assets	2,000
Add Depreciation	1,000	Increase in Stock	5,100
		Repayment of Loan	2,800
	9,000	Drawings	3,400
Increase in Creditors	400		
			13,300
	9,400		

i.e. – a decrease in cash of £3,900

ANSWER 24.8

Cash Flow Statement for 19_8

	£		£
Sources		*Uses*	
Profits	3,000	Purchase Fixed Assets	2,000
Add Depreciation	1,300	Repayment of Loan	1,000
		Decrease in Creditors	400
	4,300	Increase in Debtors	300
Decrease in Stock	600	Drawings	3,600
	4,900		7,300

i.e. a decrease in cash of £2,400 (increase in overdraft)

ANSWER 25.1

Sources and Applications of Funds Statement for 19_9

		£
Sources of Funds		
Profits before tax		4,824
Add Depreciation		34,860
		39,684
Issue of Shares		15,000
Issue of Debentures		45,000
		99,684
Application of Funds	£	
Purchase of Plant	78,750	
Purchase of Transport	9,900	
		88,650
Increase in Funds		11,034

Increase (Decrease) in Working Capital

	£
Increase in Stock	21,396
Increase in Debtors	14,934
Increase in Current Liabilities	(9,675)
Decrease in Bank	(15,621)
Net Increase	11,034

ANSWER 25.2

Statement of Source and Application of Funds for Year 2

	£	£
Source of Funds		
Profits		40,000
Add Depreciation		5,900
		45,900
Issue of Shares		20,000
Issue of Debentures		5,000
		70,900
Application of Funds	£	
Purchase of Plant	18,900	
Payment of tax (Year 1)	13,500	
Payment of dividends (Year 1)	10,500	42,900
Increase in Funds		28,000

Increase (Decrease) in Working Capital

	£
Increase in Stock	17,000
Increase in Debtors	4,000
Increase in Creditors	(4,500)
Increase in Bank	11,500
Net Increase	28,000

ANSWER 25.3

Sources and Applications of Funds Statement

	£	£
Sources of Funds		
Profit before tax	31,500	
Add items not involving movement of funds:		
Depreciation	6,000	
	37,500	
Issue of shares	20,000	
Premium on shares	3,000	
		60,500
Application of Funds		
Purchase of fixed assets	30,000	
Repayment of debentures	5,000	
Payment of tax	14,000	
Payment of dividend	9,000	
		58,000
Net Increase		2,500
Increase (Decrease) in Working Capital		
Increase in Stock		7,200
Increase in Debtors		11,800
Increase in Current Liabilities		(8,500)
Decrease in Bank		(8,000)
Net Increase		2,500

ANSWER 25.4

Statement of Source and Application of Funds

	£	£
Sources of Funds		
Profit before tax	10,000	
Adjustments for items not involving movement of funds:		
Depreciation	3,800	
Gain on sale of equipment	(400)	
	13,400	
Proceeds from sale of equipment	1,400	14,800
Applications of Funds		
Tax paid	6,000	
Purchase of equipment	9,000	15,000
Net decrease		(200)
Increase (Decrease) in Working Capital		£
Increase in Stock		1,400
Increase in Debtors		400
Increase in Creditors		(1,000)
Decrease in Bank		(1,000)
Net decrease		(200)

ANSWER 25.5

Funds Flow Statement for year ended 31st March 19_9

		£'000
Source of Funds		
Profits		53
Add Depreciation		8
		61
New Capital		24
Investment Sale		2
		87
Application of Funds	£	
Repayment of Loan	10	
Purchase of Property	5	
Purchase of Plant	10	
Purchase of Vehicles	5	
Drawings	12	
Tax paid (19_8)	20	
		62
Increase in Funds		25

Increase (Decrease) in Working Capital

Decrease in Stock	(30)
Increase in Debtors	5
Decrease in Creditors	10
Increase in Bank	40
Net Increase	25

ANSWER 25.6

Small-Capital Account

Balance c/d	29,470	Balance b/d	18,000
		Gain on Revaluation	2,900
		Cash (Legacy)	8,450
		Adjust Goodwill (Tiny)	120
	29,470		29,470
		Balance b/d	29,470

Small-Current Account

	£		£
Drawings (Stock)	800	Balance b/d	5,400
Drawings	860	Interest on Capital	1,800
Balance c/d	6,300	Share Profits	760
	7,960		7,960
		Balance b/d	6,300

Large Capital Account

	£		£
Balance c/d	27,530	Balance b/d	23,000
		Gain on Revaluation	4,350
		Adjust Goodwill (Tiny)	180
	27,530		27,530
		Balance b/d	27,530

Large Current Account

	£		£
Drawings (Stock)	600	Balance b/d	2,800
Drawings	2,140	Interest on Capital	2,300
Balance c/d	3,500	Share of profits	1,140
	6,240		6,240
		Balance b/d	3,500

Tiny – Capital Account

	£		£
Adjust Goodwill – Small	120	Cash	2,300
Adjust Goodwill – Large	180		
Balance c/d	2,000		
	2,300		2,300
		Balance b/d	2,000

(ii) *Sources & Applications of Funds Statement for year 19_9*

		£
Sources of Funds		
Profits		6,000
Add Depreciation		4,100
Add Loss on Sale of fixed asset		300
		10,400
Less Gain on Sale of Property		1,700
		8,700
New Capital – Small		8,450
New Capital – Tiny		2,300
Sale of Property		3,950
Sale of Other fixed assets		1,500
Loan from Mrs Small		1,500
		26,400
Application of Funds	£	
Purchase of Other Fixed Assets	19,400	
Purchase of Property	2,000	
Drawings – Small	1,660	
Drawings – Large	2,740	25,800
Increase in Funds		600

Increase (Decrease) in Working Capital	
Increase in Stock	4,800
Increase in Debtors	2,200
Increase in Creditors	(400)
Decrease in Bank	(6,000)
Net Increase	600

ANSWER 25.7

(a)

Sources and Applications of Funds Statement

	£	£
Sources of Funds		
Profits		15,000
Add Depreciation		3,000
		18,000
Less Gain on sale of Plant and Machinery		2,000
		16,000
Issue of Shares		30,000
Premium on Shares		5,000
Sale of Plant and Machinery		7,000
		58,000
Application of Funds	£	
Purchase of Plant and Machinery	5,000	
Purchase of Buildings	46,000	
Payment of Dividends (19_7)	2,000	
		53,000
Increase in Funds		5,000

Increase (Decrease) in Working Capital

	£
Increase in Stocks	4,000
Increase in Debtors	9,000
Decrease in Creditors	2,000
Decrease in Bank	(10,000)
Net Increase	5,000

ANSWER 25.8

(a)

Source and Application of Funds Statement for 19_1

	£	£
Source of Funds		
Profit		40,000
Add Depreciation		22,000
		62,000
Issue of Shares		10,000
		72,000
Application of Funds	£	
Purchase of Fixed Assets	44,000	
Repayment of Debentures	15,000	
Payment of Dividend (19_0)	6,000	
		65,000
Increase in Funds		7,000

Increase (Decrease) in Working Capital

Increase in Stock	16,000
Increase in Debtors	8,000
Increase in Creditors, etc.	(9,000)
Decrease in Bank	(8,000)
Net Increase	7,000

(b) Working Capital Ratio in 19_0 = 2.
Therefore current liabilities in 19_1 must equal £44,000
– therefore proposed dividend should be added of £5,000.

ANSWER 26.1

(a)

	Business X	*Business Y*
(i)	20%	15%
(ii)	13%	5%
(iii)	$3\frac{1}{3}$	8
(iv)	20%	10%

ANSWER 26.2

(1) $\frac{60}{435} \times \frac{100}{1} = 13{\cdot}8\%$

(2) $\frac{\text{Current Assets}}{\text{Current Liabilities}} = \frac{150}{60} = 2{\cdot}5$

(3) $\frac{\text{Cost of Goods Sold}}{\text{Average Stock}} = \frac{600}{30} = 20$

(4) $\frac{\text{Debtors}}{\text{Credit Sales}} = \frac{90}{720} \times \frac{12}{1}\text{(months)} = 1\frac{1}{2}\text{ months}$

ANSWER 26.3

(a) Working Capital = £5,000 (19_7); £9,000 (19_8).
(b) Stock Turnover = 25; (d) £4,000;
(e) £5,000; (f) £177,000.

ANSWER 26.4

	19_3	*19_4*	*19_5*
(i) Rate of return on capital employed	9·9%	8·5%	6·1%
On *long term* capital employed	8·5%	7·5%	5·6%
(ii) Net working capital	£280,000	£244,000	£184,000
(iii) Stock turnover (using closing stock)	3	2·6	2·02
(iv) Debtors Collection period	48 days	57 days	76 days

ANSWER 26.5

(a)

	WHIZ	*BANG*
	1:1	2·5:1
Current Ratio	0·3:1	1·17:1
Liquid Ratio	12	1·375
Stock Turnover		
Net Earnings for		
Ordinary Shareholders	40%	44%
Earnings on Long-Term Capital	40%	23½%
Net Profit as % of Sales	4%	16%

ANSWER 26.6

(a)

	MANUFACTURER	*BANK*
Current Ratio	1·08	0·95
Liquid Ratio	0·74	0·95
Return on Shareholders' Funds	9%	22%
Return on Long Term Capital	3·67%	20%
Shareholders' Stake	20%	7·2%